A FIELD GUIDE TO
THE NORTH AMERICAN
PRAIRIE

THE PETERSON FIELD GUIDE SERIES®

A FIELD GUIDE TO THE

NORTH AMERICAN PRAIRIE

STEPHEN R. JONES

AND

RUTH CAROL CUSHMAN

SPONSORED BY THE
NATIONAL WILDLIFE FEDERATION
AND THE ROGER TORY PETERSON INSTITUTE

HOUGHTON MIFFLIN COMPANY
BOSTON NEW YORK 2004

For information about permission to reproduce selections from
this book, write to Permissions, Houghton Mifflin Company,
215 Park Avenue, New York, New York 10003.

Visit our Web site: www.houghtonmifflinbooks.com.

PETERSON FIELD GUIDES and PETERSON FIELD GUIDE SERIES
are registered trademarks of Houghton Mifflin Company.

Library of Congress Cataloging in Publication Data

Jones, Stephen R., 1947–
Field guide to the North American prairie /
by Stephen R. Jones and Ruth Carol Cushman.
p. cm. — (The Peterson field guide series)
Includes bibliographical references (p.).
ISBN 0-618-17929-1
ISBN 0-618-17930-5 (pbk.)
1. Prairies—North America—Guidebooks.
I. Cushman, Ruth Carol, 1937– II. Title.
III. Series.
QH102.J54   2004
578.74'4'097—dc21   2002191338

Book design by Anne Chalmers
Typeface: Linotype-Hell Fairfield; Futura Condensed (Adobe)

Printed in Singapore

TWP 10 9 8 7 6 5 4 3 2 1

To Glenn, who drove many rough and rutted miles and
hiked many hot and dusty trails in search of Edens
on the prairie. Thank you for spotting bugs,
birds, and other wonders and for
making me laugh.

—Ruth Carol

To all the people of the plains,
and to the professional scientists
and volunteers who work daily,
against daunting odds,
to restore the prairie.

—Stephen

Contents

ACKNOWLEDGMENTS

Researchers and managers from numerous government and private agencies have been invaluable in providing information, suggesting places to visit, and critiquing portions of our manuscript. Many of them accompanied us into the field and shared their love of the prairie with us. We would especially like to thank the following people and organizations:

Marian Langan, Kevin Poague, and Paul Tebbel, from the National Audubon Society.

James Crooks, Steven Currey, Anthony Detoy, Keith Frankki, Dan Garcia, Pat Hessenflow, Jack Isaacs, John Kouns, Cristi Lockman, Ian Ritchie, Marcia Rose-Ritchie, Colleen Rufsvold, Doug Sargent, and Brian Stotts, from the national grasslands.

Ed Day, Peter Dederich, Sharon de la Rosa, Robert Exley, Denise Harmon, Maggie Johnson, Jim LaRock, Marianne Mills, Barbara Muenchau, Noel Poe, Dan Roddy, Charles Sides, Jim Staebler, Michael Stansberry, Rhonda Terry, and Wildfire Wandering, from the National Park Service.

Bill Behrends, Ken Butts, Paul Charland, Don Clapp, Bob Danley, Pauline Drobney, Nancy Gilbertson, Mike Granger, Jake Ivan, Dan Jorgensen, Mark Lindvall, Lynn Nymeyer, Dan Severson, Carol Stayer, Sam Waldstein, Gordon Warrick, and Steve Whitson, from the U.S. Fish and Wildlife Service.

Kristen Austin, Bob Hamilton, Cate Harrington, Keith Kinne, Bill Kleiman, Susan Kleiman, Clint Miller, Scott Moats, Betsy Neely, Russell Reisz, Steve Richter, Erik Rosenquist, Robert Self, Al Steuter, Tracey Vodehnal, Rod Voss, and Brian Winter, from the Nature Conservancy.

Kevin Badgley, Arthur Benson, Dennis Clark, Kathy Duttenhefner, Karl Grover, Charlene McDade, Joe Nyhoff, Lowell Pugh, Martha Pugh, Craig Pugsley, Arthur Rohr, Arik Spencer, and Valerie Wright, from various state parks, universities, and private conservation organizations.

Steve Armstead, Gregor Auble, Kathryn Bolin, Clait Braun, Linda Coates-Markle, Paula Cushing, Gene Gasiokiewicz, Ken Giesen, Joyce Gellhorn, Stephanie Harmon, David Hartnett, William Jennings, Fritz Knopf, Boris Kondratieff, Tony Leukering, Paul Opler, Fiona Reid, Randy Rogers, Virginia Scott, Steve Taylor, John Kirwin Werner, and Jeff Yost, who provided information on prairie ecology.

Christie Borkowsky, Shirley Bruised Head, Jim Campbell, Adam Cheadle, John Dunlop, Michele Kading, Peter Kingsmill, Cam Lockerbie, Sue Michalsky, Bonnie Moffet, Melody Nagel-Hissey, Laura Reeves, Colin Schmidt, Robert Sissons, and Bob Ward, from various Canadian parks and preserves.

The resources at the University of Colorado Libraries and the Boulder Public Library were invaluable, as was the assistance of their staffs.

We owe a very special debt of gratitude to the people who reviewed large portions of the manuscript. Any remaining mistakes are ours, not theirs. With heartfelt thanks we acknowledge Carl Bock, Dina Clark, Hugh Kingery, Hannan LaGarry, Lauren Livo, Carron Meaney, Curtis Nepstad-Thornberry, James Swinehart, Michael Weissmann, and Richard Wilshusen.

Lisa White, our editor; Beth Kluckhohn, editorial assistant; Sandy Sherman, copy editor; and Anne Chalmers, book designer, took our manuscript and created a book that is far more attractive than we could have imagined. They were a joy to work with.

It is with great sadness that we acknowledge the death of Sandy Sherman in June, 2003. Sandy was a superb copy editor and enthusiastic naturalist who served as the first female president of the Delaware Valley Ornithological Club.

Many friends who share our appreciation of the prairie aided and abetted this project in various ways. Thank you Dianne Andrews, David Bartholomew, Robert Bell, Galen Brown, Ron Butler, Bill Dunmire, Randy Gietzen, Merrill Gilfillan, Ruth Grant, Paula Hansley, Tim Hogan, Tom Simpson, and John Weller.

Most of all we thank our spouses, Nancy Dawson and Glenn Cushman, who helped us with all the many problems that arise in writing a book. They read and reread the manuscript, gave us invaluable suggestions and advice, smoothed out computer problems, and encouraged us throughout the adventure.

A FIELD GUIDE TO
THE NORTH AMERICAN
PRAIRIE

The legacy of America's great naturalist, Roger Tory Peterson, is preserved through the programs and work of the Roger Tory Peterson Institute of Natural History. The RTPI mission is to create passion for and knowledge of the natural world in the hearts and minds of children by inspiring and guiding the study of nature in our schools and communities. You can become a part of this worthy effort by joining RTPI. Just call RTPI's membership department at 1-800-758-6841, fax 716-665-3794, or e-mail (webmaster@rtpi.org) for a free one-year membership with the purchase of this Field Guide.

INTRODUCTION

"A sense of place" has become a cliché, but that's really what this book is about. We wrote it to give readers an enhanced awareness and appreciation of the North American prairie. This is the land that Meriwether Lewis described as "...extreemly fertile; consisting of a happy mixture of praries and groves, exhibiting one of the most beautifull and picteresk seens that I ever beheld."

It's also land that has been plowed, developed, overgrazed, and abused to the point that only fragmented remnants of the original grasslands remain. Less than 5 percent of the original tallgrass prairie still stands unplowed, and about half of the original mixed-grass and shortgrass prairies have vanished. Many prairie animals have been extirpated from the region, and grassland birds are disappearing at an alarming rate.

We have tried to tell the story of the prairie in the context of 48 very special places. Each place description contains short essays on unique features, such as prairie potholes or playa lakes, and on characteristic wildlife or plant life, such as Greater Prairie-Chickens or Buffalo Gourds. Each account also includes practical information on hiking, camping, best times to visit, weather, addresses, and a selective list of some of the wildlife you might encounter. Most of the visitor centers and museums are open daily except for certain holidays; phone ahead for the hours.

These preserves are the ones we consider among the best examples of native prairies open to the public. However, many other national parks and monuments, state parks, wildlife refuges, and privately owned preserves also contain prairies worth visiting. Brief descriptions of additional sites conclude the state and province chapters. Appendix I describes sites in Indiana, Michigan, Ohio, and Ontario—places where relatively small prairie fragments survive.

Prairies also exist in other parts of the United States and

Canada, notably the Palouse prairies of the Pacific Northwest and the Great Basin grasslands, but that would be another book. We chose to focus on the contiguous prairie region of central North America, the ocean of grass that once extended from Colorado to Ohio, from Alberta to Texas. These grasslands have been pivotal in our history, and they are at a crossroads today.

Will our prairies all become croplands and suburbia with an inevitable loss of untold grassland species? Does our future hold only a few token "museum" prairies? Or can we preserve and restore large enough expanses of grassland to contain the rich diversity of species that can, given a chance, thrive here?

This book is not intended to be used as an identification key but as a general guide to the North American prairie region. Because we could not include all the interesting plant and animal species that compose the prairie biome, we have focused on those we consider of greatest interest to people exploring the prairie and most important to the continuing vitality of the prairie.

A book is no substitute for actually experiencing the prairie. Lie hidden in the tall grasses of eastern Kansas and Oklahoma, explore the badlands of the Dakotas, or perch on the cliffs above the Missouri River and imagine how the valley looked to Lewis and Clark. Discover the secret that prairies are much more than flat lands covered in grass, and revel in the diversity of vast wetlands, wooded copses, oak savannas, and sagebrush steppes. Magic happens when, under a prairie sky, you are lulled to sleep by owls and awakened by meadowlarks.

This book can be used as a guide for a prairie odyssey, perhaps following spring north from the blooming chollas of Texas to the wild orchids of Saskatchewan, zigzagging east and west to experience the Flint Hills of Kansas, the Sandhills of Nebraska, and the prairie pothole region of North Dakota and Manitoba. Or celebrate the autumn equinox in Canada and track colors south, following the dusky pink, russet, and golden grasses. Or simply take a short side trip to one of these destinations for a glimpse of what America once was.

PRAIRIE PASSAGE ROUTE

Six states in the heart of North America (Minnesota, Iowa, Missouri, Kansas, Oklahoma, and Texas) have strung together a national prairie wildflower corridor called the Prairie Passage Route, which protects and promotes prairie remnants found along highway rights of way. A yellow Prairie Coneflower logo, shown below, designates the route, along with selected historical, archaeological, and natural sites along the route.

Coordinated by the departments of transportation for the six states and funded by the federal highway administration, this unique cooperative program began in 1993. The program oversees the planting of native grasses and wildflowers and provides interpretive signs and brochures. For more information, contact each state's department of transportation.

PERILS OF THE PRAIRIE

Don't become so soothed by the peace of the prairie that you overlook its hazards. Killing winter blizzards can swirl across the plains with little warning. "The schoolchildren's storm" hit Nebraska on January 12, 1888, just as children were leaving school. One group never made it across the 200 yards to a boarding house. Altogether, more than 200 people were killed. Temperatures can drop 50°F in 10 minutes. Dress appropriately and carry extra clothes and matches for an emergency fire when hiking or skiing, and always carry extra food, water, clothes, and blankets on car trips.

Hot, oppressive days in summer can foreshadow a tornado. If a funnel cloud approaches, get out of the car and crouch down in a ditch or low area. If you're near an underground storm shelter, take advantage of it. In a house, stay away from windows. A door lintel offers some protection. If you are caught in a hailstorm, get under an overpass if possible. We sacrificed two windshields to hail while researching this and other prairie books.

Lightning is especially dangerous on the wide open plains and kills 50 to 100 people every year in North America. In a thunderstorm, stay inside your car or a house if possible. If you are caught outside, do not seek shelter under a tree or near rocks, fences, or power lines. Instead, squat down in the lowest area you can find.

Summer temperatures can top 100°F. To avoid heat exhaustion or heat stroke, seek shade, drink lots of water, and douse exposed body parts with water. Always wear a broad-brimmed hat and sunglasses and use mosquito repellent and sun screen rated SPF 15 or higher.

Be aware of your surroundings. Watch for rattlesnakes; if one bites you, call for help or drive to the nearest hospital rather than using the old method of cut and suck. Also watch for poison ivy, common on the prairie, and check frequently for ticks in spring and summer. Brush ticks off before they dig in, and be sure to bathe thoroughly every day. If a tick, which can carry debilitating disease, becomes embedded, cover it with heavy oil and wait half an hour; if it doesn't disengage, use tweezers to pull it straight out.

Chiggers, which abound in the tallgrass region, are an invisible scourge. To discourage them, wear loose-fitting clothing, tuck pants legs into socks, and spray socks with insect repellent.

Do not eat mushrooms or any other wild foods unless you are certain of their identification and edibility. We frequently describe American Indian uses of wild plants, but that does not necessarily mean these plants are safe to eat.

One of the things we love about prairies is their remoteness and the solitude we find there. When you take the road less traveled, however, you can run into trouble. And you can get lost. Roads are frequently unpaved and treacherous when wet, and another car may not pass for hours. When we went off a back road in North Dakota, we were guiltily thankful for a cell phone. Travel hopefully, but be prepared. Carry emergency equipment and a detailed map, such as those available at national grassland offices.

SOURCES

We have used the following sources as authorities for nomenclature: *A Synonymized Checklist of the Vascular Flora of the United States, Canada and Greenland*, by John T. Kartesz; *Flora of the Great Plains*, edited by Ronald L. McGregor et al.; *Check-list of North American Birds*, prepared by the American Ornithologists' Union, 7th edition; *Revised Checklist of North American Mammals North of Mexico*, 1997, by Clyde Jones et al.; and *Scientific and Standard English Names of Amphibians and Reptiles of North America North of Mexico*, edited by Brian I. Crother.

The Internet is a rich source of information that we used extensively. Most prairie parks and preserves have excellent Web sites, often including maps and species lists. We did not include their Web addresses because they are subject to change, but the pages are easily accessed by typing the name of the preserve into a search engine. Massive amounts of information on almost every subject covered in this book can be found by typing in keywords. Departments of Natural Resources in most states and provinces maintain informative Web sites; several offer free booklets. Several outstanding prairie Web sites are listed at the end of the bibliography.

ABBREVIATIONS USED IN TEXT

CR — County Road
FS — Forest Service Road
Hwy. — Canadian Road or Highway
SR — State Road
US — United States Highway
(m) — migrant
TNC — the Nature Conservancy
(w) — winter

NOTE: Hiking distances are one way unless otherwise noted.

Part I

Ecology of the
North American
Prairie Region

Clumps of Switchgrass turn golden in the Nebraska Sandhills in early autumn.

Evolving Prairie

Grass has been around for a long time, perhaps 50 million or 60 million years. But the North American prairie as we know it evolved quite recently.

About 70 million years ago, an inland sea covered most of central North America. Its traces appear wherever erosion has laid bare the old sea bed, revealing fossils of large mollusks and ripple marks caused by wave action. In shortgrass prairies of the western plains you can find clam shell fossils scattered in the grass, striking evidence that this now arid land once lay under water.

The sea was warm and shallow but wouldn't have been inviting to humans. Fifteen-foot-long carnivorous fish patrolled its bottoms. Nodosaurs, 4-ton dinosaurs resembling overgrown armadillos, waded in its shallows. Inland, where rivers meandered through humid forests and over marshy plains, *Tyrannosaurus* hunted and *Triceratops* browsed.

This was the culmination of the age of dinosaurs. Their fossil record ends 65 million years ago. Some fossil beds dating from that time contain a thin layer of iridium-laced clay deposited when an enormous asteroid collided with the earth near the present-day Yucatán Peninsula. The impact created a dust cloud that may have blanketed the planet for years, causing sudden global cooling.

Many scientists believe that this cataclysmic event, coupled with dramatic changes in global climate during the previous several million years, caused the late-Cretaceous extinction of dinosaurs and more than half of the world's other species. Others point to the possibility that the dinosaurs were poisoned by toxic clouds of sulfur dioxide produced by major volcanic eruptions. Either way, the extinctions occurred abruptly and signaled the transition to a new era in the Earth's history: the Cenozoic, the age of mammals and flowering plants.

As the dinosaurs were dying off, the modern Rocky Mountains had begun their gradual uplift. Wind and water carried sediments from the emerging mountains eastward, raising the level of the plains. Gradually, the inland sea retreated, and the inland climate began to change.

Prior to the Rocky Mountain uplift, the central North American climate had been dominated by warm, moist air masses that swept east from the Pacific or flowed north from the Gulf of Mexico. The rising mountains created a barrier that blocked the Pacific storms, squeezing out most of their moisture before it reached the plains. This rain shadow effect helped to create the more arid conditions that can favor growth of grasses over trees.

Fossils of camels, rhinoceroses, horses, and other grass-eating herbivores unearthed on the plains suggest an erratic progression, 25 million to 14 million years ago, toward a prairie environment. Recent analysis of plant microfossils indicates that extensive grasslands covered parts of the Great Plains even earlier, perhaps beginning in the late Eocene 35 million years ago.

These early grasslands were dominated by "cool-season" grasses, species that thrive under relatively mild growing conditions. The quintessential tallgrasses, including "warm-season" bluestems and switchgrasses, did not begin to appear until about 10 million years ago. Even then, forests continued to cover much of the Great Plains, with grasslands spreading during drier climatic periods and contracting during wetter periods.

About 2.5 million years ago, a gradual cooling trend that had characterized the North American climate since the end of the Cretaceous period intensified. During at least 26 episodes of sharp cooling, mile-deep rivers of ice flowed south to present-day Nebraska, Kansas, Illinois, and Wisconsin. As the glaciers advanced, boreal forests dominated by spruces and firs spread over the plains. During warmer interglacial intervals, the forests retreated northward and the grasslands expanded.

The glaciers contributed to the establishment of grasslands by depositing thick layers of glacial till—ground up bedrock, gravel, and grit—where grasses could take hold and thrive, eventually forming the rich blacksoil prairies of the upper Midwest. Fine silt particles that blew in great clouds off extinct glacial rivers, floodplains, and sand dunes accumulated as powdery brown loess. Under dry climatic conditions, fine-rooted grasses could outcompete thick-rooted trees in deep, highly permeable loess soils.

Nevertheless, near the end of the Wisconsin glaciation (named for the southernmost extent of its glaciers), coniferous forests and savannas covered most of central North America. Pollen samples indicate that spruce forests still flourished in Kansas 18,000 years ago and in the Nebraska Sandhills 12,000 years ago.

ERA	PERIOD	EPOCH	AGE (MILLIONS OF YEARS AGO)	EVENTS
Cenozoic	Quaternary	Holocene	0–0.01	Grasses dominate. Mammoths and many other large mammals become extinct.
		Pleistocene	0.01–2	Glaciers push into northern plains. Mammoths and large carnivores flourish.
	Tertiary	Pliocene	2–5	Horses, mammoths, and saber-tooth cats roam grasslands and forests.
		Miocene	5–24	Rhinoceroses, camels, and horses abound. Ashfalls continue.
		Oligocene	24–34	Volcanoes spew ash onto plains. Tiny horses, camels, and primates appear as grasses spread.
		Eocene	34–57	Palm trees and crocodiles thrive in humid forests. Primitive horses appear.
		Paleocene	57–65	Grasses evolve. Uplift of modern Rocky Mountains begins. Sea retreats.
Mesozoic	Cretaceous		65–144	Sea covers central North America. Flowering plants evolve. Dinosaurs flourish.
	Jurassic		144–200	Humid climate supports lush vegetation and dinosaurs. Birds and primitive mammals appear.
	Triassic		200–250	Erosion of ancestral Rockies continues. First dinosaurs appear.
Paleozoic	Permian		250–290	Erosion of ancestral Rockies continues. Conifers develop and reptiles spread.
	Pennsylvanian		290–325	Ancestral Rockies uplift and begin to erode. Primitive reptiles appear.
	Mississippian		325–354	Seas deposit thick gray limestones. Fishes diversify. Coal-forming forests develop.
	Devonian		354–412	Seas deposit limestones and shales. Amphibians, the first known land vertebrates, appear.
	Silurian		412–436	First land plants and animals appear.
	Ordovician		436–513	Seas deposit limestone layers containing fossil fish, the first known vertebrates.
	Cambrian		513–530	Seas deposit sandstones and limestones. Marine invertebrates abound.
Pre-Cambrian			530 +	Periods of mountain building alternate with periods of erosion. Metamorphic and igneous rocks are formed by compression, heating, and volcanic activity.

Ripple marks ornament sandstones deposited by the Cretaceous Sea near Boulder, Colorado.

Fossil-rich sediments from the Cretaceous seabed create castle-like formations at Monument Rocks, Kansas.

Water and wind carved South Dakota's White River Badlands from volcanic ash and stream sediments deposited 28 million to 38 million years ago.

This scarp woodland of Ponderosa Pine, Limber Pine, and Rocky Mountain Juniper in northeastern Colorado may be a remnant of forests that covered the Great Plains during the Ice Age.

As the climate warmed and the glaciers retreated, the forests finally gave way to nearly continuous prairie. Over a period of a few thousand years, a blink of the eye in geologic time, more than 30 genera of large mammals that had thrived during the Ice Age vanished. These included mammoths, mastodons, and sabre-tooth cats, along with giant wolves, giant sloths, wild horses, and camels.

The coincidence of this sudden die-off with the apparent arrival of Clovis hunters in central North America about 11,000 years ago has prompted some scientists to attribute the mass extinctions to humans (see Human Impacts, p. 67). But the rapid change in environmental conditions certainly played a part. In the heart of the continent, a grassland ecosystem evolved in which certain mammals, including Elk, modern Bison, and their associated predators, seemed to gain a competitive advantage over some of the large lumbering Ice Age mammals.

The warming and drying trend continued for several millennia, reaching its maximum intensity between 8,000 and 5,000 years ago. During the height of this hot, dry period, the prairie pushed eastward, replacing forests in parts of present-day Illinois, Indiana, Michigan, Ohio, and perhaps Pennsylvania. The sands of western Nebraska, stripped of most of their vegetation, shifted in the prairie winds. All but a few isolated groves of conifers disappeared from the western plains. *Bos bison,* a smaller, more agile species than its forest-dwelling progenitor, became the dominant herbivore on the Great Plains; prairie dogs and ground squirrels proliferated; and Pronghorn populations climbed into the tens of millions.

About 5,000 years ago the climatic pendulum began to swing back toward slightly cooler and wetter conditions. By the time the first white explorers stepped out into the grasslands, the forests had begun to creep westward, filling in pockets of prairie in the Great Lakes region and upper Mississippi River Valley.

Nevertheless, all of these early travelers marveled at the expanse of grass that seemed to extend forever beyond the last islands of forest. Nineteenth-century author Washington Irving characterized the landscape as being "inexpressively lonely" and like "a desert world." Writer Francis Parkman referred to it as "a barren, trackless waste." In contrast, nineteenth-century artist George Catlin extolled a land of "soul-melting scenery...where Heaven sheds its purest light and lends its richest tints."

Whatever their opinion of the landscape, few of these writers realized that the prairie was still evolving, caught up in a struggle between sun and rain, grass and forest; or that their actions would help trigger a wave of change that would sweep this uniquely American ecosystem and the cultures that depended on it into near oblivion.

First-time visitors to the prairie sometimes complain about the monotony of a landscape seemingly bereft of trees and conspicuous landmarks. But most people who linger in the grasslands come to appreciate the subtle features—the escarpments, buttes, and hills that grow in stature when touched by the light and shadow of a prairie evening. "The grand simplicity of the prairie is its peculiar beauty," wrote explorer John Charles Frémont. "The uniformity is never sameness . . . And whatever the object may be —whether horsemen, or antelope, or buffalo—that breaks the distant outline of the prairie, the surrounding circumstances . . . give it a special interest."

In this land of unobstructed vision you can stand on a hilltop at sunrise and sense the earth turning beneath your feet, feel the full force of the westerly wind as it roars off the Rocky Mountains and scours the plains, or track racing cloud shadows to the edge of the earth. Each wrinkle in the landscape, each ravine, bluff, or hillside spring, shelters unique treasures.

"The plains, as far as the eye could see, were green, and here and there was a pretty stream," wrote Lakota Chief Luther Standing Bear. "Over the hills roamed the buffalo and in the woods that bordered the streams were luscious fruits that were ours for the picking."

The North American prairie region encompasses a mixture of distinct ecosystems, each with its characteristic assemblage of plants and animals. In the tallgrass-aspen parklands of southeastern Manitoba and northwestern Minnesota, Gray Wolves and Moose slog through fens, Sloughgrass meadows, and islands of deciduous forest. In the Flint Hills prairies of eastern Kansas, White-tailed Deer bound through 8-foot-high stands of Big Bluestem and Indian Grass. Short-horned Lizards and Western Rattlesnakes bask in bunches of Blue Grama and Buffalo Grass on the parched shortgrass plains of eastern Colorado and western Kansas. Elsewhere, there are shady Bur Oak savannas and Limber Pine woodlands; fragrant sandsage prairies; salt plains prairies; wet, mesic, and dry tallgrass prairies; and uncountable varieties of mixed-grass prairies (so named because they contain a mix of short, medium, and tall grasses).

This diversity stems from differences in climate, topography, and soils within the immense grassland region. On the western plains, where the Rocky Mountain rain shadow limits precipitation to 10 to 20 inches per year, drought-tolerant shortgrasses such as Blue Grama and Buffalo Grass predominate. Prickly Pear cactus creeps over patches of bare ground, and the landscape greens up for only a few weeks each summer.

*Tallgrass prairie,
Bluestem Prairie
Scientific and Natural Area, Minnesota*

*Mixed-grass prairie,
Badlands National
Park, South Dakota*

*Shortgrass prairie,
Black Mesa State
Park, Oklahoma*

*Tallgrass–aspen
parkland. Wallace
C. Dayton Conservation and Wildlife
Area, Minnesota.*

A couple of hundred miles east, rainfall increases to 20 to 25 inches, and the grass cover grows denser and taller. In the mixed-grass prairies of central Nebraska and central South Dakota, the Little Bluestem, Western Wheatgrass, Porcupine Grass, and Prairie Sandreed grow knee- to waist-high.

Farther east, where annual precipitation exceeds 30 inches, Big Bluestem, Indian Grass, and Switchgrass may grow 8 feet tall, and the prairie sod may become so dense that you can barely penetrate it with a shovel. This is the classic tallgrass prairie, but it is far from uniform. Within the tallgrass region, grass cover ranges from knee- to over head-high, and grassland community types range from relatively dry sand and hill prairies to wet prairies dominated by sedges and Sloughgrass.

Throughout the prairie region, local topography and soil conditions ensure that no two patches of prairie appear exactly the same. In the Loess Hills of western Iowa, in the heart of the tallgrass region, Buffalo Grass and Prickly Pear grow on well-drained, wind-dried soils. In some areas of arid eastern Colorado, head-high stands of Big Bluestem, Indian Grass, and Switchgrass ornament floodplains of trickling streams. A typical square mile of prairie, whether on the Great Plains or in the Mississippi Valley, supports a half-dozen grassland plant communities and 40 or more species of grass.

These varied plant communities shelter a correspondingly diverse array of mammals, birds, amphibians, reptiles, and invertebrates (see Wildlife, p. 41). Each community creates a universe of its own, with unique textures, smells, and sounds.

FIRE, WIND, DROUGHT, AND BISON

The Cheyenne and other Plains Indians sometimes referred to prairie fires as "red buffalo," in part because the fires roared across the grasslands bringing renewed growth in their wake. The Lakota named the winds after gods who descended from the sky to establish the Four Directions and complete the circle of life. All Plains Indian peoples held the Bison as sacred.

These reverent attitudes grew in part from an intimate understanding of how fire, wind, drought, and grazing animals shape and maintain prairie ecosystems. Without these forces, our grasslands would dwindle in size and become much less varied.

Periodic fires burned throughout the prairie region, blackening hundreds of square miles at a time. In tallgrass prairies, fires raged as fast as 40 miles per hour and sent flames 30 feet or more into the air. Elk and deer scattered before the rolling clouds of black smoke. Herds of Bison and groups of people on horseback could be swallowed up by the conflagrations.

Newcomers to the prairie found the fires both frightening and alluring. While canoeing up the Minnesota River in 1847, George Featherstonhaugh watched a fire burn for days:

> Before going to my pallet, I made another journey to the upland behind the Fort, to see the prairies on fire. It is a spectacle one is never tired of looking at: half the horizon appeared like an advancing sea of fire, with dense clouds of smoke flying towards the moon.

Many fires were started by lightning, especially on the arid plains during late summer and early fall. A high percentage of fires in the tallgrass region were deliberately set by Plains Indians —to signal, to drive game, to repel the enemy, to create a defensible perimeter around villages, or to encourage growth of new grass that attracted Bison herds. Lewis and Clark commented on the prevalence of smoke and fire in the Missouri River Valley. On March 6, 1805, Lewis wrote, " . . . a cloudy morning and smoky all Day from the burning of the plains of which was set on fire by the Minetarries for an early crop of grass, an inducement for all the Buffalow to feed on." When these explorers wanted to parlay with groups of Indians, they followed the regional custom of igniting the prairie to signal their intentions.

The effects of prairie fires vary depending on time of year, weather, fire intensity and frequency, and the type and condition of prairie. In tallgrass prairies, fires typically reduce the litter layer, allowing rainfall and nutrients in the ash to quickly enter the ground and sunlight to bake the soil. Rhizome and tiller growth of dominant grasses generally increases after a fire. Under certain conditions, particularly in late summer and early fall, fires may lead to greater diversity of native forbs. Frequent spring fires often decrease species diversity, however, by stimulating growth of dominant grasses.

In shortgrass and mixed-grass prairies, the impacts of periodic fires are less well understood. But virtually all fires in all regions of the prairie kill or damage invading trees and shrubs. Even fire-resistant trees such as Quaking Aspen and Bur Oak wither before repeated waves of flame. Vast areas of prairie, from central Nebraska, Kansas, and Oklahoma east to Ohio and Missouri, have become overgrown by trees since fire suppression began during the mid-nineteenth century.

Most prairie grasses are fire-adapted, meaning they evolved with and can benefit from fire. Since grass stems grow from the base rather than from the tip, they recover quickly after being clipped or burned away. In many prairie grasses, the apical meristem, the point from which cell growth is initiated, is located underground.

Many grasses are long-lived perennials with extensive root systems. Ninety percent or more of their mass may lie underground, insulated from disturbances. In experiments conducted at Konza Prairie in the Kansas Flint Hills, areas that were periodically burned and grazed produced a higher volume of grasses and forbs over time than did areas that were neither burned nor grazed.

Like fire, wind and drought help to create grasslands and rid them of trees. Because the North American prairie region lies in the center of the continent where major weather systems collide, it experiences some of the most violent weather on Earth. Warm, moist air from the Gulf of Mexico clashes with frigid arctic air and hurricane-force winds sweeping eastward off the Rocky Mountains. The resulting instability and turbulence cause startling temperature fluctuations and violent storms.

In Spearfish, S.D., weather watchers once recorded a 49°F temperature rise in just two minutes; Bozeman, Mont., experienced a 100°F temperature range, from +44°F to -56°F, in 24 hours. A grapefruit-sized hailstone that fell in Kansas weighed 1.67 pounds, a world record. Tornadoes strike with more frequency and fury on the southern plains than anywhere else in the world.

People who live on the prairie learn to make light of weather extremes that would drive others to despair. In *Where the Sky Began,* John Madson recounts the tale of a Nebraska farmer who died in retirement in San Diego. They took his remains to a crematorium and baked them for an hour or so. When the furnace door was opened, the farmer stepped out looking healthy and tanned. He wiped some sweat off his face, gazed up at the hazy blue sky, and said, "Sure good to be home again. But by God, another couple of weeks of this and we ain't gonna get a corn crop this year!"

The violent winds that swirl across the grasslands can uproot mature trees and flatten saplings, but the winds' desiccating effect probably causes the most damage to shrubs and trees. Torrid spring and summer winds can suck the soil dry. Even the relatively wet tallgrass prairie region experiences a net annual water deficit when you factor in evaporation, much of it caused by scorching winds. Exposure to intense sunlight and long periods of drought also dry prairie soils.

Grasses are particularly efficient at tapping and retaining moisture. The root systems of Big Bluestem extend as far as 10 feet underground; a cubic meter of Big Bluestem sod may contain more than 20 linear miles of rootlets and root hairs. Leaves of many grasses curl up in hot weather, minimizing exposure to sun and wind. Waxy coating on grass leaves reduces water loss from evaporation. Grasses' pliant yet sturdy stems can withstand the

Tornadic thunderstorm near Platteville, Colorado

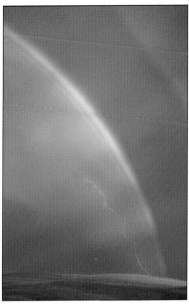

Passing thunderstorm, Nebraska Sand-hills

Prescribed burn, southeastern Colorado

Greening grasses after a burn, Konza Prairie, Kansas

fiercest gales; wind seems to flow effortlessly through fields of grass, creating a mesmerizing interplay of waves and eddies.

Some of the attributes that help prairie grasses adapt to fire and wind also help them resist damage and even benefit from grazing by large ungulates. On shortgrass prairies of the western plains, Buffalo Grass and Blue Grama react to frequent grazing by sending out roots and tillers that help to form tough sod and sodlike bunches. These drought-hearty shortgrasses carry most of their living tissue underground in extensive root systems. When ungulates clip off the upper few inches of above-ground growth, the stems and leaves grow back quickly.

Bison graze preferentially on Buffalo Grass and Blue Grama because, unlike many tallgrasses, these shortgrasses retain a high nutritional content throughout the year. Buffalo Grass was named for its wiry texture, which feels like buffalo hair, but the name could easily have derived from its mutualistic relationship with Bison.

In the tallgrass region, scientists are just beginning to understand how Bison influence prairie patterns and processes. At Konza Prairie in Kansas, Bison graze preferentially on the dominant grasses, creating room for forbs and other grasses. As a result, grazed areas support higher species diversity than ungrazed areas. Nitrogen added to the soil by urine and decaying Bison carcasses stimulates plant growth. Bison wallows provide habitat islands for moisture-loving plants in spring and for drought-resistant plants in late summer, when the wallows dry up. By trampling seedlings and rubbing against saplings, Bison help to keep the prairie free of trees.

Some of the most intriguing new research has shown how Bison and fire interact to shape prairies. At the Nature Conservancy's Tallgrass Prairie Preserve in Oklahoma, Bison prefer to graze in recently burned areas and continue to select these areas for up to two years after burning. Conversely, lightly grazed areas burn most intensely and, under natural conditions, most often. Bison diets (the percentage of various plants that they consume) are different in recently burned sites than in unburned sites.

These interactions between Bison grazing patterns and fire create a dynamic mosaic of prairie patches that fuels diversification of plant and animal life. In addition to creating and maintaining prairies, fire and Bison constantly enrich them. Plains Indians understood these relationships and wove them into their folklore.

A Pawnee story tells of a time when there were not yet Bison on Earth and the people were poor and starving. A young man sat on a hilltop above a spring, crying out for a vision. The full moon came to him in the form of an old woman. She spoke comforting words, instructed him in the proper way to build earth lodges and cultivate corn, and told him of a wonderful gift that was soon to come to his people.

The people waited for several months, growing restless from hunger. Finally, thousands of Bison streamed from the cave and flowed out onto the prairie. From that moment the Pawnee lived well, and the earth was whole.

A young Bison calf runs with its mother in early summer at Wind Cave National Park, South Dakota.

PLANTS

For a century or more the Pawnee, Ponca, Omaha, and Winnebago lived in relative prosperity at the western edge of the tall-grass prairie region, where the Platte and Niobrara Rivers meander down to the Missouri. Though these tribes depended on Bison for much of their subsistence, they and other plains peoples made good use of the native plant communities surrounding their villages.

In addition to tending gardens of corn, beans, and squash, women scoured the countryside for edible tubers, fruits, and herbs. They collected Hazelnuts, Wild Strawberries, Raspberries, Juneberries, Wild Plums, Sand Cherries, Chokecherries, Buffaloberries, Ground Cherries, and Elderberries. They made sugar from Silver Maple, Hickory, and Box Elder sap; pounded Bur Oak acorns and Buffalo Gourd seeds into flour; dug Prairie Turnips, Wild Licorice, and Jerusalem Artichokes; harvested seeds of Wild Rice and other grasses; and dried Wild Mint and New Jersey Tea for winter. In autumn, Pawnee women raided the nests of Prairie Voles, taking the Hog Peanuts the rodents had hoarded and leaving behind a handful of corn as a token of thanks.

Dozens of other plants were used medicinally or ceremonially. A decoction of Sweet Flag was drunk to fight fevers, the juice of Purple Coneflowers spread on abrasions, the dried root of Compass Plant burned to discourage lightning strikes. Nettle stalks were dried and woven into twine, Smooth Sumac leaves boiled up to make a yellow dye, cattail down stuffed into pillows and cradle boards. Children made toy tepees from cottonwood leaves, earrings from green cottonwood fruits, and chewing gum from the sap of Compass Plant and Common Milkweed.

The passage of the seasons was marked as much by the blooming of wildflowers as by the journeys of the sun, moon, and stars. In early spring, shamans prayed and sang to the first Pasque

Flowers to encourage other plants to bloom. When Wild Plums flowered, the Omaha knew it was time to plant their crops, and when parties out hunting Bison saw the first goldenrods on the western plains, they knew their corn was ripening back home. Many plains peoples scheduled their most sacred ceremony, the Sun Dance, during the Moon of Ripening Cherries, when the midsummer heat sweetened the astringent Chokecherry fruits and turned them from red to deep purple.

Perhaps because many European-Americans considered the prairie a form of desert, awareness of prairie plants diminished in the decades following white conquest. The Pawnee and most of the Ponca were removed from Nebraska to Oklahoma during the 1870s, the Omaha and Winnebago confined to tiny reservations. Other tribes suffered a similar fate, and traditional practices were discouraged throughout the plains.

Then in 1914, a University of Nebraska graduate student named Melvin Gilmore published a groundbreaking Ph.D. dissertation, *Uses of Plants by the Indians of the Missouri River Region*. Gilmore documented the use of nearly 200 native plant species by the Pawnee, Ponca, Omaha, and Winnebago.

"The people of the European race . . . have not really sought to make friends of the native population, or to make adequate use of the plants or the animals indigenous to this continent," wrote Gilmore. "[T]he surest road to contentment would be by way of gaining friendly acquaintance with the new environment."

Gilmore's dissertation sparked a renewed interest in uses of prairie plants and laid the groundwork for more recent ethnobotanical works, including Kelly Kindscher's *Edible Wild Plants of the Prairie*. With this revival has come an awareness that many of the plants that sustained generations of Native Americans served as survival food for white homesteaders as well. On late-summer evenings, descendants of these homesteaders and of the Plains Indian families that preceded them still comb prairie ravines for Chokecherries, Wild Plums, Saskatoon Serviceberries, and Buffaloberries to cook up into jams and pies.

"Nothing could be more generous, more joyous, than these natural meadows in summer," wrote Minnesota homesteader and novelist Hamlin Garland. "The flash and ripple and glimmer of the tall sunflowers, the myriad voices of gleeful bobolinks, the meadow-larks piping from grassy bogs . . . Made it all an ecstatic world to me. . . . The sun flamed across the splendid serial waves of the grasses, and the perfume of a hundred spicy plants rose in the shimmering air."

Several thousand species of vascular plants, including close to 300 grasses, bloom in the prairie region. Ecologists sometimes divide this region into three general prairie types: tallgrass, shortgrass, and mixed-grass. The highest plant species diversity often occurs in tallgrass prairies, where wildflowers unfurl in waves from May through October. Late-spring rains bring a burst of color to shortgrass prairies on the arid western plains. In mixed-grass prairies of the central plains, peak wildflower displays typically come in late spring and again in late summer.

Within each of these regions, wildflower displays and abundance of wild fruits vary from year to year, depending on moisture and sunlight. After a wet spring, Purple Locos, Scarlet Globemallows, and Prairie Evening-Primroses may carpet hundreds of square miles of shortgrass prairie in Colorado and Wyoming. If the rains fail, the grass remains brown and few wildflowers appear. In the tallgrass region, Big Bluestem and Indian Grass may grow 8 feet high during some years and only waist-high during others.

A good way to get to know the grasses and wildflowers of a given region is to keep an annual blooming chart, noting which species bloom when and where. Most of the preserves featured in this book maintain lists of blooming plants, and numerous wildflower field guides are available.

TALLGRASS PRAIRIE

When nineteenth-century explorers and settlers talked of grass as tall as a man on horseback, they were usually referring to prairies dominated by Big Bluestem and some combination of Indian Grass, Switchgrass, Little Bluestem, and Prairie Cordgrass. These "bluestem prairies" thrive on floodplains and moist hillsides from Manitoba to Missouri.

According to ecologist John Madson, Iowa homesteaders carved routes through head-high stands of bluestem prairie by dragging logs chained to teams of oxen. Herds of cattle could vanish in the jungle of grass. Unfortunately, the soil and moisture conditions favored by Big Bluestem were perfect for growing corn, and most of these lush prairies were plowed under within a few years of white settlement.

Big Bluestem was named for the bluish green color of its stems in early summer. Close-up, the 3- to 5-pronged "turkey-foot" seed head distinguishes this grass from all others. As summer progresses, the flower stalks and stems take on a reddish hue. "Winestem" seems a more appropriate name for this grass in late summer and early fall.

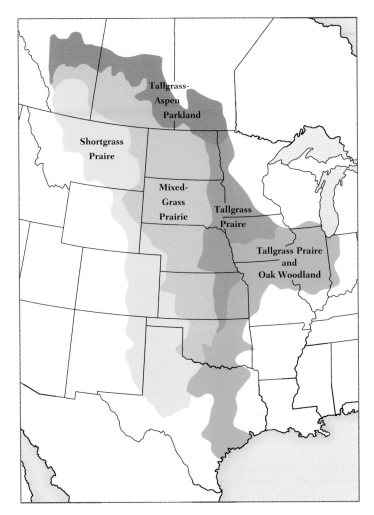

Major Prairie Types in Central North America
Sources: *Bailey, Robert G. 1995.* Descriptions of the Ecoregions of the United States; *Küchler, August William. 1977.* Potential Natural Vegetation of the Coterminous United States.

Flowering stems of Indian Grass add a golden tint to bluestem prairies in late summer. Tall, erect, and bending in the slightest breeze, this grass flourishes in wet to dry soils. The slightly velvety texture of the soft, brushlike inflorescences and the twisted awns (bristles) at the tip of each hairy seed distinguish this tallgrass from its neighbors.

Prairie Cordgrass, or Sloughgrass, forms a mat of dense sod as it grows up to 10 feet tall in wet meadows. Homesteaders cut the sod into strips and stacked them up to form the walls of their houses. Big Bluestem and Switchgrass also served this purpose, but no grass formed thicker sod than Prairie Cordgrass. No grass inspired more epithets, either, than this "rip gut," whose razor-sharp leaves bloodied the hands and faces of toiling homesteaders.

Switchgrass, which usually grows in slightly drier sites than Prairie Cordgrass, looks and feels soft. This grass sports long curling leaves and a delicate cluster of slender branches bearing oval nutlike seeds. A chest-high clump of golden Switchgrass makes a pleasant napping spot on a warm October day. It's also a likely place to encounter a resting Red Fox, White-tailed Deer, or Wild Turkey.

Spring comes late to most of the tallgrass region, and the first conspicuous wildflowers may not appear until April or early May. Pasque Flowers, Prairie Violets, Prairie Trout Lilies, and Shooting Stars provide an early burst of color, often blooming in areas where grass cover is sparse. Several orchids, including the Ragged Fringed Orchid, Grass Pink Orchid, and the exquisite Yellow Lady's-Slipper, begin blooming in April.

In June, milkweeds, coneflowers, and wild indigos color the sun-drenched hills and meadows. Butterfly Milkweed forms brilliant orange patches on sandy soils of hill prairies and savannas. Plains Indians used the roots and stems of this sometimes toxic plant as food and medicine. Homesteaders called this milkweed "pleurisy root" for its supposed ability to alleviate chest congestion.

Plains Indians coveted several species of purple coneflower, crushing the roots and leaves to treat toothaches, colds, wounds, and snakebites. The recent popularity of *Echinacea* (the generic name for purple coneflowers) as a cold remedy, along with the lure of the magenta-petaled blossoms to gardeners, has resulted in many wild stands being decimated by collectors.

Leadplant and Compass Plant have become symbols of native tallgrass prairie. Both "decrease" under grazing pressure and thrive amid stands of Big Bluestem and Indian Grass. Named for its lead-colored leaves, Leadplant, a woody shrub growing up to 3 feet high, was dubbed "prairie shoestring" by settlers who dented

Indian Grass (Sorghastrum nutans)

Prairie Cordgrass (Spartina pectinata)

Big Bluestem (Andropogon gerardii)

Switchgrass (Panicum virgatum)

Spider Milkweed (Asclepias viridis)

Butterfly Milkweed (Asclepias tuberosa)

Ragged Fringed Orchid (Platanthera lacera)

Blue False Indigo (Baptisia australis)

Pale Purple Coneflower (Echinacea pallida)

Prairie Phlox (Phlox pilosa)

Leadplant (Amorpha canescens)

Compass Plant (Silphium laciniatum)

their plow blades on its tenacious roots. The Omaha and Ponca called this member of the pea family "buffalo bellow plant" because it bloomed during the Bison rut, and they brewed a golden tea from its leaves.

Nineteenth-century explorers tied strips of cloth to the 10-foot-high stems of Compass Plants to mark their way through the grasslands. This deep-rooted sunflower gets its name from its own powers of orientation: the giant oak-shaped leaves typically align north-south, an adaptation that may reduce moisture loss on hot summer days.

If you can stand the heat and humidity, July and August are prime times for observing tallgrass-prairie wildflowers. Most of the dominant grasses in the tallgrass region are "warm-season" types that evolved in mild southerly climates and grow most vigorously during the summer months. The blooming of these grasses during the dog days of summer often coincides with impressive wildflower displays.

"You will scarcely credit the profusion of flowers upon these prairies," wrote emigrant Eliza Steele of the Illinois grasslands in 1840. "We passed whole acres of blossoms all bearing one hue, as purple, perhaps, or masses of yellow or rose; and then again a carpet of every color intermixed, or narrow bands, as if a rainbow had fallen upon the verdant slopes."

From mid-July to late August the purple flowering spikes of blazing stars attract swarms of butterflies, moths, and bees. Though they bear little superficial resemblance to sunflowers, blazing stars belong to the same family (Asteraceae). Each apparent flower head on the spike is actually a composite of tiny disk flowers similar in structure to the flowers in the central disk of an aster or sunflower.

Sunflowers bloom throughout the summer, but they come on with a rush in August. Jerusalem Artichokes unfurl along streams and lakeshores, Maximilian Sunflowers sprout 9 feet high in sandy swales, and Prairie and Common Sunflowers turn whole hillsides into gardens of light.

Early autumn wildflowers are less abundant but nevertheless provide points of gemlike radiance in the sea of golden grass. The deep blue tulip-shaped corollas of Downy and Fringed Gentians mirror the cloudless September sky, while clumps of Heath Aster and pale lavender Willow Aster freshen the dying prairie as migrating Snow Geese race south on arctic winds.

For nine months of the year, the arid steppes just east of the Rockies can appear drab and lifeless. But if the spring rains come on time and with enough frequency, the shortgrass plains transform into lush green meadows carpeted with wildflowers.

The greening begins in May or early June, when cyclonic storms swirl down from the Gulf of Alaska and thunderheads billow up along the Rocky Mountain Front. Blue Grama and Buffalo Grass spring to life, flowering and setting seed. On soft summer evenings, Pronghorn herds race through glowing fields of evening-primrose, milk vetch, and loco.

Blue Grama, a bunchgrass with eyebrow-shaped seed heads at the end of short round stems, thrives in medium and fine-textured soils of dry upland prairies. This drought-resistant, ankle-high grass "increases" under light to moderate grazing pressure, spreading in sodlike bunches.

Buffalo Grass forms sod by sending out horizontal stems called runners and rhizomes. The runners creep along above ground, and the rhizomes worm their way through the soil, producing roots and stems of their own. This method of growth and reproduction is critical during dry years when the grasses produce few seeds.

Other common grasses of the shortgrass region include Hairy Grama, Sideoats Grama, Needle-and-Thread, Junegrass, Western Wheatgrass, Three-Awn, and Indian Ricegrass. Many of these grasses are cool-season types primed for rapid growth and flowering when spring rains arrive.

During the dry winter months, persistent westerly winds blowing off the Rockies keep daytime temperatures relatively mild. On the central and southern shortgrass plains, some wildflowers begin blooming long before the vernal equinox. Early Easter Daisies may unfurl on south-facing shales in late December, while Nuttall's Violets and Sand Lilies often flower in March and early April.

On rock outcrops in eastern Colorado and New Mexico, Pasque Flowers typically appear right around Passover. Appropriately, the closed flowers look like pale lavender Easter eggs. Pasque Flowers grow on dry or rocky soils throughout the prairie region, blooming progressively later as you move north.

While mild weather conditions favor some early bloomers, the drying winds of the western plains punish plants that grow too high above the ground. The cementlike sandstones, or capstones, atop wind-buffeted buttes and escarpments, are carpeted with cushion and mat plants similar to those that grow in the alpine re-

Blue Grama (Bouteloua gracilis)

Junegrass (Koeleria macrantha)

Buffalo Grass (Buchloë dactyloides)

Sideoats Grama (Bouteloua curtipen-dula)

Early Easter Daisy
(Townsendia *sp.*)

Pasque Flower
(Pulsatilla patens)

Nuttall's Violet
(Viola nuttallii)

Ceramic Milk Vetch
(Astragalus ceramicus)

Prickly Pear (Opuntia *sp.*)

Sandwort (Arenaria hookeri), *growing on capstone*

Prairie Evening-Primrose (Oenothera albicaulus)

Rocky Mountain Bee Plant (Cleome serrulata)

gion of the central Rockies. Sandworts and milk vetches form mosslike clumps, sending thick taproots down into the rock. Plains Phlox creeps across the ground, forming a loose mat covered with fragrant white flowers.

Cactuses thrive in the shortgrass region, and their Day-Glo blossoms brighten the landscape from late spring through early summer. Prickly Pears produce magenta or waxy yellow flowers. Tiny Pincushion Cactus sport a ring of 5-petaled pink flowers. The gangly, scarecrowlike Chollas of the southern plains display a dozen or more floppy pink to purple blossoms.

No spring wildflowers are better known to cattle ranchers than milk vetches and locos. Collectively called "locoweeds" and "crazyweeds," these colorful members of the pea family often grow on selenium-rich soils, and many are poisonous to livestock. Some, however, are edible. The Lakota, Omaha, and Ponca ate the immature pods of Ground-Plum Milk Vetch after boiling or pickling them. The delicate fruit pods of Ceramic Milk Vetch were used for ornamentation. An often toxic species, Purple Loco, creates some of the high plains' most dazzling floral displays in late spring.

By midsummer most of the colors on the shortgrass plains have faded. A few blazing stars and sunflowers wilt in the heat, and drought-tolerant golden asters and Snakeweed add a faint yellow tint to the parched hills. The drying grasses curl up as much of their life energy retreats underground to await next spring's regenerative rains.

MIXED-GRASS PRAIRIE

Most of the plants found in tallgrass and shortgrass prairies also grow in mixed-grass prairies. As in other prairie types, the composition of dominant grasses varies according to slope, soils, climate, and latitude.

Throughout much of the central Dakotas and southern Saskatchewan, wheatgrasses and needlegrasses predominate. A couple of hundred miles to the south, in novelist Willa Cather's "shaggy-grass country," clumps of Little Bluestem and Sideoats Grama turn burgundy and copper in the autumn sun. "The whole prairie was like a bush that burned with fire and was not consumed," wrote Cather of these distinctive loess hills grasslands. Sandy areas of eastern Colorado and western Kansas support sandsage, a mixture of Sand Sagebrush and various midgrasses and tallgrasses.

Little Bluestem grows throughout the prairie region, often on sandy or rocky soils of hillsides and ridgetops. This warm-season

Needle-and-Thread (Hesperostipa comata)

Canada Wild Rye (Elymus canadensis)

Western Wheatgrass (Pascopyrum smithii)

Little Bluestem (Schizachyrium scoparium)

Shell-leaf Penstemon (Penstemon grandiflorus)

Crested Penstemon (Penstemon eriantherus)

Showy Milkweed (Asclepias speciosa)

Bush Morning Glory (Ipomoea leptophylla)

Fourpoint Evening-Primrose (Oenothera rhombipetala)

Black-eyed Susan (Rudbeckia hirta)

Maximilian Sunflower (Helianthus maximilianii)

Tulip Gentian (Eustoma exaltatum)

bunchgrass resembles its taller cousin, but the seed heads are much smaller and the stems rarely grow taller than 4 feet.

Western Wheatgrass, sometimes called "bluestem wheatgrass," forms nearly pure stands in the northern plains. This cool-season, sod-forming wheatgrass looks like a small version of commercial wheat, with the seed-bearing spikelets growing flat along either side of a slender stem. A dozen wheatgrasses occur in the prairie region, and all are edible if you have the patience to separate the seeds from the chaff.

Green Needlegrass, Needle-and-Thread, Porcupine Grass, and several other related grasses (placed by some taxonomists into the single genus *Stipa*) flourish in areas with moderate rainfall. Also known as "speargrass," these cool-season grasses produce sharply pointed seeds bearing long twisted awns. The awns compress and unravel with changes in humidity, literally corkscrewing the seeds into the soil.

Canada Wild Rye forms 3- to 5-foot-tall bunches in moist to moderately dry prairies from the Rocky Mountains to the Ohio River Valley. Its nodding seed heads with stiff, bristlelike awns distinguish it from other grasses. This native grass thrives in disturbed areas, such as roadsides and fallow fields.

Prairie Dropseed and Sand Dropseed bear their 1- to 3-foot-tall flowering stalks within a curled leaf, or sheaf. As the flowers mature, the panicles open out, forming a branching cluster with each flower growing on the end of an individual stalk. When the round seeds mature, they drop to the ground.

Of the hundreds of wildflower species that bloom in the mixed-grass prairie region, milk vetches and asters (about 30 species each) and milkweeds, penstemons, and evening-primroses (about 20 species each) are particularly well represented. Milkweeds flower as early as April and as late as October. Common Milkweed (eastern prairie region) and Showy Milkweed (west and central) serve as host plants for Monarch butterflies. Throughout the summer, adult Monarchs cling to the ball-shaped pink and white flower clusters. Homesteaders collected the morning dew from the fragrant flowers and spread it on their pancakes. Plains Indians ate the tender shoots and green fruits after boiling them in water to remove their toxins.

Many evening-primroses snap open just before sundown and close up the following morning. Night-flying sphinx moths hover over the trumpet-shaped flowers, extracting nectar with their long tonguelike proboscises. The white tissue-paper blossoms of Gumbo and Prairie Evening-Primroses scatter across the hillsides in late spring. From mid-July through mid-August, the lemon yellow blossoms of Fourpoint Evening-Primrose brighten thousands of square miles of the Nebraska Sandhills.

Penstemons display trumpet-shaped corollas ranging from white to deep blue to scarlet. Some species, including the 2-foot-tall Shell-leaf Penstemon, thrive in a variety of settings; others, such as Crested Penstemon (gravel and sandy soils on the northwestern plains) and Blowout Penstemon (sand dunes in Nebraska and Wyoming), cling to a narrow range of habitats.

Common Sunflowers grow throughout North America, but they do especially well in sandsage prairies of the western plains, combining with Prairie Sunflowers to transform the late summer landscape from mauve to fiery yellow. Sunflower fruits (known commonly as "seeds") were roasted and eaten by Plains Indians, and plants were selected and bred to produce the giant varieties cultivated on prairie farms today.

The Hidatsa, who lived along the upper Missouri, planted several varieties of sunflower each spring during the Sunflower Planting Moon. In late summer they ground the kernels into flour, molded the flour into thin cakes, and baked the cakes in hot ashes. According to Melvin Gilmore, the Teton Dakota used boiled sunflower heads as a remedy for pulmonary troubles. A Teton elder shared this saying: "When the sunflowers are tall and in full bloom, the buffaloes are fat and the meat good."

SPECIES DESCRIPTIONS: Aspen 444–45, Blowout Penstemon 225–26, Buffaloberry 287–88, Buffalo Gourd 145, Bur Oak Savannas 311–12, Cholla 393, Chokecherry 353–54, Cottonwoods 215–16, Death Camas 463, Eveningstars 146–47, Gentians 446, Goldenrods 128–30, Junipers 295–96, Mesquite 380–81, Orchids 168, Pasque Flower 360–61, Prairie Turnip 247–48, Prairie Wild Onion 105 and 463, Prickly Pear Cactus 393–94, Rough Fescue 455–56, Sagebrushes 415, Saskatoon Serviceberry 430–31, Shooting–Star 404–5, Snowberry 287–88, Spiderwort 112–13, Sunflowers 128–30, Sweetgrass 424–25, Three–flowered Avens 437, Western Prairie Fringed Orchid 309–11 and 444, Wild Rice 254, Wolf Willow 456, Wood Lily 181, Yucca 393–94.

WILDLIFE

On a hot afternoon in the summer of 1878, O. W. Williams led a surveying party out onto the Staked Plains of northern Texas. The party had traveled 6 to 8 miles along a muddy, shallow stream when they noticed a peculiar sound, a dull roar off to the north. When they looked in that direction, they saw what appeared to be a low-lying cloud.

As the billowing cloud swirled closer, small dark objects became visible. Williams wrote that the cry went out, "Buffaloes! A stampede!" There was no escaping the approaching herd, which now stretched across the plains from the eastern to the western horizon. With no trees to climb and the wagons a half mile away, the men stood in single file and fired their rifles at the onrushing Bison.

A few of the leaders fell, and the herd parted. The Bison thundered by on either side, some so close the men could see the glint in their eyes and almost touch them with outstretched rifles. The men continued firing, almost certain they would soon be trampled to death.

Within a few minutes the roar subsided, the dust began to clear, and the herd, numbering perhaps 50,000, rumbled away over the low hills to the south. Where they had come from or where they were going no one knew, but Williams commented that this was "almost surely the last great herd of the southern buffalo, after they had been cut off from migration to the north and after five years of the Sharp's rifle in the hands of the professional hunters."

How many Bison roamed the North American prairie? Modern estimates place the total anywhere from 20 million to 70 million. Bison were most numerous on the shortgrass and mixed-grass prairies of the western plains, but even there, distribution was spotty. Some settlers traveled from the Missouri to the Rockies without encountering a single one of the great herds. Others reported Bison blackening the plains in every direction. One pioneer rode 200 miles through a single herd of Bison in what is now northeastern Colorado. Another described a herd that was 100 miles wide and of "unknown length," and he estimated extravagantly that it contained 10 *billion* animals.

As impressive as the Bison herds were, they made up only a portion of the wildlife spectacle on the North American prairie. In 1846 journalist Francis Parkman wrote that the grasslands north of the South Platte River "teemed with wildlife." In 1832 George Catlin described the vistas along the upper Missouri River:

> One thousand miles or more of the upper part of the river, was, to my eye, like a fairy-land; and during our transit through that part of our voyage, I was most of the time rivéted to the deck of the boat, indulging my eyes in the boundless and tireless pleasure of roaming over the thousand hills, and bluffs, and dales, and ravines; where the astonished herds of buffaloes, of elks, and antelopes, and sneaking wolves, and mountain-goats [Bighorn Sheep], were to be seen bounding up and down and over the green fields.

MAMMALS

It's hard to imagine the North American prairie without Bison. Modern Bison evolved with the prairie, developing a huge digestive system to process the coarse grasses, along with the hardiness to cover great distances searching for prime forage. Their nomadic grazing activities created a mosaic of grassland conditions where other wildlife could thrive.

In some places the herds grazed and trampled the prairie to dust. Mountain Plovers nested and Greater Short-horned Lizards foraged for ants in these denuded areas, while Swainson's Hawks and Horned Larks snatched grasshoppers and beetles from the bare ground. Other expanses of prairie were left undisturbed by Bison for years. Here the lush grass cover sheltered Henslow's Sparrows and Greater Prairie-Chickens, nourished Elk and Prairie Voles, and provided fuel for regenerative fires.

Grazing by Bison stimulated new grass growth and created room for less palatable plants (see Evolving Prairie, p. 9). Bison carcasses sustained an array of predators and scavengers, such as Prairie Wolves, Swift Foxes, and Bald Eagles. Invertebrates in Bison dung helped feed a variety of birds, including Sandhill Cranes and Brown-headed Cowbirds.

The near extirpation of Bison during the last half of the nineteenth century, when the total North American population diminished to fewer than 1,000 individuals, had repercussions for many other species. Swift Foxes disappeared from much of the northern plains. Ravens retreated from the grasslands. Deciduous trees, now protected from both trampling and fire, proliferated along prairie streams, creating expanded habitat for forest-dwelling White-tailed Deer, Virginia Opossums, Fox Squirrels, and Blue Jays.

Elk, Pronghorns, and Bighorn Sheep, though not as numerous as Bison, nevertheless massed on the prairie in large herds prior to white settlement. Of the Elk grazing in tallgrass meadows along the Missouri, naturalist John James Audubon wrote, "[T]he number of this fine species of deer that are about us now is almost inconceivable . . . These animals are abundant beyond belief."

Elk, which graze and browse on grasses, forbs, and shrubs, once ranged all the way east to the Atlantic Ocean and west to the Pacific. One million or more may have inhabited the prairie region at the time of European contact. Only a few remained on the periphery of the prairie after 1920.

Small bands of Bighorn Sheep inhabited rugged buttes and canyons in the shortgrass and mixed-grass prairie regions, primarily on the western plains. All were extirpated from the plains by 1930. Though a few Elk and Bighorn Sheep have been reintroduced into national grasslands and other prairie preserves, primarily on the western plains, current populations are minuscule compared to historic numbers.

Pronghorns probably numbered in the tens of millions prior to European contact. With strong, tapered leg bones and forefeet equipped with shock absorber–like cartilaginous pads, Pronghorns race across the grasslands at speeds approaching 60 miles per hour. Enormous lung capacity and oversized hearts enable them to run miles without tiring. Their ability to go days without water and subsist on shrubs and forbs, including cactus, enables Pronghorns to thrive in arid country that is of little economic value to humans. Today close to one million remain in prairies and deserts of the Great Plains and Great Basin.

Wherever large herds of Bison, Elk, Mule Deer, or Pronghorns roamed, Grizzly Bears, Mountain Lions, and packs of Gray Wolves followed. Along the upper Missouri, wrote Meriwether Lewis, "the country in every direction and around us was one vast plain in which innumerable herds of Buffalo were seen attended by their shepherds the wolves." Artist and ethnographer George Catlin noted that wolves could be found "in gangs or families of 50 or 60 in numbers." One U.S. Fish and Wildlife Service publication estimated that the tens of millions of ungulates in the prairie region could have supported as many as 750,000 wolves.

Prior to white settlement, Gray Wolves ranged throughout almost all of North America. They were particularly suited to life on

Bison cow and calf

Pronghorn

Elk

Bighorn Sheep

Swift Fox (Photo by Michael Forsberg)

Young Red Fox

Gray Wolf
(Photo by W. Perry Conway)

Black-tailed Prairie Dog

Black-footed Ferret (Photo by Michael Forsberg)

American Badger (Photo by Michael Forsberg)

Thirteen-lined Ground Squirrel

Deer Mouse on nest

the prairie, where large herds of ungulates provided relatively easy prey. Hunters and ranchers extirpated the last prairie wolves from the badlands country of western Montana and the western Dakotas during the 1920s and 1930s. Their elimination, like that of the Bison, had repercussions that rippled across the grassland ecosystem. In many areas Coyote populations increased. More Coyotes meant more predation on Swift Foxes, ground-nesting Ferruginous Hawks, and waterfowl. Fewer large carcasses meant fewer scavenging opportunities for Swift Foxes, Bald Eagles, and Common Ravens. The prairie would never be the same once the wolves were gone.

Grizzly Bears and Mountain Lions were far less numerous than wolves, but both ranged across the prairie. Grizzly Bears ambled east beyond the Missouri River, and European settlers observed Mountain Lions in New England. Encounters between early explorers and Grizzly Bears sometimes proved fatal to one or both parties. Less aggressive Black Bears foraged along prairie streams and in the transition zones between forest and prairie.

Other mammalian predators included the Red Fox, Long-tailed Weasel, Least Weasel, Black-footed Ferret, Mink, Badger, Northern River Otter, and Bobcat. Of these species, the Red Fox, ferret, and River Otter were probably most affected by European settlement. Red Foxes, historically uncommon throughout the prairie region, proliferated as competitors were killed off and trees, shrubs, and human settlements invaded the grasslands. Fur trappers and settlers extirpated River Otters from most of the prairie region; only scattered, reintroduced otter populations remain. Black-footed Ferrets were driven to the brink of extinction as farmers and ranchers eliminated prairie dog colonies.

The Black-tailed Prairie Dog, like the Bison and Gray Wolf, plays a keystone role in prairie ecosystems. More than 150 vertebrate species make use of prairie dog colonies during some part of their life cycle. Black-footed Ferrets, Eastern Cottontails, Burrowing Owls, and Western Rattlesnakes live in prairie dog burrows. Coyotes, Badgers, ferrets, Golden Eagles, Ferruginous Hawks, and Great Horned Owls hunt prairie dogs. Mountain Plovers forage for insects, and Northern Harriers hunt mice in areas where prairie dogs have reduced the grass cover. Bison wallow where the ground has been denuded of vegetation.

The name "prairie dog" comes from the French *petit chien* (little dog) and probably was given to this highly social rodent because of its habit of "barking" alarm calls in moments of danger. Black-tailed Prairie Dogs once numbered in the billions on the Great Plains, mostly in the shortgrass and mixed-grass prairie regions. In addition to supporting dozens of species of associated wildlife, prairie dog colonies created microhabitats that enriched

SPECIES	STATUS
Gray Wolf	Prairie subspecies extirpated; a few Gray Wolves inhabit periphery of region
Coyote	Has increased throughout much of region
Red Fox	Has increased throughout much of region
Swift Fox	Has declined sharply in north and in parts of southern range. Being reintroduced in Canada
Black Bear	Small populations remain on periphery of region
Grizzly Bear	Extirpated
Black-footed Ferret	Extirpated; being reintroduced on high plains
Wolverine	Extirpated
American Badger	Unknown; has declined where crops have replaced grass
Northern River Otter	Extirpated from most of region by 1900; small populations have been reintroduced
Mountain Lion	Extirpated from most of region
White-tailed Deer	Declined initially, then increased throughout much of region and expanded range westward
Elk	Extirpated from region by 1900; mostly captive populations have been reintroduced
American Bison	Extirpated by 1900; mostly captive populations have been reintroduced
Bighorn Sheep	Prairie subspecies extirpated; small populations of other subspecies have been introduced

Sources: Samson and Knopf 1996; Licht 1997.

PRAIRIE ENDEMICS*

White-tailed Jackrabbit, Franklin's Ground Squirrel, Richardson's Ground Squirrel, Thirteen-lined Ground Squirrel, Black-tailed Prairie Dog, Plains Pocket Gopher, Olive-backed Pocket Mouse, Plains Pocket Mouse, Hispid Pocket Mouse, Plains Harvest Mouse, Northern Grasshopper Mouse, Prairie Vole, Swift Fox, Black-footed Ferret, Spotted Skunk, Pronghorn.

*Mammals whose distributions are centered in the prairie region. Source: Benedict et al. 1996.

the prairie mosaic. The rodents' burrowing activities loosened the soil. Their selective grazing of prairie grasses created room for forbs, increasing plant species diversity.

Though prairie dog populations on the Great Plains have been reduced by more than 95 percent, prairie dog colonies still function as wildlife concentration areas. In recent years observers have noted groups of Bald Eagles congregating around prairie dog colonies in Colorado's Front Range urban corridor. When a Golden Eagle or Ferruginous Hawk captures one of the rodents, a half-dozen Bald Eagles may converge on the spot to steal the prey. Great Horned and Burrowing Owls perch in these colonies by day, and families of Coyotes skulk through them at dawn and dusk.

Since the early 1990s, some of the largest remaining prairie dog colonies in the Great Plains and Great Basin have served as Black-footed Ferret reintroduction sites. The ferrets, once reduced to only 18 captive individuals, now number several hundred, and biologists cautiously hope for their long-term recovery. Although Black-tailed Prairie Dogs have not yet joined ferrets on federal endangered species lists, U.S. and Canadian fish and wildlife agencies and state and provincial governments are working to create conservation plans for these unique rodents.

If prairie dogs can be saved, along with populations of ferrets, Gray Wolves, Elk, Bighorn Sheep and Bison, future generations may experience the prairie that we know only from books and oral history: a tapestry of chalk bluffs, meandering rivers, and rippling grasses overflowing with life.

SPECIES DESCRIPTIONS: Badger 347–48, Bighorn Sheep 87 and 293, Bison 366–67 and 423–24, Black Bear 208–9, Black–footed Ferret 346–47, Black–tailed Prairie Dog 368–69, Bobcat 323–24, Coyote 348–49, Elk 214–15, Gray Wolf 179, Grizzly Bear 208–9, Moose 457, Nine–banded Armadillo 386–87, Porcupine 271–72, Pronghorn 359–60, Swift Fox 95 and 464–65, White–tailed Jackrabbit 429–30, White–tailed Deer 189–91, Wild Horse 207–8.

BIRDS

Most of the 800 or so bird species common to the United States and Canada have been observed on the prairie at one time or another. Only about 50 species actually nest in open grasslands far from marshes and trees, and only a dozen nest exclusively in grasslands. Most of these grassland-nesting birds have declined in number as farming, ranching, and urbanization have destroyed or fragmented native prairies. On remaining grassland parcels, control of fire, poisoning of prairie dogs, and uniform grazing regimes have eliminated niches for birds that typically nest in taller grasses (Northern Harrier and Henslow's Sparrow) or in denuded areas (Mountain Plover and Horned Lark).

Though the grasslands supported fewer birds than the adjacent deciduous and coniferous forests, white explorers and settlers marveled at the abundance of some species. Hundreds of thousands of Greater Prairie-Chickens boomed in the oak savannas of Illinois, Indiana, Missouri, and Ohio. Migrating Long-billed Curlews and Upland Sandpipers darkened the skies over the Ohio Valley. Passenger Pigeons streamed over the oak savannas in seemingly endless flocks. Even today, a half-million Sandhill Cranes gather along a 200-mile stretch of Nebraska's Platte River each spring, and several million migrating Snow Geese form a seething white squall line that sweeps across the northern plains each fall.

For many prairie lovers the ritualistic mating dance of prairie-chickens captures the timeless spirit of the grasslands. Greater Prairie-Chickens thrive in tallgrass prairies and adjacent oak savannas. Lesser Prairie-Chickens inhabit mixed-grass prairies, sandsage prairies, and Shinnery Oak woodlands. Both somehow survived the destruction of most of their native habitat, though in greatly reduced numbers. Many prairie preserves offer public viewing blinds where visitors can still observe and photograph the spring mating dances of these or related prairie grouse, including Sharp-tailed Grouse and sage-grouse.

Of the twenty or so birds of prey commonly seen on the prairie, Northern Harriers ("marsh hawks"), Ferruginous Hawks, Swainson's Hawks, Prairie Falcons, Short-eared Owls, and Burrowing Owls seem especially suited to life in grasslands. Ferruginous Hawks, unique to central North America, nest on the ground, on low cliff faces, or in trees. With large bodies and 53-inch wingspans, these white-tailed, usually white-breasted hawks are adept at catching cottontails, jackrabbits, and prairie dogs.

Slightly smaller Swainson's Hawks specialize in much smaller prey, including mice and grasshoppers. In fall they circle behind tractors looking for invertebrates or swirl skyward on thermal updrafts. Traveling in flocks of several hundred, they ride the thermals south to wintering areas in the pampas of Argentina. Poisoning of insect prey in Argentina has sometimes resulted in massive die-offs of these graceful hawks.

The piercing screams of nesting Prairie Falcons echo off canyon walls and drift out over adjacent grasslands, where these acrobatic falcons swoop down on rodents and songbirds. Prairie Falcons nest on cliff faces in the western plains and Great Basin.

Short-eared Owls breed in open habitats throughout much of North America, South America, and Eurasia. They typically nest

Greater Prairie-Chicken (Photo by Richard W. Holmes)

Sharp-tailed Grouse

Upland Sandpiper (juvenile)

American Avocets

Ferruginous Hawk

Swainson's Hawk

Short-eared Owl
(Photo by John B.
Weller)

Burrowing Owl
(Photo by John B.
Weller)

Horned Lark

Lark Bunting (Photo by Rick and Nora Bowers)

Western Meadowlark

Yellow-headed Blackbird

on the ground in wetlands or areas of dense grass cover. These tawny medium-sized owls may hunt throughout the day or night, but are often active around dusk, when they course low over the ground searching for voles and other small rodents. Northern Harriers nest in similar sites and glide over the grasslands in a similar manner, using sensitive hearing to detect movement of mice and voles.

Throughout the summer months, 10-inch-high Burrowing Owls perch on prairie dog mounds, bobbing up and down on spindly legs as they scan the sky for predators. They lay their eggs in the burrows of prairie dogs and other rodents. Populations of these little owls have plummeted in recent decades, in part because of loss of nesting habitat.

For an arid landscape, the prairie region supports a surprising variety of birds associated with water. American White Pelicans, Snowy Egrets, Trumpeter Swans, Sandhill Cranes, and Franklin's Gulls all nest in the region. Several shorebirds breed in the grasslands, including Long-billed Curlews, Upland Sandpipers, Marbled Godwits, Piping Plovers, Willets, and Mountain Plovers. Many others nest in wetlands or pass through in migratory flocks. Roughly half the total North American shorebird population passes through Cheyenne Bottoms Wildlife Area in Kansas during spring and fall migration.

The prairie pothole region, which encompasses a half-million square miles from Alberta, Saskatchewan, and Manitoba south through the Dakotas, western Minnesota, and Iowa, provides prime nesting habitat for waterfowl. Formed by glacial scouring during the Ice Age, the shallow pothole lakes are loaded with nutrients and rimmed with protected nesting sites. Though farmers and ranchers have drained or plowed under a majority of the potholes, this region remains North America's most important waterfowl breeding area.

Many visitors to the prairie marvel at the volume and variety of bird song in spring and early summer. Typically, the "dawn chorus" begins around 3 A.M., when ever-vigilant kingbirds erupt in clamorous chatter. A little later the hoots of Great Horned Owls and coos of Mourning Doves float through the twilight, then the flutelike notes of meadowlarks, tinkling phrases of Horned Larks, and rhythmic whistles of Common Yellowthroats. As the eastern sky brightens, the individual songs coalesce into a richly textured, life-affirming symphony.

Each species' song informs us of the condition of the prairie. The high, thin notes of Baird's Sparrows emanate from dense grass cover in northern mixed-grass prairies. The arpeggios of McCown's Longspurs enliven heavily grazed shortgrass steppes close to the Rockies. The rare cries of Upland Sandpipers and

NOTE: These species showed statistically significant ($p < 0.1$) declines in North America from 1966 to 2002.

SPECIES	DISTRIBUTION IN PRAIRIE REGION
Northern Harrier	Grasslands and wetlands, throughout
Ring-necked Pheasant	Open country, throughout
Short-eared Owl	Grasslands and wetlands, mostly north and west
Horned Lark	Shortgrass and croplands, throughout
Sprague's Pipit	Short/mixed-grass, north
Cassin's Sparrow	Short/mixed-grass, southwest
Vesper Sparrow	Mixed-grass, sagebrush, and forest edge, north and west
Lark Bunting	Short/mixed-grass and sagebrush, west
Savannah Sparrow	Moist grasslands, wetlands, croplands throughout
Grasshopper Sparrow	Grasslands, throughout
Baird's Sparrow	Mixed-grass and weedy fields, north
Henslow's Sparrow	Wet meadows, shrubby fields, east
Chestnut-collared Longspur	Moist upland prairies, north
Dickcissel	Mixed/tallgrass, central and east
Bobolink	Wet meadows and hayfields, mostly east
Eastern Meadowlark	Mixed/tallgrass, east
Western Meadowlark	Grasslands and fields, north and west

Source: Sauer et al.

PRAIRIE ENDEMICS*

Ferruginous Hawk, Mountain Plover, Long-billed Curlew, Marbled Godwit, Wilson's Phalarope, Franklin's Gull, Sprague's Pipit, Cassin's Sparrow, Baird's Sparrow, Lark Bunting, McCown's Longspur, Chestnut-collared Longspur.

*Birds whose distributions are centered in the prairie region. Source: Knopf, F. L. Prairie legacies—birds. In Samson and Knopf 1996. *Prairie Conservation.*

Long-billed Curlews drift out poignantly from isolated patches of native mixed-grass and tallgrass prairie.

Some of the sweetest singers, including Lark Buntings and Cassin's Sparrows, warble while performing graceful aerial displays. Others perch on a Yucca stalk, fence post, or swaying grass stem and raise their heads at regular intervals to send their music skyward. The songs, repeated by the same species in the same stands of grass for thousands of years, serve primarily to attract mates and warn away competitors. But each carries an underlying message: One strand of the web of life remains unsevered, one piece of prairie endures.

SPECIES DESCRIPTIONS: American White Pelican 470–71, Bald Eagle 234–35, Burrowing Owl 340–41 and 465, Black–capped Vireo 329, Chuck–will's–widow 191, Common Nighthawk 191, Common Poorwill 191, Eastern Meadowlark 138–40, Eastern Screech–Owl 329–30, Golden Eagle 277–78, Greater Prairie–Chicken 354–55, Greater Roadrunner 266–67, Greater Sage Grouse 413–15, Grebes 469–70, Henslow's Sparrow 127–28, Horned Lark 138–40, Lark Bunting 138–40, Lark Sparrow 138–40, Lesser Prairie–Chicken 144–45, Long–billed Curlew 226–27, Mississippi Kite 87, Mountain Plover 94, Northern Bobwhite 197–98, Ovenbird 240–41, Piping Plover 302–3, Prairie Falcon 277–78, Ring–necked Pheasant 106, Sandhill Crane 179–81 and 231–33, Scissor–tailed Flycatcher 196–97, Sharp–tailed Grouse 226, Snow Goose 303–4, Trumpeter Swan 252–53, Upland Sandpiper 355–56, Western Meadowlark 138–40, Whip–poor–will 191, Wild Turkey 151–52, Wood Duck 330–31, Yellow Rail 446–47.

AMPHIBIANS, REPTILES, AND FISHES

While some prairie residents mark the onset of spring by the arrival of bluebirds or the blooming of Pasque Flowers, others listen for the first peeps emanating from the nearest marsh or wet prairie. Chorus frogs, sometimes called "bubble-gum frogs" because of the size of their inflatable vocal sacs, begin calling in some prairie regions as early as February and March.

As the ground thaws and air temperatures rise, other amphibians and reptiles emerge from subterranean resting places. Eastern Collared Lizards crawl out of rock crevices to bask on boulders. Western Rattlesnakes slither from hibernacula in burrows and small caves. Ornate Box Turtles dig out of the sand and plod across the prairie, warming their blood in the sun as they search for tender shoots and insects.

In April and May, male Bullsnakes lock their heads together in sexually inspired combat, swaying and intertwining their bodies. In June algae-encrusted Snapping Turtles lumber out of the water to lay their eggs in a hole dug in the sand. Later in the summer, short-horned lizards give birth to as many as 30 live young, and masses of young leopard frogs hop across highways while dispersing from breeding ponds. Throughout the warmest months, the intermittent chirruping of the chorus frogs continues, mixing with the snorelike calls of Woodhouse's Toads and the sonorous bellows of Bullfrogs.

In an arid environment where the air temperature might fluctuate as much as 140°F in one year, ectothermic (cold-blooded) amphibians and reptiles have evolved remarkable behaviors for reproducing and surviving the elements. The Plains Spadefoot, a toad with a sharp, spadelike protuberance on each hind foot, burrows into the ground in the fall and stays buried until late the following spring. On summer evenings the toads emerge to feed, but some may remain in their burrows for weeks at a time. However, the sound of rumbling thunder stirs most of these toads to serious action. The males surface, find a pool of water left by the recent downpour, and emit a ducklike call that can be heard a mile away. Females converge to lay their eggs, which are fertilized by the males and hatch into tadpoles within two or three days. If the ephemeral pools begin to dry up, the tadpoles may become cannibalistic, ensuring that a few will survive.

Wood Frogs persevere in the frigid northeastern plains by producing a form of "antifreeze" in winter and by breeding early in spring. These light brown 1- to 3-inch-long frogs hibernate under leaves, rocks, logs, or tree roots. Hibernation sites are often insulated by snow, but temperatures may still dip to 20°F or lower. The frogs survive the cold by increasing the breakdown of glycogen stored in their livers, raising their blood glucose levels to as much as 60 times above normal. The increased glucose protects frozen tissues from damage, enabling the frogs to partially freeze without dying. Soon after they thaw out in spring, Wood Frogs return to breeding ponds and mate, giving tadpoles time to develop, metamorphose, and reach maturity before ponds and marshes freeze up again.

Since box turtles rarely travel more than 100 yards in a day, encounters between males and females are infrequent. This is no problem for females, who can store sperm in their oviducts for up to four years. In addition to ensuring that the female can fertilize her eggs almost at will, sperm storage may enable her to select her mates more carefully. Females who are not thrilled about having a particular male clasped to their backs have been known to abruptly close their plastrons (the underside of the shell), pinching the male's hind legs.

Plains Spadefoot (Photo by Glenn Cushman)

Lesser Earless Lizard

Greater Short-horned Lizard

Northern Leopard Frogs (Photo by W. Perry Conway)

Bullsnakes

Western Rattlesnake

Eastern Racer

Ornate Box Turtle

In all, the prairie region is home to about 120 species of amphibians and reptiles. More than 200 fish species swim in the region's lakes, rivers, and streams; Iowa, alone, supports at least 135. Introduced cold-water fish such as Coho Salmon and Brook Trout and cosmopolitan warm-water species such as Longnose Sucker, Common Carp, and Channel Catfish all thrive in prairie waters.

Of particular interest to many scientists are prairie endemics such as the Topeka Shiner and Fountain Darter. Several of these prairie specialists have become threatened or endangered by channelizing, dewatering, pollution, and increased turbidity of streams (see table, p. 63). In the Illinois River system, two-thirds of the native fish species are declining in number or have been eliminated from parts of their historic range.

SPECIES DESCRIPTIONS: Barking Frog 263–64, Horned Lizards 381, Northern Leopard Frog 312–13, Ornate Box Turtle 228, Pecos Pupfish 263–64, Red–sided Gartersnake 438–39, Snapping Turtle 253–54, Tiger Salamander 304–5, Topeka Shiner 157, Western Rattlesnake 122 and 246–47.

FEDERAL ENDANGERED AND THREATENED MAMMALS, BIRDS, AMPHIBIANS, REPTILES, AND FISHES IN THE PRAIRIE REGION

E - Endangered in U.S. and Canada
EC - Endangered in Canada
EU - Endangered in U.S.
T - Threatened in U.S. and Canada
TC - Threatened in Canada
TU - Threatened in U.S.
XC - Extirpated in Canada

MAMMALS	STATUS AND DISTRIBUTION IN PRAIRIE REGION
Preble's Meadow Jumping Mouse	TU; scattered populations on high plains
Northern Swift Fox	EU/XC; being reintroduced in Canada
Gray Wolf	EU; virtually eliminated from prairie region
Red Wolf	EU; extirpated from historic range in Texas
Black-footed Ferret	EU/XC; reintroduced on western plains
Grizzly Bear	TU/XC: virtually eliminated from prairie region

Bald Eagle	TU; scattered populations along rivers
Audubon's Crested Caracara	TU; declining in Texas
Ferruginous Hawk	TC; declining on northern plains
Greater Prairie-Chicken	XC; declining in eastern prairie region
Attwater's Prairie-Chicken	EU; fewer than 1 oo remain in south Texas
Whooping Crane	E; migrant, fewer than 200 remain
Eskimo Curlew	E; migrant, probably extinct
Mountain Plover	EC; fewer than 50 adults remain in Canada
Piping Plover	E; scattered populations on northern plains
Western Snowy Plover	TU; isolated populations along prairie rivers
Least Tern	EU; isolated populations along prairie rivers
Burrowing Owl	TC; declining on northern plains and elsewhere
Black-capped Vireo	EU; scattered populations on southern plains
Loggerhead Shrike	TC; declining throughout
Baird's Sparrow	TC; declining on northern plains
Henslow's Sparrow	EC; declining on northeastern prairies

AMPHIBIANS	STATUS AND DISTRIBUTION IN PRAIRIE REGION
Blanchard's Cricket Frog	EC; declining on northeastern plains
Wyoming Toad	EU; occurs along Laramie and Big Rivers

FISHES	STATUS AND DISTRIBUTION IN PRAIRIE REGION
Fountain Darter	EU; isolated population in Texas
Neosho Madtom	TU; scattered in Missouri, Kansas, Oklahoma
Arkansas River Shiner	TU; isolated populations in Arkansas River basin
Topeka Shiner	EU; scattered populations on central plains
Pallid Sturgeon	EU; scattered populations in prairie rivers
Paddlefish	XC; declining in prairie rivers

Sources: Scientific Committee on the Status of Endangered Wildlife in Canada (COSEWIC) 2002; U.S. Fish and Wildlife Service 2000.

Tens of thousands of insect and spider species inhabit the prairie region, and scientists are discovering new ones all the time. There are more than 200 grasshoppers, about 500 butterflies and dragonflies, and around 10,000 beetles. In most prairie sites that have been sampled, the total biomass of insects exceeds that of all vertebrates, excluding domestic livestock.

Insects influence the plant and animal composition of prairies by loosening the soil and breaking down nutrients; pollinating and nibbling on grasses, shrubs, and trees; and providing nourishment for wild-life. Some species play roles that seem completely out of proportion to their diminutive stature.

The 1-inch-long Pronuba Moth lays her eggs in the ovary of a yucca flower. Then she stuffs a wad of pollen previously gathered from another yucca plant down the flower's style. The fertilized ovary produces fruit for her young. The remaining seeds disperse, creating more yucca plants. No other insect pollinates yucca flowers, and no other flower supports Pronuba Moth larvae. Should these moths disappear, the grasslands would change dramatically, since yuccas help to stabilize sandy soils throughout the western prairie region.

Scarab dung beetles gather balls of animal dung and roll them around until they find an appropriate place to bury them. Ancient Egyptians believed these balls represented the earth and that the beetles' movements were directed by heavenly bodies. The balls actually provide food for the beetles and nursery sites for their young. Females of some species bury a ball and inject their eggs into it. The larvae feed on the dung and remain in the protected underground environment until they pupate into adults. Laboratory studies show that buried dung balls, which contain numerous grass seeds, provide exceptionally fertile environments for grass seed germination and growth. Besides cleaning up the prairie, dung beetles also cultivate it.

Harvester Ants build 6- to 12-inch-high conical anthills from soil and pebbles. If you search one of these hills carefully, you may find 150-year-old glass beads or million-year-old fossilized tooth and bone fragments that the ants have collected. In summer and fall, the ants scour the prairie for seeds of grasses and forbs, which they store in their mounds, along with bird dung and carcasses of dead insects. According to ecologist David Costello, the ants in one colony can collect a pint of seeds in a single day. We can only guess what impact all this activity has on prairie plant distribution and growth.

The Rocky Mountain Locust was a migratory grasshopper that

Short-horned Grasshoppers

Widow Skimmer dragonfly

Ottoe Skipper (Photo by Paul Opler)

Scarab Dung Beetles (Photo by Jon Farrar)

bred in the foothills and on the northern plains, occasionally irrupting east and south in uncountable numbers. Between 1874 and 1877, great crackling clouds of these locusts descended on prairie farms, eating everything in sight, including crops, grass, fences, window curtains, furniture, and even the green stripes of one homesteader's dress. Nebraska observers estimated the size of one swarm at nearly a mile high, 100 miles across, and 300 miles deep. The devastation caused hundreds of farmers to give up their lands and head back east.

The legendary swarms of Rocky Mountain Locusts disappeared a couple of decades later. Scientists believe that cultivation of flood plains in locust breeding areas may have helped drive the species to extinction. But it's possible there would be even less grass and more farmland on the Great Plains today if locust swarms had not swept through as westering homesteaders were beginning to extol the productivity of the prairie soils.

Because insects are so numerous and specialized, they serve as strong indicators of environmental quality and change. Like canaries in coal mines, endangered and threatened insects in the prairie region warn of the near collapse of entire ecosystems.

Dakota Skippers flit through grasslands of the northern and central plains, where the caterpillars feed on native grasses and overwinter in silken tubes lined with grass. These compact brown-and-orange skippers have disappeared from prairies that have been severely overgrazed or invaded by nonnative grasses. Although some still breed in more natural prairie remnants, scientists fear that these sites are too small and isolated to support viable populations.

Prairie Mole Crickets face a similar fate in the southeastern prairie region. These burrowing crickets, which aggregate each spring on leks to perform courtship dances, have vanished from all but a few tallgrass remnants. Other imperiled insects in the prairie region include the American Burying Beetle, Ottoe Skipper, and one of the prairie's most beautiful butterflies, the orange and silver-spangled Regal Fritillary.

SPECIES DESCRIPTIONS: Black and Yellow Garden Spider 191–92, Cicadas 157–59, Convergent Ladybird Beetle 272–73, Dragonflies and Damselflies 264–65, Fireflies 107, Monarch 169–70, Prairie Mole Cricket 196, Regal Fritillary 122–23 and 127, Texas Brown Tarantula 278–79.

Human Impacts

Since the waning days of the Ice Age, humans have helped shape the North American prairie. For more than 10,000 years they have hunted big game animals, driving some species to extinction. They have set fire to the grasslands, killing trees and shrubs and altering the composition of the grasses and forbs. Beginning 5,000 to 3,000 years ago, they introduced exotic plants—first squash, then corn and beans, and eventually dozens of garden plants and Eurasian weeds. Within the past 150 years, farmers and ranchers have plowed under two-thirds of North America's native grasslands and irrevocably altered the rest.

Large spearpoints found scattered among the bones of mammoths and ancient Bison establish the presence of human hunters in the evolving grasslands around 11,500 years ago. Paleo-Indians known as Clovis hunters—for the New Mexico site where some of their long, fluted spearpoints were unearthed—lived on the Great Plains for several hundred years. Groups of Clovis hunters ranged over the plains, ambushing or scavenging mammoths that had become mired in swamps or sand dunes. These people may have specialized in big game hunting or they may have pursued large mammals while engaging in a much wider range of hunting and foraging activities.

Until recently, Clovis hunters were widely recognized as the first people to colonize the New World. They presumably walked from Asia to Alaska across the Bering Land Bridge and then followed an ice-free corridor south into the Great Plains and Great Basin. Recent discoveries have called this theory into question.

Hints of human activity dating to several thousand years before the appearance of Clovis culture have surfaced throughout the Western Hemisphere. Artifacts recovered near Monte Verde, Chile, date back 12,500 years or more. On the Great Plains, scientists have found 12,000- to 17,000-year-old mammoth bones

Oregon Trail ruts, Guernsey, Wyoming

Rebuilt sod house, Oglala National Grassland, Nebraska

that appear, at least to some researchers, to have been fractured by blunt instruments.

In addition, the distribution of Clovis sites suggests that these people may actually have spread from south to north across the prairie. Some recent research indicates that the ice-free corridor through present-day Canada did not exist until well after Clovis culture became established in central North America. Some anthropologists have proposed that the first people to colonize the New World may have followed the Pacific Coast southward from Alaska or even crossed the Atlantic from Western Europe.

For decades scientists noted the apparent coincidence of the arrival of Clovis hunters in North America with the extinction of more than 30 genera of large mammals, including mammoths, mastodons, sloths, and camels. Did the hunters cause these extinctions? "Overkill" proponents point out that extinction rates were higher among the large game animals than among other genera of mammals; that similar extinctions occurred in other parts of the world, particularly islands, when humans first arrived; and that post–Ice Age extinctions were not nearly so severe in Eurasia or Africa, where humans were already established.

Skeptics point to the relative scarcity of Clovis sites and conclude that Clovis hunters were not numerous enough to wipe out so many large mammals. They cite the mounting evidence that many of the mammals were already extinct before Clovis culture developed. The mass extinctions occurred, they argue, because of sudden changes in global climate that triggered a reordering of plant and animal communities. Nevertheless, few scientists dispute that hunting by humans contributed to the extinction of at least some species.

As the mammoths disappeared between 11,000 and 10,500 years ago, big game hunters on the prairie shifted to other prey, using slightly thinner Folsom-style spearpoints to hunt Bison, deer, and Pronghorns. From 10,500 to 8,000 years ago, Paleo-Indians killed large numbers of Bison by driving herds over cliffs. Bones of hundreds of animals have been unearthed at the base of some of these "Bison jumps." These peoples also ate Pronghorns, deer, rabbits, prairie dogs, fish, and mollusks.

This apparent trend toward diversification continued for several thousand years, producing what some scientists describe as the most stable cultural complex to occupy the prairie. Plains Archaic hunter-gatherers lived in the region from about 8,500 to 500 years ago. They used notched projectile points to hunt large and small game, harvested wild plants, fished, and gathered snails and mussels.

The small simple huts and hearths at the campsites of these

seminomadic people suggest a life on the move. Many of their possessions were probably made of lightweight and perishable materials such as leather, wood, sinew, and bone and are not preserved at archaeological sites. However, the various stone tools and elegant ornaments found buried with the dead offer a picture of a society rich in ceremony and with strong ties to other groups, including cultures in the Great Basin and Mississippi River Valley.

About 2,500 years, ago new technologies from the eastern woodlands infiltrated the prairie region. People learned to hunt with bows and arrows, make fine pottery, and grow corn and other crops. In the eastern Great Plains and upper Midwest, people adopted the custom of burying their dead in giant effigy mounds on hills overlooking river valleys. People slowly became more sedentary, establishing permanent villages and farms.

Village Farmers, who inhabited parts of the eastern and central plains from roughly 900 to 1880 A.D., constructed large earth lodges overlooking the Missouri, Platte, and other rivers. They stored their food in pits, made smoking pipes from red clay, and molded globular jars and bowls with ornamented rims and handles. They cultivated corn, beans, squash, and sunflowers. They also collected wild plants, hunted Bison and other mammals, and caught fish and freshwater mussels.

Based on the size and number of village sites unearthed, human populations over much of the plains increased during the early part of this period. However, many villages decreased in size or vanished after about 1300, and others became heavily fortified. Drought, accompanied by warfare and disease, may have afflicted these agricultural societies, or rapid population growth may have taxed scarce resources in a limited number of farmable river valleys.

Nevertheless, Village Farmer culture persisted until very recently, especially in the Missouri and Mississippi River Valleys. Many of the peoples first encountered by European explorers, including the Mandan, Arikaree, and Hidatsa along the upper Missouri and the Pawnee along the Platte, still lived in earth lodges, farmed the river bottoms, and dispersed across the plains in early summer and fall to hunt Bison. Other peoples who would also come to be known as Plains Indians, including the Lakota and Cheyenne, migrated onto the plains from deciduous forests in the Mississippi and Ohio Valleys, some arriving as recently as the mid-eighteenth century.

European culture had transformed Plains Indian life long before American explorers ventured onto the plains. On their journey up the Missouri in 1804, Lewis and Clark encountered people riding European horses, using European knives and rifles, and mourning the loss of countless relatives to European diseases. Many of these plains peoples had been displaced westward as Europeans annexed lands east of the Mississippi River. The immense Bison herds, victims of increasing trade between Native Americans and Europeans, had begun their stampede toward extinction long before white hunters initiated the final slaughter during the mid-1800s.

PREHISTORIC PEOPLES OF THE PRAIRIE REGION

CULTURE	YEARS AGO	CHARACTERISTICS
Paleo-Indian (Includes Clovis, Folsom, and later cultures)	11,500–8,000	Nomadic hunter-gatherers; used large fluted spear points to kill big game animals; made tools from bone and ivory; used red ocher and bison skulls in ceremonies
Plains Archaic	8,500–500	Seminomadic; built simple huts; hunted a variety of game using notched projectile points; fished and gathered shellfish and wild plants
Plains Woodland	2,500–500	Used bow and arrow to hunt a variety of game, also gathered wild foods and tended gardens; made ceramics and complex tools; buried dead communally in effigy mounds
Village Farmer	1,050–120	Built permanent villages containing large earth lodges; grew a variety of crops; hunted and gathered; made finely decorated pottery, bone adornments, and effigy pipes

Source: Wood 1998.

BROKEN AND SCATTERED

When artist and ethnographer George Catlin sailed up the Missouri River in 1832, he wrote poetically of the "velvet hills," picturesque bluffs, and "enameled plains," and he praised the "happy and flourishing people" who lived and hunted on the prairie:

> No man's imagination . . . can ever picture the beauty and wildness of scenes that may be daily witnessed in this romantic country; of hundreds of these graceful youths . . . their long black hair mingling with their horses' tails, floating in the wind, while they are flying over the carpeted prairie . . .

Abandoned houses at Comertown, Montana (Photo by Glenn Cushman)

Drifting dust and sand, eastern Colorado

A Great Horned Owl, a habitat generalist that benefits from human disturbance of prairie ecosystems, perches beside a winter wheat field in Montana (Photo by Glenn Cushman)

Boarded-up church at Scenic, South Dakota (Photo by Glenn Cushman)

Signature Rock, Guernsey, Wyoming

Prairie View Community Building, Pawnee National Grassland, Colorado

Within 60 years these scenes lived only in memory. Even as Catlin embarked on his historic trip into "Indian country," imported diseases had decimated Native American populations. In the Great Lakes region, smallpox had infiltrated Ojibwe, Menomenee, and Potawatomi villages by 1650. A 1781 smallpox outbreak may have killed half the Indians on the Great Plains.

Trading parties and warring bands spread the pox. Raiders took scalps from dying victims and plundered stricken camps, taking the disease home with them. One Piegan survivor said, "We had no belief that one man could give it to another any more than a wounded man could give his wound to another."

The scourge returned in the 1830s, destroying the Mandans who had housed and fed Lewis and Clark 30 years earlier. Out of a village of 1,600 only 30 or 40 were left alive. Catlin wrote that the few survivors were enslaved by the Arikara and some months later brought about their own death in a battle with the Lakota. "They wielded their weapons as desperately as they could to excite the fury of their enemy, and they were cut to pieces," he wrote.

Imported horses and cattle had a more subtle but no less disruptive impact on traditional Native American life. Horses were introduced into the continent by the Spanish during the sixteenth century, but most plains peoples did not acquire them until after the 1680 Pueblo Indian revolt. As the Spanish fled from New Mexico, their captured steeds scattered with the winds. Within a century, almost all the Plains Indian tribes possessed horses, as well as rifles.

These new technologies rendered people more mobile and much more efficient at killing Bison and each other. Trade and warfare intensified, and Bison populations began to diminish. By the time land-hungry homesteaders and cattle ranchers began to overwhelm remaining tribal lands during the 1860s and 1870s, Plains Indian culture had been transformed by technology, warfare, and disease, and the prairie had been blackened more than usual by war-related fires.

The final chapters of this story are painfully familiar. In 1864 Major John Chivington and his regiment of volunteers launched an unprovoked attack on a camp of Cheyenne and Arapaho at southeastern Colorado's Sand Creek. Two hundred or more women, children, and old men were killed even as they tried to surrender. Soldiers hacked off the women's breasts and took them home to be used as tobacco pouches.

After twenty-six more years of bloodshed, the Plains Indian wars ended for good at Wounded Knee, South Dakota. Nervous federal troops fired on an encampment of ghost dancers, mes-

Approximate location of Plains Indian Peoples around 1800

sianic pilgrims committed to restoring the old ways of life. Nearly 200 people, mostly noncombatants, were killed. Forty years later Oglala shaman Black Elk remembered the moment: "A people's dream died there. It was a beautiful dream...[Now] the nation's hoop is broken and scattered. There is no center any longer, and the sacred tree is dead."

The prairie nearly died as well. By 1875 settlers had broken the soils throughout the tallgrass region, where land sold for around $1.25 an acre. The promise of free, arable land farther west lured homesteaders into the mixed-grass prairies of the Dakotas, Nebraska, and central Kansas. During the 1870s Texas ranchers began to drive their herds up into the central plains to fatten on the prairie grasses before being shipped east to market. During the dry year of 1885 tens of thousands of cattle died on overgrazed lands.

Wildlife populations dwindled. Hunters killed off the last Elk in Indiana in 1818. Greater Prairie-Chickens, which once numbered in the millions, disappeared from most of Ohio, Illinois, and Iowa by 1900. Audubon's Bighorn Sheep were gone by 1905, Prairie Wolves by 1930.

Market and sport hunters finished off most of the Bison before the settlers even arrived. Millions of animals were shot from passing trains, their carcasses left to rot in the sun. One hunter claimed an unofficial record when he killed 120 Bison in 40 minutes. By 1895 fewer than 1,000 Bison remained in all of North America.

Prairie flora and fauna gained a reprieve of sorts during the 1890s when drought and depression forced many homesteaders off their lands. By the early 1900s new technologies, new crops, expanding markets, and an unusually wet climatic cycle enabled a second wave of settlers to push westward. As they plowed marginal lands on the high plains, most failed to consider what would happen to the bare soil when the wind began blowing in earnest.

The black blizzards struck in 1932, blotting out the sun. On May 11, 1934, one storm scoured an estimated 300 million tons of topsoil from the plains. Dirt clogged the engines of cars, tractors, and trains. Birds, jackrabbits, and cattle suffocated. Grit from some storms blew clear across the country and settled on decks of ships out in the Atlantic Ocean.

In 1935 hearings were being held in Washington, D.C., on a bill to establish the Soil Conservation Service. A shadow passed over the hearing room, and one senator muttered, "It's getting dark." Hugh Bennett, nicknamed the "Father of Soil Conservation," thundered, "There, gentlemen, goes Oklahoma!"

Every year in October, volunteers from the Missouri Prairie Foundation gather at Stillwill Prairie to clear brush and trees, sing prairie songs under the stars, and celebrate the resurrection of tallgrass prairies in their state. In January, young Cheyenne men run 400 miles from Fort Robinson, Nebraska, to a cemetery in Busby, Montana, to commemorate their people's heroic flight to freedom in 1879. Throughout the prairie region, people come together at campouts, relay runs, powwows, and sun dances to renew spiritual and cultural bonds and give thanks for nature's gifts.

In small Kansas towns, residents plant Indian Grass and Switchgrass in their gardens; some even sow prairie wildflowers on their roofs. In Chicago, volunteers are working to restore 200,000 acres of urban grasslands and woodlands. A group in eastern Nebraska, after losing their fight to save a remnant grassland from the bulldozer, dug up the entire prairie and moved it to a protected location. Prairie Web sites have sprouted like sunflowers, providing information on native plant cultivation and prairie restoration.

It took the Dust Bowl disaster of the 1930s to awaken most North Americans to the dire plight of the prairie. In 1933 Congress passed the National Restoration Act, allowing the government to buy out the most severely damaged land for 50 cents to 8 dollars an acre. Reclamation workers planted windbreaks and seeded Crested Wheatgrass, a Eurasian import, to stabilize the soil and provide forage. The Soil Conservation Act, passed in 1935, laid the groundwork for the national grasslands, which were formally established in 1960. The U.S. Forest Service now manages 20 such grasslands, covering about 4 million acres, in 11 western states.

However, most of the national grasslands lie on the high plains — shortgrass and mixed-grass prairie country. With the exception of Sheyenne National Grassland in eastern North Dakota and Caddo National Grassland in northeastern Texas, no sizable preserves existed in the tallgrass region until the 1970s. In addition, from the outset, national grasslands were managed primarily for cattle production, with limited focus on re-establishing native plant and animal communities.

The 8,600-acre Konza Prairie, established by Kansas State University and the Nature Conservancy in the northern Flint Hills during the 1970s, became the first relatively large preserve dedicated to conserving tallgrass prairie. Several smaller preserves followed, including 4,000-acre Prairie State Park in Missouri,

5,000-acre Bluestem Prairie in Minnesota, 2,900-acre Goose Lake Prairie State Natural Area in Illinois, and the 6,000-acre Manitoba Tallgrass Prairie Preserve.

During the late 1980s and 1990s a new wave of enthusiasm for prairie conservation contributed to the establishment of larger preserves. In 1989, the Nature Conservancy announced the acquisition of the 29,000-acre Barnard Ranch in Oklahoma's Osage Hills. This historic ranch became the cornerstone for the Tallgrass Prairie Preserve, the largest area of protected tallgrass in North America.

At the same time, conservationists were proposing a series of new prairie initiatives on the high plains. Most controversial was a proposal by Rutgers University professors Frank and Deborah Popper to create a several-million-acre "Buffalo Commons" stretching from Montana to Texas.

The Poppers noted that many counties on the high plains suffer from economic depression, dying towns, and declining populations. Their plan, along with several more modest ones offered by western conservationists, proposed restoring lands in economically impoverished areas to expanses of native prairie where Bison and wolves can run free and tourism can thrive. In 2001, the Rosebud Sioux Tribal Council endorsed a version of the Poppers' proposal set forth by the Denver-based Great Plains Restoration Council. Meanwhile, the Nature Conservancy initiated a program to conserve several hundred thousand acres of shortgrass prairie, and Saskatchewan established 118,000-acre Grasslands National Park in the mixed-grass prairie region.

While plans for conversion of private lands on the western plains to public prairie preserves have moved forward slowly, often encountering angry resistance from prairie residents, restoration efforts in the tallgrass region have quietly accelerated. These efforts have benefited from the development of herbicide-resistant crops and the establishment of native seed banks.

In 2001, biologists at the Nature Conservancy's Glacial Ridge preserve near Crookston, Minnesota, began restoring more than 20,000 acres of croplands and degraded pastures to native tallgrass. Using light tillage and herbicides to control weeds between rows of soybeans, they drill native grass and forb seeds harvested from nearby Nature Conservancy properties right into the crop stubble. Later, they broadcast additional forb seeds onto the soil surface.

Once the prairie begins to grow, biologists use mowing, burning, and selective spraying to control weeds. When restoration work is completed, Glacial Ridge will become part of a 35,000-acre national wildlife refuge that will provide habitat for Western

Restored tallgrass prairie from soybean field, Bluestem Prairie Scientific and Natural Area, Minnesota

Suburban Pronghorns, Cheyenne, Wyoming

High-quality mixed-grass prairie on private grazing lands, Nebraska Sandhills

Cultivated sunflowers in former prairie, Nebraska Panhandle

Prairie Fringed Orchids, Trumpeter Swans, Sandhill Cranes, Sharp-tailed Grouse, Moose, and Gray Wolves.

To the north, Minnesota and Manitoba biologists are using fire and grazing to restore more than 50,000 acres of tallgrass-aspen parklands. Another Nature Conservancy project, anchored by the 4,000-acre Dunn Ranch in northern Missouri, will create a 32,000-acre mosaic of restored grasslands and private pasture lands straddling the Missouri-Iowa border.

These prairie restorations represent a giant first step toward re-establishing functioning tallgrass ecosystems in North America. None of the existing tallgrass preserves, however, is large enough to sustain a full range of natural processes. For example, large predatory mammals, such as Gray Wolf and Mountain Lion, are absent from all but the Canadian and northern Minnesota preserves, and none of the preserves supports truly free-ranging Bison herds.

Conservationists have established public-private partnerships throughout the prairie region to expand areas of protected grasslands. In Kansas, Nature Conservancy land stewards and private landowners created the Flint Hills Initiative, a venture aimed at conserving grasslands and enhancing their productivity. A similar partnership in Nebraska, known as the Sandhills Task Force, has protected several thousand acres of wetlands and organized seminars on grazing management.

In the Prairie Coteau region of the eastern Dakotas, government agencies and conservation groups are working with private landowners to conserve a half-million acres of tallgrass prairie on unplowed glacial moraines. These and similar efforts in Missouri, Illinois, and other states and provinces have been aided by several federal initiatives, including the Conservation, Wetlands, and Grassland Reserve Programs.

These federal programs compensate private landowners for converting croplands to grass, conserving wetlands, and maintaining healthy grazing lands. The Conservation Reserve Program has received mixed reviews from environmentalists. Thousands of acres of converted lands have been seeded in nonnative grasses, including Smooth Brome, Crested Wheatgrass, and Tall Fescue. The program has even stimulated some landowners to plow native prairie so that they can later convert it back to grass and claim a subsidy.

The Wetlands Reserve Program and Canada's Prairie Habitat Joint Venture program have contributed to the protection of more than a million acres of wetlands in the United States and Canada; however, existing programs tend to encourage preservation of small fragmented wetlands without providing mechanisms for consolidating them into larger, naturally functioning ecosystems.

Habitat fragmentation plagues the prairie region. The national grasslands, which make up roughly half of all protected prairie lands, generally consist of checkerboard arrangements of public and private parcels. Most protected lands within the tallgrass region are tiny seminatural islands surrounded by cultivated fields.

Fragmentation creates imbalances that jeopardize native-species populations. In its 2002 report, "The Status of Biodiversity in the Great Plains," the Nature Conservancy identified 464 plains species that are either "critically imperiled," "imperiled," or "globally rare." The organization estimated that only half of the prairie's natural plant community types are represented on lands owned by public agencies or conservation groups.

Other environmental problems in the prairie region include pollution of soils and aquifers by pesticides, herbicides, commercial fertilizers, and feedlots; depletion of aquifers (the level of the High Plains [Ogallala] Aquifer has dropped 100 feet in some high plains locations); soil depletion and erosion; and invasion by exotic plants. Knapweed, a prickly Eurasian tumbleweed introduced to North America during the early 1900s, has overrun millions of acres of rangeland in Montana, Wyoming, and Colorado. In North Dakota, the extent of Leafy Spurge infestation increased from 200,000 acres in 1962 to more than one million acres in 1990. Russian Olive trees and Purple Loosestrife have invaded wetlands from Minnesota to Colorado, choking out native plants. Recently, development of genetically modified crops has accelerated conversion of native prairie to farmland. Particularly frightening are the potential impacts of global warming, which could convert much of the prairie region to desert within a few decades.

These myriad threats can breed discouragement, especially among those working to protect or restore small patches of prairie surrounded by towns and croplands. But it's hard to witness the surge of recent interest in prairie conservation without feeling some optimism.

The prairie has always been a place of hope. For the Plains Indians it was, in the words of historian N. Scott Momaday, the "immeasurable meadow of North America . . . the sacred ground of sacred grounds." For westering homesteaders it was a new universe of possibility, a fruitful wilderness where poor and landless immigrants could carve out a life. For city-weary travelers, remaining prairies provide islands of serenity in a frenetic, materialistic world.

It takes only a few fiery sunsets, ear-splitting thunderstorms, or dead-quiet nights under the circling stars to ignite the passion for place that most prairie residents have known. "We could feel the peace and power of the Great Mystery in the soft grass beneath our feet and the blue sky above us," writes Lakota Chief Luther Standing Bear. "All this made great feeling within us, and this is how we got our religion."

REMAINING PRAIRIES IN CENTRAL NORTH AMERICA

PRAIRIE TYPE	ORIGINAL EXTENT (ACRES)	PERCENT UNPLOWED	PERCENT PROTECTED*
Tallgrass	165 million	3–4	0.3
Mixed-Grass	190 million	40–55	1.8
Shortgrass	190 million	55–65	8.0

*Federal, state and provincial, or private conservation lands.

Sources: Licht 1997, Samson and Knopf 1996, The Nature Conservancy 2002.

Tallgrass prairie, early September, at Five Ridge Prairie, Iowa

Part II
Where to See the Prairie

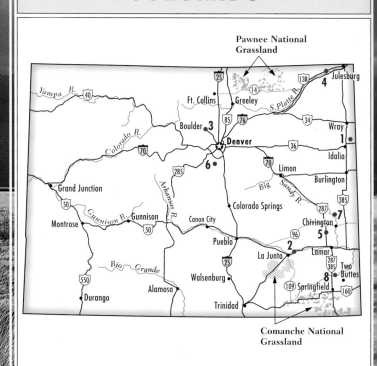

COLORADO

Pawnee National Grassland

Yampa R.
40
Ft. Collins
Greeley
S. Platte R.
138
Julesburg
4
14
Boulder
3
85
76
Colorado R.
70
Denver
36
Wray
1
6
285
70
Limon
Idalia
Grand Junction
50
Big
Sandy R.
Burlington
Gunnison R.
Gunnison
50
Arkansas R.
Colorado Springs
287
385
Montrose
Canon City
96
Chivington
7
Pueblo
La Junta
2
5
Lamar
Rio Grande
25
Walsenburg
287
385
Two Buttes
550
Alamosa
109
Springfield
8
160
Durango
Trinidad

Comanche National Grassland

COMANCHE NATIONAL GRASSLAND

PAWNEE NATIONAL GRASSLAND

OTHER COLORADO SITES:

1. Beecher Island Battleground National Historic Site
2. Bent's Old Fort National Historic Site
3. Boulder Open Space and Mountain Parks
4. Julesburg (Jumbo) Reservoir State Wildlife Area
5. Nee Noshe and Nee Granda Reservoirs State Wildlife Areas
6. Roxborough State Park
7. Sand Creek Massacre National Historic Site
8. Two Buttes Reservoir State Wildlife Area

COMANCHE NATIONAL GRASSLAND

Dinosaurs, Swift Foxes, Long-billed Curlews, and other extraordinary creatures have all left tracks at Comanche National Grassland. Plains Indians left mysterious and haunting petroglyphs on canyon walls, and homesteaders left cabin ruins, testimony to heartbreak, on broken fields.

This corner of southeastern Colorado was one of the areas hardest hit by the Dust Bowl drought. During the late 1930s, the federal government began purchasing badly eroded and overgrazed land in order to aid destitute farmers and to rehabilitate severely damaged grasslands. Comanche was established in 1960.

Today, more than 400,000 acres of public land are interspersed with privately owned land to form a crazy quilt of more than a million acres of shortgrass and mixed-grass prairie. About 2,000 Lesser Prairie-Chickens dance on leks in April and May. They can be observed from a photographic blind, available by reservation, and from a drive-in viewing area. Riparian woodlands, rimrock canyons, and scattered groves of Ponderosa Pine and Plains Cottonwood shelter Bighorn Sheep, Wood Ducks, Wild Turkeys, and Mississippi Kites.

Above: Picture Canyon.

AERIAL ACROBATS

Among the most graceful of raptors, Mississippi Kites have expanded their range westward from the Mississippi River Valley as human settlers have introduced cottonwood groves and shelterbelts into once treeless grasslands. The first breeding pair in Colorado was reported in 1971. Now several pairs nest in cottonwood groves in Cottonwood, Tecolote, and Furnish Canyons, southeast of Kim, and several dozen pairs nest in urban parks in the nearby towns of Pueblo and Lamar.

Mississippi Kites arrive on the Comanche in early May and begin nest-building in June. They usually return to the same location each year, often using or reconstructing the same nest. Look for them overhead as they swoop and dive for grasshoppers, other flying insects, and occasionally, bats. Centuries ago, people playing with wind-hovering paper toys noticed that the toys fluttered in the wind, much as kite wings flutter when the birds hang in the air. They called their toys "kites."

BIGHORN SHEEP

The crashing of Bighorn dueling starts in December. Grunting and snorting, the rams push and kick each other and then pace slowly away. Suddenly they turn and rear up on stiff hind legs. They charge and collide with a mighty bang that can be heard for up to a mile. The cartilage at the base of the horns absorbs most of the shock, and after a few dazed moments, the rams resume the fight. Observers have counted up to 48 clashes in a single battle with impact speeds of more than 50 miles per hour. The weaker combatant usually gives way, and the victor, weighing up to 350 pounds, mates with the ewes. Lambs are born about six months later.

The ram's spiral horns, weighing up to 35 pounds, grow larger and more curled each year. Like tree rings, the grooves around the horns reveal his age. In contrast to the massive horns, Bighorn hooves are dainty. The hollow front part acts like a suction cup, and the rough and springy sole gives purchase on slippery slopes.

In the early 1800s some two million Bighorn Sheep roamed the West, but only those living in remote areas of the mountains survived western settlement and loss of habitat. With no immunity to diseases spread by domestic sheep, Bighorns are especially vulnerable to lungworm pneumonia. In the 1970s, the Colorado Division of Wildlife initiated a capture-and-transplant program to limit the spread of this disease in susceptible mountain herds and reintroduced Bighorns to Carrizo Canyon. They often graze near the southern end of the canyon, where Cottonwood Creek joins West Carrizo Creek. The North American population currently stands at about 20,000.

SPRINGS AND SEEPS

Just north of the New Mexico and Oklahoma borders, tongues of lava spewed out by ancient volcanoes form high mesas that resist erosion. Rain and spring water trickle through gaps in the lava and wear away the underlying Dakota sandstone to create narrow rimrock canyons. Shortgrass prairie carpets the parched mesa tops; mixed-grass prairie, cottonwood groves, and oak woodlands thrive in the moister canyon bottoms.

Small springs and seeps at the heads of these canyons create oases of greenery where Eastern Phoebes nest on moss-covered cliffs and Great Blue Herons stalk bluegills in placid pools. Cottonwood, Carrizo (Spanish for "reed"), Pat, and Holt Canyons contain dozens of springs and seeps. Sadly, many springs are drying up as irrigation of southeastern Colorado tablelands draws the aquifer down.

Several wind-sculpted arches and windows, formed where wind and water have eroded the soft sedimentary rock, rise above one of the natural springs in Holt Canyon. Locations of springs are shown on topographic maps.

DINOSAUR TRACKS

The longest set of dinosaur tracks in North America follows the Purgatoire River in Picket Wire Canyonlands, about 25 miles south of La Junta. These tracks are part of a "dinosaur freeway" where dinosaurs walked along the shoreline of an interior seaway extending from the Front Range of Colorado into Oklahoma. According to paleontologist Martin Lockley, this migration route contains billions of tracks, some of which are in parallel rows, suggesting that some dinosaurs traveled in herds.

More than 1,300 tracks made 150 million years ago by the enormous plant-eating *Apatosaurus* and by smaller meat-eating dinosaurs pockmark areas of the Morrison Formation along the Purgatoire River. Fossilized clams and plants, trampled by the dinosaurs, are also visible. The only way to get there is to bike, hike, or ride a horse down Withers Canyon or to join a jeep tour conducted by the Forest Service. To register, contact the Comanche office listed on p. 91.

Apatosaurus *tracks at Comanche National Grassland are part of one of the longest dinosaur trackways in the world. (Photo by Glenn Cushman)*

ROCK ART, METATES, AND INDIAN RUINS

Rock art, remnants of ancient houses, projectile points, stone tools, turquoise beads, and other artifacts indicate that humans have inhabited the canyons of Comanche since the end of the Ice Age. The earliest inhabitants were hunters and gatherers, but by about 1 000 A.D., people of the Apishipa Culture were farming and living in small villages. Hut foundations still exist on the northern rim of Picture Canyon. Tepee rings found throughout the area were probably made by Apaches.

An etching of a long-necked horse under an overhang in Picture Canyon sets our imagination galloping back to a time when historic Plains Indians carved and painted rock art panels here. Outstanding petroglyphs on the walls near the picnic area also include "Spotted Woman," "Black Buffalo," and "Warrior with Two Spears." Rock art also decorates cliff faces in Carrizo and Vogel Canyons.

Other signs of early habitation include the "birthing stone" and adjacent cavities (located in Picture Canyon) thought to be associated with birth rituals. Along the dirt track from Picture Canyon to the Oklahoma border, *metates*, bowl-shaped depressions made by women grinding grain, were worn into the stones at the base of the cliffs. Some of these relics are on private lands.

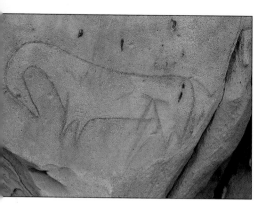

A horse petroglyph in Picture Canyon indicates that some rock art was created after Spanish contact. (Photo by Glenn Cushman)

HISTORIC SITES

Cabin ruins, some dating back to the 1880s, lie scattered throughout the grassland. The Westbrook homestead in Vogel Canyon is among the most accessible. A Spanish cemetery and the Rourke Ranch, founded by Eugene Rourke in 1869 and inhabited by three generations of the family, are included on the Forest Service jeep tour of Picket Wire Canyon.

Place names often reveal a lot about the history of an area. Originally, French beaver traders called the river *Rio de las Animas Perdidas en Purgatorio* (River of Lost Souls) because Spanish soldiers reportedly died in the valley. Later the name became simply *Purgatoire*, which cowboys gradually changed to the more familiar words "Picket Wire."

A section of the Santa Fe National Historic Trail stretches south from La Junta. You can drive to Sierra Vista Overlook from SR 71. Iron Spring (27 miles southwest of La Junta on CR 9) was an important stop along the Santa Fe Trail and the site of a stagecoach station. Look for trail ruts west of the parking lot. A spur of the Santa Fe Trail goes through the Vogel Canyon Picnic Area, where sections of the stagecoach road and ruins of the station can be seen.

HIKING

Hiking is permitted everywhere in the grassland, and delightful small paths wind through the following areas. Most of these paths are not marked.

PICTURE CANYON TRAILS (4 and 8 miles) start at the picnic area and loop through dusty rimrock canyons containing old homesteads, petroglyphs, springs, and natural arches. See directions below under Camping.

CARRIZO CANYON TRAIL (0.5 miles) follows a cool, spring-fed creek flowing between 50-foot-high sandstone walls. More than 80 species of birds have nested in Carrizo Canyon, and the unique Gilia Penstemon blooms here in June. See directions below under Camping.

PURGATOIRE CANYON DINOSAUR TRACKWAY (5.3 miles from Pipe Gate) descends a rough and rocky road down Withers Canyon to the Purgatoire River and the main dinosaur trackway. Length of the hike depends on the condition of the access road, which begins 23 miles south of La Junta off David Canyon and Rourke Roads.

SANTA FE NATIONAL HISTORIC TRAIL (3 miles) follows a section of the famous trail to the Sierra Vista Overlook. Begins at the Timpas Picnic Area Nature Trail 16.5 miles southwest of La Junta off US 350 and is marked with stone posts.

CAMPING

Camping is permitted at three picnic/parking areas:

CARRIZO CANYON PICNIC AREA. From Springfield go south on US 287 for 17 miles; turn west on CR M and continue for 22 miles.

PICTURE CANYON PICNIC AREA. From Springfield go south on US 287 for 20 miles to Campo; turn west on CR J; continue for 10 miles to CR 18; turn south for 5 miles and follow signs.

VOGEL CANYON PICNIC AREA, 15 miles south of La Junta off SR 109.

BEST TIMES TO VISIT

Lesser Prairie-Chickens dance and neotropical migrant birds begin to arrive in April and May. Penstemons, evening-primroses, and prickly pear cactus bloom in May and June, depending on the frequency of spring rains. Female Pronghorns defend their tiny fawns from Coyotes and other predators in June. Young Mississippi Kites fledge in July. In October, flocks of Sandhill Cranes stream over silent, nearly deserted canyons, and in December, Bighorn Sheep battle and mate.

INFORMATION

COMANCHE NATIONAL GRASSLAND, Box 817, 1420 East Third St., La Junta, CO 81050; 719-384-2181; or 27204 Highway 287, Springfield CO 81073; 719-523-6591.

Drive south from La Junta on SR 109; east from Trinidad on US 160; or south from Springfield on US 287. Watch for signs and explore on various county roads. **NOTE:** A Comanche National Grassland map, available at the Springfield and La Junta offices, is essential for exploring this grassland.

COMANCHE NATIONAL GRASSLAND

WEATHER
MEAN TEMPERATURES AND PRECIPITATION

MONTH	HIGH (°F)	LOW (°F)	PRECIP.	SNOW
January	44	13	0.4"	5.0"
April	70	38	1.2"	1.8"
July	94	64	2.2"	0.0"
October	72	37	0.7"	0.0"

Hot weather can occur throughout the year. Intense thunderstorms during July and August make some roads impassable. Data are for Lamar, Colorado, which is slightly drier and warmer than the national grassland.

SELECTED WILDLIFE OF SPECIAL INTEREST

MAMMALS: Rock Squirrel, Thirteen-lined Ground Squirrel, Swift Fox, Ringtail, Badger, Black Bear, Mountain Lion, White-tailed Deer, Pronghorn, Bighorn Sheep.

BIRDS: Mississippi Kite, Ferruginous Hawk, Golden Eagle, Prairie Falcon, Lesser Prairie-Chicken, Wild Turkey, Scaled Quail, Long-billed Curlew, Greater Roadrunner, Western Screech-Owl, Burrowing Owl, Black-chinned Hummingbird, Ladder-backed Woodpecker, Ash-throated Flycatcher, Chihuahuan Raven, Canyon Towhee, Cassin's Sparrow, Blue Grosbeak.

AMPHIBIANS AND REPTILES: Plains Leopard Frog, Plains Spadefoot, Eastern Collared Lizard, Greater Short-horned Lizard, Western Hog-nosed Snake, Western Rattlesnake.

PAWNEE NATIONAL GRASSLAND

"Grass no good upside down" reads a sign in Pawnee National Grassland, quoting a long-ago Pawnee chief. In the 1930s, farmers found out the hard way that he was right.

Believing that rain follows the plow, early settlers optimistically turned under the shortgrass prairie sod and planted wheat and corn. Then came drought, and relentless winds carried off the good loamy topsoil. And the next layer. And continued to carry off the soil until dust clouds rose more than 20,000 feet into the air. Ten-foot drifts closed roads and buried fences, which were often rebuilt over their predecessors, three fences deep. Dozens of fallen-down cabins, flattened barns, and two-story Victorian homes in ruins still endure on the grassland, testifying to broken dreams and broken lives. The plow did indeed break the plains.

What was once a dust bowl is now a mosaic of public and private lands totaling 193,060 acres. Plowing is prohibited, grazing is regulated, and native grasses once again shelter prairie birds and mammals at Pawnee National Grassland.

Northeastern Colorado's most prominent landmark, the Pawnee Buttes, was created by erosion of sandstones and volcanic ash deposited on the plains during the Rocky Mountain uplift.

Despite their name, Mountain Plovers are quintessential birds of the shortgrass prairie and the high desert. Historically, they were associated with Bison and prairie dogs and later with cattle, all of which grazed the grasses short. Patches of bare ground interspersed among islands of shortgrass turf appear to provide optimal nesting habitat.

Starting in May, the females, colored like prairie sand, excavate small depressions between clumps of grass where they lay 3 well-camouflaged eggs. The male takes over the first nest, and she lays another clutch of 3 eggs in a second nest that she incubates—a good example of the adage "Never put all your eggs in one basket."

To keep large lumbering animals from stepping on the nest, plovers will fly up even into the face of the intruder, according to Fritz Knopf who has studied Mountain Plovers extensively. Male plovers also have a flight display called the "falling leaf," in which they drop 15 to 30 feet in the air and then perform the "butterfly display" with slowly beating wings. Later in summer the birds form large flocks. By mid-September most have left for their wintering grounds in California and central Mexico.

More than half the world's population nests on the heavily grazed prairies of eastern Colorado. In 1990 researchers counted 77 Mountain Plovers at permanent survey sites in Pawnee National Grassland, but only 2 were found in 1995, none in 1999, and only 2 in 2001. Knopf believes decreased grazing, a paucity of prairie dogs, and several wet springs during the late 1990s virtually eliminated the areas of bare ground necessary for nesting. He

Mountain Plovers nest on bare ground in close-cropped shortgrass prairies. Cultivation of grasslands and the elimination of Prairie Dogs and Bison have placed this upland shorebird in peril.

is working with area farmers to determine if the birds are nesting on private lands left fallow in spring and is investigating the hypothesis that the birds may benefit from heavy grazing.

The North American Breeding Bird Survey indicates the North American population declined more than 60 percent from 1966 to 1991 and continues to decline by 2.7 percent annually, a higher rate than for any other grassland bird. In 1999 the Mountain Plover population was estimated to be about 10,000 birds. In 2002 a coalition of conservation groups sued the U.S. Fish and Wildlife Service to have Mountain Plovers listed as a threatened species under the Endangered Species Act.

SWIFT FOXES

Swift Foxes feed on Mountain Plovers and other ground-nesting birds, prairie dogs, other small rodents, insects, berries, seeds, and carrion. Before wild bison were wiped out, their carcasses may have been a major component of the diet of this long-legged, cat-sized canid.

They mate from late December through February. Both parents care for the kits that are born from late March to early May and emerge above ground four to five weeks later. Their preferred habitat is a prairie dog colony, where they often den in the pre-dug burrows. They also inhabit agricultural lands but in lower densities than on the prairie.

Swift Foxes are holding their own at Pawnee but have been extirpated in other places. In 1995 they were designated "warranted but precluded" from the U.S. Fish and Wildlife Threatened and Endangered List. They have been successfully reintroduced in Saskatchewan and Alberta, and other reintroduction programs are underway.

Loss of shortgrass and mixed-grass habitat dooms them, and they are also vulnerable to Coyote and Red Fox predation. Coyotes kill them outright but usually don't eliminate the entire population, whereas Red Foxes harass them, driving them from their dwindling territories. Red Foxes may actually be a bigger menace than Coyotes because the encounters are more frequent. In fact, some recent studies suggest Swift Foxes may actually fare better when Coyotes keep Red Foxes in check. Wolves might be even more effective. Historically, wolves were the dominant canid in North Dakota's grasslands. When the wolves, major predators of both Coyotes and Red Foxes but not Swift Foxes, disappeared, so did Swift Foxes. (See Grasslands National Park, Saskatchewan, for more information.)

Many lists of birding hotspots in the country include Pawnee's Crow Valley Recreation Area, a cottonwood oasis with an intermittent stream running through it. It's one of the few places for many miles where migrating birds can find trees, shrubs, and water. Warblers that are rare in the West—such as Golden-winged, Northern Parula, Cape May, Blackburnian, and Chestnut-sided—are reported here during spring and fall migration, and Brown Thrashers and Northern Mockingbirds sing from the treetops. A wetland north of the group camping area attracts Long-billed Curlews and various waterfowl.

Throughout the Pawnee more than 300 bird species have been recorded. A self-guided birding tour, keyed to a pamphlet, begins about 3 miles north of Crow Valley at the intersection of Weld County roads 77 and 96. It takes three to four hours to drive the 36 miles; avoid it in wet weather. Lark Buntings, Colorado's state bird, and McCown's and Chestnut-colored Longspurs nest in this area and often perch on barbed-wire fences.

Among the abundant birds of prey living in the grassland, some of the most fascinating are the cliff-nesting raptors, which do not tolerate large numbers of people within a half mile of their nests. Both Golden Eagles and Prairie Falcons nest at Pawnee Buttes.

PAWNEE BUTTES AND CHALK BLUFFS

James Michener called the twin formations "Rattlesnake Buttes" in his novel *Centennial*, which adeptly captures the flavor of this prairie. (Recreational use of Pawnee Grassland rose 50 percent in

Cliff Swallows (shown here), Golden Eagles, Prairie Falcons, and Ferruginous Hawks all nest on the Chalk Bluffs of Pawnee National Grassland.

the year following publication.) When a television studio wanted to film the *Centennial* series here in 1978, the district ranger at the time, Steward Adams, refused because of the nesting raptors. "I'd rather see an eagle than a movie," he said.

The 300-foot-tall Pawnee Buttes dominate the grassland like two "signal towers on the ramparts of a castle," in Michener's words. When the Cretaceous Sea dried up around 65 million years ago, the seabed was gradually buried under stream sediments, volcanic ash, and glacial dust. The sediments hardened into sandstone and siltstone, which were carved by wind and water into buttes and chalk cliffs.

The White River Formation has been called one of the finest sources of vertebrate fossils in the world. Among the 100-plus species discovered here are fossils of horses, rhinoceroses, camels, and ancient pigs. It's still possible to find clams and other fossils, but removing them is forbidden.

Stunted Limber and Ponderosa Pines grow alongside Rocky Mountain Junipers in canyons cutting through the Chalk Bluffs. These "scarp woodlands," possible remnants of more extensive forests that covered this region during the Ice Age, are now isolated by many miles from their relatives. Nevertheless, they provide homes for some of the same species that live in the mountains, such as Red-breasted Nuthatches and Porcupines.

Some of the vegetation clinging to the buttes is similar to that of the alpine tundra. In both environments blazing sun and high winds favor plants that grow low to the ground. Sandworts, milk vetches, and Plains Phlox form mosslike mats atop the hard capstones that hold the buttes together.

HIKING

Cross-country hiking is permitted on public lands throughout the grassland, except for areas that are closed seasonally. There are a few short trails:

BIRDWALK (0.25 miles) heads north into a wetland from the group picnic area in Crow Valley Campground. See directions under Camping.

TRAIL OF THE MOURNING DOVE (0.25 miles) starts at the Farm Implement Museum in the campground and meanders into a pasture.

PAWNEE BUTTES TRAIL (1.5 miles) begins at the parking area near the terminus of FS 685 and goes to the West Butte. The Pawnee Buttes Overlook and off-trail hiking areas near the Buttes are closed during raptor nesting season.

CAMPING

CROW VALLEY CAMPGROUND, located about a quarter-mile north of the intersection of SR 14 and CR 77, is the only official campground, but dispersed camping is allowed throughout the grassland except on privately owned land and at the Pawnee Buttes Overlook.

BEST TIMES TO VISIT

Migrating warblers and curlews pass through Crow Valley Campground from April through June, when White Penstemon, Purple Loco, Lupine, Spiderwort, and Scarlet Globemallow bloom. Watch for Pronghorn and deer fawns and for Prairie Dog, Coyote, and Swift Fox pups in May and June. July and August can be very hot, but in August shorebirds pass through and the spectacular Plains Eveningstar blooms. Many stargazers escape the light pollution of metropolitan areas to enjoy dark skies at Pawnee. It's a favorite spot to view the Perseid Meteor Shower around August 11–12 and the Leonids in November.

INFORMATION

PAWNEE DISTRICT OFFICE, 660 "O" Street, Greeley, CO 80631; 970-353-5004. Brochures, including bird checklists and the self-guided birding tour, are available here and at the Crow Valley Recreation Area.

HOW TO GET THERE

The two units of this grassland are located about 90 miles northeast of Denver, 30 miles east of Fort Collins, and 20 miles northeast of Greeley. SR 14 skirts the southern boundary of the grassland, and numerous Weld County roads also give access. **NOTE:** A Pawnee National Grassland map, available at the above office, is essential for exploring this grassland.

PAWNEE NATIONAL GRASSLAND

WEATHER
MEAN TEMPERATURES AND PRECIPITATION

MONTH	HIGH (°F)	LOW (°F)	PRECIP.	SNOW
January	42	12	0.3"	2.1"
April	63	30	1.2"	1.3"
July	90	55	2.5"	0.0"
October	66	33	0.7"	0.4"

Annual precipitation is 13.5 inches. May and June downpours often leave back roads impassable. Strong westerly winds blow from October through May. The shortgrasses are usually greenest in June and often turn brown by July 4. A weak "monsoon" in August sometimes produces enough moisture to green-up the prairie a second time.

SELECTED WILDLIFE OF SPECIAL INTEREST

MAMMALS: Black-tailed Prairie Dog, Porcupine, Coyote, Swift Fox, Red Fox, Badger, Mule Deer, White-tailed Deer, Pronghorn.

BIRDS: Ferruginous Hawk, Golden Eagle, Prairie Falcon, Mountain Plover, Long-billed Curlew, Burrowing Owl, White-throated Swift, Horned Lark, Rock Wren, Canyon Wren, Lark Bunting, Grasshopper Sparrow, McCown's Longspur, Chestnut-collared Longspur.

AMPHIBIANS AND REPTILES: Great Plains Toad, Woodhouse's Toad, Plains Spadefoot, Greater Short-horned Lizard, Western Rattlesnake, Western Hog-nosed Snake, Milk Snake, Spiny Softshell, Ornate Box Turtle.

BEECHER ISLAND BATTLEGROUND NATIONAL HISTORIC SITE (no address or phone). Several thousand acres of protected shortgrass prairie surround this historic site on the Arikaree River. Eastern Screech-Owls and Northern Cardinals nest in woodlands. Camping. From US 385, 14 miles south of Wray, go east on CR 22 for 3 miles, then south on CR KK for 2 miles.

BENT'S OLD FORT NATIONAL HISTORIC SITE (35110 Highway 194 East, La Junta, CO 81050; 719-383-5010). This reconstructed fort, originally built by William and Charles Bent in 1833 along the old Santa Fe Trail, was once the most important trading post between Independence, Missouri, and Santa Fe, New Mexico. It is surrounded by about 638 acres of shortgrass prairie and wetlands. About 7 miles northeast of La Junta on SR 194.

BOULDER (CITY) OPEN SPACE AND MOUNTAIN PARKS (66 S. Cherryvale Road, Boulder, CO 80303; 303-441-3440). Thirteen thousand acres of protected grasslands surrounding Boulder include the Tallgrass Prairie State Natural Area along South Boulder Creek. Prairie dog colonies attract Golden Eagles, wintering Bald Eagles, and Ferruginous Hawks. Wetlands support threatened Ute Ladies'-Tresses orchids. Hiking.

JULESBURG (JUMBO) RESERVOIR STATE WILDLIFE AREA (Colorado Division of Wildlife, 122 E. Edison, Brush, CO 80723; 970-842-6300). Burrowing Owls nest and American Badgers hunt in prairie dog colonies surrounding this large reservoir. American White Pelicans, Sandhill Cranes, Snow Geese, and shorebirds pass through in spring and fall. Camping. Twenty miles west of Julesburg off US 138.

NEE NOSHE AND NEE GRANDA RESERVOIRS, IN QUEENS STATE WILDLIFE AREA (Colorado Division of Wildlife, 1204 E. Olive, Lamar, CO 81052; 719-336-6600). Between 5,000 and 10,000 Snow Geese winter here. Sandhill Cranes pass through in March and October. Ferruginous Hawks, Burrowing Owls, and Mountain Plovers nest in surrounding shortgrass prairie. Camping. Twenty-five miles north of Lamar on US 287.

ROXBOROUGH STATE PARK (4751 Roxborough Drive, Littleton, CO 80125; 303-973-3959). Enormous red rock formations are the chief attraction of this foothills park, which also contains prairie grasses, wet meadows, oak brush, aspen groves, and a mix of prairie and mountain species. Hiking. From Denver take Wadsworth Boulevard (SR 121) south past Chatfield State Park; turn left on Waterton Road and follow signs.

SAND CREEK MASSACRE NATIONAL HISTORIC SITE. Peaceful Cheyenne and Arapaho, still sleeping at their camp along Sand Creek and believing themselves under military protection, were killed and mutilated by the Colorado militia under Colonel John Chivington in 1864. The site, in sandsage prairie north of Chivington, was authorized to become a National Historic Site in 2000 and is expected to open to the public sometime after 2004. See p. 74 in Human Impacts for more information, and check the Internet for current status.

TWO BUTTES RESERVOIR STATE WILDLIFE AREA (Colorado Division of Wildlife, 1204 E. Olive, Lamar, CO 81052; 719-336-6600). Barn Owls and Beavers inhabit a box canyon below a small reservoir. Surrounding shortgrass prairie supports Pronghorns, Burrowing Owls, and Horned Larks. Camping and hiking. Drive south from Lamar about 25 miles on US 287/385; turn east on CR C and follow signs for about 3 miles.

Boulder's open space system protects 13,000 acres of mixed-grass and tallgrass prairie at the base of the Rocky Mountain foothills.

ILLINOIS

Goose Lake Prairie State Natural Area

Nachusa Grasslands

Other Illinois Sites:

1. Ayers Sand Prairie Nature Preserve
2. Fults Hill Prairie Nature Preserve
3. Illinois Beach State Park
4. Indian Boundary Prairies
5. Iroquois County Conservation Area
6. Midewin National Tallgrass Prairie
7. Revis Hill Prairie Nature Preserve

GOOSE LAKE PRAIRIE
STATE NATURAL AREA

As they skirted the southern shores of Lake Michigan, nine-teenth-century immigrants walked out of the forest and squinted in the harsh light, imagining they could see all the way to the edge of the earth. "I started with surprise and delight," wrote Eliza Steele in 1840. "A world of grass and flowers stretched around me, rising and falling in gentle undulations, as if an enchanter had struck the ocean swell, and it was rested forever."

Now almost all of Illinois' tallgrass prairies and oak savannas are gone. The largest remnant, the 2,900-acre Goose Lake Prairie State Natural Area, lies sandwiched among a nuclear power plant, a busy highway, and the Kankakee River, 50 miles south of Chicago.

These four square miles of grassland were saved by their soggy, rock-strewn soils. About 400 acres of the preserve once lay en-tirely underwater. Settlers drained Goose Lake and mined its bot-tom for clay and coal. Most of the remaining 2,500 acres were heavily grazed but never plowed.

Volunteer naturalists enjoy leading lines of schoolchildren through these stands of virgin prairie in late summer, when the Big Bluestem, Indian Grass, and Switchgrass grow over head-high. As White-tailed Deer bound through cordgrass meadows and Henslow's Sparrows sing from concealed perches, this small

Above: Morning mist shrouds Goose Lake Prairie in early June.

prairie remnant begins to feel like the real thing, a place where you can lose yourself in a world of grass.

Chica'go

The name of Illinois' largest city derives from the Menomini *shika'ko,* meaning roughly, "skunk place." The odor apparently came from fields of Prairie Onions growing in grasslands that stretched westward from Lake Michigan.

The Cheyenne name for wild onions is *kha-a'-mot-ot-ke'-wat,* which ethnobotanist Kelly Kindscher renders as "skunk testes; probably a polite translation for something more derogatory." Nevertheless, many Plains Indians included wild onions in their diets. They boiled the bulbs with meat, roasted them over fires, or pickled them. They nibbled on the young leaves or added them to stews. Children sometimes dug up the bulbs and ate them on the spot.

The Prairie Onion *(Allium stellatum)* produces striking magenta flower heads in dry tallgrass prairies from midsummer through fall. Nearly a dozen related species, including the widely distributed Nodding Onion and Textile Onion, thrive throughout the prairie region.

Wild onions are among several members of the lily family that bloom at Goose Lake Prairie. Michigan Lily, a 6-petaled reddish orange beauty with protruding orange stamens, blossoms on moist sites in June and July. Yellow Stargrass, a tiny lily with 6-petaled flowers, blooms in moist to dry prairies from April through July.

Prairie Onions (Allium stellatum) *bloom from July through September throughout most of the tallgrass prairie region.*

Michigan Lilies (Lilium michiganense), *also known as Turk's Cap Lilies, grow in moist swales and seepage areas.* (Photo by Joseph Kayne)

PHEASANTS

On summer mornings dozens of Ring-necked Pheasants loiter along preserve roads, scratching for seeds and insects. These Asian game birds are a welcome sight to hunters, who harvest millions in Illinois and other prairie states each year. Many conservationists react less favorably, since pheasants compete with and sometimes dump their eggs into nests of Greater Prairie-Chickens and Sharp-tailed Grouse.

Ring-necked Pheasants were introduced to North America in 1881, when the American consul general at Shanghai shipped 30 birds to Oregon's Willamette Valley. They took hold, and after several more reintroductions the species spread across the continent. By the 1920s, several million inhabited grain fields, hayfields, shelterbelts, grasslands, and woodlots from British Columbia and Nova Scotia south to Nevada, Texas, and Virginia.

Pheasants do best in areas with an abundance of seeds and insects, along with cover for nesting and hiding from predators. The mosaic of croplands, tallgrass prairies, and shrub thickets along the Kankakee River provides excellent habitat. Pheasant populations elsewhere have decreased as modern farming techniques have eliminated the weedy and shrubby areas favored by these birds.

Pheasant courtship begins in early spring when multicolored males strut and crow before groups of females. The male raises his ear tufts, the bare skin around his eyes turns bright red, and he walks with a stiff, bobbing motion. He spreads his tail, stretches one or both wings, and turns his head to display his striking colors. Dominant males mate with several females, who hide their nests deftly under shrubs or weeds. The female's cryptic plumage enables her to "sit tight" when potential predators pass by.

A single nest can produce 12 or more young, who soon follow their mother off in search of food. Adults use broken-wing acts and conspicuous, whirring flight to distract predators. It's not unusual, while walking through tallgrass and mixed-grass prairies, to nearly step on a resting male, who explodes from the grass with a loud metallic whir before gliding a short distance to another resting spot.

FIREFLIES

On summer evenings, courting fireflies create mesmerizing light effects in marshes and wet meadows. Fireflies are beetles in the family Lampyridae, from the Greek word for "bright." There are 23 genera and about 200 species of fireflies in North America.

Firefly larvae and eggs are bioluminescent, and adults of most species also produce light. The larvae live underground or under bark and leaves, where they feed on snails, slugs, and other invertebrates. They kill their prey by crunching down with their powerful mandibles, injecting a poison, and sucking out the insides. The adults spend most of their short lives searching for mates.

Males of most flashing species fly several feet off the ground, emitting greenish white, yellow, or orange flashes at regular intervals. Females typically perch on a leaf or grass stem, flashing a short response. Both sexes continue blinking until they find each other and mate. The light is produced in the firefly's abdomen when a compound known as luciferin oxidizes in the presence of a second compound called luciferase.

Until the 1940s, many species within the two most common North American genera, *Photuris* and *Photinus,* remained undiscovered. Then researchers in Virginia began documenting differences in the flashing patterns of *Photuris* males. They found that each species had a slightly different signature: Some flashed in dots, others in zigzags or sine waves. Within a few years, scientists studying these flashing patterns had nearly doubled the number of known *Photuris* species.

Biologists also discovered that females of some species emit "false" flashes (patterns used by other species) in order to attract males of different species and eat them. The hapless males contain defensive chemicals that the females need to repel spiders and other predators. Now biologists are beginning to document similar behavior among some males, who use false female flashes to distract competing suitors.

For centuries scientists have known about "firefly trees" in Southeast Asia, where thousands of male fireflies blink on and off in synchrony. Only recently has such behavior been documented in North America. In the southern Appalachian Mountains, *Photinus carolinus* males gather in shrubs and trees and flicker in unison.

Some biologists posit that synchronous flashing in fireflies, much like coordinated croaking in frogs, may evolve as females react to the first stimulus they see or hear. It's to each male's advantage to be the first flasher or croaker, so eventually the laggards catch up, creating a synchronous performance.

Fireflies begin displaying at Goose Lake Prairie on warm evenings in May and continue into August. Several species, including the Big Dipper Firefly *(Photinus pryalis)*, inhabit wet prairies and wetlands at the preserve. Big Dipper males inscribe an incendiary "J" as they swoop above the ground shortly after sunset. The males flash every five to eight seconds; the females, perched in the grass, respond a few seconds later with a half-second flash.

HIKING

A 7-mile trail network, including a signed nature loop, begins at the visitor center off Jugtown Road. One loop is universally accessible.

CAMPING

No camping is permitted. Nearby public campgrounds include:

DES PLAINS FISH AND WILDLIFE AREA, along River Road 1 mile northwest of I-55 Exit 241.

CHANNAHON STATE PARK, off US 6/34, on the Illinois River just south of Channahon. From Channahon, take Canal Street south to Story Street and go right for 2 blocks.

BEST TIMES TO VISIT

Waves of ducks and geese pass through in early spring and late fall. Shooting Stars, Yellow Stargrass, and Blue-eyed Grass bloom in April and early May. Fireflies display from late May through early August, and Prairie Blazing Stars bloom in profusion in July and August. Closed and Downy Gentians flower among russet and wine-colored grasses from August through October. With adequate moisture and sunlight, Prairie Cordgrass may grow as high as 12 feet in late summer and early fall.

GOOSE LAKE PRAIRIE STATE NATURAL AREA, 5010 N. Jugtown Road, Morris, IL 60450; 815-942-2899.

HOW TO GET THERE

From Morris go 1 mile south on SR 47, then about 7 miles east on Pine-Lorenzo Road. From I-55 Exit 240, go west about 7 miles on Pine Bluff/Lorenzo Road. The visitor center is 1 mile north on Jugtown Road.

GOOSE LAKE PRAIRIE STATE NATURAL AREA

WEATHER
MEAN TEMPERATURES AND PRECIPITATION

MONTH	HIGH (°F)	LOW (°F)	PRECIP.	SNOW
January	30	12	1.4"	6.8"
April	60	39	3.8"	1.8"
July	85	63	4.0"	0.0"
October	65	42	2.6"	0.2"

Mean annual precipitation is 33.3 inches. June and July are the wettest months. Severe thunderstorms can occur from May through September. Data are for Joliet, Illinois.

SELECTED WILDLIFE OF SPECIAL INTEREST

MAMMALS: Coyote, Red Fox, Badger, Mink, White-tailed Deer.

BIRDS: Great Egret, Northern Harrier, Ring-necked Pheasant, Northern Bobwhite, Eastern Screech-Owl, Barred Owl, Short-eared Owl, Eastern Bluebird, Henslow's Sparrow, Grasshopper Sparrow, Dickcissel, Eastern Meadowlark.

AMPHIBIANS AND REPTILES: Northern Cricket Frog, Boreal Chorus Frog, Spring Peeper, Eastern Hog-nosed Snake, Eastern Racer, Ornate Box Turtle.

NACHUSA GRASSLANDS

During the 1960s, prairie enthusiasts Doug and Dorothy Wade heard an Upland Sandpiper calling amidst corn fields and rolling pastures near Nachusa, Illinois. When they searched for its likely nesting habitat, they found remnants of native prairie growing on several low hilltops near Franklin Creek. In 1986 the Nature Conservancy purchased this land just 15 minutes before it was slated to be auctioned off as five-acre homesites.

The conservancy set out to protect and buffer these hill prairie remnants, purchasing surrounding lands and restoring old corn and soybean fields to native prairie. By 2003 the preserve encompassed 1,500 acres, and a corps of volunteer stewards were putting in more than 10,000 hours a year counting birds, clearing brush, removing weeds, carrying out prescribed burns, and re-seeding native plants. An annual "Autumn on the Prairie" festival, held the third Saturday of September, draws hundreds of people to Nachusa Grasslands to celebrate the conservation of this unique landscape.

Nachusa's sandstone outcrops, meadows, and stream corridors support 11 natural community types, including gravel hill prairie, mesic tallgrass prairie, Bur Oak and Black Oak savanna, calcareous fen, and streamside marsh. Naturalists have documented

Above: Autumn sunlight illuminates stands of Little Bluestem on Nachusa Grasslands' gravel hills. (Photo by Joseph Kayne)

more than 700 plant species. Large populations of the federally threatened Prairie Bush Clover grow here, along with four federal candidate species: Rough-seeded Fameflower, Hill's Thistle, Kittentails, and Forked Aster. Badgers waddle through clumps of Little Bluestem and Porcupine Grass, and Wild Turkeys scratch for acorns and insects in the oak savannas and sedge meadows.

GRAVEL HILL PRAIRIES

Shimmering stands of Little Bluestem, Sand Dropseed, and Porcupine Grass have persevered on Nachusa's gravel hills for thousands of years, bearing silent witness to the destruction of almost all of the surrounding grasslands. These islandlike patches of natural vegetation survived because the underlying soils were too rocky or too steep to plow.

Hill prairies usually grow on steep south- or southwest-facing slopes where dry soils and frequent fires enable grasses to outcompete trees and shrubs. Suppression of natural fire has threatened remaining hill prairies throughout the Midwest. Between 1940 and 1988 the total area of these prairies in Illinois declined by more than 50 percent.

Ecologists denote four types of hill prairie in Illinois: loess, glacial drift, gravel, and sand. Gravel hill prairies are among the least common and have been designated as globally rare by the Nature Conservancy. Nachusa's gravel hills formed about 150,000 years ago when glacial meltwater carved tunnels in the Illinois ice sheet. The tunnels filled with coarse sediments, creating eskers, long, molded ridges of sand and gravel that were exposed when the glacier melted away.

Remaining gravel hill prairies support an abundance of wildlife and wildflowers. In late spring and early summer, Ornate Box Turtles and Blanding's Turtles lay their eggs in the sandier soils. Badgers, Woodchucks, Thirteen-lined Ground Squirrels, and Meadow Jumping Mice burrow and forage. Eastern Meadowlarks, Dickcissels, and Henslow's Sparrows sing from grassy perches. A midsummer display of Bigflower Coreopsis, Pale Purple Coneflower, and Purple Prairie Clover offers a glimpse of the palette of colors that once illuminated the Illinois prairies.

BRINGING INSECTS BACK

Prairie restoration at Nachusa involves much more than establishing native grasses and forbs. Since remnants are surrounded by altered lands, they are constantly being invaded by nonnative and weedy species. Smooth Brome, Bird's-Foot Trefoil, Leafy

Spurge, and Wild Parsnip thrive on bare or disturbed soils. Within the animal kingdom, prairie interlopers range from conspicuous Fox Squirrels and Ring-necked Pheasants to easily overlooked European Leafhoppers and Meadow Spittle Bugs. Some of these animals compete with hill prairie specialists, and their foraging, nesting, and burrowing activities alter the composition of native plant communities.

In 1988 Illinois naturalist Ron Panzer and a corps of volunteers initiated an ambitious project to restore native invertebrates to Nachusa Grasslands. After determining that dozens of native insects were missing from Nachusa's gravel hill prairies, they began translocating insects from nearby prairie remnants that were threatened by development. They netted Bunchgrass Grasshoppers, Great Plains Froghoppers, Angelica Moths, Gorgone Checkerspot butterflies, and a half-dozen other species, transported them in coolers, and released them on Doug's and Schaefer's Knobs, near the western boundary of the preserve.

Within a few years some of the translocated species appeared to have taken hold. In 1991 volunteers found two dozen freshly emerged Gorgone Checkerspots fluttering over the hilltops. The following year they found a dozen Prairie Dock Moth larvae feeding on stems of Prairie Dock and Compass Plant.

Other species fared less well. After releasing 1,015 Great Plains Froghoppers in 1989, 1990, and 1991, volunteers could find only 2 individuals on the release site during a 30-minute survey in 1992. They feared that European Spittle Bugs pouring in from surrounding farmlands were outcompeting the translocated froghoppers.

The process of reintroducing invertebrates becomes a balancing act when fire is added to the equation. Many prairie insects depend on periodic fires to maintain the grasses and forbs on which they feed; however, isolated insect populations can be set back by a single blaze. While rotating prescribed fires through the preserve, Nachusa biologists have maintained rotating "fire-free zones" within the native prairie remnants to serve as refugia for insects and other invertebrates.

SPIDERWORTS

In early summer, love-struck Lakota and Cheyenne youths would pick spiderwort blossoms, rub them between their palms, and then shake hands with their sweethearts, hoping to cast a romantic spell. It's easy to appreciate how these delicate wildflowers, with their slender, arching leaves and cluster of bluish purple three-petaled blossoms, could inspire such feelings of magic and devotion.

Common Spiderwort (Tradescantia ohiensis) *plants may bloom for several weeks in late spring and summer, but the individual flowers last for a single day.*

At least four species of spiderwort grow in the prairie region. Common Spiderwort (*Tradescantia ohiensis*) sprouts 3 feet high in tallgrass prairies from Texas to Wisconsin. This showy species blooms in profusion at Nachusa Grasslands from late May through June. Prairie Spiderwort (*T. occidentalis*), less than 2 feet tall with slightly smaller flowers, blooms in late spring and early summer in dry and sandy prairies from the Missouri River to the Rocky Mountains and from North Dakota to central Texas.

Named for the threadlike, mucilaginous slime that oozes from the stems when they are broken and pulled apart, these plants were occasionally eaten by Native Americans. The Cherokees used the young stems and leaves as a potherb, and children nibbled on the sweet-tasting flowers.

HIKING

A half-mile nature trail takes off from the visitor parking area on Lowden Road, and a network of mowed trails and two-track roads make for easy walking.

CAMPING

Camping is not permitted. Nearby public campgrounds include:

LOWDEN STATE PARK, 1411 N. River Road, in the town of Oregon.

CASTLE ROCK STATE PARK, 3 miles south of Oregon on SR 2, offers riverside camping for canoeists only.

BEST TIMES TO VISIT

Wildflowers bloom from April through October. Spiderwort is prominent in late May and early June. Pale Purple Coneflowers and Bigflower Coreopsis display in June and July, and Prairie Blazing Stars proliferate in August. Grassland birds, including Grasshopper Sparrows, Henslow's Sparrows, Dickcissels, and Bobolinks, begin singing in early May. The gravel hill prairies are at their fiery best in October, when clumps of Little Bluestem glow in the clear autumn light.

INFORMATION

NACHUSA GRASSLANDS, 8772 S. Lowden Road, Franklin Grove IL 61031; 815-456-2340.

HOW TO GET THERE

From Dixon take SR 2 north for 2 miles, go east 1 mile on Lost Nation Road, right a short block on Maples Road, then left 3.5 miles on Naylor Road. Go left 1 mile on Lowden Road to the visitor parking area on your left.

From Franklin Grove, go north on Daysville Road (1700E) 1.5 miles to Naylor Road. Go left 2.2 miles to Lowden Road. Turn right on Lowden Road and go 1 mile to the visitor parking area.

NACHUSA GRASSLANDS

WEATHER
MEAN TEMPERATURES AND PRECIPITATION

MONTH	HIGH (°F)	LOW (°F)	PRECIP.	SNOW
January	28	9	1.4"	9.0"
April	60	38	3.5"	1.5"
July	85	63	3.6"	0.0"
October	63	40	2.7"	0.3"

Mean annual precipitation is 35.7 inches. Record temperatures range from 110°F to −27°F. June is the wettest month. Watch for severe thunderstorms throughout the summer. Data are for Dixon, Illinois.

SELECTED WILDLIFE OF SPECIAL INTEREST

MAMMALS: Eastern Chipmunk, Franklin's Ground Squirrel, Thirteen-lined Ground Squirrel, Meadow Jumping Mouse, Coyote, Red Fox, Badger, White-tailed Deer.

BIRDS: Northern Harrier, Ring-necked Pheasant, Barred Owl, Eastern Bluebird, Grasshopper Sparrow, Henslow's Sparrow, Northern Cardinal, Dickcissel, Bobolink, Eastern Meadowlark.

AMPHIBIANS AND REPTILES: Boreal Chorus Frog, Spring Peeper, Wood Frog, Western Hog-nosed Snake, Eastern Hog-nosed Snake, Ornate Box Turtle, Blanding's Turtle.

AYERS SAND PRAIRIE NATURE PRESERVE (Department of Natural Resources, One Natural Resources Way, Springfield, IL 62702-1271; 309-597-2212). Dry sand prairie and sand dune communities grow on 109 acres of protected land. Carolina Anemone and Puccoon bloom in spring and summer. From Savannah take SR 84 south 2.7 miles to Airport Road, then go east 0.5 miles.

FULTS HILL PRAIRIE NATURE PRESERVE (Department of Natural Resources, c/o Randolph County SRA, 4301 S. Lake Drive, Chester, IL 62233; 309-597-2212). The largest remaining complex of high-quality Illinois loess hill prairie clings to Mississippi River bluffs at this 532-acre National Natural Landmark. Nature trail. Monroe County, 1.6 miles southeast of Fults on Bluff Road.

ILLINOIS BEACH STATE PARK (Lake Front, Zion, IL 60099; 847-662-4828). On the shores of Lake Michigan, this 829-acre park protects a remnant of wet to dry sand prairie. Interpretive center, camping, and hiking. From Zion, take Sheridan Road south about 1 mile to Wadsworth Road. Go east to the park entrance.

INDIAN BOUNDARY PRAIRIES (The Nature Conservancy, 800 South Michigan Avenue, Chicago, IL 60603; 312-580-2100). A cluster of high-quality blacksoil prairies perseveres on 252 protected acres on Chicago's urban fringe. The largest, Gensburg-Markham, offers striking wildflower displays throughout the summer. In Markham, east of Kedzie Avenue, west of I-294, and between 155th and 159th streets. To reach Gensburg-Markham, take 159th Street to Whipple Avenue and go north for three blocks.

IROQUOIS COUNTY CONSERVATION AREA (2803E 3300N Road, Beaverville, IL 60912-7020; 815-435-2218). Seventeen hundred acres of protected tallgrass prairie and marsh include some of the best preserved sand dune and prairie marsh habitat in the state. Mink, Beavers, and Southern Flying Squirrels. Hiking. Kankakee County, 5 miles northeast of Beaverville on county roads.

MIDEWIN NATIONAL TALLGRASS PRAIRIE (30071 South State Route 53, Wilmington, IL 60481; 815-423-6370). Restoration of 19,000 acres on the Joliet Arsenal, a former ammunition factory, began in 1996. *Midewin* means "healing" in Potawatami, and it will take careful ministrations to bring this degraded landscape back to life; the restoration is expected to take 20 years or more. Hiking trails and visitor center. SR 53, 40 miles south of Chicago and 3 miles north of Wilmington. Call or write for updated information before visiting.

REVIS HILL PRAIRIE NATURE PRESERVE (Department of Natural Resources, Sangchris Lake State Park, RR #1, Rochester, IL 62563; 217-498-8543). More than 400 acres of loess hill prairie and oak savanna survive on steep bluffs overlooking central Illinois' Sangamon River. Hiking. From 0.5 miles north of Kilbourne on SR 97, turn east on blacktop road 7.5 miles to gravel road, then turn right and go southeast 1 mile. The preserve is on the northeast side of the road.

Prairie Blazing Stars (Liatris pycnostachya) *and goldenrods bloom in profusion at Gensburg/Markham Prairie in midsummer. (Photo by Joseph Kayne)*

IOWA

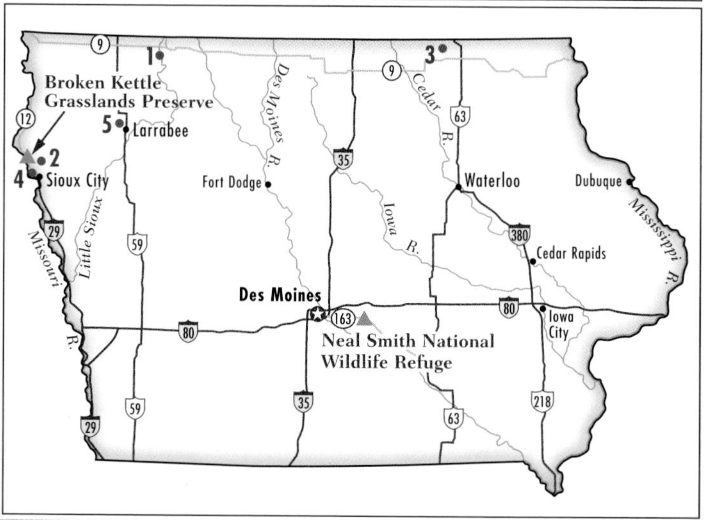

1
2
3
4
5
Broken Kettle Grasslands Preserve
Larrabee
Sioux City
Fort Dodge
Des Moines R.
Cedar R.
Waterloo
Dubuque
Mississippi R.
Iowa R.
Cedar Rapids
Iowa City
Des Moines
Neal Smith National Wildlife Refuge
Missouri R.
Little Sioux
9
12
63
35
380
59
29
80
163
218

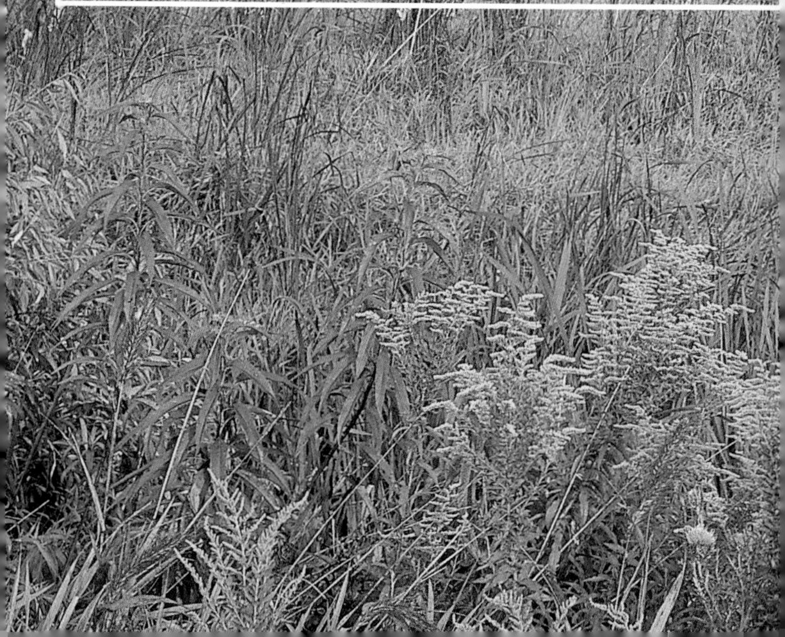

**BROKEN KETTLE GRASSLANDS
PRESERVE**

**NEAL SMITH NATIONAL WILDLIFE
REFUGE**

OTHER IOWA SITES:
1. Cayler Prairie State Preserve
2. Five Ridge Prairie
3. Hayden Prairie State Preserve
4. Sioux City Prairie
5. Steele Prairie

BROKEN KETTLE GRASSLANDS PRESERVE

In the Loess Hills of western Iowa, fine silt particles known as "glacial flour" have piled up 200 feet deep, forming some of the richest soils on earth. These well-drained soils once supported several hundred square miles of Loess Hills prairie, a unique grassland dominated by Little Bluestem, Big Bluestem, Sideoats Grama, Hairy Grama, Indian Grass, Junegrass, and various needlegrasses. Since European contact, suppression of natural fire has enabled woodlands to creep up from ravines and riverbottoms, nearly elimating the native prairie.

The Nature Conservancy's Broken Kettle Grasslands Preserve, named after thousand-year-old shards of pottery found along a nearby stream, protects the largest remaining patch of prairie in the Loess Hills. The preserve encompasses about 3,000 acres and is surrounded by an additional 3,000 acres of lands that have been protected through conservation easements. Woodlands still cover parts of the preserve; conservancy staff and neighboring landowners use prescribed fire and heavy equipment to keep the trees and shrubs at bay.

Wild Turkeys wander over the ridgetops, and Western Rattlesnakes bask among yuccas and clumps of Hairy Grama on dry, west-facing slopes. Western Rattlesnakes, along with several drought-tolerant plant species, reach the eastern limit of their

Above: Mixed-grass prairie, early September.

range on this island of mixed-grass prairie between the Missouri River floodplain to the west and the rich blacksoil prairies to the east.

One of the largest remaining populations of the Federally threatened Regal Fritillary resides in these hills in summer. The fritillaries nectar on Dotted Gayfeathers, purple coneflowers, and Purple Locos, and they lay their eggs on leaves of Prairie and Bird's-Foot Violets. In winter Long-eared Owls roost communally in the draws, and Bald Eagles glide over the hills searching for carrion.

LOESS HILLS

Retreating glaciers left behind immense quantities of ground-up rock, sand, and silt, known as glacial till. Floodwaters from the melting glaciers washed away the lighter sediments and deposited them in river floodplains as layers of fine, pulverized silt. Eventually, westerly winds blew great clouds of this "glacial flour" eastward, where the silt particles settled and oxidized to form the yellowish brown material known as loess. Although layers of loess cover much of the Great Plains and upper Midwest, the deepest deposits occur along a 3- to 10-mile-wide strip of land east of the Missouri River. Only in China are deeper deposits of loess found.

The Loess Hills extend 200 miles from northern Iowa to northwestern Missouri. Because loess (from the German word for "loose") is extremely stable when cut vertically but falls apart when exposed to water, stream channels tend to erode straight downward, cutting deep gullies. The gullies create relatively moist and cool microhabitats where deciduous trees thrive. The sunbaked, windswept uplands support more drought-resistant

Badgers and other mammals excavate burrows in loess embankments. Western Rattlesnakes sometimes use these burrows as hibernacula.

grasses. Since European contact, more than 95 percent of these grasslands have been destroyed by farming, overgrazing, urban development, mining, and woodland invasion.

RATTLESNAKES, MAGPIES, AND YUCCAS

Like ocean waves, grasslands have advanced and retreated across central North America for millions of years. During the mid-Holocene, about 8,000 to 4,000 years ago, hot, dry conditions enabled tallgrass prairies to expand eastward, displacing deciduous forests in the Ohio River Valley. During the 1930s Dust Bowl drought, expanding shortgrass and mixed-grass prairies temporarily replaced tallgrass prairies in eastern Kansas, Nebraska, and the eastern Dakotas.

Just as tide pools on the beach shelter flora and fauna left behind by retreating waves, some hills and valleys on the Great Plains nurture plants and animals that became isolated as prairies advanced and retreated. Scarlet Globemallow (*Sphaeralcea coccinea*), an orange-blossomed wildflower of dry prairies and waste places, grows east of the Missouri River only in the Loess Hills. Geographically isolated populations of Plains Pocket Mice, Ornate Box Turtles, Plains Spadefoot Toads, and Prairie Racerunners also inhabit the drier regions of the hills.

Some western species have migrated southeastward into the Loess Hills, following a narrow band of mixed-grass prairie that extends along the wind-buffeted bluffs east of the Missouri River. Distributional maps for Buffaloberry, *Yucca glauca,* and Giant Eveningstar suggest that they followed this route. Black-billed Magpies have expanded their range eastward into the hills during historic times.

The only Western Rattlesnake population east of the Missouri River inhabits south- and west-facing slopes in the northern Loess Hills. Broken Kettle biologists estimate that more than 200 breeding adults live within the boundaries of the preserve. From April through October they bask in the sun or lie curled up in patches of ankle-high grass waiting to ambush a passing mouse or vole. During winter, groups of rattlesnakes hibernate in rodent or badger burrows in sandstone embankments (see Oglala National Grassland, Nebraska, for more on rattlesnakes).

REGAL FRITILLARIES

Dozens of male Regal Fritillaries flit over the ridgetops of Broken Kettle in July and August looking for mates. Once the male finds a female he flutters up to her. Depending on her mood and her

Regal Fritillaries seek sustenance from milkweeds, thistles, blazing stars, and even Coyote scat. Violets serve as host plants for their eggs and larvae.

assessment of his fitness, she either launches into a repertoire of evasive aerial maneuvers or settles onto a perch where they copulate. Later, the fertilized female zigzags across the grasslands, depositing several hundred eggs on or near violets, which serve as host plants for the larvae. The caterpillars overwinter without feeding until the following summer.

Regal Fritillaries are to the prairie as Boreal Owls and Pine Martens are to the north woods. If you see a Regal, you are probably standing in a relatively healthy prairie. The farther east you go, the fewer you see.

These giant fritillaries have disappeared from large areas of their historic range, including parts of New England, where they inhabited wet meadows and forest openings, and all of the Ohio Valley, where only tiny remnants of prairie remain. They are endangered or declining in Illinois, Wisconsin, and Missouri.

Because Regal Fritillaries are so large (up to a 3.5-inch wingspan) and have prominent black patterning on their hind wings, people sometimes mistake them for Monarchs. But the Regal's hind wings appear almost entirely black and white, with very little orange, and their orange forewings are marked with blue-black spots as compared to the Monarch's long black lines. Their rapid, erratic flight is typical of fritillaries and renders them tricky to observe and photograph once the morning sun has warmed their wings and flight muscles.

HIKING

There are no hiking trails, but the entire preserve is open to cross-country travel. Beware of electric fences, ticks, and rattlesnakes.

Camping

No camping is permitted. Nearby Stone State Park (4 miles north of I-29 Exit 151 on SR 12) has developed campgrounds and hiking trails.

Best Times to Visit

The Loess Hills sparkle in October, when reddish and amber clumps of Little Bluestem, Big Bluestem, Junegrass, and Sideoats Grama cure under azure skies. Rattlesnakes emerge from hibernation and amorous Wild Turkeys gobble in late March and early April. Grassland sparrows begin nesting in late May. Bald Eagles roost along the adjacent Big Sioux River throughout the winter, and a few pairs remain to nest each spring.

Information

THE NATURE CONSERVANCY, 24764 Hwy. 12, Westfield, IA 51062; 712-568-2596.

How to Get There

From I-29 Exit 51, go 10.5 miles north on SR 12 to CR K 18. Continue straight on SR 12 for another 4 miles to Butcher Road (gravel). Turn right and go about 2 miles to the top of the hill. Watch for the yellow TNC signs. The office is on the east side of SR 12, 0.5 miles north of its intersection with Butcher Road.

BROKEN KETTLE GRASSLANDS PRESERVE

WEATHER
MEAN TEMPERATURES AND PRECIPITATION

MONTH	HIGH (°F)	LOW (°F)	PRECIP.	SNOW
January	28	8	0.6"	6.3"
April	62	38	2.3"	1.5"
July	87	65	3.3"	0.0"
October	64	40	1.9"	0.1"

Mean annual precipitation is 26.0 inches. May, June, and July are the wettest months, with occasional severe thunderstorms. Data are for Sioux City, Iowa.

SELECTED WILDLIFE OF SPECIAL INTEREST

MAMMALS: Virginia Opossum, Woodchuck, Franklin's Ground Squirrel, Thirteen-lined Ground Squirrel, Badger, White-tailed Deer.

BIRDS: Bald Eagle, Wild Turkey, Northern Bobwhite, Upland Sandpiper, Long-eared Owl, Short-eared Owl, Red-headed Woodpecker, Western Kingbird, Black-billed Magpie, Horned Lark, Summer Tanager, Grasshopper Sparrow, Rose-breasted Grosbeak, Indigo Bunting, Bobolink.

AMPHIBIANS AND REPTILES: Great Plains Toad, Northern Leopard Frog, Plains Spadefoot, Great Plains Skink, Western Rattlesnake.

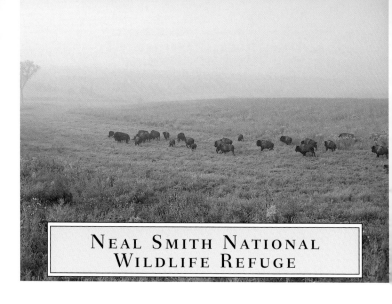

NEAL SMITH NATIONAL WILDLIFE REFUGE

Each spring and fall, as many as 18,000 Iowa children come to this refuge to help re-create the tallgrass prairie. The children plant forbs and bunchgrasses, collect and scatter seeds, and monitor the progress of previous plantings. They observe butterflies, birds, and Bison and take in an inspiring multimedia presentation that ends with words from ecologist John Madson: "Be patient, have faith, and don't mind the dirt under your fingernails."

Located 20 miles east of Des Moines, this ambitious prairie restoration sits on the site of a proposed nuclear power plant. When the the power company decided not to build the plant in 1990, the U.S. Fish and Wildlife Service acquired 3,600 acres of croplands and small prairie remnants in the Walnut Creek drainage. By 2003 the refuge had expanded to 5,500 acres, of which 3,000 had been restored to grass and native forbs. Congress has authorized acquisition and restoration of up to 8,600 acres at the site.

Refuge managers and volunteers are attempting to replicate the prairie landscape that European settlers encountered 150 years ago. They start by inventorying and restoring small degraded prairie remnants scattered throughout the refuge. These remnants contain pieces of the original prairie fabric, bits of informa-

Above: Bison graze in recently established tallgrass prairie at Neal Smith National Wildlife Refuge.

tion that scientists use to characterize the prairie's plant and animal composition. Downy Gentians and Showy Orchis bloom in some of these remnants. A wealth of invertebrates, including a previously undescribed ant species, feed on the native vegetation and burrow in the soil.

As these remnants become healthier, scientists and volunteers connect them with plantings of grasses and forbs. Because less than 0.1 percent of Iowa's tallgrass prairies and oak savannas remain, finding native seed sources poses a challenge. To preserve species and genetic integrity, seed collecting is limited to remnant prairies within 38 counties near the refuge.

Small herds of Bison and Elk have been reintroduced to the refuge. Coyotes and Northern Harriers have made it back on their own. Upland Sandpipers, Henslow's Sparrows, Grasshopper Sparrows, and Bobolinks have begun to stop over or nest.

The refuge's Prairie Learning Center features more than a dozen interactive exhibits, including a walk-in model of an underground burrow system. Visitors who write ahead often can join refuge staff and volunteers in seed collecting, brush cutting, or planting activities.

REGAL FRITILLARY INTRODUCTION

Beginning in the early 1990s refuge staff and volunteers worked with Dr. Diane Debinski and her graduate students to establish Prairie Violets, a Regal Fritillary host plant, in plots at the refuge. They also monitored nearby Regal populations to determine whether any were large enough to tolerate the removal of pregnant females. In 2000 and again in 2001 two pregnant females trapped from outside the refuge were placed in mesh cages over the violets in hopes they would lay eggs.

In 2002 researchers observed adult Regals flying over the refuge and estimated that 20 were present. They don't know how many of these butterflies hatched out on site, but they hope that as restored prairies mature, Regal Fritillary populations will become self-sustaining (see Broken Kettle Grasslands Preserve, Iowa, for more on Regal Fritillaries).

SPARROWS IN THE GRASS

Flee-sic, tsee-slick. The song, like a soft hiccough or a Dickcissel with laryngitis, can easily go unnoticed. To prairie biologists it's beautiful music, a sign that native grasses and wildflowers are coming back.

Henslow's Sparrows have disappeared from most of the Midwest, where their prime nesting habitat, damp meadows filled with tall grasses and wildflowers, has been decimated. Once one of the most abundant birds of the tallgrass region, this small, secretive sparrow now nests only in isolated grassland remnants from Oklahoma and Minnesota east to Québec and Virginia.

Late-nineteenth-century observers described the Henslow's Sparrow as a common summer resident throughout Iowa. By the 1930s most of the sparrows were gone, and during the early 1990s observers confirmed breeding at only two sites in the state, Hayden Prairie and the Lake Sugema area in Van Buren County. Beginning in the late 1990s, scientists at Neal Smith National Wildlife Refuge began seeing or hearing Henslow's Sparrows every summer in burned and unburned portions of the preserve.

These greenish-headed, streak-breasted songbirds are more easily heard than seen. They forage for seeds and insects in dense grass cover, where they build a cup-shaped ground nest protected by an arched roof of dead grass. In Iowa, Henslow's Sparrows begin singing in May and remain on their breeding grounds until early fall. They winter from the Virginia coast south and west to Florida and Texas.

At least four other sparrow species also nest in the refuge's grasslands and marshes. Grasshopper Sparrows, whose weak song resembles the buzz of their namesake, like areas of clipped grass and bare ground for foraging and conspicuous perches on shrubs or fence posts for singing. Field Sparrows also sing from exposed perches, but they nest and forage primarily in tallgrass meadows. Song Sparrows gravitate toward wetlands and shrub thickets, while Vesper Sparrows prefer a mix of grasses, shrubs, and small trees.

Though drab and sometimes difficult to see, these grassland-nesting sparrows tell fascinating stories about the composition and quality of prairie ecosystems. Their absence in former breeding areas speaks volumes about our stewardship of native grasslands.

SUNFLOWERS AND GOLDENRODS

Sunflowers and goldenrods brighten the refuge's restored prairies from early July through September. Their blossoms attract tiny wheel spiders, fearsome-looking tiger beetles, and graceful swallowtail butterflies. Gregarious flocks of American Goldfinches chatter their way from one glowing meadow to another.

Common Sunflowers, Maximilian Sunflowers, and Jerusalem Artichokes grow up to 8 feet tall in the refuge's fallow fields and wetlands. Common Sunflowers bear giant flowers with reddish

*A long-horned beetle (*Megacyllene *sp.) feeds on Canada Goldenrod (*Solidago canadensis*) pollen in late summer.*

brown central disks. Maximilian Sunflowers produce a cluster of yellow-centered flowers aligned vertically near the top of the stem. Jerusalem Artichoke stems bear large hairy leaves and a horizontal cluster of yellow-centered flowers.

A slightly smaller member of the sunflower family, the Bur Marigold, frames the refuge's roads in late summer with fields of 2-inch-wide yellow-centered flowers. The Compass Plant sprouts in prairies and waste places in June and July; look for its giant oak-shaped basal leaves and slender stalk topped by one or more large yellow-centered flowers. A close relative, Rosin Weed, grows 2 to 3 feet tall in mesic tallgrass prairies.

Archaeologists have found evidence that people used sunflowers for food as early as 5800 B.C. Plains Indians relished Common Sunflower fruits, and they dug up the nutritious roots of Jerusalem Artichokes and ate them raw or boiled or roasted them. When Common Sunflowers were introduced into Europe during the sixteenth and seventeenth centuries, they caused a sensation. English herbalist John Gerard wrote that sunflower buds, when boiled and eaten like artichokes, surpass the artichoke "in procuring bodily lust."

A half-dozen goldenrod species bloom in the refuge's marshes, wet meadows, and upland prairies. Canada Goldenrods sprout nearly 7 feet tall in wet sites, their golden flowers forming a pyramid at the top of the stalk. Slightly shorter Showy Goldenrods bear a cylindrical cluster of bright yellow flowers. Stiff Goldenrods produce a flattened inflorescence and broad, thick basal leaves.

Goldenrods have been unjustly accused of causing hay fever, probably because their blooming coincides with that of less conspicuous wind-pollinated ragweeds. The ragweeds' microscopic pollen grains fill the air, irritating eyes and nasal passages. Goldenrods produce relatively large, sticky pollen grains that adhere to body parts of visiting insects.

The showy inflorescences attract scores of insect species. Black Blister Beetles, soldier beetles, and yellow and black long-horned beetles graze on the pollen. Yellowish green ambush bugs grasp passing insects with their front legs, penetrate their bodies with a sharp-tipped soda-straw mouth, and suck out their body fluids. Pale yellow goldenrod spiders skitter crab-fashion across the flower heads to pounce on ants and lacewings.

Other insects burrow into or lay their eggs on the succulent stems. Round galls on the upper stems contain gall fly larvae, and oblong galls house tiny moth caterpillars. The galls provide protection from predators and food for the growing insect larvae. Most larvae emerge in the spring to mate and seek out a goldenrod host for their eggs.

HIKING

OVERLOOK TALLGRASS TRAIL (3-mile loop) takes off from the visitor center and traverses recently re-established bluestem prairie.

SAVANNA TRAIL (0.5-mile loop) begins 0.5 miles east of the visitor center and passes through an oak woodland. Listen for Barred Owls and Wild Turkeys.

BASSWOOD TRAIL (1-mile loop) explores wetlands and prairie remnants at the south end of the preserve. 112th Avenue, 0.3 miles east of 119th Street.

CAMPING

No camping is permitted. Elk Rock State Park is 15 miles southeast on SR 14, 7 miles south of Monroe.

BEST TIMES TO VISIT

Bison and Elk calve in April and May. Black-eyed Susans, Prairie Blazing Stars and Pale Purple Coneflowers bloom in profusion from late June through early August. Sunflowers, goldenrods, and flowering grasses display throughout August and September. Northern Harriers migrate through in early spring and again in early autumn, when Elk bugle and prairie grasses take on their richest hues.

NEAL SMITH NATIONAL WILDLIFE REFUGE, Box 399, Prairie City IA
50228; 515-994-3400.

HOW TO GET THERE

From Des Moines take SR 163 east 20 miles to the Prairie City
exit and go southwest on the refuge entry road (Pacific Street).

NEAL SMITH NATIONAL WILDLIFE REFUGE

WEATHER
MEAN TEMPERATURES AND PRECIPITATION

MONTH	HIGH (°F)	LOW (°F)	PRECIP.	SNOW
January	28	11	1.0"	8.3"
April	62	40	3.4"	1.8"
July	87	66	3.8"	0.0"
October	64	43	2.6"	0.3"

Mean annual precipitation is 34.2 inches. The record high is
108°F, the record low -26°. Watch for severe thunderstorms
throughout the late spring and summer. Data are for Des
Moines, Iowa.

SELECTED WILDLIFE OF SPECIAL INTEREST

MAMMALS: Coyote, Red Fox, Badger, Mink, Long-tailed Weasel,
White-tailed Deer, Elk, Bison.

BIRDS: Wood Duck, Northern Harrier, Ring-necked Pheasant, Wild
Turkey, American Woodcock, Yellow-billed Cuckoo, Eastern
Screech-Owl, Barred Owl, Short-eared Owl, Yellow-throated
Vireo, Horned Lark, Cedar Waxwing, Scarlet Tanager,
Henslow's Sparrow, Rose-breasted Grosbeak, Indigo Bunting,
Dickcissel, Bobolink.

AMPHIBIANS AND REPTILES: Northern Cricket Frog, Cope's Gray
Treefrog, Western Chorus Frog, Northern Leopard Frog, Eastern Racer, Milk Snake.

CAYLER PRAIRIE STATE PRESERVE (Department of Natural Resources, Wallace State Office Building, 900 East Grand, Des Moines, IA 50319; 515-281-8524). A National Natural Landmark, this high-quality 160-acre mixed-grass prairie remnant grows on a glacial end moraine west of Spirit Lake. From the intersection of SR 86 and SR 9, take SR 9 west for 3.5 miles and go south 2.5 miles on 170th Avenue. The Nature Conservancy Iowa Web site lists several other small preserves in this area.

FIVE RIDGE PRAIRIE (Plymouth County Conservation Board, Box 1033, Hinton, IA 51024; 712-947-4270). Three hundred acres of remnant dry-mesic prairie on steep ridges give visitors a glimpse of the once magnificent Loess Hills ecosystem. Rare butterflies, including Regal Fritillaries, gather in summer. From I-29 Exit 151, take SR 12 north 10.5 miles to CR K18 *North*. Turn northeast and continue 3 miles to a gravel road 0.5 miles south of CR C 43. Turn left 1 mile to preserve entrance. Walk in 0.8 miles.

HAYDEN PRAIRIE STATE PRESERVE (Iowa Department of Natural Resources, Wallace State Office Building, 900 East Grand, Des Moines, IA 50319; 515-281-8524). Iowa's best-preserved black-soil prairie, designated a National Natural Landmark, survives on this 240-acre parcel. Shooting Stars, Common Spiderwort, Prairie Phlox, and Prairie Smoke bloom in late May. Howard County. From intersection of SR 9 and US 63, take SR 9 west about 4 miles, then turn north on Jade Avenue and continue for 5 miles.

SIOUX CITY PRAIRIE (Woodbury County Conservation Board, 4500 Sioux River Road, Sioux City, IA 51109; 712-258-0838). Touted as the "largest known prairie preserve within an urban environment," this 150-acre remnant is used by area schools as an outdoor classroom. Between Talbot Road and Briar Cliff College, 3 miles north of downtown Sioux City.

STEELE PRAIRIE (Cherokee County Conservation Board, 629 River Road, Cherokee, IA 51012; 712-225-6709). Mesic tallgrass prairie dominates this 200-acre preserve in the glaciated Northwest Iowa Plains. From US 59 and CR C 16 just north of Larrabee, take C 16 west 1 mile. Turn north on gravel road 1.5 miles and go west 0.7 miles to the main tract south of the road.

Three-flowered Avens (Geum triflorum), *also known as Prairie Smoke, is one of dozens of native wildflowers that bloom at Hayden Prairie State Preserve. (Photo by Glenn Cushman)*

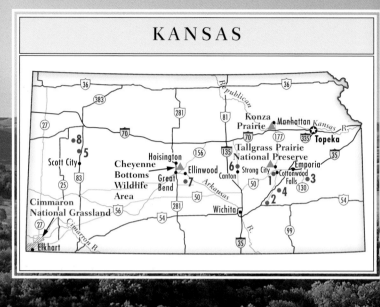

KANSAS

Republican
36
36
383
81
27
70
Konza
Prairie
Manhattan
Kansas R.
281
177
335
Topeka
156
135
Tallgrass Prairie
National Preserve
35
8
Hoisington
5
Cheyenne
Ellinwood
6
Emporia
Scott City
Bottoms
Canton
Strong City
3
83
Wildlife
Great
7
Cottonwood
25
Area
Bend
Arkansas
1
Falls
130
Cimmaron
281
50
4
National Grassland
56
54
54
2
Wichita
27
Cimmaron R.
R.
99
Elkhart
35

Cheyenne Bottoms Wildlife Area

Cimmaron National Grassland

Konza Prairie

Tallgrass Prairie National Preserve

Other Kansas Sites:

1. Chase State Fishing Lake
2. El Dorado State Park
3. Flint Hills National Wildlife Refuge
4. Flint Hills Tallgrass Prairie Preserve
5. Lake Scott State Park
6. Maxwell Wildlife Refuge and MacPherson State Fishing Lake
7. Quivira National Wildlife Refuge
8. Smoky Valley Ranch

CHEYENNE BOTTOMS WILDLIFE AREA

Sapphire pools below reflect sun-diamonds as White-faced Ibis wheel overhead. Thousands of white pelicans sail across the sky and settle on a pond like an eiderdown comforter wafting down. Yellow-headed Blackbirds cackle discordantly from the cattails as a watersnake swims silently by.

With almost 20,000 acres consisting of more water than grass, Cheyenne Bottoms Wildlife Area is a prairie paradox. It's part of a natural land sink where trapped water is channeled into pools and marshes forming the largest interior marsh in the United States. In the 1970s and 1980s the Manomet Bird Observatory conducted an international shorebird survey and named Cheyenne Bottoms the top shorebird spring staging area in the contiguous United States. In 1988 the United Nations designated it a "Wetland of International Importance."

About 3,300 acres of this wetland are set aside as a refuge where no disturbance of the wildlife is allowed. More than 320 bird species have been recorded here, including such rarities as Whooping Cranes, Piping Plovers, Peregrine Falcons, Bald Eagles, and Least Terns. More than 100 species nest in the area,

Above: White Pelicans at dusk.

Thousands of American White Pelicans converge on Cheyenne Bottoms' lakes and marshes each summer.

and 63 species are permanent residents along with 31 mammals, 19 reptiles, and 8 amphibians. A driving tour, with numbers keyed to a brochure, can be completed in 45 minutes, but most people will want to allow much more time for this magical marsh.

Biologist John Zimmerman catches the spirit of the place in his book *Cheyenne Bottoms*: "Marsh wrens rattled above my head, least bitterns braced their legs akimbo between the stalks of the cattails while they hunted, young zebra-striped grebes rode the backs of their parents, diving beetles hurried past with bright red mites inserted in the sutures of their exoskeletons, turtles swam by to raise their snouts above the water almost at my fingertips, and leeches measured my trouser leg, searching for entry. Close up, a marsh is a joy."

A Managed Marsh

Cheyenne Bottoms is part of a larger 41,000-acre basin formed about 100 million years ago. This "dish," bordered by rocky bluffs to the north and south, collects water and filters out pollutants as the water slowly percolates through rich-smelling mud and ooze.

This paradise was almost lost several times during the past century. In 1899 land promoters diverted water from the Arkansas River into the basin attempting to create an enormous lake where pleasure steamers would attract thousands of tourists. This project was doomed by too little natural water flow and by the 1902 flood that washed out the diversion dam. (Natural flooding has actually created large lakes here several times since that fiasco.) Another ill-fated plan called for draining the Bottoms for farming.

After purchasing the land in the 1940s, the Kansas Department of Wildlife and Parks built canals and dams to divert water from the Arkansas River and Wet Walnut Creek to augment the flow into the marsh from two intermittent streams. Wildlife officials built dikes to impound water in five major pools and later installed pumps to manipulate the water, filling and draining the ponds as needed. They store water in spring and slowly release it during dry periods. They also plant millet and wheat in mud flats to provide food for fall migrating birds.

Nowadays the streams that feed the Bottoms flow sluggishly and only in spring. About 60 inches of water evaporate from the marsh each year, with only about 24 inches being replenished through precipitation. Water diversion projects continue to drain the High Plains (Ogallala) Aquifer. If the water dries up, the future of Cheyenne Bottoms as a refuge for migrants will be doomed.

A MIGRATION STOPOVER

Ornithologists estimate that 45 percent of the North American shorebird population stops at the Bottoms during spring migration to probe the mud for bugs, blood-worms (midge larvae), and other tasty bits. Charles Darwin would have enjoyed observing the different shapes of beaks, evolved for slightly different feeding habits. American Avocets sweep long, up-curved bills through shallow water; Long-billed and Short-billed Dowitchers probe the mud with stout, straight beaks; White-faced Ibis wield decurved bills; and Common Snipe "feel" the mud with soft, pliable beaks.

Only 349 shorebirds of 16 species had been banded in all of North America when Edmund Martinez started banding at Cheyenne Bottoms in 1966. John Zimmerman writes that in 12 years Martinez banded 58,159 birds, documenting the incredible long-distance journeys made by many migrants. Semipalmated Sandpipers were recovered on Alaskan breeding grounds as well as on their Brazilian wintering grounds; a Long-billed Dowitcher and a Pectoral Sandpiper were recovered from Siberia and a White-rumped Sandpiper from Argentina. Without stopovers like Cheyenne Bottoms, these migrants would have no place to rest and refuel.

SONG OF THE LARK

Five quintessential prairie birds that nest at Cheyenne Bottoms have the word "lark" embedded in their name: Horned Lark, Lark Bunting, Lark Sparrow, Western Meadowlark, and Eastern Meadowlark. Only one, the Horned Lark, is actually a member of the

Lark Sparrows were named for their complex, melodious songs, often delivered from a low shrub or fence post.

lark (Alaudidae) family. All, however, sing melodious, larklike songs, often delivered in flight.

Horned Larks perform dramatic song flights, ascending steeply up to 825 feet. At the pinnacle of flight, the male starts singing and gliding. On finishing the song, he folds his wings and plummets to earth, sometimes finishing off with an upward loop. The tinkling, "lisping" song is weaker and not as complex as songs of other larking birds.

Flashy black and white male Lark Buntings sing while ascending and descending in delirious courtship flights aimed at nondescript brownish females. In researching his master's thesis on Lark Buntings, Bill Ervin discovered a fact that goes against traditional bird lore: "The windier it is, the longer the song and display…Conventional wisdom doesn't hang together on the prairie." Lark Buntings use the wind to save energy by orienting into it. Consequently, on windy days the bunting has a shorter ascent but a much longer glide during which he sings longer than on a calm day. There is nothing on the prairie to block the sound, so downwind you can hear it for miles.

The Lark Sparrow "sings a long medley of sweet warbles and trills, interspersing it every so often with rude and embarrassing snorts," writes Ron Lambeth in *Colorado Breeding Bird Atlas*. During courtship, the male struts with upright tail like a turkey, and he often passes a twig to the female during copulation. The male sometimes rearranges song elements to produce a slightly different song, and he sometimes sings with regional dialects. When they gather for fall migration, males may burst into song again. With bold chestnut, black, and white face markings and a dark breast spot, Lark Sparrows are one of our most handsome sparrows. Sadly, they are also one of many grassland birds whose numbers appear to be declining.

Even non-birdwatchers recognize and love the flutelike song of the Western Meadowlark, a member of the blackbird family, who perches conspicuously on fences, wires, treetops, and the tips of yuccas to deliver his concert. Some researchers recognize a repertoire of 48 different meadowlark songs. Because primary songs are learned from experienced birds, a male isolated from his own species during critical learning periods will imitate another species instead. Western Meadowlarks have learned to sing like Red-winged Blackbirds, Common Yellowthroats, and Cardinals.

Eastern Meadowlarks look almost identical to the Western, but their song is not so glorious to most ears. Where both species occur, they can learn each other's song, and sometimes the eastern species is identified only by its *zert* call note. Since 1960 their range has expanded westward. They are still considered uncommon at Cheyenne Bottoms, whereas Westerns are listed as abundant. Cheyenne Bottoms provides a chance to hear and compare the two species.

HIKING AND BOATING

Although there are no designated trails at Cheyenne Bottoms, hiking is allowed on several of the dikes, and hand-powered boats are permitted on some ponds at certain times. Check at the office for current restrictions.

CAMPING

Camping is permitted only in a primitive campground, shaded with lots of big cottonwoods, a half-mile west of the office. In spring the dawn bird chorus makes an alarm clock unnecessary. Listen for Eastern Screech-Owls and Great Horned Owls, and bring mosquito repellent! Joy-riders on the adjacent county road can be a problem on weekends.

BEST TIMES TO VISIT

Sandhill Cranes arrive as early as February, followed by wading birds such as herons and egrets. Migrating duck numbers peak from late March to early April, and migrating shorebird numbers in late April to mid-May. "Lark" singing crescendoes in May and June. Thousands of American White Pelicans and hundreds of Snowy and Great Egrets converge on the ponds in August. Fall shorebird migration extends from July into October, when peak duck migration occurs. In late October hundreds of thousands of Canada and Greater White-fronted Geese return. Whooping Cranes are most likely from late October into early November, and Bald Eagles overwinter from November to March.

INFORMATION

CHEYENNE BOTTOMS WILDLIFE AREA, 56 NE 40 Road, Great Bend, KS 67530; 620-793-7730 (24-hour hotline) or 620-793-3066 (office).

HOW TO GET THERE

Halfway between Hoisington and Great Bend (five miles from each city) turn east off US 281 onto CR 60 and follow the signs two miles to the headquarters and the inlet canal. Or, from Great Bend drive 4 miles east on US 56 and 7 miles northeast on SR 156 to reach the outlet canal on the southeast end of the area and start the driving tour.

CHEYENNE BOTTOMS WILDLIFE AREA

WEATHER
MEAN TEMPERATURES AND PRECIPITATION

MONTH	HIGH (°F)	LOW (°F)	PRECIP.	SNOW
January	42	19	0.6"	4.6"
April	70	44	2.2"	0.9"
July	94	69	3.3"	0.0"
October	73	46	2.1"	0.2"

Mean annual precipitation is 25.9 inches, with much of the moisture falling from May through October. Severe thunderstorms can occur from late spring through early fall. Data are for Great Bend, Kansas.

SELECTED WILDLIFE OF SPECIAL INTEREST

MAMMALS: Virginia Opossum, Thirteen-lined Ground Squirrel, Black-tailed Prairie Dog, Beaver, Coyote, Long-tailed Weasel, Mink, Badger, Eastern Spotted Skunk, Striped Skunk, Mule Deer, White-tailed Deer.

BIRDS: American White Pelican (m), American Bittern, White-faced Ibis, Cinnamon Teal, Mississippi Kite, Bald Eagle (m), Northern Harrier, Golden Eagle, Prairie Falcon, Wild Turkey, Northern Bobwhite, Sandhill Crane (m), Upland Sandpiper, Burrowing Owl, Red-headed Woodpecker, Lark Bunting, Grasshopper Sparrow.

AMPHIBIANS AND REPTILES: Plains Leopard Frog, Plains Spadefoot, Great Plains Skink, Western Rattlesnake, Northern Water-snake, Massasauga, Snapping Turtle, Painted Turtle, Yellow Mud Turtle.

Cimmaron, Spanish for "wild" or "untamed," seems an odd name for a river that runs dry much of the year. Early-nineteenth-century travelers on the Santa Fe Trail, which paralleled the river for many miles, often had to dig down through the sand or seek out rare riverside springs to find any water at all.

But the Cimmaron revealed its potential fury on May 1, 1914, when a rainstorm produced a 12-foot-high flash flood that swept away the Point of Rocks Ranch, killing the foreman's two young children. The ranch, headquartered near the point where Spanish explorer Francisco Vásquez de Coronado etched his signature on a chalk bluff in 1541, once supported 30,000 head of cattle and extended west to Colorado and south to the Texas Panhandle.

After the onset of drought in 1933, the Point of Rocks Ranch fell into foreclosure. Farmers abandoned neighboring lands as windstorms swept up the parched soil and sent it swirling eastward. In 1936 the U.S. Department of Agriculture purchased more than 108,000 acres in the region and began reclaiming the devastated lands.

Today about 100 ranchers graze some 5,000 cattle on the

Above: Though dry throughout much of the year, the Cimmaron River supports a verdant riparian woodland populated by Elk, White-tailed Deer, and Wild Turkeys.

shortgrass, mixed-grass, and sandsage prairies of this national grassland. Ranger district personnel and range riders maintain 33 stock ponds and 125 windmills. Private companies operate more than 400 oil and gas wells.

This grassland supports a free-roaming Elk herd, along with Pronghorns, Swift Foxes, Lesser Prairie-Chickens, Wild Turkeys, and Long-billed Curlews. A three-person blind for observing and photographing Lesser Prairie-Chickens is available March through May.

DANCING PRAIRIE-CHICKENS

Lesser Prairie-Chickens strut on leks, or "booming grounds," during early spring. The males circle and stomp, emitting a high, turkeylike call as they puff out their rose-colored throat sacs. Females choose a dominant male to mate with before dispersing into the surrounding grasses and shrubs to scratch out a nest and lay their eggs.

Lesser Prairie-Chickens once numbered in the millions on the southern plains, and their ritualistic dance was widely imitated by Plains Indian peoples. In *My Indian Boyhood,* Lakota Chief Luther Standing Bear writes that no human dancing is as orderly as that of prairie-chickens: ". . . the marvelous thing is that every bird makes a sound in his throat that is something like the double beat of a tom-tom."

During the nineteenth century hundreds of thousands of these easily hunted birds were shipped back east to be served as delicacies in the finest restaurants. Since then, droughts, conversion of rangeland to cropland, woodland invasion of grasslands, herbicide poisoning of sagebrush and scrub oak, and overgrazing by livestock have degraded or eliminated nesting habitat. By 1990 only about 50,000 Lesser Prairie-Chickens, approximately 3 percent of the historic population, remained in North America. During the 1990s numbers continued to decline despite efforts to preserve nesting habitat in national grasslands and on adjacent lands.

In Oklahoma, numbers declined more than 75 percent from 1988 to 1999. At Cimmaron National Grassland, estimated populations dropped from 12.6 birds per square mile in 1990 to 1.4 birds per square mile in 1994, and they remained low throughout the 1990s.

Unusually dry conditions during the 1990s and early 2000s may have contributed to this decline. Biologists also blame continued habitat degradation. Lesser Prairie-Chicken populations have increased slightly in areas of west-central Kansas where

In April male Lesser Prairie-Chickens face off to establish dominance and win the right to mate with females. (Photo by Richard W. Holmes)

farmers enrolled in the Conservation Reserve Program have planted native grasses in close proximity to existing mixed-grass prairie.

BUFFALO GOURDS

No prairie plant carries a more apt scientific name than the Buffalo Gourd (*Cucurbita foetidissima*). The arrow-shaped leaves of this sprawling member of the cucumber family emit a nauseating, fetid odor that falls somewhere between smoldering tennis shoes and road-killed badger.

Despite its rank odor, the Buffalo Gourd has many uses. The Osage refer to this plant as *monkon tonga* ("big medicine"), and the Dakota call it *wagamun pezhuta* ("pumpkin medicine"). Seeds from the baseball-sized gourds can be ground for mush, and the bitter roots can be processed for their starch and protein. The Omaha, Ponca, and Dakota all used the roots medicinally.

Harvesting the taproot of this squash requires some effort. In *Edible Wild Plants of the Prairie*, Kelly Kindscher reports that one exceptionally large root weighed 178 pounds. Many Plains Indians took special care when digging up the mammoth roots, fearing that injury to any part of this magical plant might bring bad luck to themselves or their relatives.

Buffalo Gourds grow throughout the southwestern and central plains. At Cimmaron National Grassland look on either side of the main highway for the long, dark green tendrils that extend out like the legs of an octopus from the giant taproot.

On late summer evenings, one of the prairie's gangliest weeds metamorphoses into a wildflower of breathtaking beauty. Few people ever witness this transformation, since the saucer-sized cream and lemon blossoms of the Giant Eveningstar (*Mentzelia decapetala*) usually unfurl after sunset and close up before sunrise.

The star-shaped flowers of this 2-foot-high member of the stick-leaf family (Loasaceae) have evolved to attract night-flying moths. Sphinx moths (also known as "hummingbird moths") hover over the deep-throated corollas, probing for nectar with their long tonguelike proboscises.

In addition to enabling eveningstars to attract the right pollinators, night blooming helps them thrive in arid environments. During the heat of the day, while other forbs are losing precious water through their open petals, the flowers of eveningstars are rolled up into tight, evaporation-resistant bundles.

Giant Eveningstars bloom from early August to late September on shale outcrops, including the Point of Rocks area at Cimarron National Grassland. The Plains Eveningstar, similar in appearance to the Giant Eveningstar but with shorter, narrower petals, proliferates on sand dunes from eastern Montana south to the Texas Panhandle. A half-dozen other *Mentzelia,* most with smaller yellow blossoms, grow on the Great Plains.

Plants of the stick-leaf family are covered with stiff, bristly "pagoda-form" hairs (under the microscope they look like tiny Japanese pagodas). These hairs adhere like Velcro to almost anything they touch, including human clothing and animal fur. Some

Night-blooming Giant Eveningstars (Mentzelia decapetala) *thrive on bare shales north of the Cimmaron River.*

sheep ranchers say that once the foliage from eveningstars becomes entangled in sheep's wool, the wool loses all commercial
value.

HIKING

The Turkey Trail (9 miles) takes off from the Cimmaron River
Picnic Area, where SR 27 crosses the river, and follows the south
bank eastward. Look for Wild Turkeys, Ring-necked Pheasants,
and White-tailed Deer. **NOTE:** Hunting and target shooting are
popular activities along the river on weekends.

CAMPING

Dispersed camping is permitted throughout this national grassland. Cimmaron Recreation Area, 6 miles east of SR 27 on a
county road, includes a developed campground and a nearby fishing pond.

BEST TIMES TO VISIT

Lesser Prairie-Chickens dance and Burrowing Owls begin nesting
in April and May. During wet years, wildflowers bloom in profusion in late May and again in August. Giant Eveningstars, Plains
Eveningstars, and Tulip Gentians bloom from early August to
mid-September. Elk bugle and Eastern Screech-Owls wail at dusk
in late autumn.

INFORMATION

CIMMARON NATIONAL GRASSLAND, 242 Highway 56 East, Box J,
Elkhart, KS 67950; 620-697-4621.

HOW TO GET THERE

From Elkhart, Kansas, take SR 27 north for 8 miles. Gravel roads
with interpretive signs follow both sides of the Cimmaron River.
Note: Because federal lands are remote and scattered, you will
need a Cimmaron National Grassland map, available at the
Elkhart office, to find your way around.

CIMMARON NATIONAL GRASSLAND

WEATHER
MEAN TEMPERATURES AND PRECIPITATION

MONTH	HIGH (°F)	LOW (°F)	PRECIP.	SNOW
January	49	19	0.4"	2.3"
April	71	39	1.5"	0.2"
July	94	65	2.8"	0.0"
October	74	43	1.2"	0.0"

Mean annual precipitation is 17.67 inches, but amounts have ranged from a high of 32.83 inches to a low of 7.09 inches. Thunderstorms are frequent and sometimes severe in July and August. Summer daytime temperatures often exceed 100°F. Data are for Elkhart, Kansas.

SELECTED WILDLIFE OF SPECIAL INTEREST

MAMMALS: Black-tailed Prairie Dog, Beaver, Coyote, Swift Fox, Badger, Elk, White-tailed Deer, Mule Deer, Pronghorn.

BIRDS: Swainson's Hawk, Lesser Prairie-Chicken, Wild Turkey, Northern Bobwhite, Mountain Plover, Long-billed Curlew, Eastern Screech-Owl, Burrowing Owl, Horned Lark, Cassin's Sparrow, Grasshopper Sparrow, Dickcissel.

AMPHIBIANS AND REPTILES: Woodhouse's Toad, Lesser Earless Lizard, Greater Short-horned Lizard, Massasauga, Western Rattlesnake, Ornate Box Turtle.

KONZA PRAIRIE

Sooner or later, most prairie lovers come to Konza. They come for the head-high stands of Big Bluestem, lush gallery forests, herds of Bison, and Greater Prairie-Chickens strutting on limestone-cobbled ridgetops. They come, as well, to pay homage to prairie philanthropist Katherine Ordway, Kansas State University professor Lloyd C. Hulbert, and other visionaries who created Konza at a time when the entire tallgrass ecosystem seemed headed toward oblivion.

This 8,600-acre Nature Conservancy property in the northern Flint Hills was the first major tallgrass prairie preserve in North America. Using funds donated by Ordway, the Nature Conservancy acquired the original 916 acres in 1971 and the adjacent 7,220-acre Dewey Ranch in 1977. Kansas State University established its Konza Prairie Biological Station on the site in 1971.

Discoveries made at Konza contribute to prairie conservation efforts throughout the world. The historic Dewey ranch house serves as a research center that houses visiting scientists from as far away as Argentina, South Africa, and Mongolia. More than 4,000 schoolchildren participate in day hikes, classes, and long-term monitoring projects each year.

In 1980 the National Science Foundation designated Konza

Above: Konza Prairie in late May.

one of its first Long-Term Ecological Research Sites (LTER). LTERs were created to track ecological processes over decades or centuries. Long-term studies at Konza focus on topics ranging from soil microorganisms to landscape ecology.

Much of the work revolves around the vital roles of fire and grazing in tallgrass ecosystems. Beginning in 1973, Kansas State University scientists divided Konza into 60 watersheds, each of which is subjected to a different prescribed burning regime. Units are burned at various intervals (from 1 to 20 years, or not at all) and at various seasons. Within their respective pastures, Bison and cattle roam freely from one burn unit to another, allowing scientists to observe the natural interplay of fire and grazing.

The research has confirmed that without periodic fire there would be no tallgrass prairie in the Flint Hills, and without grazing the prairie would lose much of its plant species diversity. Periodic fire combined with moderate grazing generally leads to increased cover of grasses and forbs and higher plant species diversity.

Beyond these conclusions, Konza scientists have shown how fire and grazing interact with weather, soil types, topography, and each other to create an infinitely complex patchwork of prairie types. This dynamic prairie system and the riparian woodlands that cut through it support more than 600 plant species, more than 200 resident and migratory birds, 36 mammals, and several dozen fishes, amphibians, and reptiles.

Walking the hills and valleys of Konza Prairie is like traversing a giant, billowing quilt whose pieces continually shift and transform. As wind, fire, and Bison herds flow over this grassland mosaic, the prairie diversifies and re-creates itself.

THE FLINT HILLS

The Flint Hills were formed by erosion of westward-dipping sedimentary rocks deposited on the floors of ancient seas 200 million to 300 million years ago. The white limestones exposed on the hillsides and ridgetops contain bands of chert, or flint, a fine-grained sedimentary rock composed of silica. The flint is less soluble than the limestones, so weathering action creates clayey soils riddled with small flint particles. White settlers found these soils virtually impossible to plow, and the Flint Hills became rangeland while prairies to the west and east were tilled under.

Today these hills, which stretch from near the Nebraska-Kansas border southward into northeastern Oklahoma, support 4 million acres of tallgrass prairie. Though overgrazing, too-frequent burning, and introduction of nonnative grasses and forbs have degraded portions of these grasslands, native tallgrasses still cover much of the region.

The gravelly ridgetop soils also helped create the striking topography of Konza Prairie. Over millions of years, the Kansas River and its tributaries carved deep valleys through adjacent softer limestones while the gravelly hilltops resisted erosion. The resulting dissected landscape supports a wide range of prairie types, from dry hill prairies where Eastern Collared Lizards scurry among Prickly Pear and Pincushion Cactus, to wet bottomland prairies dominated by Prairie Cordgrass and sedges.

Springs are a byproduct of this topography. Groundwater accumulates between layers of the westward-tilting strata and flows gently downhill until it emerges from hillsides where the strata have been exposed by erosion. Some Flint Hills springs flow at more than 1,000 gallons per minute. Diamond and Lost Springs, 40 miles south of Manhattan, were important watering stops along the Santa Fe Trail.

The springs that trickle from the steep hillsides of Konza Prairie feed five creeks, including King's Creek, the only North American stream whose entire watershed lies within a protected tallgrass prairie. The clear waters of King's Creek support 19 species of fish and several aquatic insects that have only recently been discovered. Gallery forests of Bur Oak, Chinkapin Oak, Silver Maple, Hackberry, American Elm, and a mixture of shrubs and forbs provide habitat for Bobcats, White-tailed Deer, Wild Turkeys, and Barred Owls.

WILD TURKEYS

Wild Turkeys gobble and trill throughout the year at Konza. These dark-feathered game birds have made a spectacular comeback on the Great Plains and in the Mississippi Valley after being extirpated from most of North America during the late nineteenth century. Now, thanks to successful reintroduction programs, habitat preservation efforts, and control of diseases once spread by domestic poultry, the North American population has grown to more than 4 million. Flocks inhabit every prairie state and even wander through some prairie towns.

Wild Turkeys feed on acorns, grass seeds, wild fruits, and insects. During the spring mating season toms gather on strutting grounds where they gobble, fan their feathers, and fight for the affections of discriminating hens. The hens lay 6 to 20 eggs in a shallow depression lined with dead leaves or grass stems. After the young have matured, the turkeys coalesce into fall and winter flocks of 50 or more birds.

Wild Turkeys mate in spring. Elimination of natural predators has contributed to a population explosion in some regions. (Photo by Glenn Cushman)

Some Wild Turkeys in the prairie region have lost their natural fear of humans. Individuals stroll down busy highways or strut through campgrounds pecking at table scraps. Some of these "uptown" birds are turkeys that imprinted on humans while being raised in captivity; others have simply learned where to find the easy pickings.

KATHERINE ORDWAY, THE WOMAN WHO SAVED THE PRAIRIE

When the Nature Conservancy completed its acquisition of the Dewey Ranch in 1977, it reported that the purchase had been made possible by a gift from an anonymous donor. It was typical of Katherine Ordway, a quiet, somewhat frail woman with an iron resolve, to make as little noise as necessary while doing as much good as possible. She asked only that the prairies she helped preserve be named after the Plains Indian peoples who lived on them prior to white conquest.

Born in 1899, she grew up in St. Paul, Minnesota. As a child and young woman she watched in dismay as remaining tracts of tallgrass prairie disappeared from the upper Midwest. She graduated from the University of Minnesota with degrees in botany and art, and she did graduate work in biology and land-use planning at Columbia.

After Ordway and her four brothers inherited nearly 20 million dollars from their father's home-heating and mining businesses in 1948, she set about saving the landscape she loved. During the 1960s and 1970s, Ordway donated money that helped to preserve more than 31,000 acres of tallgrass prairie. Prairie State Park and

Wah' Kon-Tah Prairie in Missouri, Nachusa Grasslands in Illinois, and dozens of nature preserves throughout the United States trace their existence to her generosity and vision.

HIKING

Seven miles of hiking trails, including a 2.8-mile interpretive loop, originate from the kiosk at the preserve entrance. These trails provide dawn-to-dusk access to the northern portion of the preserve. Konza staff and volunteers offer classes and group tours of the remainder of the preserve throughout the year. Reservations can be made through the Konza office.

CAMPING

No camping is permitted. Nearby public campgrounds include:

TUTTLE CREEK STATE PARK, 7 miles north of Manhattan on SR 13.

POTTAWATOMIE STATE FISHING LAKE NO. 2, 6 miles north of Manhattan on SR 13.

BEST TIMES TO VISIT

Wild Turkeys display, Greater Prairie-Chickens dance, and Bison calve from late March through May. Wildflowers carpet the green hills in late spring. Showy species include Missouri Evening-Primrose, Cobaea Penstemon, Blue False Indigo, and Spider Milkweed. The tallgrasses reach their full height, moisture permitting, in late August and early September. After the heat and humidity of summer, October days seem especially pleasant, and the grasses show their most striking colors.

INFORMATION

KONZA PRAIRIE BIOLOGICAL STATION, Division of Biology, Kansas State University, 232 Ackert Hall, Manhattan, KS 66506-4901; 785-587-0441.

HOW TO GET THERE

From I-70 Exit 307, take McDowell Creek Road north 4.5 miles. The preserve entrance is signed on your right. From Manhattan, take SR 177 south across the Kansas River, then turn immediately right on McDowell Creek Road and drive 7 miles to the entrance on your left.

KONZA PRAIRIE

WEATHER
MEAN TEMPERATURES AND PRECIPITATION

MONTH	HIGH (°F)	LOW (°F)	PRECIP.	SNOW
January	38	17	0.8"	5.2"
April	68	44	3.0"	0.5"
July	91	69	3.3"	0.0"
October	70	46	3.1"	0.0"

Mean annual precipitation is 33.0 inches. Record temperatures range from 116°F to -31°F. Summers are hot and muggy with occasional severe thunderstorms. January is the driest month. Data are for Manhattan, Kansas.

SELECTED WILDLIFE OF SPECIAL INTEREST

MAMMALS: Virginia Opossum, Prairie Vole, Plains Harvest Mouse, Thirteen-lined Ground Squirrel, Coyote, Bobcat, Badger, White-Tailed Deer, Bison.

BIRDS: Greater Prairie-Chicken, Wild Turkey, Northern Bobwhite, Upland Sandpiper, Yellow-billed Cuckoo, Eastern Screech-Owl, Great Horned Owl, Barred Owl, Red-headed Woodpecker, Red-bellied Woodpecker, Sedge Wren, Eastern Bluebird, Northern Mockingbird, Grasshopper Sparrow, Northern Cardinal, Dickcissel.

AMPHIBIANS AND REPTILES: Western Chorus Frog, Bullfrog, Great Plains Skink, Eastern Collared Lizard, Texas Horned Lizard, Eastern Racer.

TALLGRASS PRAIRIE NATIONAL PRESERVE

In late summer, Big Bluestem and Indian Grass grow 7 feet high along the nature trail that winds through part of this preserve. Cicadas, orb spiders, and Common Buckeye butterflies glisten in the morning dew as they cling to the gently swaying stalks. Endangered Topeka Shiners swim in the clear waters of a spring-fed creek.

The historic Spring Hill Ranch was purchased by the National Park Trust in 1994 and renamed the Tallgrass Prairie National Preserve when it became a unit of the National Park System in 1996. In a unique private/public partnership, the trust retains ownership of all but 180 acres of land on the preserve. However, the National Park Service manages the entire 10,894-acre preserve through a cooperative agreement with the trust.

Plans are afoot to introduce a small Bison herd. Cattle will continue to graze on the preserve, which will be managed both to sustain a tallgrass prairie ecosystem and to acknowledge the historic uses of the Flint Hills by ranchers. Much of the land within the preserve is slowly recovering from years of intensive grazing.

The Spring Hill Ranch dates back to the early 1880s, when Stephen F. Jones and his family purchased the land and built their Second Empire–style 11-room house out of the finest hand-cut Cottonwood Limestone. The house and outbuildings, so im-

Above: Bluestem prairie, looking toward hilltop schoolhouse.

posing that nineteenth-century passersby often mistook them for a hotel complex, still dominate the site. A one-room stone school-house constructed on land donated by Jones sits on a nearby hill.

National Parks staff offer guided tours of the ranch house and outbuildings several times a day. A 7-mile bus tour through the preserve takes visitors to a hilltop affording a sweeping view of the Flint Hills.

THE WIND PEOPLE

> You white people treat the Kansa like a flock of turkeys. You chase us from one stream and then you chase us to another stream, so that soon you will chase us over the mountains and into the ocean.

> —Chief Al-le-ga-wa-ho, 1872

When federal agent George Sibley visited the Kansa Indians' main village where the Blue River joins the Kansas River in 1811, he was impressed by what he saw. Above the north bank of the Kansas River were 128 lodges, "rather neat and cleanly" in ap-pearance, with American flags flying from their pole rafters. Fields of corn, beans, and pumpkins grew nearby. Children herded horses in meadows of head-high grass. With a "bustle busy hum and merriment," the Kansa prepared to ride west on their summer buffalo hunt.

Thirty-four years later, newly appointed Kansa agent John Montgomery wrote that the Kansa were sick and starving, that their crops were dying, and that they were stealing from everyone in sight: ". . . their tendency is downward, and, in my opinion, they must soon become extinct, and the sooner that they arrive at this period, the better it will be for the rest of mankind."

Montgomery later recanted and became an advocate for these persecuted people. By then it was too late. Hemmed in by the Pawnee and Cheyenne to the north, the Comanche and Kiowa to the south, and American settlers on all sides, the Kansa had no choice but to trade their remaining lands for a trickle of Federal annuities.

In 1846 the thousand or so Kansa who had not been struck down by smallpox and other European-introduced diseases moved to a 256,000-acre reservation in the Neosho Valley near Council Grove. Within 25 years, squatters and land speculators had overrun the reservation, and the remaining Kansa were relo-cated to "Indian country" in northeastern Oklahoma.

No one knows the exact meaning or origin of the word "Kansa," but it was used in relation to a clan within the tribe known as "the Wind People" or "Southwind People." This social order, which was responsible for carrying out rites honoring the four winds and other sky deities, probably existed long before the Kansa broke away from the Omaha, Osage, and other Mississippi Valley peoples and migrated westward.

The Kansa (also known as Konza or Kaw) probably arrived in the Kansas River Valley during the early eighteenth century. Though never prosperous and often at war with their neighbors, they experienced several decades of relative stability, subsisting on their crops, Bison and other wild game, and goods delivered in trade with French fur trappers.

Today the Kaw Nation, headquartered in Kaw City, Oklahoma, provides its 2,500 enrolled members with health, educational, and cultural benefits under the governance of an elected executive council. In early 2000 the Nation purchased 150 acres of former reservation land near Council Grove, and they are developing the land into an historical park.

TOPEKA SHINERS

Biologists have found these federally endangered minnows in three unnamed creeks that flow through the Tallgrass Prairie National Preserve. Topeka Shiners depend on clear running water and are intolerant of sedimentation and stream channelization. Urban development, dam and pond construction, stocking of predatory fish, and loss of streamside vegetation have eliminated habitat throughout the tallgrass region.

The presence of these finger-sized minnows testifies to the purity of the preserve's spring-fed creeks. Though Topeka Shiners are uncommon and difficult to spot, you might catch a flash of silver in the fall, when streams flow low and clear, or glimpse the bright orange-red coloring on the males' heads and fins during the late spring spawning season.

CICADAS

Many Midwesterners no doubt can intuit the time of year, time of day, and temperature from the rhythms and intensities of cicada choruses. Since different species hatch out during different years and each has a distinct call, a truly dedicated observer could use recordings of calls to construct an audio "cicada calendar" that would span decades, or perhaps millennia.

Cicada species in the genus *Magicicada* are "periodical," meaning that almost all the members of each brood emerge as adults

A Giant Grassland Cicada (Tibicen dorsatus) *warms its wings in the morning sun along the Southwind Nature Trail.*

after a fixed number of years living underground as nymphs. Some periodical cicadas emerge after 13 years, others after 17 years. These long life cycles may help cicadas to avoid being wiped out by predatory mammals and songbirds, who become sated before they can consume all the cicadas hatching out during a given year.

Periodical cicadas (*Magicicada* spp.) can be identified by their striking black bodies, red eyes, and red wing veins.

Most North American cicada species, however, are not periodic. Though their life cycles span several years, hatching years are not synchronized within broods, and some adults of most species hatch out each summer.

On August mornings, 2-inch-long yellow and black cicadas of the nonperiodic genus *Tibicen* cling to stalks of Big Bluestem and Indian Grass at the Tallgrass Prairie Preserve. Only luck keeps them from being eaten, for they remain lethargic until the sun has warmed their wings. As the morning heat builds, the males fly up to "chorus centers" in sunlit branches of deciduous trees. The males flex strong muscles in their thoraxes, causing stiff ribs to bend rapidly over a resonating chamber. The resulting buzzy, rasping sound, which can exceed 80 decibels, is apparently as rhapsodic to female cicadas as it is annoying to some heat-weary humans.

Adult cicadas live for just a few weeks. After mating, the female deposits her oblong white eggs on stems and branches of woody vegetation. A few weeks later the eggs hatch, and the nymphs

*Big Bluestem gener-
ally blooms in August
and develops seeds a
few weeks later. How-
ever, the bare ground
needed for germina-
tion is scarce in tall-
grass prairies, so
plants depend on
tillering to establish
new stems.*

drop to the ground, attaching themselves to the root of a grass or
forb and using their piercing mouth parts to suck out its sustenance. Recent research suggests the ebb and flow of sap within
the root serves as a sort of biological clock influencing the matu-
ration and timing of emergence of cicada nymphs.

PERIODICAL CICADA EMERGENCE DATES

This table gives emergence dates for 13- and 17-year cicadas in the
prairie region. Some variation may occur, since groups of individuals
within broods of 17-year cicadas occasionally switch to 13-year cycles
and others may emerge after only 16 years. This life cycle switching
may help periodical cicada broods avoid genetic isolation.

STATE	17-YEAR	13-YEAR
Illinois	2004, 2007, 2014	2011, 2015
Indiana	2004, 2007, 2008	2011, 2015
Iowa	2007, 2014, 2015	
Kansas	2015	
Michigan	2004, 2007	
Missouri	2014, 2015	2015
Nebraska	2015	
Ohio	2008, 2016, 2019	2011
Oklahoma	2015	2011
Texas	2015	
Wisconsin	2007	

Sources: University of Michigan Museum of Zoology 2002. Cicada Web Site; Williams and Simon 1995.

HIKING

The Southwind Nature Trail (1.75-mile loop) takes off 50 yards north of the preserve entrance and winds through restored tall-grass prairie and across a spring-fed stream to the 1882 Lower Fox Creek Schoolhouse. Look for Northern Cardinals, Upland Sandpipers, and Eastern Collared Lizards in the meadow and White-tailed Deer along the creek.

CAMPING

CHASE STATE FISHING LAKE, 8 miles south of the preserve, has primitive campsites and a swimming beach. From Cottonwood Falls, take Main Street west and continue for 2.6 miles.

BEST TIMES TO VISIT

Greater Prairie-Chickens boom and migrating warblers pass through in late April and May. Tallgrasses usually bloom and reach maximum height in late August. Butterflies, including Eastern Black Swallowtails, Tiger Swallowtails, Viceroys, Monarchs, and Common Buckeyes, are abundant throughout the summer, but chiggers and mosquitoes can be annoying. By October most of the biting insects are gone, and the turning grasses and leaves create a Monet-like canvas of reds, russets, and golds.

INFORMATION

TALLGRASS PRAIRIE NATIONAL PRESERVE, Route 1, Box 14, Strong City, KS 66869; 620-273-8494. Ranch buildings and interpretive facilities are open daily except holidays; the nature trail is open from dawn to dusk.

HOW TO GET THERE

From the intersection of US 50 and SR 177 near Strong City, go north about 2 miles. The preserve entrance is on the west side of the highway.

TALLGRASS PRAIRIE NATIONAL PRESERVE

WEATHER
MEAN TEMPERATURES AND PRECIPITATION

MONTH	HIGH (°F)	LOW (°F)	PRECIP.	SNOW
January	38	17	0.9"	2.0"
April	67	43	3.4"	0.0"
July	91	68	4.6"	0.0"
October	70	45	2.9"	0.0"

Mean annual precipitation is 34.84 inches. Summers are very humid with periodic severe thunderstorms. Temperatures can fluctuate wildly in spring and fall. Data are for Emporia, Kansas.

SELECTED WILDLIFE OF SPECIAL INTEREST

MAMMALS: Plains Pocket Gopher, Black-tailed Jackrabbit, Coyote, Bobcat, Badger, White-tailed Deer.

BIRDS: Wood Duck, Greater Prairie-Chicken, Upland Sandpiper, Black-billed Cuckoo, Yellow-billed Cuckoo, Barred Owl, Common Nighthawk, Red-bellied Woodpecker, Scissor-tailed Flycatcher, Grasshopper Sparrow, Northern Cardinal, Indigo Bunting.

REPTILES AND AMPHIBIANS: Great Plains Narrow-mouthed Toad, Eastern Collared Lizard, Great Plains Skink, Texas Horned Lizard, Copperhead, Massasauga, Ornate Box Turtle.

OTHER KANSAS SITES

CHASE STATE FISHING LAKE (State Parks, 6232 E. 29th Street, Wichita, KS 67220; 316-683-8069). Several hundred acres of tallgrass prairie, including some ungrazed mesic hillside prairies, surround this small lake in the Flint Hills. Camping, swimming. From Cottonwood Falls, take Main Street west for 2.6 miles.

EL DORADO STATE PARK (618 NE Bluestem Road, El Dorado, KS 67042; 316-321-7180). A total of 4,600 acres of protected lands include several tallgrass remnants. Greater Prairie-Chickens strut here in spring. Camping, hiking. Thirty-five miles northeast of Wichita, off I-35.

FLINT HILLS NATIONAL WILDLIFE REFUGE (Box 128, Hartford, KS 66854; 620-392-5553). These 18,500 acres of farmlands, grasslands, and wetlands at the upper end of John Redmond Reservoir host migrating ducks and geese, along with wintering Bald Eagles. Camping. From Emporia go east on I-35 to Exit 141, then 10 miles south on SR 130.

FLINT HILLS TALLGRASS PRAIRIE PRESERVE (The Nature Conservancy, 820 SE Quincy, Suite 301, Topeka, KS 66612; 785-233-4400). This outstanding example of Flint Hills upland prairie occupies 2,188 acres of protected land. Greater Prairie-Chickens, Short-eared Owls, Henslow's Sparrows, Topeka Shiners. Butler and Greenwood Counties. Tours and visits by appointment only.

LAKE SCOTT STATE PARK (Route 1, Scott City, KS 67871; 620-872-2061). Elk and Bison herds, a labeled nature trail, and a restored Pueblo Indian ruin are some of the attractions at this shortgrass prairie oasis. The nearby Monument Rocks illustrate the evolution from inland sea to prairie. Campground and swimming beach. Off US 83 about 14 miles north of Scott City.

MAXWELL WILDLIFE REFUGE AND MACPHERSON STATE FISHING LAKE (Department of Wildlife and Parks, 3300 SW 29th Street, Topeka, KS 66614; 620-628-4592). Bison and Elk graze on 2,560 acres of prairie. Regal Fritillary butterflies nectar on Butterfly Milkweeds in June. Camping, nature trail. From Canton go north 6 miles on CR 304.

QUIVIRA NATIONAL WILDLIFE REFUGE (RR 3, Box 48A, Stafford, KS 67578; 620-486-2393). Salt marshes, woodlands, and grasslands attract hundreds of thousands of migratory ducks and geese. American White Pelicans and Sandhill Cranes also pass through; Mississippi Kites and Swainson's Hawks nest. Hiking. From Great Bend go south about 13 miles on US 281, then east 13 miles on CR 484.

SMOKY VALLEY RANCH (The Nature Conservancy, 820 SE Quincy, Suite 301, Topeka, KS 66612; 785-233-4400). This 16,800-acre preserve, a potential Black-footed Ferret reintroduction site, encompasses bluffs and shortgrass prairie along the Smoky Hill River. Logan County. Tours and visits by appointment.

Big Bluestem and Indian Grass grow head high around Chase State Fishing Lake in late summer.

MINNESOTA

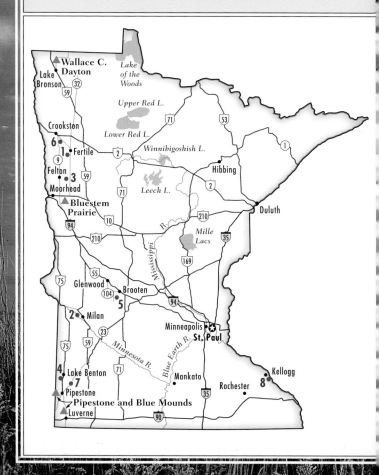

Wallace C.
Dayton

Lake
Bronson

Lake
of the
Woods

Upper Red L.

Crookston

Lower Red L.

Fertile

Winnibigoshish L.

Felton

Hibbing

Moorhead

Leech L.

Bluestem
Prairie

Duluth

Mille
Lacs

Mississippi R.

Glenwood

Brooten

Milan

Minneapolis
St. Paul

Minnesota R.

Blue Earth R.

Lake Benton

Mankato

Rochester

Kellogg

Pipestone

Pipestone and Blue Mounds

Luverne

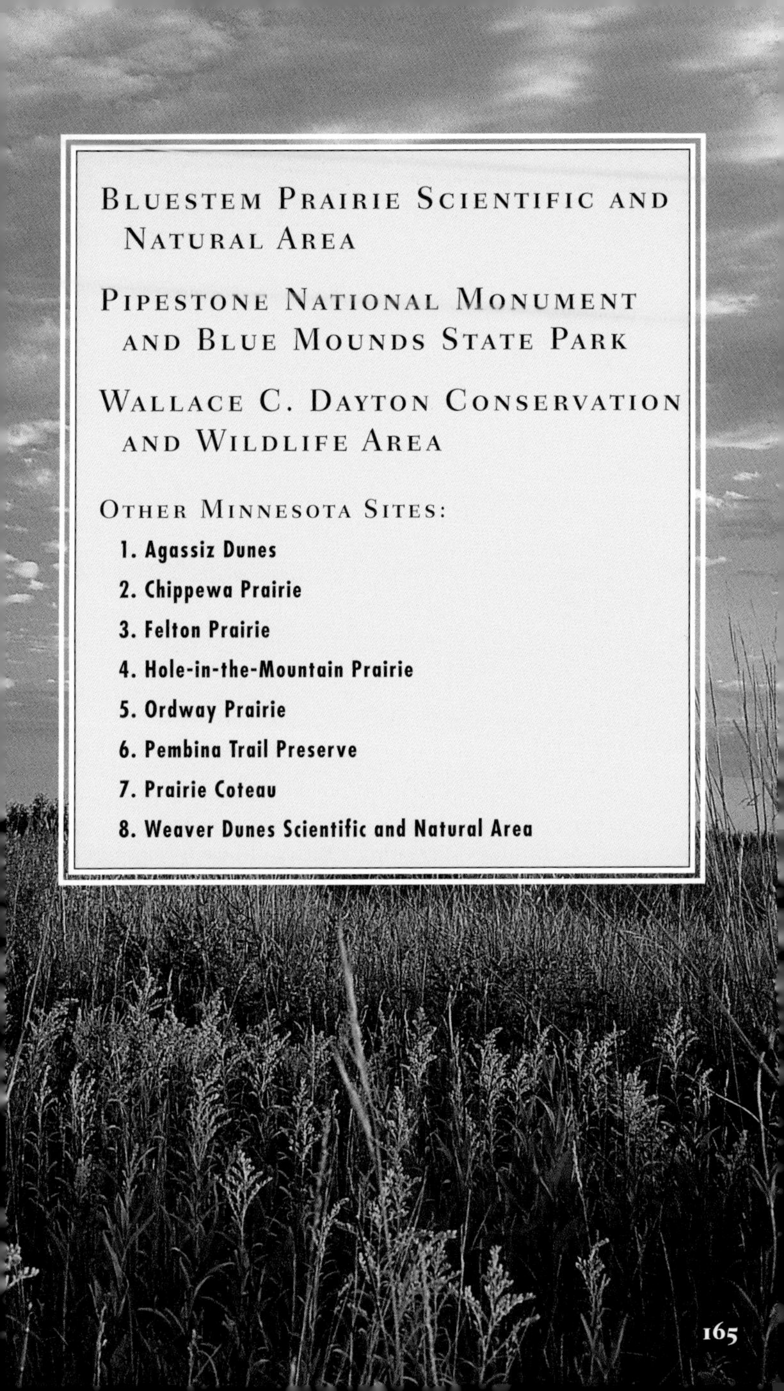

BLUESTEM PRAIRIE SCIENTIFIC AND
  NATURAL AREA

PIPESTONE NATIONAL MONUMENT
  AND BLUE MOUNDS STATE PARK

WALLACE C. DAYTON CONSERVATION
  AND WILDLIFE AREA

OTHER MINNESOTA SITES:
  1. Agassiz Dunes
  2. Chippewa Prairie
  3. Felton Prairie
  4. Hole-in-the-Mountain Prairie
  5. Ordway Prairie
  6. Pembina Trail Preserve
  7. Prairie Coteau
  8. Weaver Dunes Scientific and Natural Area

BLUESTEM PRAIRIE
SCIENTIFIC AND NATURAL
AREA

Of the nearly 20 million acres of tallgrass prairie that once stretched across western Minnesota, only about 150,000 acres remain. Many of the largest prairie remnants lie on beach ridges of Glacial Lake Agassiz. This enormous lake formed at the end of the Ice Age as retreating glaciers created a natural dam that held back waters flowing northward toward Hudson Bay.

At its peak, Glacial Lake Agassiz was larger than all the current Great Lakes combined. Wave action sorted and deposited sand and gravel on its shores, creating a series of beach ridges as the lake level rose and fell. Farmers found these ridges difficult to plow, so some remained in grass.

At Bluestem Prairie Scientific and Natural Area, more than 5,000 acres of tallgrass prairie thrives among several of these beach ridges. Like groundswells far out at sea, the 40-foot-high ridges rise almost imperceptibly above the surrounding floodplain. You could easily miss them, were it not for the differences in vegetative cover. In summer the dry prairie on the gravel ridges appears duller in color than the dark green tallgrasses growing in the intervening swales.

The beach ridges support an impressive array of grasses, including Little Bluestem, Porcupine Grass, Big Bluestem, Indian Grass, Sideoats Grama, and Blue Grama. Blanket Flowers and Prairie

Above: Glacial erratic and tallgrass prairie, Bluestem Prairie Scientific and Natural Area.

Coneflowers bloom beside granite boulders left behind by Ice Age glaciers. Grasshopper Sparrows and Western Meadowlarks sing from Chokecherry and willow bushes.

Mesic tallgrass prairie with head-high stands of Big Bluestem dominates the swales between the ridges. In July and August, Monarch, Orange Sulphur, and Wood Nymph butterflies flit from one Prairie Blazing Star to another, while Sedge Wrens chatter in the concealing vegetation. This luxuriant prairie also supports the state-threatened Regal Fritillary and Dakota Skipper butterflies, along with nesting Greater Prairie-Chickens, Marbled Godwits, and Upland Sandpipers.

Wet tallgrass prairie, dominated by Prairie Cordgrass and sedges, thrives in low areas with saturated soils. The federally threatened Western Prairie Fringed Orchid blooms in these wet swales in late June and early July.

The 4,658-acre Bluestem Prairie preserve is owned and managed by the Nature Conservancy and leased to the Minnesota Department of Natural Resources. Biologists from both organizations work to restore croplands and hay meadows to native prairie. On the south side of the preserve just north of CR 12, a 100-acre field was seeded in native grasses and forbs and restored to lush bluestem prairie in only five years.

The preserve is bordered to the north by the 1,100-acre Buffalo River State Park and to the east by the 300-acre University of Minnesota Moorhead Regional Science Center. The preserve is open to day use only. A free blind for observing and photographing Greater Prairie-Chickens can be reserved in April and May.

GLACIAL FOOTPRINTS

Giant granite boulders stranded on the prairie alert travelers to the fact that most of Minnesota lay under ice only 12,000 years ago. These boulders, known as glacial erratics, were swept along in the rivers of ice and left behind when the glaciers retreated. (See photo in Felton Prairie, p. 185.) Some are polished smooth where Bison rubbed against them or are encircled by distinctive troughs where Bison hooves trampled the surrounding soil.

Many other signs of glacial advance and retreat are visible in western Minnesota. Prominent striations on granite outcrops reveal where rocks and gravel embedded in the glacial ice scratched against the underlying rock. Moraines, hilly deposits of glacial debris deposited underneath or at the terminus of glaciers, rise hundreds of feet above the surrounding plains. Hundreds of kettle lakes, or potholes, remain where giant chunks of ice melted, leaving collapsed pits. Small conical hills called "kames" were created when some of these meltout depressions filled with debris.

At least four orchid species bloom at Bluestem Prairie. Small White Lady's-Slippers grow in moist areas on the edge of wetlands and begin blooming in May. Less than 1 foot tall with 1-inch-long purple-veined flowers, these delicate orchids are easily missed, or worse, stepped on by careless hikers. Yellow Lady's-Slippers grow in similar habitat and also begin blooming in late spring. The flowers of both these lady's-slippers have prominent, inflated lips that help direct nectaring insects to the orange-yellow pollen sacs.

Few wildflowers are more striking than the Western Prairie Fringed Orchid (see Sheyenne National Grassland, North Dakota, and Manitoba Tallgrass Preserve). Up to 2 feet tall, with a raceme of showy white flowers, this federally threatened species blooms in late June or early July in damp swales, often mixed in with sedges, Prairie Blazing Stars, and Blue-eyed Grass.

In late summer and early fall, the sweet fragrance of Nodding Ladies'-Tresses wafts up from roadside ditches and wet meadows. The pearly white flowers of this exquisite orchid spiral up a slender 6- to 12-inch-high stalk.

Though often associated in our minds with jungles and exotic places, orchids are among the most widely distributed plants. Tiny windborne orchid seeds have colonized continents and islands around the world. Only the sunflower family contains more species than the orchid family.

Unfortunately, many orchids, with their highly specialized growing requirements and their attractiveness to collectors, have become rare or endangered. This is especially true on the prairie, where most orchid habitat has been drained or plowed under.

*Yellow Lady's-Slipper orchids (*Cypripedium calceolus*) bloom in moist lowlands in May and early June.*

On midsummer mornings, hundreds of Monarch butterflies nectar from Prairie Blazing Stars, purple Prairie Coneflowers, and other wildflowers at Bluestem Prairie, but it's the milkweeds that are the prime attraction. Monarchs choose milkweeds as host plants for their eggs and caterpillars. The milkweeds contain toxins called cardiac glycosides, which, though harmless to Monarchs, render the caterpillars and adults virtually inedible to birds and other predators.

If Monarchs were as tasty as some other butterflies, it's unlikely that they could perform their annual migration. Some of the Monarchs that hatch out at Bluestem Prairie may winter as far as 2,000 miles to the south in the highlands of the central Mexican state of Michoacán. Recent research suggests that the migrants use an internal sun compass and sensitivity to the Earth's magnetic field to navigate across great distances.

A single adult Monarch can fly all the way from Minnesota to Michoacán, but it takes two or three generations to complete the northward trip. Most of the Monarchs that arrive at Bluestem Prairie in June and July probably hatched out somewhere along the way in the southern United States.

Once they reach the greening prairies of western Minnesota, adult Monarchs set to work looking for partners. After mating, the female lays up to 500 eggs, one to a leaf, on milkweed plants. The caterpillars hatch after a few days and begin gorging themselves on milkweed. After gaining full size, they transform into jade green chrysalises ornamented with flecks of gold. Late-summer larvae hatch out as supersized, long-living adults capable of flying all the way to Mexico.

Monarch butterflies take nectar from and mate on Prairie Blazing Stars (Liatris pycnostachya) *in early August.*

Seeing flurries of orange Monarchs shimmering in the evening light at Bluestem Prairie, you might conclude that this species is in no danger. However, concentrations of this kind are misleading. Although milkweeds grow along irrigation ditches, in fallow fields, and in remaining prairie fragments, most of the Monarch's breeding habitat in western Minnesota and throughout the Great Plains has been destroyed.

In addition, wintering areas in Mexico and along the California coast are under siege. In Michoacán, logging continues to encroach on a 6,400-square-mile reserve that harbors 10 million to 50 million Monarchs per acre. Pesticides sprayed on agricultural crops in the United States and Mexico kill bucketfuls of Monarchs each year.

HIKING

Several two-track roads, suitable for hiking, traverse the preserve. A 0.7-mile mowed nature trail originates at the north parking area (see How to Get There, below) and follows a prominent beach ridge, eventually connecting with the hiking trail system maintained by Buffalo River State Park.

CAMPING

BUFFALO RIVER STATE PARK, immediately north of the preserve on US 10, has 44 somewhat crowded campsites, a swimming beach, and hiking trails.

BEST TIMES TO VISIT

Greater Prairie-Chickens boom and Pasque Flowers bloom in April and early May. Orchids begin blooming in late May. Marbled Godwits and Upland Sandpipers aggressively defend nesting sites in June. Tallgrasses flower and butterflies cluster on Prairie Blazing Stars in early August. Thousands of Sandhill Cranes pass through in early fall.

INFORMATION

THE NATURE CONSERVANCY NORTHERN TALLGRASS PRAIRIE OFFICE, 15337 28th Avenue South, Glyndon, MN 56547; 218-498-2679.

From the junction of US 10 and SR 9, 14 miles east of Moorhead, go south 1.5 miles. Turn east on 17th Avenue South, a gravel road, and continue 1.5 miles to the parking area on the left side of the road. To reach a second parking area on the south side of the preserve, continue south on SR 9 to CR 12 (50th Avenue South), turn east, and drive about 3.5 miles.

BLUESTEM PRAIRIE SCIENTIFIC AND NATURAL AREA

WEATHER
MEAN TEMPERATURES AND PRECIPITATION

MONTH	HIGH (°F)	LOW (°F)	PRECIP.	SNOW
January	15	-4	0.7"	8.6"
April	54	32	1.8"	3.1"
July	83	59	2.7"	0.0"
October	57	35	1.7"	0.7"

Mean annual precipitation is 19.45 inches. Severe thunderstorms and tornadoes are possible from May through August. Data are for Fargo, North Dakota.

SELECTED WILDLIFE OF SPECIAL INTEREST

MAMMALS: Richardson's Ground Squirrel, Plains Pocket Gopher, Plains Pocket Mouse, Prairie Vole, White-tailed Deer, Moose.

BIRDS: Northern Harrier, Greater Prairie-Chicken, Sandhill Crane (m), Upland Sandpiper, Marbled Godwit, Red-headed Woodpecker, Loggerhead Shrike, Sedge Wren, Marsh Wren, Grasshopper Sparrow, Henslow's Sparrow, Dickcissel, Bobolink, Eastern Meadowlark.

AMPHIBIANS AND REPTILES: Boreal Chorus Frog, Western Chorus Frog, Northern Leopard Frog, Wood Frog, Tiger Salamander.

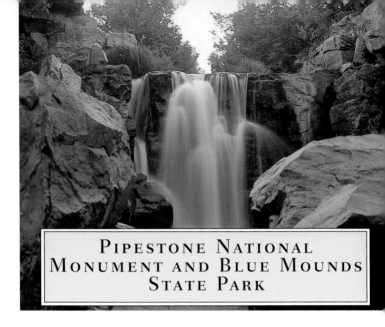

PIPESTONE NATIONAL MONUMENT AND BLUE MOUNDS STATE PARK

A Lakota story tells how the Great Spirit grew angry with the people and unleashed a cataclysmic flood upon the earth. The people scrambled up to the highest hills but could not escape the rising waters. As they died, their blood congealed into a great pool and later hardened into red rock.

At the height of the flood, only one Lakota, a beautiful young woman, remained alive. She was struggling in the swirling waters when a spotted eagle swooped down and snared her in his talons. He took her to a tree atop the highest of the Black Hills, the only remaining island of land. The eagle and the maiden mated, and their descendants became the Lakota Nation.

Many years later, the Great Spirit, assuming the form of a large bird, perched above a waterfall on a wall of red rock and called the people around him. He broke away a piece of the stone, molded it into a pipe, and began to smoke.

"This red stone is your flesh," he said. "You were made from it, and you must all smoke to me through it. And as this rock belongs to all the peoples, this ground is sacred, and no weapons must be used or brought upon it."

Above: Pipestone Creek tumbles over giant boulders of Sioux Quartzite, the source of the red rock used to make sacred pipes.

So the people learned to make pipes from the red stone. Now whenever people smoke the sacred pipe, they hold in their hands the blood of their ancestors. The smoke they exhale is their ancestors' breath. That breath mingles with the essence of all life, creating a perfect union.

The beauty of the Pipestone quarries matches the beauty of the story. The 30-foot-high Sioux Quartzite escarpment still glows crimson in the light of the setting sun. Pipestone Creek plunges over the cliff face and meanders west through tallgrass meadows, as it has for thousands of years. People from all the tribes still come to quarry the precious pipestone with hand implements.

Inevitably, some things have changed. A Bur Oak woodland, benefiting from the suppression of wildfires, crowds up against the cliffs where there was once mostly grass. The waterfall has lowered a few feet, the result of an effort by a local Indian school during the early 1900s to bring more land into cultivation. Less than a mile from the quarries, the obligatory mishmash of fast food restaurants, gas stations, and chain motels clutters the main highway into the town of Pipestone.

Managed by the National Park Service, Pipestone National Monument strives to protect the physical resources and cultural history of one of the Great Plains' most sacred places. All visitors are welcome, but only Native Americans are permitted to quarry the stone.

A visitor center provides information about the history of the quarries and the cultural significance of the red pipestone. Visitors can rub their fingers across the soapy-textured pipestone and walk beneath the "leaping rock," where young Plains Indian men impressed their sweethearts with death-defying jumps across a 12-foot-wide chasm.

About 260 acres of the national monument has been restored to native tallgrass prairie. Monument staff burn prairie parcels on a rotating basis to control weeds and stimulate growth of native grasses. A larger area of restored tallgrass prairie and a small Bison herd are maintained by the Minnesota Department of Natural Resources at Blue Mounds State Park, 20 miles to the south (see Blue Mound, below).

SIOUX QUARTZITE AND PIPESTONE

Over 1.5 billion years ago, a thin layer of muddy clay was deposited on an ancient riverbed. Later, vast quantities of sand settled on top of the clay layer. Over time, pressure, heat, and chemical action transformed the sandstone into a hard rose-colored quartzite, known to geologists as Sioux quartzite. The blood red clay, finer grained and containing lower concentrations of silica, metamorphosed into a solid but malleable rock. Plains Indians called this rock pipestone. Nineteenth-century geologists named it catlinite, after the artist and writer George Catlin.

Catlin was one of the first European-Americans to visit the pipestone quarries and write about them. His eloquent descriptions of the quarries and their spiritual significance to Plains Indian peoples, first published in 1841, helped inspire later efforts to preserve the area as a national monument.

Quarrying along Pipestone Creek may have begun during the seventeenth century when Plains Indians acquired metal tools from European traders, but stone pipes had been used by North American peoples for at least 2,000 years. Throughout the seventeenth century, tribes journeyed from hundreds of miles away to quarry the pipestone. By around 1700 the Lakota had taken control of the quarries and distributed the stone to other tribes through trade.

Mistakenly called "peace pipes" by European-Americans, sacred pipes have a wide variety of ceremonial uses. Pipes were smoked prior to battle, prior to important meetings, during welcoming ceremonies, and during sweat-lodge ceremonies. Demand for the pipes has increased recently with the revival of traditional Plains Indian spiritual practices.

BLUE MOUND

When white settlers traveled westward across the flat Minnesota prairies, they marveled at a bluish-hued escarpment rising up through the summer haze. They referred to this 100-foot-high Sioux quartzite outcrop as "the Blue Mound."

This prominent landmark apparently held special significance to earlier peoples as well. At the southern end of the mound a 1,250-foot-long line of rocks aligns east-west, pointing directly to the rising and setting sun on the vernal and autumnal equinoxes. No one knows who put these rocks in place, but lichens growing on their upper surfaces suggest they have been there for a long time. Each year on the first day of spring, pilgrims and prairie lovers hike up to the top of the mound to watch the rising sun illuminate this mysterious stone feature.

Prairie views from atop the escarpment are captivating in August when the Big Bluestem and Indian Grass are in bloom and in late September when the grasses turn every shade of yellow and red. Patches of prickly pear cactus, rare on the eastern plains, grow in shallow crevices among the quartzite outcrops. Glacial striations mark the rose-colored rock. An introduced herd of 40 to 80 Bison grazes in fenced pastures.

The "Blue Mound" is actually a massive dome of Sioux Quartzite that has been exposed by millions of years of erosion.

HIKING

PIPESTONE NATIONAL MONUMENT maintains a single 0.75-mile nature trail originating at the visitor center.

BLUE MOUNDS STATE PARK maintains 13 miles of hiking trails, all originating at the interpretive center or at the picnic area 2 miles to the north. A 3-mile self-guided nature trail begins at the interpretive center and winds through a Bur Oak woodland along the cliff line.

CAMPING

BLUE MOUNDS STATE PARK has drive-in, walk-in, and handicapped accessible campsites, and a swimming beach.

SPLIT ROCK CREEK STATE RECREATION AREA, 7 miles southwest of Pipestone off SR 23, has drive-in campsites and a swimming beach.

BEST TIMES TO VISIT

Prairie wildflowers peak in July and early August. Grasses bloom in August. A walk across the Blue Mound or among the pipestone quarries on a moonlit October evening or snowy winter morning is delightful.

INFORMATION

PIPESTONE NATIONAL MONUMENT, 36 Reservation Avenue, Pipestone, MN 56164; 507-825-5464.

BLUE MOUNDS STATE PARK, RR 1, Box 52, Luverne, MN 56156; 507-283-1307.

How to Get There

PIPESTONE: On US 75, northern outskirts of Pipestone, Minnesota.

BLUE MOUNDS: 20 miles south of Pipestone and 4 miles north of Luverne on US 75.

PIPESTONE NATIONAL MONUMENT AND

BLUE MOUNDS STATE PARK

WEATHER
MEAN TEMPERATURES AND PRECIPITATION

MONTH	HIGH (°F)	LOW (°F)	PRECIP.	SNOW
January	22	1	0.5"	5.0"
April	56	34	2.3"	2.1"
July	85	59	3.1"	0.0"
October	61	35	1.8"	0.5"

Mean annual precipitation is 25.11 inches. Summer days can be hot and sticky with occasional severe thunderstorms. Data are for the town of Pipestone, Minnesota.

SELECTED WILDLIFE OF SPECIAL INTEREST

MAMMALS: Northern Pocket Gopher, Prairie Vole, Coyote, Red Fox, White-tailed Deer, Bison.

BIRDS: Northern Harrier, Short-eared Owl, Upland Sandpiper, Sedge Wren, Gray Catbird, Savannah Sparrow, Grasshopper Sparrow, Blue Grosbeak, Bobolink, Western Meadowlark, Orchard Oriole.

REPTILES AND AMPHIBIANS: American Toad, Western Chorus Frog, Northern Leopard Frog, Tiger Salamander, Prairie Skink.

WALLACE C. DAYTON CONSERVATION AND WILDLIFE AREA

This Nature Conservancy preserve in northwestern Minnesota lies on the edge of wildness, where the flat farmlands of the Red River Valley give way to tallgrass-aspen parkland. In this hybrid landscape, trumpeting Sandhill Cranes fly over white farmhouses and Moose wander through golden hay meadows, while Gray Wolves and domestic dogs howl in discordant chorus.

Tallgrass-aspen parkland, a mosaic of deciduous forest, tallgrass prairie, and marsh, covers 1.2 million square miles of Minnesota and Manitoba. Because this ecosystem is remote and its soils difficult to cultivate, it has remained relatively undisturbed. Nearly 200,000 acres are under federal, state, or private protection in Minnesota. The 14,500-acre Wallace Dayton preserve lies at the southwestern edge of these wild lands and forms a bridge of natural habitat between two large state wildlife management areas.

In addition to the cranes, wolves, and Moose, the preserve and adjacent state lands shelter River Otters, Black Bears, Elk, and an occasional Mountain Lion. Marbled Godwits, Yellow Rails,

Above: "Mima mounds," oblong-shaped mounds in wet tallgrass prairies, are probably created in part by burrowing activities of pocket gophers and other mammals.

Sharp-tailed Grouse, and Nelson's Sharp-tailed Sparrows nest in marshes and grasslands. Biologists have documented 36 rare plant species within the preserve, including Western Prairie Fringed Orchid and Wood Lily.

Core lands for the preserve were acquired in 1999, and additional land acquisitions continue. Working in partnership with the U.S. Fish and Wildlife Service and the Minnesota and Manitoba Departments of Natural Resources, Nature Conservancy staff have begun a program of prescribed burns to restore the natural dynamic of grasslands and woodlands.

In the absence of fire, or under a regime of infrequent fires, aspens and Balsam Poplars would dominate this landscape. Periodic burning keeps the deciduous trees from encroaching farther into tallgrass meadows and removes ground litter, creating room for new growth. Biologists also use prescribed burns to restore hay meadows to more natural prairie.

Visitor services at this new preserve are limited, and protected lands are interspersed with private farms. Visitors should contact the Nature Conservancy's Karlstad office (see Information, p. 182) for a map and directions to the preserve.

MIMA MOUNDS

When pioneers observed 30- to 100-foot diameter mounds rising 2 to 4 feet above surrounding wet prairies, they christened these features "Mima mounds," thinking they had been constructed by primitive peoples, possibly as burial sites. Now many scientists believe these mounds are created partly by earth-moving activities of pocket gophers and other vertebrates.

During its lifetime, a single pocket gopher can displace several tons of soil. The loosened soil expands, forming small rises on the flat prairie. Over time, blowing dust and other organic matter may accumulate on these mounds of reworked soil, increasing their height. Many creatures take advantage of the loosened soil to burrow and nest, possibly enlarging the mounds in the process. In a Minnesota study, W. J. Breckenridge and John Tester found as many as 3,000 Canadian Toads overwintering in a single Mima mound. Some of these toads had burrowed 3 feet or more into the ground.

As the soil is loosened, water permeability increases, favoring shrub growth. Many mounds are crowned with shrub willows, which provide nesting habitat for sparrows and other songbirds. Look for Mima mounds (about 1 per acre) in wet prairies throughout the Dayton preserve.

Minnesota, which supports 80 percent of all the Gray Wolves found in the the lower 48 states, is one of the few places where it's still possible to see wolves on the prairie. These highly social predators are most concentrated in the remote forested regions of northeastern Minnesota, but a few small packs roam through the tallgrass-aspen parklands.

After wolves received Federal protection in 1973, the Minnesota population increased from a few hundred individuals to an estimated 2,400 in 1998. Wolves have been successful enough in Minnesota that they are currently listed as threatened, not endangered, and federal trappers are mandated to kill individuals that depredate livestock.

Although Gray Wolves do kill some sheep and cattle, their presence has been good for Minnesota's wild lands. In the Great Lakes region, wolves prey on White-tailed Deer, Moose, Beavers, Snowshoe Hares, and other mammals. Since they generally cull the weakest and oldest individuals from ungulate herds, their predatory activities contribute to herd fitness while keeping ungulate populations in check. The presence of ungulate carcasses increases scavenging opportunities for foxes, ravens, and Bald Eagles. Wolves also kill Coyotes. As Coyote numbers decline, small rodents become more plentiful, and birds of prey benefit.

Wolf packs in Minnesota contain from about 4 to 16 individuals. Packs hunt over territories of 50 square miles or more, and dispersing individuals can travel hundreds of miles. The dominant female in each pack generally gives birth to 5 to 14 pups in early spring.

NESTING SANDHILL CRANES

In late March tens of thousands of Sandhill Cranes stream northward over Minnesota. Most continue on toward nesting areas south of Hudson Bay, but a few thousand pairs remain in the region to rear their young.

On spring evenings at the Dayton preserve, groups of cranes gather in wet meadows to perform their timeless courtship dance. They strut in circles, leap into the air with outstretched wings, and crane their long necks skyward, croaking excitedly. As the season progresses, pairs establish nesting territories of 100 acres or more in protected woods and marshes.

Adults build a bulky nest of grass, reeds, rushes, and other aquatic vegetation on an island, tussock, knoll, or muskrat lodge, surrounded by water. The female lays 1 to 3 eggs and incubates

Preening Sandhill Cranes often rub reddish brown mud into their feathers. This "painting" may help breeding birds blend in with russet-colored marsh vegetation during early spring. (Photo by John B. Weller)

them for 29 to 32 days. The Killdeer-sized mahogany-colored chicks quickly learn to stay hidden while foraging for invertebrates in the surrounding marshes and grasslands. To protect their young, cranes must square off with a host of potential nest predators, including foxes, Coyotes, and Bobcats. Adults may lose several pounds during the stressful nesting period.

Sandhill Cranes breed primarily in northern North America and northeastern Siberia, and they winter in the southern United States and Mexico. Nonmigratory populations live in Mississippi, Florida, Georgia, and Cuba. The total North American population currently stands at more than a half-million. About 10,000 to 15,000 nest in the tallgrass-aspen parklands of northwestern Minnesota, southwestern Ontario, and southern Manitoba. Most of the birds that nest in this prairie region winter along the Texas gulf coast.

Loss and degradation of wetlands in nesting areas, wintering grounds, and in the Platte River Valley migration stopover area (see Lillian Annette Rowe Sanctuary, Nebraska) continue to threaten crane populations. However, Midwest populations have increased dramatically in recent decades. In Wisconsin, breeding numbers climbed from a low of around 25 during the 1930s to more than 11,000 in 1999.

WOOD LILIES

With their bell-shaped, dusky orange-red corollas, Wood Lilies are among the showiest of prairie wildflowers. They also are among the most threatened, partially because their natural habitat in moist prairies and woods has been greatly reduced, but also because people thoughtlessly pick them.

Wood Lilies grow to a height of up to 3 feet. Their flowers have 6 petals and 6 stamens, and their narrow leaves alternate up the stem, forming a small whorl below the corolla. They begin blooming in early July as young Sandhill Cranes are leaving their nests and clouds of mosquitoes are swarming over the fens and wet prairies of northwestern Minnesota. Their range extends from Québec to British Columbia and south to Arizona, New Mexico, and Texas.

Wood Lily (Lilium philadelphicum)

HIKING

There are no designated hiking trails within the preserve, but the adjacent Skull Lake and Beaches State Wildlife Areas contain several two-track roads suitable for hiking:

SKULL LAKE: Take SR 15/4 north from the town of Lake Bronson. After 13 miles, where the road bends sharply right, turn left on a county road. Follow this road for 1 mile until it becomes a two-track road. From here you can hike several miles into the wildlife area.

BEACHES: From SR 15/4, 14 miles north of the town of Lake Bronson, turn right (south) on CR 51. Follow this road south for 2 miles to the fork, then turn left and drive about 2 miles. From here you can walk east or west on the two-track road that traverses the wildlife area.

CAMPING

LAKE BRONSON STATE PARK, 2 miles east of Lake Bronson off SR 28, has a large campground with a swimming beach.

BEST TIMES TO VISIT

Thousands of Snow Geese and Sandhill Cranes pass through in March and again in October. Sharp-tailed Grouse dance on leks in April. Small White Lady's-Slippers and Western Prairie Fringed Orchids bloom from mid-June through early July. Wood Lilies bloom from early July through early August. Aspen woodlands and wet meadows are usually most accessible in early fall, when the mosquito population shrinks and groundwater levels recede.

INFORMATION

THE NATURE CONSERVANCY, Tallgrass Aspen Parkland Office, Box 139, Karlstad, MN 56732.

HOW TO GET THERE

From the town of Lake Bronson drive north 11 to 15 miles on SR 15/4 and explore on adjacent county roads. Nature Conservancy parcels are marked with yellow signs. **NOTE:** Since protected lands are scattered, you will need a map, available at the Nature Conservancy's Glyndon office, to find your way around (see Information on p. 170).

WALLACE C. DAYTON CONSERVATION AND WILDLIFE AREA

WEATHER
MEAN TEMPERATURES AND PRECIPITATION

MONTH	HIGH (°F)	LOW (°F)	PRECIP.	SNOW
January	15	-7	0.5 "	9.1"
April	52	29	1.4"	1.8"
July	81	56	2.8"	0.0"
October	56	34	1.4"	0.7"

Mean annual precipitation is 19.87 inches. This area experiences some of the greatest temperature extremes found in the lower 48 states; the record high is 105°F; the record low, -51°F. Severe thunderstorms can occur from May through September. Data are for Thief River Falls, Minnesota.

SELECTED WILDLIFE OF SPECIAL INTEREST

MAMMALS: Beaver, Gray Wolf, Coyote, Red Fox, Gray Fox, Black Bear, Fisher, River Otter, Bobcat, Elk, White-tailed Deer, Moose.

BIRDS: Red-necked Grebe, Bald Eagle, Northern Harrier, Ruffed Grouse, Sharp-tailed Grouse, Yellow Rail, Sandhill Crane, American Woodcock, Great Gray Owl, Short-eared Owl, Pileated Woodpecker, Black-billed Magpie, Sedge Wren, LeConte's Sparrow, Nelson's Sharp-tailed Sparrow.

AMPHIBIANS AND REPTILES: Canadian Toad, Boreal Chorus Frog, Northern Leopard Frog, Wood Frog, Smooth Green Snake.

OTHER MINNESOTA SITES

AGASSIZ DUNES (The Nature Conservancy, 15337 28th Avenue South, Glyndon, MN 56547; 218-498-2679). Oak savanna and dry sand prairie grow on the state's largest dune field. Polk and Norman Counties. A hiking trail winds through this 435-acre preserve. From Fertile go 0.6 miles south on SH 32, west 0.5 miles on gravel road, and turn left into the grass parking area.

CHIPPEWA PRAIRIE (Department of Natural Resources, Box 25, St. Paul, MN 55155; 651-296-6157). This 1,102-acre preserve protects one of the few prairies in southwestern Minnesota that was never plowed. Swift County. From Milan go northwest about 3 miles on US 59, then 2 miles west on a gravel road.

FELTON PRAIRIE (Department of Natural Resources, Box 25, St. Paul, MN 55155; 651-296-6157). Considered the state's most important gravel prairie complex, Felton Prairie encompasses 761 acres in four parcels. Greater Prairie-Chickens, Upland Sandpipers, Marbled Godwits, Baird's Sparrows, and Chestnut-collared Longspurs nest. To reach the largest parcel, go south from Felton 2 miles on SR 9, then east 3 miles on CR 108. Continue on the gravel road about 0.25 miles, following turns to the right.

HOLE-IN-THE-MOUNTAIN PRAIRIE (The Nature Conservancy, 15337 28th Avenue South, Glyndon, MN 56547; 218-498-2679). This 590-acre preserve is part of 4,300 protected acres on the Prairie Coteau. From Lake Benton go 1.5 miles south on US 75. Park on the west side of the highway.

ORDWAY PRAIRIE (The Nature Conservancy, 15337 28th Avenue South, Glyndon, MN 56547; 218-498-2679). A mosaic of grasslands, woods, and wetlands covers 581 acres of rolling, glacially deposited hills. Pope County. From Brooten, take CR 8 west about 7 miles, then go south on SR 104 for 3 miles. The preserve and a historical marker are on the east side of the road.

PEMBINA TRAIL PRESERVE (The Nature Conservancy, 15337 28th Avenue South, Glyndon, MN 56547; 218-498-2679). This Lake Agassiz beach ridge includes 2,360 acres of high-quality tallgrass prairie. Western Prairie Fringed Orchids bloom in early July. Restoration of an additional 24,000 acres is in progress at the adjacent Glacial Ridge property, managed by TNC and federal agencies. Nearby Rydell National Wildlife Refuge has nesting Sandhill Cranes and abundant waterfowl. From Crookston take SR 102 southeast to CR 45. Turn east, drive for 6.5 miles, and look for the yellow TNC signs.

PRAIRIE COTEAU (Department of Natural Resources, Box 25, St. Paul, MN 55155; 651-296-6157). Two rare prairie communities, the southwestern dry hill prairie and dry sand-gravel prairie, grow on steep slopes and valleys of a glacial moraine. Rare Dakota and Ottoe Skipper butterflies inhabit the 329 acres. Ten miles northeast of Pipestone on SR 23.

WEAVER DUNES PRESERVE (The Nature Conservancy, 80 County Road 84, Kellogg, MN 55945; 507-767-4502). Sand prairie and oak savanna grow on a sand terrace formed by the ancient Mississippi River. The state-endangered Rough-seeded Fameflower blooms in midsummer. Wabasha County. From Kellogg take Dodge Street (CR 84) south and east for 5.5 miles. Turn left on a small sand road, Township Road 141, to the preserve.

This granite boulder at Felton Prairie was left behind by retreating glaciers more than 10,000 years ago. Bison rubbed against the rock, creating a trough around it.

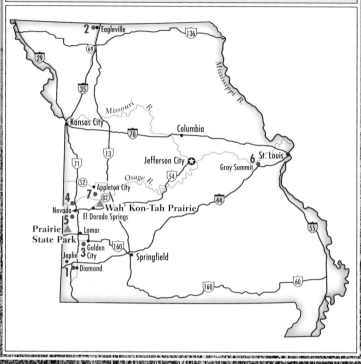

MISSOURI

Prairie State Park

Wah' Kon-Tah Prairie

Other Missouri Sites:

1. Diamond Grove Preserve
2. Dunn Ranch and Pawnee Prairie
3. Golden Prairie
4. Marmaton River Bottoms Prairie
5. Osage Prairie Conservation Area
6. Shaw Nature Reserve
7. Taberville Prairie

PRAIRIE STATE PARK

At Prairie State Park you can experience a little of author Laura Ingalls Wilder's world, "the enormous, empty prairie, with grasses blowing and waves of light and shadow across it, and the blue sky above it, and the birds flying out from it and singing with joy because the sun was rising."

The vistas have contracted as trees and shrubs have encroached on this prairie remnant on the Osage Plains, just 70 miles northeast of Independence, Kansas, and Wilder's "Little House." But each May the songs of Dickcissels and Grasshopper Sparrows float over meadows speckled with paintbrushes and penstemons. Bison snort and bellow in the golden dawn, and White-tailed Deer bound through tallgrasses dripping with dew.

Most of this park's nearly 4,000 acres have never been plowed, and four parcels of high-quality prairie have received State Natural Area designation. East Drywood Creek, one of the last pristine prairie headwater streams in Missouri, forms shallow pools as it meanders through sandstone outcrops. A reintroduced Elk herd grazes in the West Drywood Creek drainage in the northwest corner of the park.

The more than 500 wildflower species recorded at the park in-

Above: Common Nighthawks are surprisingly approachable as they sleep by day on fence posts or tree limbs. At dusk they swoop overhead, catching insects in their oversized mouths.

clude paintbrush, Rose Vervain, Mead's Milkweed, Shooting Star, and Ragged Fringed Orchid. Arrowhead Violets and Bird's-Foot Violets host eggs and larvae of hundreds of Regal Fritillary butterflies.

Up to 50 Greater Prairie-Chickens perform each spring on strutting grounds throughout the park. Northern Harriers, Rough-legged Hawks, and Short-eared Owls converge to hunt rodents and songbirds in fall and winter.

White-tailed Deer

A Cheyenne story tells of a hunter who came upon a beautiful young woman in a forest clearing. As he walked toward her, she turned and dissolved into the shadows. He ran in her direction, only to discover a graceful White-tailed Deer bounding away. The hunter ran faster and faster, following the deer maiden deep into the woods. But the faster he ran, the farther she fled. Finally, she vanished completely and he became hopelessly lost, racing around in circles until he was crazy with despair.

Other Plains Indian stories told of does that adopted infants and raised them as their own; bucks who could repel arrows with their thoughts; or deer maidens who seduced young men, led them away, and stomped them to death with their hooves. White-tailed Deer seem to bewitch nearly everyone who lives among them.

The aura of magic that surrounds these graceful ungulates derives in part from their ability to appear and vanish almost at will. With ultrasensitive hearing, sight, and smell, White-tails can detect danger several hundred yards away and slip away unseen. However, when startled, they often bound off noisily, with indignant snorts and a clatter of hooves. "I've seen you, look how fast and fit I am; I'm healthy and not worth pursuing," offers British ecologist Rory Putnam, interpreting the implied message of conspicuous flight.

When guarding their fawns, White-tail does quietly place themselves between their young and potential danger. If a Coyote or White-tail buck gets too close, a doe will rear up and strike with her sharp hooves. At Prairie State Park, the first fawns, one or two per doe, appear from mid-May to early June. The 5- to 7-pound youngsters spend their first few days lying motionless and nearly scentless in the grass while their mother browses alertly nearby.

Later, as they follow her through shrublands and open forests, young White-tails absorb a wealth of botanical information. Their dietary preferences follow the seasons: wild roses, dandelions,

White-tailed Deer form small herds during the fall and winter, but does with young fawns maintain and defend breeding territories during late spring and early summer.

and other succulent forbs in spring; pond lilies, mushrooms, and fallen fruits in summer; willow stems, roots, and evergreen leaves in winter. In farming areas, up to half their intake may consist of cultivated crops.

Since European-American settlement of the prairie region, White-tails have expanded their range westward, following riparian woodlands that spread in the absence of natural fire. After being decimated by indiscriminate hunting during the late nineteenth century, their numbers rebounded as Gray Wolves and Mountain Lions were extirpated, dense forests cleared, crops planted, and woodlots created around farms. An "edge species," they have managed to fill a niche in our untidy world.

The proliferation of White-tailed Deer during the last few decades, combined with recent expansion of human settlements into deer habitat, has begun to cause problems for people. Lyme disease carried by deer ticks has infiltrated towns in the eastern United States and Canada. Automobile-deer collisions kill dozens of people and thousands of deer each year. The appearance of chronic wasting disease in deer herds from the desert Southwest to the upper Midwest has raised alarm.

This brain-destroying disease, which causes symptoms similar to those of Creutzfeldt-Jacob and Mad Cow diseases, was first detected in captive deer herds in the central Rockies during the late 1960s. The causes of the disease are poorly understood, but many biologists believe that unnatural crowding of deer populations has contributed to its spread.

NIGHTJARS

Plains Indians called nighthawks "fart birds," after the sound that displaying males make with their wing feathers as they dive earthward. European settlers used the more polite "bull bat." In Europe and New England, nightjars were known as "goatsuckers," presumably because these large-mouthed insectivores were thought to sneak into barnyards at night and suck the teats of goats.

On summer evenings Common Nighthawks, Chuck-will's-widows, and Whip-poor-wills swoop over Prairie State Park, seining insects from the air with their oversized mouths. By day, these nightjars (members of the family Caprimulgidae) seem oblivious to passersby while perching on fence posts, tree limbs, or the ground.

Common Nighthawks, which range over most of North America, lay their eggs on bare ground, on stumps, in old robin nests, or on gravel rooftops. Chuck-will's-widows, which range throughout the southeastern United States and the Ohio River Valley, typically lay their eggs on leaf litter in open woodlands. Whip-poor-wills breed in open woodlands in eastern North America and the desert Southwest. Common Poorwills breed from the high plains westward to the Pacific Coast and throughout northern Mexico.

Since none of these nightjars build nests, incubating females depend on their cryptic coloration to fool predators. They'll sit perfectly still on their eggs until you're about 10 feet away, then flit silently off on mothlike wings.

ORB WEAVERS

On dewy summer mornings, wheel-shaped spider webs hang like miniature galaxies in a universe of glistening grass. These intricate webs are the work of orb web spiders, members of the Araneidae, a family that contains 2,500 species worldwide.

Among the largest and most colorful of the orb weavers is the Black and Yellow Garden Spider, sometimes called the Golden

A Black and Yellow Garden Spider dangles from her wheel-shaped web suspended from 7-foot-high stalks of Big Bluestem.

Orb Weaver (*Argiope aurantia*), a resident of backyards and grasslands throughout the United States and southern Canada. The 1-inch-wide females have shiny, egg-shaped abdomens with striking yellow or orange markings on a black background. The males are similar in appearance but much smaller. Both sexes have three claws per foot, one more than most spiders. They use the extra claw to help handle threads while spinning intricate, 2-foot-diameter webs.

Black and Yellow Garden Spiders use their webs to capture flying insects, including flies, grasshoppers, and wasps. The female hangs head-down in the hub or hides in a nearby leaf or grass stem. She usually eats the entire web each night and constructs a new one the following morning.

The male builds a much smaller web adjacent to the female's. After mating, the female weaves a papery egg sac containing up to 1,400 eggs and attaches it to the web. The eggs hatch in the fall, but the spiderlings remain in the egg sac until the following spring.

When threatened, the Black and Yellow Garden Spider may vibrate its web aggressively or drop to the ground. This fearsome-looking spider may bite if treated roughly, but its venom has little effect on most people.

HIKING

Nearly 11 miles of hiking trails radiate from the visitor center. Trails may be closed in Bison grazing areas. Check with park staff before hiking, and be careful when crossing electric fences.

DROVER'S TRAIL (1-, 2-, and 4-mile loops) takes off from the visitor center and heads east toward East Drywood Natural Area. A short spur crosses the railway tracks and follows East Drywood Creek upstream.

GAYFEATHER TRAIL (1.5-mile loop) takes off from the west side of NW 150th Lane, a half-mile south of the visitor center, and winds through the Regal Prairie Natural Area, where wildflowers and butterflies abound in late spring and summer.

CAMPING

There are two primitive campsites at the north entrance to the park and a single backcountry campsite, available by reservation. Register at the visitor center.

BEST TIMES TO VISIT

Greater Prairie-Chickens strut from late February through April; call ahead for information about viewing opportunities and tours. In late April and May, Bison calve and paintbrushes color the grasslands. White-tail fawns are born from mid-May to mid-June. Wildflowers abound throughout May and June. In winter, when raptors glide overhead and Bison crunch through frosted meadows, this small park can feel like a prairie wilderness.

INFORMATION

PRAIRIE STATE PARK, Box 97, Liberal, MO 64762; 417-843-6711.

HOW TO GET THERE

From Lamar, Missouri, take US 160 west about 14 miles to Hwy. NN. Turn north for 1 mile, then west on Central Road for 3 miles. Turn north on NW 150th Lane and proceed 1 mile to the visitor center.

From Pittsburg, Kansas, take US 69 north 2 miles, turn right on US 160 for 7 miles to Mindenmines, and follow the signs north to the park.

PRAIRIE STATE PARK

WEATHER
MEAN TEMPERATURES AND PRECIPITATION

MONTH	HIGH (°F)	LOW (°F)	PRECIP.	SNOW
January	41	20	1.5"	5.0"
April	70	45	3.8"	0.5"
July	92	69	3.4"	0.0"
October	72	47	4.4"	Trace

Mean annual precipitation is 43.7 inches. Severe thunderstorms and tornadoes occur from April through August. Warm daytime temperatures linger into November. Data are for Pittsburg, Kansas.

SELECTED WILDLIFE OF SPECIAL INTEREST

MAMMALS: Virginia Opossum, Woodchuck, Prairie Vole, Coyote, Red Fox, Bobcat, Badger, Mink, Elk, Bison.

BIRDS: Green Heron, Northern Harrier, Greater Prairie-Chicken, Northern Bobwhite, Upland Sandpiper, American Woodcock, Barred Owl, Short-eared Owl, Common Nighthawk, Chuck-will's-widow, Whip-poor-will, Scissor-tailed Flycatcher, Yellow-billed Cuckoo, Grasshopper Sparrow, Henslow's Sparrow.

AMPHIBIANS AND REPTILES: Northern Cricket Frog, Gray Treefrog, Spring Peeper, Green Frog, Southern Leopard Frog, Prairie Skink, Slender Glass Lizard, Eastern Fence Lizard, Eastern Mud Turtle, Ornate Box Turtle.

WAH' KON-TAH PRAIRIE

Great Spirit. Great Mystery. Sun, moon, stars. In Osage religion, *Wah' Kon-Tah* describes all that is sacred, unfathomable. Like a flock of golden-plovers flying through a shimmering rainbow, a Scissor-tailed Flycatcher ascending into a fiery sky, or a Prairie Mole Cricket dancing in the moonlight.

Amid the rolling farmlands of Missouri's Osage Plains, the Nature Conservancy and the Missouri Department of Conservation are piecing together scattered shards of Wah' Kon-Tah's prairie. The Nature Conservancy purchased the first parcel, 320 acres of unplowed grasslands, in 1973. Since then it has added more than 4,100 acres, and land stewards hope eventually to create a network of protected lands encompassing 20 square miles.

The grasslands here range from high-quality virgin prairie carpeted with native wildflowers to degraded pastures dominated by Tall Fescue and annual weeds. Land stewards spray the fescue and weeds with herbicides, clear trees and shrubs, plant native seeds, and burn each parcel every two to three years. In addition, staff are working with University of Missouri scientists to see if warm-season grasses can be re-established in Tall Fescue pastures without removing cattle. If their efforts succeed, private

Above: Tube-flowered Penstemons (Penstemon tubiflorus) *and Bigflower Coreopsis* (Coreopsis grandiflora) *bloom in late May at Wah' Kon-Tah Prairie, in Missouri's Osage Plains.*

Mead's Milkweed (Asclepias meadii) once flourished in midwestern tallgrass prairies. Now only isolated populations survive in prairie remnants of Missouri, eastern Kansas, and southern Iowa.

landowners will have stronger incentives to convert pasture lands to native prairie.

Greater Prairie-Chickens dance each spring, but numbers have declined. In 2000, 14 males were observed on strutting grounds; in 2002, only 4. Populations are more stable at Taberville Prairie, 8 miles to the north (see Other Missouri Sites, p. 201). Habitat fragmentation and invasion of prairies by nonnative species have contributed to a decline in Greater Prairie-Chicken populations throughout Missouri. Biologists hope that by forming networks of mostly natural grassland habitat, they can reverse this trend.

Tiny Prairie Mole Crickets perform their own mating dance, beginning in late April. This rare insect is the only member of the order Orthoptera known to aggregate on leks. The males chirp a strident territorial song (a series of loud *beeps* reminiscent of some fire alarms) from their burrows in tallgrass meadows. The song, audible just after sunset for up to a quarter-mile, creates vibrations that warn other crickets away from the singer's burrow.

SCISSOR-TAILED FLYCATCHERS

In spring male Scissor-tailed Flycatchers zigzag skyward, displaying their salmon-colored flanks and wing linings and emitting a soft cackling call. After fluttering as high as 100 feet above the ground, they stall out and somersault earthward, using their long forked tails to balance and right themselves.

If suitably impressed, the female consents to mate and builds a flimsy nest on a low tree branch or human structure. In *Life Histories of North American Flycatchers*, A. C. Bent describes watching a Scissor-tail attempt to nest on one of the wings of a wind-

Like most flycatchers, Scissor-tailed Fly-catchers perch in the open where they can flutter out to nab passing insects. (Photo by Glenn Cushman)

mill. When the windmill turned, the nest would fall off, but the flycatcher, undeterred, resumed construction whenever the wind subsided. Nests placed in trees often are blown away by thunderstorms or washed away by downpours.

The young hatch after 12 or 13 days and leave the nest about two weeks later. Adults become particularly conspicuous in early summer as they nab grasshoppers, beetles, wasps, and other insects in midair and carry them to their fledglings. Families flock together in September before migrating to southern Mexico and Central America.

These handsome flycatchers nest from southeastern Colorado and southeastern Nebraska south to Texas, western Arkansas, and western Louisiana. Though most abundant in Mesquite and oak savanna country of Oklahoma and Texas, they have gradually expanded their range eastward into central Missouri, Arkansas, and Louisiana. Clearing of forests for farms and pastures may have facilitated this range expansion.

BOBWHITE QUAIL

Bob–White! Every Midwesterner knows that sound. It's most prevalent in spring, when males call from fence posts and haystacks, advertising their nesting territories. It's becoming less audible throughout North America, however, as bobwhite populations plummet.

This decline is puzzling, since Northern Bobwhites seem perfectly at home in fragmented forests and grasslands, the rural agricultural setting that dominates central North America. They feed on grass seeds, cultivated grains, wild fruits, and insects.

Northern Bobwhite males often sing their 2-note song from fence posts, where they are clearly visible to rivals and potential mates.

They nest on the ground in depressions lined with grasses. Both sexes work on the nest, weaving an arch of grasses and weeds to conceal it and shelter the young. A single pair can produce as many as 25 young during one breeding season, but a high percentage of young and adults die in winter—from exposure, starvation, or from hunting. Kansas hunters killed nearly 2 million bobwhites during a recent year.

According to the North American Breeding Bird Survey, North American populations dropped an average of 2.9 percent per year from 1966 to 2000. Some scientists believe that "clean farming" practices, which lead to removal of nearly all weeds and shrubs, have contributed to the decline. Some implicate overhunting and genetic weakness resulting from release of captive-reared flocks.

At Wah' Kon-Tah Prairie, listen for Northern Bobwhites in the early morning and late afternoon, and look for the males on fence posts along the gravel entrance road.

Hiking

A half-mile interpretive trail takes off from Lake Hill Road, on the south side of the preserve 1.8 miles east of downtown El Dorado Springs. Signs lead from the the Wah' Kon-Tah Prairie display in the city park to the trailhead kiosk. From the interpretive trail you can follow a 1-mile hay road deeper into the preserve. All of the preserve is open to cross-country hiking, but beware of electric fences.

Camping

No camping is permitted. Primitive camping is available 13 miles north at the Shell-Osage Conservation Area. From El Dorado Springs take SR 82 north and east 3 miles to Road H, go north about 6 miles to Road Y, then west 2.5 miles to CR SW 401. Drive north 1.5 miles and follow the signs to the camping areas.

Best Times to Visit

As many as 100 American Golden-Plovers stop over during April. Greater Prairie-Chickens dance from late March through May, and Prairie Mole Crickets call at dusk from late April through early June. Wildflowers generally peak in early May, when paintbrushes, Spiderwort, Shooting Stars, and Grass Pink Orchids put on impressive displays; and in early June, when Tube-Flowered Penstemons, Pale Purple Coneflowers, Bigflower Coreopsis, and Federally threatened Mead's Milkweeds bloom. In September, Downy Gentians unfurl on knolls and dry hillsides; their bell-shaped 5-petaled corollas, bluer than the autumn sky, may persist long after the first frost.

Information

WAH' KON-TAH PRAIRIE, 3860 East 02 Road, El Dorado Springs, MO 64744; 417-876-2340.

How to Get There

From downtown El Dorado Springs, take SR 82 north and east for 3 miles to the intersection with Road H. Turn right on the gravel road that heads south up the incline. Follow it for 1 mile to the preserve headquarters on your right. To access high-quality prairie north of SR 82, continue northeast 0.5 miles from the intersection of SR 82 and Road H, and park on the left by the Wah' Kon-Tah Prairie sign.

WAH' KON-TAH PRAIRIE

WEATHER
MEAN TEMPERATURE AND PRECIPITATION

MONTH	HIGH (°F)	LOW (°F)	PRECIP.	SNOW
January	40	16	1.5"	5.0"
April	68	42	3.7"	0.5"
July	91	66	3.0"	0.0"
October	71	44	4.3"	Trace

Mean annual precipitation is 45.3 inches. Summers are hot and muggy with temperatures as high as 115°F. The record low of -21°F occurred in February. Data are for Nevada, Missouri.

SELECTED WILDLIFE OF SPECIAL INTEREST

MAMMALS: Virginia Opossum, Woodchuck, Coyote, Red Fox, Bobcat, Badger, White-tailed Deer.

BIRDS: Cooper's Hawk, Greater Prairie-Chicken, Wild Turkey, Northern Bobwhite, Upland Sandpiper, Scissor-tailed Flycatcher, Horned Lark, Eastern Bluebird, Grasshopper Sparrow, Henslow's Sparrow, Northern Cardinal, Dickcissel, Eastern Meadowlark.

AMPHIBIANS AND REPTILES: Northern Cricket Frog, Spring Peeper, Crawfish Frog, Plains Leopard Frog, Eastern Fence Lizard, Ring-necked Snake, Eastern Mud Turtle, Ornate Box Turtle.

DIAMOND GROVE PRAIRIE (Department of Conservation, Box 180, Jefferson City, MO 65102; 417-895-6880). Upland prairie covers 611 acres of cherty soils. Spring wildflowers bloom in profusion. Narrow-mouthed Toads bleat out courtship calls after June thunderstorms. Four miles west of Diamond on SR V, then 1.5 miles north on unpaved county road.

DUNN RANCH AND PAWNEE PRAIRIE (The Nature Conservancy and Department of Conservation, 21495 West Highway 46, Eagleville, MO 64442; 660-867-3866). This 4,000-acre site anchors a 32,000-acre prairie restoration that will eventually extend north across the Iowa state line. Topeka Shiners and Bison are being reintroduced, and a visitor center is planned. Greater Prairie-Chickens, Upland Sandpipers, Regal Fritillaries. From I-35 Eagleville exit, go west to SR 69. Go north to CR M, turn left, and continue 6.3 miles to the parking area on your right.

GOLDEN PRAIRIE (Missouri Prairie Foundation, Box 200, Columbia, MO 65205). A total of 345 plant species have been recorded on this 500-acre upland prairie, a National Natural Landmark. Greater Prairie-Chickens live here year-round. From Golden City go west 3 miles on SR 126, then south 2 miles on SE 80 Lane to "T" intersection with SE 90 Road.

MARMATON RIVER BOTTOMS PRAIRIE (The Nature Conservancy, 2800 South Brentwood Boulevard, St. Louis, MO 63144; 314-968-1105). The largest unplowed wet prairie in Missouri encompasses 609 acres of grasslands and bottomland forest. Double-crested Cormorants nest here. Wildflowers include Royal Catchfly, Swamp Dock, and White Turtlehead. Three miles northwest of Nevada off Road O (inquire locally for directions).

OSAGE PRAIRIE CONSERVATION AREA (The Nature Conservancy, 2800 South Brentwood Boulevard, St. Louis, MO 63144; 314-968-1105). This 1,547-acre preserve contains a variety of prairie types that support Greater Prairie-Chickens, Upland Sandpipers, Short-eared Owls, Coyotes, and White-tailed Deer. From Nevada go south 6 miles on US 71, then 0.5 miles west (turn west at intersection of US 71 and Road E) and 0.5 miles south on gravel roads.

SHAW NATURE RESERVE (Missouri Botanic Gardens, Box 38, Gray Summit, MO 63039; 636-451-3512). This 2,400 acre Arboretum and natural area includes 100 acres of restored tallgrass prairie and 14 miles of hiking trails through forests, wetlands, and grasslands. Visitor center and historic buildings. In the town of Gray Summit, off I-44, 35 miles southwest of St. Louis.

TABERVILLE PRAIRIE (The Nature Conservancy, 2800 South Brentwood

Boulevard, St. Louis, MO 63144; 314-968-1105). Nearly 400 plant species have been recorded at this 1,680-acre preserve, designated a National Natural Landmark. Greater Prairie-Chickens and Regal Fritillaries. From SR 52, 1.5 miles east of Appleton City, go south 2 miles on Road A and continue south 8 miles on Road H. The preserve is on the east side of Road H.

In late spring, Foxglove Penstemons (Penstemon digitalis) *bloom in profusion at Golden Prairie.*

Missouri Evening-Primroses (Oenothera macrocarpa) *bloom on limestone prairie hillsides throughout southwestern Missouri in late spring and early summer.*

MONTANA

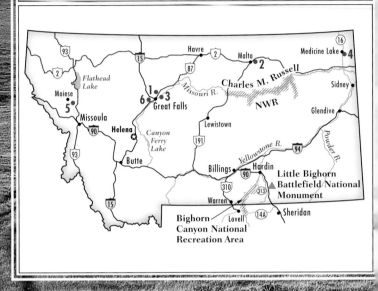

Flathead Lake

Moiese **5**

Missoula

Helena

Butte

Havre

Malta **2**

Medicine Lake **4**

Charles M. Russell

1

6 **3**
Great Falls

Missouri R.

NWR

Sidney

Glendive

Lewistown

Powder R.

Yellowstone R.

Billings

Hardin

Little Bighorn Battlefield National Monument

Warren

Lovell

Sheridan

Bighorn Canyon National Recreation Area

Canyon Ferry Lake

Bighorn Canyon National Recreation Area and Little Bighorn Battlefield National Monument

Charles M. Russell National Wildlife Refuge

Other Montana Sites:

1. Benton Lake National Wildlife Refuge and Wetland Management District

2. Bowdoin National Wildlife Refuge

3. Giant Springs Heritage State Park

4. Medicine Lake National Wildlife Refuge

5. National Bison Range

6. Ulm Pishkun State Park

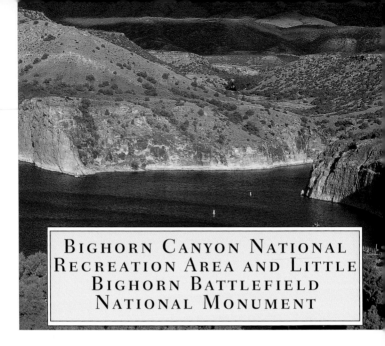

BIGHORN CANYON NATIONAL RECREATION AREA AND LITTLE BIGHORN BATTLEFIELD NATIONAL MONUMENT

Bighorn Canyon cuts a vermilion, beige, and gray gash through the high prairies of southeastern Montana and north-central Wyoming. Canyon walls—more than 2,000 feet high in places—enclose deep, blue water. Along the rim a mosaic of grasses, sagebrush, and Greasewood provides food and shelter for birds and mammals.

The most pristine prairie in this part of the state can be seen a few miles east of the canyon at Little Bighorn Battlefield National Monument, where more than 700 acres have never been plowed. No grazing has been allowed on the Custer Battlefield since 1891 nor on the Reno-Benteen site since 1954. Bluebunch Wheatgrass, Blue Grama, Idaho Fescue, Green Needlegrass, Junegrass, and other native species blanket the hills.

The Lakota and Cheyenne, led by Chiefs Sitting Bull and Crazy Horse, won their last major victory here over the 7th Cavalry under the command of George Custer. Crosses and gravestones mark where more than 200 soldiers, including Custer, died. A memorial on Last Stand Hill honors the Indian tribes. A 5-mile auto tour winds across the prairie ridges to the battle sites.

Above: The walls of Bighorn Canyon reflect late afternoon light. (Photo by Glenn Cushman)

The Pryor Mountain National Wild Horse Range borders and overlaps the western side of Bighorn Canyon. Named for Nathaniel Pryor of the Lewis and Clark Expedition, this range is actually an extension of the Bighorn Mountains. It contains one of the most diverse plant communities in Montana because rainfall varies from less than 5 inches in the foothills to 20 inches in the high mountains. Limestone cliffs and caves, multicolored canyon walls, 10 bat species, and Bighorn Sheep are additional attractions.

About 60 million years ago as the Pryor and Bighorn Mountains began to thrust up, the Bighorn River began cutting through the northern end of the uplift to form the canyon. Exposed in the Madison limestone on the upper canyon walls are fossils dating back to when the land was covered by the Cretaceous Sea. Later, dinosaurs lumbered through tropical marshes. Now desert shrubs, shortgrass prairie, junipers, pines, and Douglas-firs cover the hills, while cottonwoods, willows, and Box Elders grow in riparian areas. At the heart of the canyon lies 71-mile-long Bighorn Lake, created by Yellowtail Dam, which was built to provide electric power, irrigation, flood control, and recreation.

The 120,296-acre Bighorn Canyon National Recreation Area, with more than 1,500 acres classified as grassland or sagebrush/grassland, is divided into two units connected by a roadless area and the lake. Most of the north unit lies within the Crow Indian Reservation, closed to the public. This section, more remote than the south unit, requires a boat to see such features as Black Canyon and Yellowtail Dam. The south unit contains the spectacular Devil Canyon Overlook.

WILD HORSES

Horses evolved in North America starting with the 2-foot-tall *Eohippus* about 50 million years ago. Its descendants migrated across the Bering Strait to Asia beginning about 10 million years ago. When the Ice Age ended, horses became extinct in the Americas, possibly because of climate change and the actions of human hunters.

The early Spanish explorers brought horses back to America and revolutionized the way of life for the Plains Indians. Horses facilitated hunting and made war parties more effective. In bad times they were even used for food. Plains Indians bought, stole, and traded with the Spanish for the sturdy mustangs (from the Spanish *mesteno*, meaning "wild") that were so well adapted to the western landscape.

Many horses escaped, and by the middle of the nineteenth century, two million to three million roamed the western prairies. Be-

Between 120 and 160 wild horses roam the rugged slopes of the Pryor Mountain National Wild Horse Range. (Photo by Richard W. Holmes)

cause the horses overgrazed the range and competed with domestic livestock, the government put bounties on them. By the middle of the twentieth century, they had been reduced to a few scattered herds. Horse lovers rode to the rescue and lobbied Congress to protect the animals. In 1971 the Wild Free-Roaming Horse and Burro Act was passed.

Many of the horses at the 38,000-acre Pryor Mountain Range consist of duns, grullas, bays, and roans and have zebra stripes on the legs, a dorsal stripe down the back, and stripes on the withers. Genetic testing shows the presence of several genes signifying horses of Spanish ancestry.

The herd is managed at 120 to 160 horses, large enough that inbreeding is not a problem. Excess horses are available for adoption by qualified owners. Look for wild horses near the junction of Burnt Timber Ridge Road and Sykes Ridge Road in the Pryor Mountains and at Mustang Flats beyond the Devil Canyon Overlook in Bighorn Canyon. When hiking, look for fresh manure where stallions have made huge "stud piles" to advertise their presence.

Bears

The Short-faced Bear, once the largest land carnivore in North America, terrorized other denizens of the prairie during the Ice Age. However, Black Bears and Grizzlies eventually replaced the Short-faced Bear, which became extinct. Its fossils can be seen at Natural Trap Cave just east of Bighorn Canyon.

Both Black and Grizzly Bears roamed the plains until Europeans arrived in large numbers. The Lewis and Clark Expedition often encountered Grizzlies in Montana in 1805–1806. Because Grizzlies were so numerous near Great Falls, Lewis forbade anyone to go alone through the brush and ordered all hands to sleep with rifles nearby. He recorded that it took eight balls to kill one enraged Grizzly. As late as 1897, Alexander Henry wrote that along the Sheyenne River in North Dakota, "grizzly bears are to be seen in droves."

Grizzlies no longer inhabit the prairie east of the Rocky Mountain foothills, and Black Bears are found in only a few places, usually where prairie merges into foothills and forests. Bighorn Canyon is one of those places. In fact, some campgrounds provide strong metal lockers for overnight food storage to avoid bear problems. Bears are especially active as summer draws to a close. Omnivorous eaters, they feast on ripening berries and anything else they can find in preparation for a long winter nap.

PICTURES FROM THE PAST

Prehistoric humans arrived in the Bighorn Canyon area more than 10,000 years ago, and ancestors of the Crow people were settled here by the early 1700s. Both groups drove game over steep cliffs and used caves in the Bighorn area for winter shelter and for storage. They painted and chiseled out images of game animals and warriors with shields in nearby Pictograph Cave State Park.

The people we now call Crow called themselves *Absaroke,* meaning "people of the large-beaked bird." A member of the Lewis and Clark Expedition, which came through the area in 1806, called them "the finest horsemen in the world." Nevertheless, they were pushed west off their lands by the Lakota and Cheyenne and served as government guides and scouts during the Indian Wars.

Following the wars they were able to live in peace in the Bighorn Valley. "The Crow country . . . is a good country. The Great Spirit has put it exactly in the right place," said their chief Arapooash. By 1904 they were successfully farming and ranching the semiarid land, and they built an irrigation system at the mouth of the canyon.

The tumultuous Bighorn River thwarted attempts at navigation, although explorer Jim Bridger claimed to have rafted it early in the nineteenth century. Instead, travelers took overland routes such as the Bad Pass Trail, first used by prehistoric peoples 10,000 years ago, and the Bozeman Trail, built during the Civil War and used for only a few years. Parts of these trails are still visible. After the Civil War, open range cattle ranching became the predominant way of life until the advent of barbed wire and the demands of settlers curtailed the activities of the most powerful cattle barons.

HIKING AND BOATING

The best hiking is in the southern part of Bighorn Canyon where several trails offer spectacular canyon views. We have listed only four here; for additional hikes, pick up a detailed leaflet with maps at the visitor center.

STATE LINE TRAIL (1-mile loop) begins at a cairn along SR 37 just north of the Montana state line and follows cairns across limestone plateaus and through juniper forests to one of the best canyon overlooks.

LOCKHART RANCH TRAIL (1.5-mile loop) goes to the historic ranch, starting 2.5 miles north of Barry's Landing.

MOUTH OF THE CANYON TRAIL (3-mile loop) starts at the Horseshoe Bend Campground and offers views of the Pryor and Bighorn Mountains and of the surrounding red badlands.

OM-NE-A TRAIL (3 miles) connects the Yellowtail Dam Parking Area and the Ok-A-Beh Marina, following the canyon rim. It is poorly marked.

LITTLE BIGHORN BATTLEFIELD has self-guided walking trails that wind across the prairie connecting various battle points.

Canoeing, kayaking, sailing, and motorboating get visitors into the depths of the canyon. The stretch from Horseshoe Bend to Devil's Canyon is considered the most spectacular.

CAMPING

In addition to these campgrounds, there are also several boat-in or hike-in campgrounds. Check at the visitor center. There is no camping at Little Bighorn Battlefield.

AFTERBAY, a developed campground adjacent to Afterbay Lake on CR 313.

BARRY'S LANDING, a developed campground at the end of SR 37.

HORSESHOE BEND, a developed campground accessed from the first turn-off from SR 37 about 1 mile from the south entrance.

TRAIL CREEK, a primitive campground along Barry's Landing Road off SR 37.

SAGE CREEK CAMPGROUND, a primitive campground on FS 23085 in the Pryor Mountains.

Mustang foals, Mule Deer and Pronghorn fawns, and early-blooming wildflowers highlight a spring visit. The weather from May to October is pleasant for boating, hiking, and camping, but fierce thunderstorms occur in summer, and relentless winds can blow at any time. Be aware of lightning, and stay away from the edge of the canyon during severe weather because of falling rock. Golden grasses and smaller crowds make September a lovely time to visit Little Bighorn Battlefield.

INFORMATION

THE BIGHORN CANYON VISITOR CENTER (20 Highway 14A East, Lovell, WY 82431; 307-548-2251) serves the south unit and has exhibits on the canyon's history and natural features.

THE YELLOWTAIL DAM VISITOR CENTER AND PARK HEADQUARTERS (5 Avenue B, Box 7458, Fort Smith MT 59035; 406-666-2412) serves the north unit and has exhibits describing the Crow Indians and the dam. Power plant tours originate here.

LITTLE BIGHORN BATTLEFIELD VISITOR CENTER (Box 39, Crow Agency, MT 59022; 406-638-2621) has excellent exhibits on the Plains Indians and on the Battle of Little Bighorn.

THE BUREAU OF LAND MANAGEMENT (5001 Southgate Drive, Box 36800, Billings, MT 59107; 406-896-5013) provides information about the Pryor Mountains and wild horses. Call any BLM office to find out about adoption procedures.

HOW TO GET THERE

For the north unit of Bighorn Canyon National Recreation Area, take SR 313 south from Hardin, Montana, to Yellowtail Dam and Park Headquarters. There is no road connecting Yellowtail Dam and Barry's Landing in the south unit.

For the south unit, take US 310 south from Billings or US 14 and 14A west from I-90 near Sheridan, Wyoming, to Lovell, Wyoming. A few miles east of Lovell, SR 37 heads north paralleling Bighorn Lake to Barry's Landing.

Little Bighorn Battlefield is just east of I-90, 15 miles south of Hardin.

Several roads lead into the Pryor Mountains, but many require four-wheel drive and high clearance. One of the most beautiful is Crooked Creek Road, connecting SR 37 and the town of Warren. This road is impassable when wet; inquire locally about conditions, take along a map, and beware of muddy stretches across the red Chugwater Formation.

BIGHORN CANYON NATIONAL RECREATION AREA AND
LITTLE BIGHORN BATTLEFIELD NATIONAL MONUMENT

WEATHER

MEAN TEMPERATURES AND PRECIPITATION

MONTH	HIGH (°F)	LOW (°F)	PRECIP.	SNOW
January	35	9	0.6"	9.1"
April	63	32	1.4"	7.9"
July	92	55	0.9"	0.0"
October	66	32	1.1"	3.7"

The northern section of the N.R.A. receives 18 to 20 inches of rain annually and is classified as semiarid, whereas the southern section, in the rain shadow of the Rockies, receives only 5 to 10 inches annually and is classified as high desert. Data are for St. Xavier, Montana (temperatures and precipitation), and Billings, Montana (snow).

SELECTED WILDLIFE OF SPECIAL INTEREST

MAMMALS: Beaver, Porcupine, Coyote, Black Bear, Mountain Lion, Elk, Mule Deer, Bighorn Sheep, feral horse.

BIRDS: Wood Duck, Ferruginous Hawk, Gray Partridge, Sharp-tailed Grouse, Upland Sandpiper, Marbled Godwit, Black-billed Cuckoo, Short-eared Owl, Red-headed Woodpecker, Sedge Wren, Cedar Waxwing, Lark Bunting, Grasshopper Sparrow, Baird's Sparrow, Snow Bunting (w).

AMPHIBIANS AND REPTILES: Woodhouse's Toad, Northern Leopard Frog, Plains Spadefoot, Tiger Salamander, Pigmy Short-horned Lizard, Common Sagebrush Lizard, Western Rattlesnake.

CHARLES M. RUSSELL
NATIONAL WILDLIFE REFUGE

A wild and scenic river flows through native prairies, badlands, forested coulees, and marshy wetlands. Named for the cowboy artist Charles M. Russell, this refuge contains scenes resembling his paintings come to life. Covering 1.1 million acres, including the 245,000-acre Fort Peck Reservoir, it's the second largest National Wildlife Refuge in the lower 48 states. The refuge is adjacent to the Upper Missouri River Breaks National Monument and encompasses the last 35 miles of the free-flowing Missouri River.

Members of the Lewis and Clark Expedition camped along the Missouri on their way west in 1805 and again on their return in 1806, passing through what is now the refuge and exulting in "immence hirds" of deer, Elk, Pronghorn, Bighorn Sheep, and Black-tailed Prairie Dogs, which Lewis described as "new to science." Bighorns were introduced in 1980 to replace the now extinct Audubon's subspecies discovered by Lewis and Clark. The Grizzlies and wolves are gone, but most other birds and mammals seen in 1805 still thrive along this stretch of the Missouri River.

The river and its tributaries also provide habitat for the endangered Pallid Sturgeon and for one of the few remaining Paddlefish populations in the United States. The mixed-grass prairies sur-

Mixed-grass prairie stretches down to Fort Peck Reservoir at Charles M. Russell National Wildlife Refuge. (Photo by Glenn Cushman)

rounding the riparian areas contain Western Wheatgrass, Needle-and-Thread, Green Needlegrass, Junegrass, Sandberg's Blue-grass, and Blue Grama.

The refuge was created to protect wildlife habitat, so recreational facilities are minimal. A 20-mile self-guided auto tour, starting a few miles north of where US 191 crosses the river, is an all-weather road and one of the few improved roads on the refuge. The tour passes a meadow where Elk often graze.

ELK

In his book *Grassland,* Richard Manning tells the story of Earl, a Montana Elk who wandered away from his home in the Sweet Grass Hills almost on the Canadian border. Earl moseyed up to Alberta's Cypress Hills, back down to Montana, and then he probably followed the Missouri River south and east. He grazed his way through prairies, zigzagging down to Independence, Missouri, a distance of 1,800 miles.

Earl had reverted to the ways of Elk before European settlement. In those days Elk were common from Virginia to California and abundant throughout the Great Plains. Meriwether Lewis repeatedly mentioned immense herds of Elk in his journals, and John Madson says they were once the most widespread of any American hoofed animal. But farming and indiscriminate hunting destroyed them. By early in the twentieth century most of the remaining prairie Elk survived in mountain refugia such as the Black Hills, the Cypress Hills, and the Sweet Grass Hills.

In the state of Missouri, Earl's destination, and in the Upper Missouri region of Montana, they were exterminated by the early 1900s. Stock from Yellowstone was reintroduced in the Upper Missouri region in 1951. That herd now numbers 5,000 to 6,000.

The bugling of Elk, also called Wapiti (a Shawnee word meaning "white rump"), is the fanfare that heralds autumn. Listen at dawn and dusk for an eerie, high-pitched whinny ending in a series of snorts. Larger bulls have deeper calls, so their size and status can be guessed from the pitch.

During the rut, or mating season, bulls undergo physiological changes, possibly triggered by decreasing periods of daylight. Their necks and shoulders become swollen, and they vent their lust and stress through bugling and frenzied displays. They attack trees and shrubs. They urinate copiously, drenching themselves and rolling in urine-soaked grass and wallowing in mud.

The purpose of this sound and fury is to collect and keep a harem of five to thirty cows. To do this, each male must fend off other males vying for the same females. If bluffing fails, combat ensues. Then the two massive males circle, charge, and clash antlers, pushing and shoving until the weaker one gives way. Antlers are occasionally ripped loose along with portions of the skull, and sometimes antlers become so entangled that both Elk die. Between brawling and mating, the dominant male has little time to eat or sleep and may lose up to 100 pounds. When the rut ends in October, he will be a shadow, an echo, of the royal stag that bugled in September.

COTTONWOODS

Plains Indians ate cottonwood bark and buds, which contain chemicals similar to those in aspirin, to relieve pain. Valery Havard, assistant surgeon for the 7th Cavalry, reported in 1877 that entire groves in Montana "were seen with their trunks stripped by the Indians, who use the inner layers of the bark as a mucilaginous and anti-scorbutic food." The Lakota called the tree *canya'hu,* meaning "peel off wood" and fed it to their horses, and

Plains Cottonwoods (Populus deltoides) *grow up to 70 feet high and 10 feet in diameter but generally live for less than 150 years.*

the Blackfeet prepared a bark tea for general discomfort and to help women in labor.

Cowboys and westering pioneers watched eagerly for the large trees that delineated creek and river beds. Following European settlement, cottonwoods proliferated as natural fires were suppressed and rivers were dammed, creating a more uniform water flow. Species typical of eastern deciduous forests, including Blue Jays, White-tailed Deer, opossums, and fireflies, migrated westward following these gallery forests.

Recently, however, many streams have been channelized and many wetlands have been drained. Cottonwoods, which need flowing water or moist, bare surfaces for optimal germination, are not reproducing well. In many places they are also beset by overgrazing and by the spread of introduced species such as Russian Olives, which shade out seedlings and adapt better to altered habitats.

Once started, Plains Cottonwoods (*Populus deltoides*) grow fast and become enormous. According to the National Register of Big Trees, the largest of this species in the United States is in Boulder County, Colorado, at the edge of foothills and plains. It stands 105 feet tall and measures more than 35 feet in circumference. Cottonwoods grow rapidly, and huge branches fall without warning. River runners are advised not to camp under these giants.

"FIGHT NO MORE FOREVER"

Several nearby prehistoric sites, including petroglyph panels, campsites, and buffalo jumps, show Plains Indians lived here for thousands of years. Blackfeet and Gros Ventre were the dominant tribes at the time of the Lewis and Clark Expedition, but the area was also inhabited by Assiniboin, Crow, Plains Cree, and Plains Ojibwe. The Nez Percé National Historic Trail, which crosses through the Upper Missouri Breaks National Monument upstream from the refuge, traces the 1,170-mile route of the Nez Percé in their attempt to reach Canada and freedom.

In 1877, several bands of Nez Percé, who had befriended Lewis and Clark and other whites, were forced off their homeland in the Northwest—lands that had been promised to them in an 1855 treaty. To avoid war with the United States, some 750 people led by Chief Joseph tried to flee to Canada, crossing the Missouri River into the Breaks country. After eluding United States troops for more than four months, they were discovered and defeated in the Cow Island Skirmish just 45 miles from the Canadian border. They surrendered after the Battle of Bear Paw just north of the monument. Chief Joseph handed over his rifle saying, "I am tired;

my heart is sick and sad. From where the sun now stands, I will fight no more forever."

HIKING AND BOATING

Although there are no designated hiking trails, you can hike along the shore of the reservoir or on access roads.

Canoeing, kayaking, and rafting are popular on the river, which runs 3 to 4 miles per hour, and on the reservoir; however, Montana has suffered severe droughts since the late 1990s. In 2001 the Crooked Creek boat launch was about a quarter-mile from water, and tumbleweeds filled the flats. Check with refuge headquarters if you plan to launch a boat on the reservoir.

CAMPING

Campgrounds, which are accessed by gravel roads, dot the edge of the reservoir. Watch for signs and check with refuge headquarters regarding road conditions and to obtain a map. A map is also available on the refuge's Internet site. The refuge also encompasses three state parks:

ROCK CREEK STATE PARK on eastern end of Fort Peck Reservoir, west of SR 24.

HELL CREEK STATE PARK, southern part of reservoir north of Jordan Wildlife Station on SR 200.

JAMES KIPP STATE PARK at Robinson Bridge on US 191.

BEST TIMES TO VISIT

The best weather for river running generally occurs from late May through August. although the season officially stretches from March to November. The rainiest period is May to early July, and in September blizzards can descend unexpectedly. Mid-April through June is the best time to see migrating, courting, and nesting birds, with Sharp-tailed Grouse performing in April and May. Northern Harriers begin nesting in mid-May. Migrating shorebirds pass through again in August. In late September cottonwoods turn golden, and Elk bugle.

INFORMATION

CHARLES M. RUSSELL NATIONAL WILDLIFE REFUGE, Box 110, Lewistown, MT 59457; 406-538-8706.

U.S. 191 crosses the western part of the refuge 43 miles south of Malta and 36 miles north of Grassrange. SR 24 skirts the east side, accessing Fort Peck Recreation Area and the reservoir. Several gravel and dirt roads also access the refuge but may be impassable when wet. Inquire locally.

Young Northern Harriers on the nest.

CHARLES M. RUSSELL NATIONAL WILDLIFE REFUGE

WEATHER
MEAN TEMPERATURES AND PRECIPITATION

MONTH	HIGH (°F)	LOW (°F)	PRECIP.	SNOW
January	32	10	0.8"	12.5"
April	54	29	1.4"	10.6"
July	81	49	2.0"	0.0"
October	59	31	1.2"	4.9"

Mean annual precipitation is 18.5 inches. Blizzards can occur as late as June and as early as September. Data are for Lewistown, Montana.

SELECTED WILDLIFE OF SPECIAL INTEREST

MAMMALS: Black-tailed Prairie Dog, Coyote, Elk, Mule Deer, White-tailed Deer, Pronghorn, Bighorn Sheep.

BIRDS: American White Pelican, Osprey, Bald Eagle (w), Golden Eagle, Northern Harrier, Prairie Falcon, Sharp-tailed Grouse, Greater Sage-Grouse, Sandhill Crane (m), Piping Plover, Mountain Plover, Upland Sandpiper, Burrowing Owl, Short-eared Owl, Loggerhead Shrike.

AMPHIBIANS AND REPTILES: Great Plains Toad, Woodhouse's Toad, Northern Leopard Frog, Tiger Salamander, Greater Short-horned Lizard, Eastern Racer, Western Rattlesnake, Western Hog-nosed Snake, Milk Snake, Spiny Softshell.

OTHER MONTANA SITES

BENTON LAKE NATIONAL WILDLIFE REFUGE AND WETLAND MANAGEMENT DISTRICT (Box 450, Black Eagle, MT 59414; 406-727-7400). High mountains surround 12,383 acres of shallow marsh and native shortgrass prairie. Shorebirds and grouse nest here, and Tundra Swans, Snow Geese, and Bald Eagles migrate through. From US 87, 1 mile north of Great Falls, turn onto Bootlegger Trail and follow signs. Seven Waterfowl Production Areas also lie within this district.

BOWDOIN NATIONAL WILDLIFE REFUGE (HC 65, Box 5700, Malta, MT 59538; 406-654-2863). American White Pelicans, White-faced Ibis and many other water- and shorebirds nest on this 15,550-acre refuge. Up to 100,000 ducks and geese pass through during migration, and Sharp-tailed Grouse, Ring-necked Pheasants, and Pronghorn inhabit the surrounding native prairie. A self-guided auto tour circles Lake Bowdoin. Seven miles east of Malta off US 2.

GIANT SPRINGS HERITAGE STATE PARK (4600 Giant Springs Road, Great Falls, MT 59405; 406-454-5840). Meriwether Lewis passed through here in 1805 and speculated that this was one of the world's largest springs. He was right. The park includes an outstanding interpretive center for the Lewis & Clark National Historic Trail and a specimen garden of prairie plants. Camping.

MEDICINE LAKE NATIONAL WILDLIFE REFUGE (223 North Shore Road, Medicine Lake, MT 59247; 406-789-2305). More than 2,000 American White Pelicans hatch each year on Big Island, one of the largest pelican rookeries in the United States. Piping Plovers and Sharp-tailed Grouse also breed here, and Sandhill Cranes, Whooping Cranes, and Tundra Swans pass through on migration. A self-guided auto tour circles the lake, marshes, and mixed-grass and shortgrass prairies on this 31,457-acre refuge. One mile south of the town of Medicine Lake and two miles east of SR 16.

NATIONAL BISON RANGE (U.S. Fish and Wildlife Service, 132 Bison Range Road, Moiese, MT 59824; 406-644-2211). A self-guided auto tour loops through 18,500 acres of Palouse prairie where 350 to 500 Bison graze on Western Wheatgrass, Rough Fescue, and Idaho Fescue. Black Bears, Bighorn Sheep, Mountain Goats, Pronghorns, and Elk forage in mountain forests, prairies, and river bottoms. Located about 37 miles north of Missoula, east of US 93, and southeast of Moiese between SR 200 and CR 212. Pablo and Ninepipe National Wildlife Refuges, featuring marshes, prairie potholes, and upland grasslands, are a few miles north, just off US 93.

ULM PISHKUN STATE PARK (342 Ulm-Vaughn Road, Ulm, MT 59485;

406-866-2217). Bison bones piled up nearly 13 feet deep below one of the largest buffalo jumps in the world. Excellent exhibits, a prairie dog town, and interpretive trails. Open Memorial Day through September 30; by appointment the rest of the year. Ten miles southwest of Great Falls off I-15; follow signs.

Curious Pronghorns pause for a moment at Bowdoin National Wildlife Refuge. (Photo by Glenn Cushman)

NEBRASKA

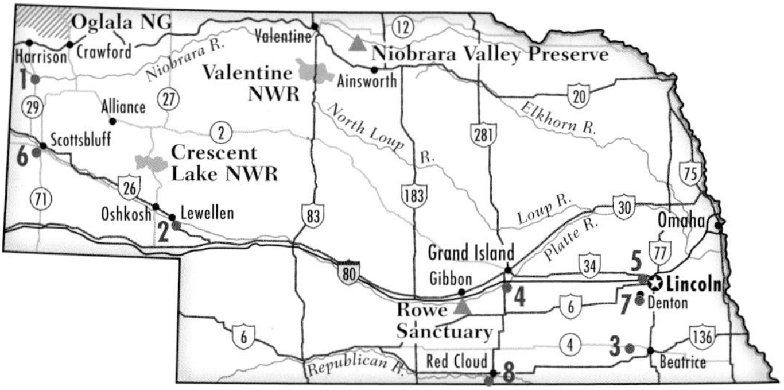

Oglala NG
Harrison
Crawford
Niobrara R.
Valentine
12
Niobrara Valley Preserve
Valentine NWR
Ainsworth
1
29
Alliance
27
20
North Loup R.
Elkhorn R.
2
281
Scottsbluff
6
Crescent Lake NWR
75
26
183
71
Oshkosh
Lewellen
83
Loup R.
30
Omaha
2
Platte R.
Grand Island
5
77
34
80
Gibbon
Lincoln
4
6
7
Denton
Rowe Sanctuary
6
4
3
136
Republican R.
Red Cloud
8
Beatrice

CRESCENT LAKE NATIONAL
  WILDLIFE REFUGE

LILLIAN ANNETTE ROWE SANCTUARY

NIOBRARA VALLEY PRESERVE

OGLALA NATIONAL GRASSLAND

VALENTINE NATIONAL WILDLIFE
  REFUGE

OTHER NEBRASKA SITES:

1. Agate Fossil Beds National Monument
2. Ash Hollow State Park
3. Homestead National Monument
4. Mormon Island Crane Meadows
5. Nine-Mile Prairie
6. Scotts Bluff National Monument
7. Spring Creek Prairie
8. Willa Cather Memorial Prairie

CRESCENT LAKE NATIONAL WILDLIFE REFUGE

The country road north from Oshkosh, Nebraska, to Crescent Lake National Wildlife Refuge passes through some of the most stunning prairie in North America. Grass-covered dunes roll away toward the edge of the earth. Mule Deer and Pronghorns stand on the dune crests, while flocks of pelicans, ducks, and shorebirds swirl over shallow lakes and ponds.

This sandhills prairie, a unique blend of sand-loving tallgrasses and midgrasses, covers 20,000 square miles of west-central Nebraska. Dominant grasses include Prairie Sandreed, Sand Bluestem, Big Bluestem, Little Bluestem, Switchgrass, Indian Grass, and Blowout Grass. Badgers, Long-billed Curlews, and Sharp-tailed Grouse inhabit the wind-buffeted dunes; White-tailed Deer, Mink, and American Bitterns thrive in the wetlands.

The refuge protects 70 square miles of grass-covered dunes, lakes, and wetlands. More than 30 miles of sand trails (two-track roads suitable for four-wheeling or walking) traverse the dunes. There's a shady picnic area at the refuge headquarters, but most of the nearly treeless landscape is fully exposed to sun, wind, and violent summer thunderstorms.

Above: White Pelicans on Lower Harrison Lake.

Scientists believe that the dunes that now cover much of western and central Nebraska were molded from sand deposited over millions of years by rivers flowing down from the Rocky Mountains. About 15,000 years ago, toward the end of the Ice Age, a lush savanna of grass and conifers covered these sands. As the high plains climate became drier and hotter, the conifers disappeared and vegetative cover on the dunes diminished. Fierce northwesterly winds reactivated the crescent-shaped dunes and elephant-backed ridges, pushing some as high as 400 feet.

Much of this dune formation probably occurred 5,000 to 8,000 years ago, during a relatively dry period of the early to mid-Holocene. But there's evidence, obtained by geologists who have drilled down into the muck of lake bottoms and marshes, that many of the dunes were moving as recently as 800 years ago. When the next extended drought hits, the cycle will continue, transforming large areas of these grasslands into sand desert.

Even under today's conditions, powerful northwesterly winds hew away some dune crests, creating craters of sand. These blowouts provide denning sites for Badgers and Coyotes, along with competitor-free growing sites for drought-resistant plants. Blowout Penstemon, knee-high with a showy stalk of lavender to white flowers, grows only in sand dunes within a half-dozen counties of western Nebraska and eastern Wyoming.

Paradoxically, improvements in range management practices in the Sandhills have contributed to this Federally endangered plant's decline. As the Sandhills grass cover has thickened, blowouts have become less common, and these penstemons have become rare.

Blowout Penstemon (Penstemon haydenii) *comes in two colors: lavender (shown here) and white.*

Sometimes you can find Blowout Penstemons by following your nose. The plants emit a vanilla-like scent. The aroma often leads to a blowout, where clusters of the bright flowers huddle in the wind. Blowout Penstemons bloom in late May and early June.

SHARP-TAILED GROUSE

In April and early May, Sharp-tailed Grouse perform their ritualistic mating dance on several dozen leks scattered throughout the refuge. Displaying males face off while making a soft cooing sound as they inflate the violet-tinted air sacs on both sides of the throat. They spread their wings, stomp their feet, and leap into the air in mock combat. Females gaze on complacently or scurry out onto the lek to select a suitor, usually the most dominant male. After mating, the females head off into the dunes to lay 10 to 15 speckled brown eggs under a shrub or in a clump of thick grass.

The Sandhills are one of the last strongholds for Sharp-tailed Grouse, which were once fairly common in tallgrass prairies and sagebrush uplands throughout the Great Plains and Rocky Mountain region. Their numbers have been reduced by hunting, habitat loss, and competition with introduced Ring-necked Pheasants. In the Sandhills, populations have remained relatively stable, but a recent decline in numbers of birds observed on strutting grounds has raised concern.

Most leks are located on hilltops where dancing grouse have unobstructed views of potential predators. Refuge staff have erected a three-person photographic blind, available by reservation, on one of these leks.

LONG-BILLED CURLEWS

The haunting cries of curlews evoke images of wild coastlines and pounding surf. But these 2-foot-tall shorebirds are perfectly at home on their prairie breeding grounds, where they lay their eggs in a shallow nest concealed by tufts of grass.

Since curlews nest on the ground, they rely largely on bluff and bravado to deter predators. If you walk across the dunes in early June when the young have just hatched, you'll likely attract a squadron of low-flying adults who zoom toward you, one by one, before veering off at the last second. The chances of actually being struck by a strafing curlew are minimal, but the experience may cause a heart palpitation or two.

Long-billed Curlews prefer medium-high grass for nesting and shorter grass and mudflats for foraging. They use their 9-inch-

Long-billed Curlews wail from dune crests throughout Crescent Lake National Wildlife Refuge.

long downcurved beaks to probe in mud and soft sand for invertebrates and to nab crickets and grasshoppers. They arrive in the sandhills in April and leave in late summer for wintering areas along the Gulf coast, in Mexico, and in Central America.

According to some nineteenth-century naturalists, migrating Long-billed Curlews once proliferated over parts of New England and the Midwest. Now their nesting range has shrunk to remaining patches of prairie west of the Mississippi River.

CATTAIL MARSHES

Nearly half of the 83 species of breeding birds that have been documented at the refuge nest or forage in cattail marshes. Eared Grebes build floating nests from cattails and aquatic vegetation. Look for them in June along the western shore of Island Lake. American Bitterns, medium-sized herons with camouflaging vertical stripes, lay their eggs in a shallow nest of grass and twigs constructed among tall emergent vegetation. At dawn and dusk, listen for their distinctive call, an *ook-a-loonk* reminiscent of the sound made by a hand-operated water pump.

Marsh Wrens chatter incessantly as they scurry up and down cattail stalks while constructing spherical nests of reeds, grass, cattail fluff, and feathers. The male, who does much of the nest building, will construct as many as 10 "dummy nests" to confuse predators. Pied-billed Grebes, Blue-winged Teal, Short-eared Owls, and Yellow-headed Blackbirds also nest in refuge marshes.

These marshes also harbor Muskrats, Meadow Voles, and Mink. Muskrats use cattails to build their haystack-like lodges. Trumpeter Swans and Canada Geese sometimes construct their nests right on top of these structures. Around dawn or dusk you may see a Mink posed on a shoreside log or swimming into a muskrat lodge looking for an easy meal.

ORNATE BOX TURTLES

In early June the most common pedestrians on Sandhills roads are Ornate Box Turtles. Many of these colorful turtles are females inching their way from home ranges near water to nesting sites in the dunes. To find their way, they use knowledge of local topography, awareness of the position of the sun, and, possibly, sensitivity to the earth's magnetic field.

Females lay a clutch of 2 to 8 eggs in the soft sand. After the young hatch, they seek cover under logs, rocks, or in a self-made burrow. They feed on insects, berries, tender shoots, and leaves. In late fall, box turtles burrow as deep as 5 feet into the sand to sleep out the coldest months.

Ornate Box Turtles have a hinged plastron (the underside of the shell) that enables them to completely enclose themselves under their brightly colored carapaces (upper shells). This defense system serves them well, for these slow-moving turtles can live for 40 years or more.

HIKING

A short nature trail takes off from refuge headquarters. Other possibilities include the following two-track roads:

LOWER HARRISON LAKE. A 2-mile sand trail heads south from the West Mail Road about one mile east of the western refuge boundary. The trail follows a narrow valley filled with small lakes, marshes, and mesic tallgrass prairie.

ISLAND LAKE LOOP. A 4-mile two-track begins at the south end of Island Lake, at the southern refuge entrance, heads northeast to Crane Lake, continues northwest to Roundup Lake, and returns to the main road northwest of Island Lake.

CAMPING

Overnight camping is prohibited. The nearest public campgrounds are located at the west end of Lake McConaughy, 45 miles southeast of the refuge.

Best Times to Visit

Ducks gather on lakes and Sharp-tailed Grouse dance during the blustery month of April. The winds settle down in mid-May just as Trumpeter Swans, Long-billed Curlews, Upland Sandpipers and Marsh Wrens begin to nest. June wildflowers include Sand Verbena, Bush Morning-Glory, and Shell-leaf Penstemon. A second wave of wildflowers, including several species of sunflower and the night-blooming Plains Eveningstar, brightens the prairie in August. Migrating shorebirds pass through in late summer, and migrating raptors abound in September.

Information

CRESCENT LAKE NATIONAL WILDLIFE REFUGE, 10630 Road 181, Ellsworth, NE 69340; 308-762-4893. Refuge maps are available at the southern and northern entrance stations. The refuge headquarters, open irregular hours on weekdays, has small interpretive displays.

How to Get There

Drive north 28 miles from Oshkosh on State Spur 27 (mostly sand and gravel). Watch for cattle on the road, and beware of slippery conditions during wet weather. Or drive east 25 miles from Alliance on SR 2 and then south 28 miles on one-lane Lakeside Road.

CRESCENT LAKE NATIONAL WILDLIFE REFUGE

WEATHER
MEAN TEMPERATURES AND PRECIPITATION

MONTH	HIGH (°F)	LOW (°F)	PRECIP.	SNOW
January	37	11	0.43"	5.8"
April	59	32	1.77"	6.4"
July	88	58	2.10"	0.0"
October	64	34	0.95"	2.3"

Average annual precipitation is 16.37 inches. May is the wettest month. March, April, and May can be very windy, with frequent gusts over 50 miles per hour. Data are for Alliance, Nebraska.

SELECTED WILDLIFE OF SPECIAL INTEREST

MAMMALS: Black-tailed Jackrabbit, White-tailed Jackrabbit, Ord's Kangaroo Rat, Coyote, Mink, Badger, Mule Deer, White-tailed Deer, Pronghorn.

BIRDS: Eared Grebe, American White Pelican, American Bittern, Trumpeter Swan, Wood Duck, Bald Eagle, Swainson's Hawk, Sharp-tailed Grouse, American Avocet, Upland Sandpiper, Long-billed Curlew, Short-eared Owl, Common Nighthawk, Marsh Wren, Yellow-headed Blackbird.

AMPHIBIANS AND REPTILES: Northern Leopard Frog, Bullsnake, Western Rattlesnake, Snapping Turtle, Ornate Box Turtle.

Ecologist Aldo Leopold described the call of the Sandhill Crane as "the trumpet in the orchestra of evolution . . . our closest link to prehistoric times." Ancestral cranes flew over the dinosaurs, and Sandhill Cranes have been flying over central North America for at least six million years.

Each morning in March and early April immense flocks of Sandhill Cranes lift off from their island and sandbar roosts in the Platte River and stream out toward feeding areas in wetlands, grasslands, and cornfields. The spectacle repeats each evening as the cranes gather in meadows and fields beside the river, flock skyward in the crimson light, and glide down to the water.

From the public viewing blinds at the National Audubon Society's Rowe Sanctuary, you can see as many as 30,000 cranes at one time. Nearly everyone who experiences the flight of the cranes and their rhythmic, trumpeting calls comes away changed by the experience. Sanctuary manager Paul Tebbel describes a memorable evening in early March:

> It was blowing 40 to 50 miles per hour out of the northwest, and the cranes were coming back, or they were trying to come

Above: The setting moon illuminates thousands of Sandhill Cranes flying up from their roosts in the Platte River just before dawn.

Sandhill Cranes begin performing their courtship dance while still gathered at migration stopover points along the Platte River. (Photo by Michael Forsberg)

back, to the river. I walked out of the sanctuary office and there was no one around, and the cranes were flying from the east to the west and they were battling their way upstream, and they were literally 10 feet above my head, almost stationary, all of them calling in the dim light. They were looking right down at me, and they were beating their wings as hard as they could and hardly moving.

A half-million Sandhill Cranes, about 80 percent of the world population, gather along a 200-mile stretch of the Platte each spring to rest and refuel before continuing their northward migration. Sandhill Cranes begin arriving at the Platte in late February. By mid-April most have headed north to nesting areas in the northern United States, Canada, and eastern Siberia. A few migrating Whooping Cranes mix in with the Sandhill Crane flocks during early April. The Whoopers, members of the world's only remaining wild flock, fly up from the Gulf Coast and continue on to Wood Buffalo National Park in Canada's Northwest Territories.

Islands and sandbars in the river provide night roosts where the cranes seek protection from predators. Historically, roosting sites abounded in the shallow, braided channels of the Platte. In places the river flowed a mile wide. Frequent spring floods and wildfires swept away woody vegetation, leaving many sandbars and islands free of thick brush and trees.

Since the late nineteenth century, water projects, control of natural fire, and other human activities have converted the Platte into a relatively tame and narrow river flanked by dense riparian woodlands. In many areas the cranes' remaining island roosts have become choked with vegetation.

Each summer and fall Rowe Sanctuary staff use heavy equipment to clear brush and small trees from the islands. They also negotiate agreements with private landowners to protect wetlands, grasslands, and corn fields where the cranes forage during the day. The 1,250 acres of land owned by the sanctuary, along with leases and conservation easements on an additional 800 acres, protect more than 5 miles of riverine habitat.

Sanctuary staff lead tours to the observation blinds on early mornings and late evenings, from early March through early April. A fee is charged, and it's a good idea to reserve well in advance. A smaller photo blind can be rented overnight.

You can also watch the cranes lifting off from or flying into their roosts from inside the brand-new visitor center (reservations required); from the Gibbon Bridge, 2 miles south of I-80 Exit 285; and from the Fort Kearny Hike-Bike Trail. Arrive at least a half-hour before sunrise or a half-hour before sunset. There are several designated pullouts along county roads south of the Platte where you can watch and photograph cranes foraging in corn fields and wetlands.

Although the cranes are present only in spring and fall, there's always much to see at the sanctuary. A 250-acre restored tallgrass prairie on the north side of the river shimmers in the soft light of spring and early fall. Upland Sandpipers nest, along with Short-eared Owls, Bobolinks, and Dickcissels. White-tailed deer bound through wetlands and woodlands at the river's edge, and beavers swim in the Platte's shallow channels.

RAINWATER BASIN

The Rowe Sanctuary lies within the Rainwater Basin, a 4,200-square-mile waterfowl stopover area south of the Platte River. Formerly a mosaic of grasslands, potholes, and swamps, the basin has been converted to farmland and many of its wetlands drained. Of more than 4,000 wetlands that occurred historically in the basin, fewer than 400 remain, and the total wetland area has shrunk from 94,000 to 22,000 acres. Removal of water for irrigation has lowered the groundwater level as much as 30 feet in some areas.

In early March and again in late October, millions of migrating Greater White-fronted Geese, Snow Geese, Canada Geese, and ducks crowd into the remaining wetlands. At the Funk Waterfowl Production Area, 25 miles southwest of Kearney, the whirring wings of tens of thousands of Greater White-fronted Geese and Snow Geese make a rolling, muffled roar as the birds circle over a four-square-mile oasis of shallow ponds and cattail marshes.

This concentration of waterfowl into small areas is great for birdwatchers, but it takes a toll on the birds. Diseases such as avian cholera spread quickly among these artificially crowded

In early March tens of thousands of Snow Geese and Greater White-fronted Geese swirl over Funk Waterfowl Production Area in central Nebraska's Rainwater Basin.

populations. During the unusually dry spring of 1980, avian cholera killed an estimated 80,000 ducks and geese in the basin, and some losses are reported each year.

To obtain a map of remaining wetlands in the basin, contact the Rainwater Basin Wetland Management District, Box 1686, Kearney, NE 68848; 308-236-5015, or check its Web site. To reach the Funk Waterfowl Production Area, take US 8/34 west from Minden through Funk, turn north 0.3 miles west of town on Funk Odessa Road, turn east after 2.3 miles on CR E-4, and continue east for 1 mile.

BALD EAGLES

At the Rowe Sanctuary it's not unusual to see thousands of wildly trumpeting cranes swirl up from their sandbar roosts as a white-headed eagle glides by in the dawn mist. The number of Bald Eagles that winter along the Platte River has increased dramatically since 1972, when DDT was banned in the United States. This insecticide accumulated in the fatty tissues of fish and other prey species. When ingested by Bald Eagles, the DDT disrupted the eagles' calcium metabolism, causing them to lay eggs with thin, breakable shells. Osprey, Peregrine Falcons, and pelicans were similarly affected.

Now several hundred Bald Eagles winter along the Platte and several thousand winter along rivers throughout the prairie region. As many as 200 congregate below the Lake McConaughy dam, near Ogallala. Most of these eagles migrate north in March, but a few pairs remain to nest. Nesting pairs begin building large

Subadult (3- to 4-year-old) Bald Eagle. The dark streak on its head indicates that this bird's plumage is transitional between the brown-headed immatures and white-headed adults.

stick nests in giant old cottonwoods during the winter months. Their young usually fledge in June or July. Though Bald Eagles may occasionally prey on cranes, their diet consists mostly of fish, carrion (often dead deer or prairie dogs), and injured waterfowl.

HIKING

TRIPLETT TRAIL (1.5 mile loop) takes off from a parking area 1.2 miles east of the visitor center and follows the south bank of the Platte. Look for Coyotes, White-tailed Deer, and Northern Bobwhites.

BOWLIN NATURE TRAIL (1.5 mile loop) winds through the tallgrass prairie north of the river. This trail is closed during crane migration. Take Kilgore Road east from SR 10 about 1 mile south of I-80 (Exit 279). After 1.5 miles, look for a large wooden sign on the south side of the road.

FORT KEARNY HIKE-BIKE TRAIL (2 miles) takes off from Fort Kearny State Park. The trail crosses the Platte on an old railway bridge. See directions below.

CAMPING

FORT KEARNY STATE RECREATION AREA, 5 miles southeast of Kearney on SR L50A (Turn east off SR 44 2 miles south of I-80 Exit 272).

WINDMILL STATE RECREATION AREA, 3 miles south of Gibbon on SR L10C (drive north 0.3 miles from I-80 Exit 285).

NOTE: A State Parks Pass, available at convenience and department stores, is required for all Nebraska state parks.

BEST TIMES TO VISIT

The first two weeks in March are optimal for seeing Snow Geese and Bald Eagles. Sandhill Crane numbers are highest in late March. A few Whooping Cranes usually pass through in early April. Grassland-nesting birds, including Upland Sandpipers, Bobolinks, and Dickcissels, arrive in mid-May. The cranes pass through again for a shorter period in late October and early November.

INFORMATION

LILLIAN ANNETTE ROWE SANCTUARY, 44450 Elm Island Road, Gibbon, NE 68840; 308-468-5282. The new visitor center on Elm Island Road offers exhibits, nature classes, and a chance to see the cranes and other wildlife from indoors.

HOW TO GET THERE

From I-80 at Gibbon (Exit 285) take SR L10C south 2 miles past the second bridge and turn west on Elm Island Road. Proceed about 2 miles to the visitor center.

LILLIAN ANNETTE ROWE SANCTUARY

WEATHER
MEAN TEMPERATURES AND PRECIPITATION

MONTH	HIGH (°F)	LOW (°F)	PRECIP.	SNOW
January	37	14	0.49"	4.2"
April	65	38	2.41"	2.5"
July	91	64	3.00"	0.0"
October	69	41	1.40"	0.5"

Mean annual precipitation is 23.66 inches. The record high is 114°F; the record low, -34°F. Early spring days can be very cold, with subfreezing temperatures and high winds, or pleasant with highs in the 70s. Sudden spring snowstorms can cause whiteout conditions. Data are for Kearney, Nebraska.

SELECTED WILDLIFE OF SPECIAL INTEREST

MAMMALS: Beaver, Coyote, Red Fox, Badger, Mink, Bobcat, White-tailed Deer.

BIRDS: American White Pelican, Snow Goose (m), Bald Eagle, Northern Harrier, Ring-necked Pheasant, Northern Bobwhite, Sandhill Crane (m), Whooping Crane (m), Piping Plover, Upland Sandpiper, Least Tern, Eastern Screech-Owl, Short-eared Owl, Red-headed Woodpecker, Northern Cardinal, Dickcissel, Bobolink.

AMPHIBIANS AND REPTILES: Northern Cricket Frog, Northern Leopard Frog, Eastern Racer, Bullsnake, Snapping Turtle.

NIOBRARA VALLEY PRESERVE

Located at the "biological crossroads" of North America, this 56,000-acre Nature Conservancy preserve protects one of the continent's most unusual plant associations—a mixture of grasslands, western coniferous forest, eastern deciduous forest, and northern boreal forest found only along a 30-mile stretch of the Niobrara River.

This complex community supports an astonishing diversity of plants and wildlife. River Otters and Wood Ducks swim in the river's spring-fed current. In shady side-canyons above the river, Bobcats and Wild Turkeys skulk through forests of Bur Oak, Basswood, American Elm, Paper Birch, and Eastern Red Cedar.

Above: Smith Falls is one of dozens of spring-fed cataracts that tumble down to the Niobrara River, creating unique springbranch canyon ecosystems.

Sandhills Prairie, a unique mix of tall-grasses and midgrasses, covers 20,000 square miles of western Nebraska, including these bluffs above the Niobrara River.

Up above the canyon rim, Bison graze in tallgrass meadows, and chattering flocks of Red Crossbills flit through Ponderosa Pine woodlands.

The mixing of forest types in the Niobrara Valley has created a zone of hybridization where eastern and western species overlap and sometimes interbreed. Indigo and Lazuli Buntings, Baltimore and Bullock's Orioles, and, possibly, Western and Scarlet Tanagers hybridize within the valley. The narrow strip of forest provides a movement corridor for mammals dispersing upstream from the Missouri River Valley or downstream from the High Plains. At least 150 plant and animal species reach the edge of their distributional range here.

Though it is the largest Nature Conservancy property in the prairie region, this preserve encompasses a small fraction of the Nebraska Sandhills grassland system, the largest expanse of uninterrupted prairie in North America. The stewardship of ranching families, many of whom have lived on the same tracts of land for over a century, has kept most of the 20,000 square miles of Sandhills grassland intact. For this reason the Sandhills are often cited as a model for private lands conservation. Throughout the Sandhills region, the Nature Conservancy and other conservation groups work cooperatively with ranchers to protect and restore native prairie.

Income generated from agricultural leases and sale of surplus Bison at the preserve supports prairie restorations and other conservation work. Research conducted on-site has generated more than two dozen publications on topics from butterflies to geomorphology.

The preserve extends 25 miles along the south side of the Niobrara River Canyon, from Smith Falls State Park to below Norden Bridge, where a visitor center and nature trails are located. The neighboring Fort Niobrara National Wildlife Refuge, between Valentine and Smith Falls, offers hiking trails and a driving tour through herds of Bison and Elk.

SPRINGBRANCH CANYONS

The Niobrara River carves a 200-foot-deep canyon along the northern edge of the Sandhills. The river's steady current is ideal for canoeing, and a 76-mile stretch below Valentine has been accorded National Scenic River status. Numerous springs issue from the south side of the gorge, where cold water from the immense aquifer that underlies the Sandhills gushes from the contact between Ogallala sandstone and White River siltstone and tumbles through narrow side canyons.

These cool, humid springbranch canyons support a flora more reminiscent of Minnesota than of the central plains. Beneath a canopy of Bur Oak, Basswood, Paper Birch, and Ponderosa Pine grow northern species such as Wild Sarsaparilla, wintergreen, and Saskatoon Serviceberry. A lone stand of aspen—a hybrid of Bigtooth Aspen and Quaking Aspen—nestles into one of these ravines near the western boundary of the preserve.

In late spring, wild mushrooms poke up through the leaf litter under the forest canopy. Cardinals, Ovenbirds, and Blackpoll Warblers whistle from the oaks and elms. The treeless, windswept prairie seems a world away—until you take a five-minute walk up the hillside and emerge in the rolling grasslands above the canyon rim.

OVENBIRDS

To many naturalists, the insistent *tea-churr, tea-churr, tea-churr* of these drab warblers suggests verdant forests dripping with moss. Ovenbirds, named for their habit of building ground nests with oven-shaped entrances, thrive in mature deciduous forests of southern Canada and the eastern United States. West of the Mississippi River, they nest in pockets of dense deciduous growth, including shady ravines in the Colorado Front Range, South Dakota's Black Hills, and the Niobrara River Valley.

The springbranch canyons on the south side of the valley contain the lush vegetation cover that Ovenbirds prefer. These warblers conceal their ground nests amid shrubs and leaf litter, and they forage on the ground for insects. Dense leaf litter and shade seem critical to their nesting success.

Ovenbird populations have declined in areas where deciduous forests have been altered by logging or urban development; in these fragmented environments, breeding pairs seem vulnerable to nest predation and nest parasitism (egg dumping) by cowbirds. Some scientists consider Ovenbirds an indicator of undisturbed deciduous forests. Their abundance in the Niobrara River Valley reflects the vitality of the valley's forest ecosystems.

NVADING CONIFERS

Throughout the high plains, islands of Ponderosa Pine grow on escarpments and in rocky canyons. Extensive stands occur on the Mesa de Maya of southeastern Colorado, the Platte River bluffs of eastern Wyoming and western Nebraska, and along the Niobrara River. Some scientists believe these isolated groves are Ice Age relicts, holdovers from cooler, wetter times. Growing on rocky soils may enable the conifers to compete with grasses for water and nutrients, escape the worst heat of prairie fires, or avoid having their seedlings trampled by ungulates.

Since white settlement of the Sandhills region during the late nineteenth century, prairie fires have been suppressed, and the pines have spread. In some areas the Ponderosas have crept nearly a mile out into the grasslands south of the Niobrara River. These southernmost groves are small and nearly isolated, but they still attract mammals and birds typical of Rocky Mountain Ponderosa Pine forests, including Porcupines, Northern Saw-whet Owls, and Red Crossbills.

A walk along the rim of the canyon, where these shady groves spill out onto the grassland sea, brings home the timelessness of the forest-grassland dynamic. Twelve thousand years ago coniferous forests thrived on the Great Plains; now grass covers the region. Natural and human-induced climatic fluctuations, along with the prevalence of fire, will help determine what grows here in another 12,000 years.

HIKING AND CANOEING

The 30-mile stretch of river from Fort Niobrara National Wildlife Refuge through Smith Falls State Park to Norden Bridge is popular with canoeists and tubers; river flows are generally highest in May and June. Two self-guided nature trails originate near the preserve headquarters:

SOUTH TRAIL (0.75 and 1.75-mile loops beginning at the visitor center) passes through springbranch canyons, sandhills prairie, and wetlands along the river.

NORTH TRAIL (3-mile loop beginning a few hundred yards north of Norden Bridge) traverses Ponderosa Pine woodlands, mixed-grass prairie, and floodplains, offering impressive views of the river valley.

CAMPING

Camping is prohibited within the preserve. Several private campgrounds are located upstream on the north side of the river. Nearby public campgrounds include:

SMITH FALLS STATE PARK, 15 miles east of Valentine off SR 12.
KELLER PARK STATE RECREATION AREA, 14 miles south of Springview on US 183.

BEST TIMES TO VISIT

Warbler migration peaks and Bison young are born in May. White-tailed Deer fawns appear in early June, and Wild Turkeys typically nest from May through June. The river, crowded with canoeists from mid-June through early August, can be almost deserted in fall. Migrating Sandhill Cranes pass through in October.

INFORMATION

NIOBRARA VALLEY PRESERVE, Route 1, Box 348, Johnstown, NE 69214; 402-722-4440. A small visitor center has displays and brochures describing grassland and forest ecology, plant life, and wildlife.

HOW TO GET THERE

From Valentine take SR 12 east 32 miles to Norden, turn south on Norden Road (gravel and dirt) and follow it 8 miles across the river bridge to the preserve entrance (on the left near the top of the hill). From Ainsworth go west 9.5 miles on US 20. Turn right on Norden-Johnstown Road (0.5 miles east of Johnstown) and continue 16 miles to the preserve. Access roads are often impassable in wet weather.

NIOBRARA VALLEY PRESERVE

WEATHER
MEAN TEMPERATURES AND PRECIPITATION

MONTH	HIGH (°F)	LOW (°F)	PRECIP.	SNOW
January	33	7	0.29"	4.6"
April	60	33	1.67"	3.9"
July	89	60	3.06"	0.0"
October	64	34	0.91"	1.0"

Mean annual precipitation is 19.23 inches. Severe thunderstorms and tornadoes may occur, mid-May to late August. Data are for Valentine, Nebraska; summer temperatures in the Niobrara River Canyon are typically several degrees lower, but humidities are higher.

SELECTED WILDLIFE OF SPECIAL INTEREST

MAMMALS: Beaver, Coyote, Mink, Badger, River Otter, Bobcat, Mule Deer, White-tailed Deer, Bison.

BIRDS: Wood Duck, Osprey (m), Wild Turkey, Yellow-billed Cuckoo, Black-billed Cuckoo, Eastern Screech-Owl, Great Crested Flycatcher, Red-eyed Vireo, Bell's Vireo, Red-breasted Nuthatch, Ovenbird, Northern Cardinal, Lazuli Bunting, Indigo Bunting, Red Crossbill.

AMPHIBIANS AND REPTILES: Northern Leopard Frog, Eastern Racer, Bullsnake, Ornate Box Turtle.

OGLALA NATIONAL GRASSLAND

The parched badlands, pine-scented canyons, and expansive up-land prairies of this national grassland are haunted by images of courage and conquest. On a hill overlooking Warbonnet Creek, Buffalo Bill Cody and the 5th U.S. Cavalry held off a band of Cheyenne warriors in a decisive skirmish only three weeks after the 1876 rout at Little Bighorn. Ten miles to the south, in a blood-soaked ravine near Hat Creek, 34 outnumbered Northern Cheyennes fought their tribe's last battle for freedom in 1879. Somewhere along the pine-studded escarpment that cuts through the heart of this grassland are said to lie the remains of Crazy Horse, the legendary Oglala chief stabbed to death by soldiers at Fort Robinson in 1877.

Although dotted with herds of cattle, the landscape appears much as it might have 130 years ago. When summer thunderstorms rumble eastward and the evening light sets the prairie grasses aglow, it's easy to understand why the Lakota and Cheyenne fought so desperately for these sacred lands.

The 92,000-acre Oglala National Grassland is virtually surrounded by other public lands, including the 51,000-acre Pine Ridge National Recreation Area to the south and east, the 7,800-acre Soldier Creek Wilderness to the southwest, and the

Above: Toadstool Park after an early summer rain.

591,000-acre Buffalo Gap National Grassland to the north. You can spend days exploring this quintessential western landscape without encountering another soul.

TOADSTOOL PARK GEOLOGIC AREA

Sandstone slabs perched atop pedestals of clay and volcanic ash create a jumble of mushroom-shaped objects at this aptly named geologic site. Many of the larger slabs have been vandalized and have tumbled to the ground since Toadstool Park was named during the late 1800s, but new toadstools are slowly being formed.

These badlands are sculpted from sediments of the White River Group, also prominent in Badlands National Park to the north. They were created when wind and water cut through layers of sand, silt, clay, and volcanic ash deposited 28 million to 38 million years ago. Where an erosion-resistant sedimentary layer, or capstone, overlays softer sediments, differential rates of erosion create buttes, cliffs, and other top-heavy features, including toadstools.

In places, the badlands erode away at a rate of one inch per year, continually uncovering fossil bones of long-extinct creatures. Fossils of giant tortoises, rhinoceroses, and giant warthoglike mammals, called enteledonts, have been found at Toadstool Park. A 30-million-year-old fossil trackway made by rhinoceroses and enteledonts is visible from the 1.3-mile nature trail. It is illegal for individuals without museum permits to collect vertebrate fossils at Toadstool Park.

Other marvels at this otherworldly site include fossil duck tracks, a prominent geologic fault, and "desert pavement," a

Within the White River Badlands of Oglala National Grassland, erosion has created jumbles of boulders and toadstool-shaped rocks.

gravel composed of dark crystals filled with fossil bone fragments. A reconstructed sod house sits on an island of grass beside the campground. For directions to Toadstool Park, see Hiking, p. 248.

HUDSON-MENG BISON BONEBED

Nearly 10,000 years ago, several hundred ancient bison (*Bison antiquus*) died suddenly in a box canyon at the base of Nebraska's Pine Ridge. During the early 1950s, rancher Albert Meng came across some of the bones weathering out of an eroding bank. After several setbacks, he and his friend Bill Hudson convinced archaeologists to excavate what turned out to be the largest bison bonebed of its age in the Western Hemisphere.

When scientists found stone artifacts near the bones, they hypothesized that the bison had been driven off a nearby cliff by Paleo-Indians of the ancient Alberta culture. Later, however, researchers determined that the bison bones and human artifacts lay in separate strata of rock and that the cliff had been no more than a gentle knoll at the time when the bison were killed. Now some scientists believe a sudden natural calamity such as a prairie fire or lightning bolt killed these animals.

These new theories are being tested as excavations continue at the site. Excavations are open to public viewing daily from May 15 to September 30 and by appointment off-season. A 3-mile hiking trail links the site to Toadstool Park.

To reach the Hudson-Meng Bison Bonebed follow SR 2/71 four miles north from Crawford, turn left on Toadstool Road (gravel), and follow the signs for about 15 miles. For information, call 308-432-0300.

WESTERN RATTLESNAKES

On hot summer days Western Rattlesnakes curl up in the shade of the giant boulders of Toadstool Park. Since they are ectothermic, rattlesnakes spend much of the day thermoregulating, holing up in the shade when it's hot, basking in the sun when it's cool. Retiring by nature, they catch most of their prey by lying in wait, often beside a mouse or vole run. Western Rattlesnakes and other pit vipers locate their prey using heat-sensitive loreal pits on the sides of their heads, along with their eyesight and their constantly flicking, odor-sensing tongues.

In early fall Western Rattlesnakes slither into rodent burrows and small caverns to sleep out the winter. As many as 100 rattlesnakes may share a single hibernaculum. No one fully understands why these cold-blooded reptiles hibernate en masse. Winter aggregation may help individuals to conserve moisture and a small amount of heat. But it's possible that the practice of aggregation offers no particular advantages, and that the snakes simply share a limited number of favorable denning sites. Herpetologists have determined that young Western Rattlesnakes, typically born in late summer or early fall, often follow their mothers' scent trails to the hibernacula.

When the rattlesnakes emerge from their dens in early spring, they disperse to summer foraging areas as far as 10 miles away. Males and females get back together in early summer to mate. During the breeding season males engage in a sort of dance. Two jousting males rear up, entangle their necks, and weave from side to side. Stronger males or males with a prior history of dominance usually prevail in these mock battles, winning the right to mate with a nearby female.

Of the more than 20 North American rattlesnake species, only 4 inhabit the prairie region. The Western Rattlesnake (or Prairie Rattlesnake) frequents shortgrass and mixed-grass prairies from southern Alberta and Saskatchewan southeastward to western Iowa and south through western Oklahoma, western Texas, and New Mexico. The Massasauga occupies a narrow band of habitat running northeastward from central Texas through parts of Oklahoma, Colorado, Kansas, and the upper Midwest. The Western Diamond-backed Rattlesnake ranges across much of New Mexico, Texas, and Oklahoma. The Timber Rattlesnake occurs in greatly reduced numbers in the eastern prairie region from eastern Texas and Kansas north to the Great Lakes and the Ohio River Valley.

PRAIRIE TURNIPS

The Prairie Turnip (*Pediomelum esculentum*) was a staple food of Plains Indian peoples, including the Lakota, who called it *tipsinna,* meaning roughly, "the little wild rice of the prairie." When Prairie Turnips bloomed in late spring, Plains Indian women staked out the blooming sites, returning a couple of months later to dig up the roots when their starch content was high.

In parts of the Oglala National Grassland, particularly mixed-grass prairies of moist ravines and valleys, Prairie Turnips bloom in profusion in late May. They can be distinguished from other legumes by their short hairy stems, alternate leaves divided into 5 fingerlike segments and covered with glandular dots, and elliptical clusters of purple flowers growing among the leaves.

Digging up the roots of this plant is not recommended, how-

Prairie Turnips (Pediomelum esculentum) *produce goose-egg sized taproots loaded with starch. Plains Indians strung the roots together, dried them, and traded them for corn and buffalo robes.*

ever. Some poisonous members of the bean family are similar in appearance; and mice, pocket gophers, and other prairie wildlife may depend on the nourishment provided by this legume, which has been severely reduced through overgrazing.

Hiking

TOADSTOOL PARK INTERPRETIVE TRAIL. A universally accessible 1-mile trail weaves through jumbled sedimentary strata and grassy ravines. A 3-mile spur connects to the Hudson-Meng Bison Bonebed to the south. Take SR 2/71 north from Crawford for 4 miles, turn left on Toadstool Road (CR 904) and continue 15 miles to the trailhead. CR 904, a gravel road, can be impassable in wet weather.

SOLDIER CREEK WILDERNESS. Trooper Trail (8-mile loop) and Boots and Saddles Trail (8-mile loop) climb up shady canyons and traverse pine bluffs frequented by deer and Wild Turkeys. This area is recovering from a 1989 wildfire. From US 20 at Fort Robinson, turn west on Soldier Creek Road and continue 6 miles to the trailhead.

Camping

TOADSTOOL PARK GEOLOGIC AREA. This six-unit campground (see directions above under Hiking) offers shade and trails through the geologic formations.

SOLDIER CREEK WILDERNESS. Semiprimitive campsites are available at the trailhead, located 6 miles west of Fort Robinson on Soldier Creek Road. Primitive camping is permitted throughout the wilderness area.

FORT ROBINSON STATE PARK. Located 2 miles west of Crawford on SR 20, this state park offers camping, fishing, and self-guided tours of the fort, an important nineteenth-century outpost.

Best Times to Visit

In late May and early June, screaming Prairie Falcons soar over the badlands, and colorful penstemons carpet the greening grasslands. Intense sun and scorching south winds bake the nearly treeless prairie from late June to mid-August. In late September, the colors of turning grasses contrast with blue autumnal skies, and a variety of raptors, including Swainson's Hawks, Ferruginous Hawks, and Golden Eagles, soar southward.

Information

OGLALA NATIONAL GRASSLAND, 270 Pine Street, Chadron, NE 69337; 308-432-0300.

How to Get There

Take SR 2/71 north from Crawford, Nebraska, or take Monroe Canyon Road north from Harrison, Nebraska. **NOTE:** Because federal lands are remote and widely scattered, you will need an Oglala National Grassland map, available at the Chadron office, to find your way around.

OGLALA NATIONAL GRASSLAND

WEATHER
MEAN TEMPERATURES AND PRECIPITATION

MONTH	HIGH (°F)	LOW (°F)	PRECIP.	SNOW
January	34	8	0.39"	7.5"
April	70	33	1.84"	7.7"
July	90	59	2.23"	0.0"
October	65	34	0.75"	1.9"

Mean annual precipitation is 15.23 inches. May and June can be quite wet and windy. Severe thunderstorms are common from June through August. Data are for Chadron, Nebraska.

SELECTED WILDLIFE OF SPECIAL INTEREST

MAMMALS: Black-tailed Prairie Dog, Badger, White-tailed Deer, Pronghorn, Bighorn Sheep (Pine Ridge).

BIRDS: Swainson's Hawk, Golden Eagle, Prairie Falcon, Sharp-tailed Grouse, Wild Turkey, Long-billed Curlew, Burrowing Owl, Rock Wren, Ovenbird (Pine Ridge), Lark Bunting, Blue Grosbeak.

AMPHIBIANS AND REPTILES: Great Plains Toad, Plains Spadefoot, Eastern Fence Lizard, Western Hognosed Snake, Western Rattlesnake, Ornate Box Turtle.

VALENTINE NATIONAL WILDLIFE REFUGE

Eared Grebes nest within hailing distance of Badger dens, and Wild Rice grows within a stone's throw of yucca and prickly pear in this sprawling refuge in the heart of the Nebraska Sandhills. The refuge encompasses 71,252 acres of grass-covered dunes, shallow lakes, and cattail-bulrush marshes. Tallgrass prairie, dominated by Switchgrass, Indian Grass, Prairie Cordgrass, and Big Bluestem, flourishes in the wet valleys; more drought-tolerant grasses such as Prairie Sandreed, Sand Bluestem, Little Bluestem, and Blowout Grass cling to the dunes.

Sharp-tailed Grouse and Greater Prairie-Chickens display here in the spring, sometimes on the same leks, and a photographic blind is available by reservation. Gravel roads and two-track sand trails traverse remote wetlands bursting with waterfowl and wind-scoured dunes covered with waving grasses. When you watch the sunset from one of these hilltops, you can pretty much count on having only the Coyotes and grassland birds for company.

SANDHILLS LAKES

The High Plains (Ogallala) Aquifer stretches from South Dakota to Texas, but a major portion of the water in the aquifer lies beneath the Nebraska Sandhills. In a dune environment there is vir-

Above: Shallow lakes at Valentine National Wildlife Refuge provide nesting habitat for Trumpeter Swans, Eared Grebes, American Bitterns, and Wood Ducks.

tually no runoff, so the precipitation that escapes evaporation and transpiration percolates down through the sand into underlying layers of porous sandstone. Between 100 and 900 feet down, the water collects above more impermeable sandstone strata.

Lakes form in Sandhills valleys wherever the aquifer lies near or above ground level. Paradoxically, geologists think most of the lake basins were formed during several dry periods over the last 15,000 years, when shifting sands dammed natural stream drainages. The number of lakes varies from year to year as the groundwater rises or recedes, but there are at least a couple of thousand permanent lakes and ponds in the Sandhills. During the 1990s the number increased as above-average precipitation caused groundwater levels to rise, leaving some school yards, campgrounds, and grazing lands underwater.

On the banks of Sandhills lakes, archaeologists have found evidence of hunting and fishing camps that are thousands of years old. The lakes support 75 species of fish and 5 species of turtle, along with Muskrats, Beaver, Mink, American White Pelicans, Trumpeter Swans, Osprey, and Black Terns. Many lakes in the eastern Sandhills are rich in aquatic vegetation, including such edibles as arrowhead, Wild Rice, and cattail.

TRUMPETER SWANS

At least three bodies of water in the Sandhills go by the name "Swan Lake." Since most geographic features in the region were named between 1875 and 1890, it's likely that Trumpeter Swans nested on these lakes sometime during that period.

However, Trumpeter Swans disappeared from most of the Great Plains during the first two-thirds of the twentieth century. By the 1950s these 5-foot-long birds had grown very rare. Protection from hunting, along with reintroduction programs in the northern Rockies and northern plains, have helped populations to recover.

Now if you pay a summer visit to one of the Swan Lakes in the Sandhills, you are likely to see a pair of Trumpeter Swans cruising through the water with their fluffy young trailing behind. The fidelity of these birds to these nesting locations points out the importance of preserving specific habitats for species that depend on them.

In the Sandhills, Trumpeter Swans typically breed in cattail/bulrush marshes on the borders of shallow lakes. They build bulky nests in tall emergent vegetation or on top of muskrat houses. The female lays 2 to 9 creamy white eggs and incubates them for five weeks. Shortly after the young hatch, they fall in line behind their parents and begin probing the shallows for aquatic invertebrates.

As the cygnets grow older, their diet broadens to include leaves, seeds, roots of aquatic vegetation, and crustaceans. In autumn families migrate to wintering areas along ice-free rivers. Hundreds of swans winter in the Greater Yellowstone Basin, where rivers are thermally heated year-round. More than 100 winter on the Snake River where it enters Merritt Reservoir 20 miles west of the refuge.

WILD RICE

The abundant groundwater in the Sandhills region permits the growth of plants that normally would not survive in such an arid, seasonally hot environment. South and west of the Valentine refuge, in Cherry County, Sensitive Ferns, Marsh Marigolds, Wood Lilies, Bog Asters, and Cottongrass (a sedge with fluffy seed heads) flourish in marshes known as fens, a type of peat bog (see Chiwaukee Prairie, Wisconsin). They are remnants of the boreal flora of the Ice Age, trapped in refugia maintained by the constant upwelling of cool groundwater in the interdune valleys. Within the refuge, Wild Rice grows in the shallows of several lakes.

Wild Rice (*Zizania aquatica*) was a staple food of Indians living in the northeastern prairie region. According to ethnobotanist Melvin Gilmore, the Dakota name for the final moon before the autumnal equinox was *psin-hna-ketu-wi*, "the moon to lay rice up to dry." The Omaha and Ponca of present-day Nebraska also harvested this cereal.

A member of the grass family, Wild Rice grows up to 10 feet tall in solitary stems with wide leaves. The much-branched panicle is bright yellow-green when in flower. The purple-black seeds fall off when the plant is brushed or shaken. Although it is most abundant in the Great Lakes region, Wild Rice occurs along the margins of streams and lakes from Manitoba, Ontario, and Québec south to Louisiana and Florida.

SNAPPING TURTLES

In early summer, 2-foot-long Snapping Turtles emerge from the water to lay their eggs. Before dawn, the female waddles up toward the dunes until she finds an area of soft sand suitable for easy excavation. She digs down 8 inches or so and deposits a clutch of 15 to 60 leathery-shelled eggs. Most clutches of eggs are dug up and eaten by Raccoons and other predators, who scatter the eggs like Ping-Pong balls around the refuge's lakes and ponds.

On June mornings female Snapping Turtles waddle up into areas of soft sand to lay their eggs.

Those that survive hatch into 2-inch-long versions of their fearsome-looking parents.

Snapping Turtles spend much of their time resting underwater, where plant growth and the algae on their shells conceal them from predators. They eat crayfish, snails, insects, fish, frogs, salamanders, reptiles, birds, and mammals, as well as aquatic plants. They range from the Rocky Mountains eastward and have been introduced into lakes and ponds in California and Nevada, where they wreak havoc on nesting duck populations.

Four other turtles inhabit the lakes, marshes, and dunes of the refuge. Painted Turtles forage underwater but often can be seen sunning on logs or rocks. Ornate Box Turtles (see Crescent Lake National Wildlife Refuge, Nebraska) frequent marshes and grasslands and nest high in the dunes. Yellow Mud Turtles live in ponds where they feed on invertebrates and aquatic plants. Blanding's Turtles frequent ponds, shallow streams, and marshes where they feed on crustaceans, insects, snails, small fish, frogs, and plants.

Hiking

There are 40 miles of sand trails suitable for hiking or four-wheeling, and 40 miles of service trails open to hiking only. Pick up a map at refuge headquarters or any refuge entrance. A short nature trail takes off just west of refuge headquarters and climbs to an observation tower that affords a sweeping view of the Sandhills prairie.

Camping

Camping is prohibited within the refuge. Nearby public campgrounds include:

BALLARD'S MARSH STATE WILDLIFE AREA, 20 miles south of Valentine on US 83.
MERRITT RESERVOIR, 28 miles southwest of Valentine on SR 97.

Best Times to Visit

Greater Prairie-Chickens and Sharp-tailed Grouse dance and waterfowl crowd lakes in April and early May. In August Fourpoint Evening Primroses and Common, Maximilian, and Nuttall's Sunflowers paint the hills yellow. In early fall up to 150,000 ducks gather on refuge lakes; migrating hawks drift through cobalt skies; and grasses turn to russet, sienna, and amber.

Information

VALENTINE NATIONAL WILDLIFE REFUGE, HC 14 Box 67, Valentine, NE 69201; 402-376-3789. Pick up a refuge map at the Hackberry Headquarters on State Spur 16B, 13 miles west of US 83; or at the Valentine/Fort Niobrara National Wildlife Refuge Complex 5 miles east of the city of Valentine.

How to Get There

The refuge is located east and west of US 83, about 20 miles south of Valentine. To reach the refuge headquarters, go south from Valentine 17 miles on US 83 and west 13 miles on State Spur 16B.

VALENTINE NATIONAL WILDLIFE REFUGE

WEATHER
MEAN TEMPERATURES AND PRECIPITATION

MONTH	HIGH (°F)	LOW (°F)	PRECIP.	SNOW
January	33	7	0.29"	4.6"
April	60	33	1.67"	3.9"
July	89	60	3.06"	0.0"
October	64	34	0.91"	1.0"

Mean annual precipitation is 19.23 inches. Temperatures recorded in Valentine range from a high of 114°F (July) to a low of -39°F (February). Severe thunderstorms and tornadoes may occur from mid-May to late August. Data are for the city of Valentine, Nebraska.

SELECTED WILDLIFE OF SPECIAL INTEREST

MAMMALS: Beaver, Coyote, Mink, Badger, Mule Deer, White-tailed Deer.

BIRDS: Eared Grebe, American White Pelican, American Bittern, Trumpeter Swan, Wood Duck, Northern Harrier, Sharp-tailed Grouse, Greater Prairie-Chicken, Wild Turkey, Virginia Rail, Sora, Upland Sandpiper, Wilson's Phalarope, Black Tern, Short-eared Owl, Bell's Vireo, Grasshopper Sparrow, Chestnut-collared Longspur.

REPTILES AND AMPHIBIANS: Northern Leopard Frog, Eastern Racer, Bullsnake, Snapping Turtle, Blanding's Turtle, Ornate Box Turtle.

NOTE: A state parks pass, available at convenience and sporting goods stores, is required to camp in any Nebraska state park.

AGATE FOSSIL BEDS NATIONAL MONUMENT (301 River Road, Harrison, NE 69346-2734; 308-668-2211). A one-mile botanical trail leads to a 519-million-year-old fossil bed containing hundreds of rhinoceros skeletons. The visitor center displays Lakota artifacts and art. On SR 29 about 40 miles north of Scottsbluff.

ASH HOLLOW STATE PARK (Game and Parks, Box 30370, Lincoln, NE 68503; 308-778-5651). Oregon Trail ruts, a sod house, a flowing spring, and a prehistoric cave shelter have been preserved at this peaceful park along the North Platte River. The adjacent Clear Creek Wildlife Area has River Otters, Wild Turkeys, Bald Eagles in winter, and 5,000 Sandhill Cranes in March. One mile south of Lewellen on US 26.

HOMESTEAD NATIONAL MONUMENT (RFD 3, Box 47, Beatrice, NE 68310; 402-223-3514). Founded in 1936, this national monument includes an original homestead and cabin, along with more than 100 acres of restored tallgrass prairie. Nature trails. From Beatrice take US 136 west for 2 miles, then go north and west 4 miles on SR 4.

MORMON ISLAND CRANE MEADOWS (Platte River Whooping Crane Maintenance Trust, 6611 West Whooping Crane Drive, Wood River, NE 68883; 308-384-4633). Twenty-five hundred acres of wet meadows and tallgrass prairie host thousands of Sandhill Cranes during early spring. From I-80 Exit 312, near Grand Island, go south 1 mile to Elm Island Road. Turn west, and park along the road.

NINE-MILE PRAIRIE (402-472-2971). This 260-acre tallgrass remnant, owned and managed by the University of Nebraska–Lincoln, was the main research site for Professor John Weaver, a pioneer in grassland ecology. From I-80 Exit 401 take US 34 west about 5 miles to NW 48th Street. Go south 0.5 miles and then west 1 mile on West Fletcher Avenue.

SCOTTS BLUFF NATIONAL MONUMENT (Box 27, Gering, NE 69341-0027; 308-436-4340). This sandstone and siltstone bluff, a prominent natural landmark along the Oregon Trail, is surrounded by 2,000 acres of protected mixed-grass prairie. The museum contains a collection of watercolors by William Henry Jackson. SR 71 and SR 92, 2 miles south of Scottsbluff.

SPRING CREEK PRAIRIE (Nebraska Audubon Society, Box 117, Denton, NE 68339; 402-797-2301). More than 620 acres of nearly virgin tallgrass prairie, woodlands, and wetlands lie on a glacial moraine. More than 350 plant species and 150 bird species have been documented. Three-and-a-half miles south of Denton (southwest of Lincoln) on SW 98th Street. Look for the Audubon mailbox on the east side of the road just south of the double curve.

WILLA CATHER MEMORIAL PRAIRIE (The Nature Conservancy, 1722 St. Mary's Avenue #403, Omaha, NE 68102; 402-342-0282). A 610-acre remnant of the "shaggy grass country" (mixed-grass prairie) portrayed in Cather's books. US 281, 6 miles south of Red Cloud.

The chalky cliffs, mixed-grass prairies, and forested ridgetops of Scotts Bluff National Monument rise 500 feet above wetlands in the North Platte River valley.

Spring Creek Prairie. Located on a glacial moraine 15 miles south of Lincoln, this Nebraska Audubon sanctuary protects one of eastern Nebraska's largest tallgrass prairie remnants.

Wild Turkeys forage in the mixed-grass prairies and riparian woodlands of Ash Hollow State Park.

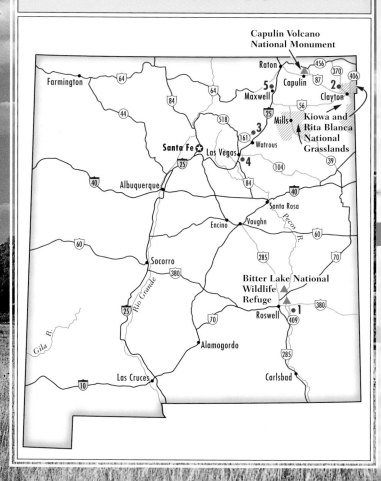

NEW MEXICO

Farmington

64

84

44

64

518

161

Maxwell 5

Santa Fe ★

Las Vegas

3

Watrous

4

104

Raton

456

370

87

406

Capulin

56

2

Clayton

Capulin Volcano
National Monument

Mills

Kiowa and
Rita Blanca
National
Grasslands

39

Albuquerque

40

25

Santa Rosa

60

40

Encino

Vaughn

Pecos R.

60

Socorro

380

285

70

Bitter Lake National
Wildlife Refuge

1

Roswell

380

409

70

Rio Grande

Gila R.

25

70

Alamogordo

285

60

Las Cruces

10

Carlsbad

BITTER LAKE NATIONAL WILDLIFE REFUGE

CAPULIN VOLCANO NATIONAL MONUMENT

KIOWA AND RITA BLANCA NATIONAL GRASSLANDS

OTHER NEW MEXICO SITES:
1. Bottomless Lakes State Park
2. Clayton Lake State Park
3. Fort Union National Monument
4. Las Vegas National Wildlife Refuge
5. Maxwell National Wildlife Refuge

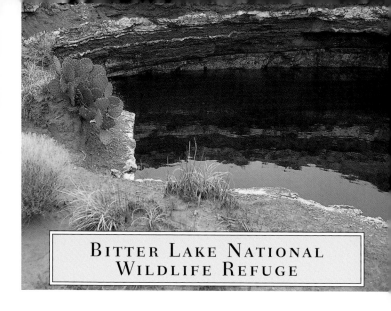

BITTER LAKE NATIONAL WILDLIFE REFUGE

"Rare" and "bizarre" are words that repeat endlessly in your mind on a visit to this place where the Chihuahuan Desert meets the shortgrass steppe. The playas, seeps, springs, and sinkholes in this semiarid land create unique small worlds where Barking Frogs, Pecos Pupfish, dragonflies, damselflies, tiny spring snails, and other wonders thrive.

More than 10,000 Sandhill Cranes, 20,000 Snow and Ross's Geese, and thousands of other waterfowl migrating along the Central Flyway overwinter on the playa lakes of this refuge, where 355 bird species have been recorded. The Federally endangered Interior Least Tern nests on the salt flats, its only breeding site in New Mexico. Snowy Plovers, Black-necked Stilts, and Scaled Quail also nest here.

The refuge is famous for its sinkholes, formed when underground water dissolves salt and gypsum deposits to create subterranean caverns. When the roofs collapse, the resultant cuplike basins range in depth from shallow puddles to 70-foot-deep Lake Francis. The surrounding vegetation, substrate, temperature, and water chemistry also vary. Some sinkholes are three times saltier than the ocean and contain green marine algae normally found in the Gulf of Mexico, while nearby sinkholes hold fresh water. Col-

Above: Brilliant red bluffs contrast with dark water at the Inkpot sinkhole in the wilderness section of Bitter Lake National Wildlife Refuge. (Photo by Glenn Cushman)

ors range from Caribbean turquoise to inkwell black. These intriguing pools shrink and expand as the Roswell artesian basin water table fluctuates.

Over millions of years, some invertebrates, such as Noel's Amphipod (a shrimplike crustacean) and several spring snails, became isolated in disconnected sinkholes and evolved in different ways, like Darwin's finches. However, when the refuge was established in 1937, the emphasis was on managing habitat for waterfowl and other migratory birds. Canals, built between sinkholes, shunted water into impoundments for the cranes and inadvertently ended species isolation. The canals are now silted in, so hybridizing is prevented and species uniqueness preserved.

The difference between playas and sinkholes is that playas are not formed by gypsum dissolution and tend to be bowl-shaped rather than straight-sided like most sinkholes. Generally, playas are filled from above by surface water; sinkholes are filled from below by ground water.

The largest playa was called "Bitter Lake" because of its alkaline water, and that became the name of this 24,536-acre refuge that encompasses three units along the Pecos River in eastern New Mexico. The 12,000-acre Salt Creek Wilderness, open for horseback riding and hiking, includes sinkholes, shortgrass prairie, sand dunes, orange cliffs, and brush bottomlands. The middle unit includes refuge headquarters, an 8-mile auto tour, and the Bitter Creek/Sago Springs research area. The southern unit, closed to public access, is planted to provide crops for overwintering birds.

Refuge staff attempt to eradicate the invasive tamarisk, or salt cedar, and conduct controlled burns to promote native grasses, such as Alkali Sacaton, Gyp Grama, and Black Grama. These warm-season bunchgrasses grow well in saline, gypsum soils not hospitable to most plants. Densely tufted sacaton growing up to 3 feet high is an eye-catcher in sparsely vegetated areas of the Southwest.

PECOS PUPFISH AND BARKING FROGS

Pecos Pupfish tolerate conditions that kill most fish. They can survive water above 100°F with high salinity and low oxygen content. Although other pupfish species are common throughout the Southwest, the Pecos Pupfish is now found only in the salty sinkholes of the refuge, at Bottomless Lakes State Park, and in backwater areas of the Pecos River. Less than 2 inches long, Pecos Pupfish are gray to brown except during breeding season, when males turn iridescent blue or purple. They are relics of the Pleistocene when Lake Otero filled the Pecos River Valley.

Although tolerant of harsh conditions, the Pecos Pupfish might succumb to a friendly relative. In the early 1980s an angler dumped a bucket of bait consisting of Sheepshead Minnows into the Pecos River. Female pupfish preferred the nonnative minnows to male pupfish, and the resultant hybrids quickly took over the Pecos River. By 1984 no pure Pecos Pupfish were found in the river.

Other unusual fish include Mexican Tetra, Greenthroat Darter, Pecos Bluntnose Shiner, and the endangered Pecos Gambusia. Most of the 26 fish species in the refuge are native to the Pecos River drainage.

Barking Frogs live in gypsum burrows or limestone crevices and are relicts from more than 200 million years ago. In spring or during the summer monsoon breeding season, the males yap like small dogs. Their amorous calls bounce off the burrow walls, making it hard to find the noisy suitors. This secretive ventriloquist protects himself by puffing up when attacked by a snake or other predator.

Greenish, tan, gray, and occasionally purplish in color, Barking Frogs look more like toads than frogs. They are also unusual in that froglets bypass the tadpole stage, hatching directly from eggs laid in moist underground microhabitats. In New Mexico, they live in only three counties and may be jeopardized by the lowering water table of the Pecos River. They also occur in extreme southern Arizona and from the Edwards Plateau in Texas south into Mexico.

DRAGONFLIES: AERIAL JEWELS

Two dragonflies form a wheel—or maybe a heart—as they fly above a reed-lined sinkhole. Often mating on the wing, with the male clasping the female behind her head, these delicate-looking insects have successfully propagated since Carboniferous times. Ancestral dragonflies pre-date dinosaurs by more than 100 million years, and some were giants, the largest insects ever known to fly. One fossil specimen has a wingspan of 30 inches.

Following the nuptial flight, the female deposits her eggs into water, floating debris, mud, or an aquatic plant. Some pairs continue flying in tandem while the female releases her eggs. Some females use their ovipositors to cut slits in plants where they insert the eggs.

Gilled larvae hatch in a few weeks and live underwater for several months to several years, depending on the species. During this stage they feed voraciously on other aquatic invertebrates, tadpoles, and fish spawn. After undergoing several instars (stages between molts), the nymph climbs up a plant stem out of the wa-

A male damselfly (front) clasps a female's head with his terminal abdominal appendages prior to mating.

ter. The exoskeleton splits, and an adult emerges. This event usually happens in early morning as temperatures rise; so rise early to see the magic of metamorphosis.

When the diaphanous wings expand and harden, the jewel-hued insects can fly up to 35 miles per hour. The wings can move independently, enabling dragonflies to hover and to fly backward, an ability useful in evading predators and in capturing prey, such as mosquitoes. Males perform territorial and courtship displays, often flashing body parts of metallic blue, red, or gold.

Bitter Lake National Wildlife Refuge may host the greatest diversity of dragonflies and damselflies in North America. Tropical dragonflies make up 69 percent of the species here, and some highly specialized species are found in only a single sinkhole. The world's largest known dragonfly and the largest damselfly, as well as the smallest dragonfly and the smallest damselfly, occur here.

Refuge researchers have identified 54 species bearing such evocative names as Firecracker Skimmer, Black Saddlebags, Halloween Pennant, Tiger Dragonlet, and Lace-winged Skimmer, which has been called the most beautiful dragonfly in the world.

IS IT A DRAGON OR A DAMSEL?

Dragonflies and damselflies are similar in appearance and are both members of the insect order Odonata. However, dragonflies are usually larger than damselflies, are stronger fliers, and have huge, compound eyes that often touch on top of the head. At rest, most dragonflies hold their wings almost horizontally, whereas damselflies fold their wings over the body.

Also called Medicine Bird, Snake Killer, and Paisano (fellow countryman), the Greater Roadrunner is revered in folklore. Because roadrunners can reach speeds of 18 miles per hour, the Tarahumara Indians, famed runners of Mexico, ate them, hoping to gain their speed and endurance, and the Hopis tied roadrunner feathers to their horses to invest them with such qualities.

Unlike most birds, roadrunners have two toes pointing forward and two back, making an ×-shaped track. Because the track does not show direction, many southwestern Indians used an "×" to confuse evil spirits. They drew ×'s around houses of the dead and hung roadrunner skins over lodges to ward off demons.

According to folk tales, the Snake Killer sometimes builds a Cholla corral around a snake and drops thorns on its head, making it thrash itself to death against the Cholla. The truth is strange enough: The roadrunner whacks a snake or lizard with its beak, then whams the stunned victim against the ground at a rate of about 21 slams per minute, sometimes continuing for 45 minutes.

Roadrunners also catch small mammals and birds and can even snag low-flying hummingbirds and White-throated Swifts. According to Janice Hughes in *The Birds of North America* (see Poole and Gill, p. 493), one adult was observed consuming 336 grasshoppers, 17 scorpions, 7 caterpillars, 39 moths, 14 centipedes, 14 angleworms, 18 spiders, 3 toads, 17 lizards, 1 mouse, and 35 other assorted tidbits during the course of one day.

A food offering is part of the courtship ritual for these monogamous birds. The male, food in beak, dances up to the female with crest erect, show-

A Greater Roadrunner perches on a fence post near the start of the auto tour at Bitter Lake National Wildlife Refuge. (Photo by Glenn Cushman)

ing off red and blue patches near his eyes. He alternates tail wagging with dignified bowing and then takes a flying leap onto her back. During copulation the female reaches up to take the food from the male. The nest, made of thorny sticks, is often built in Cholla or other thorny bushes. Hughes reports that lethargic nestlings are tossed into the air and swallowed whole by the parent or fed to healthier nestlings. Nature is not sentimental.

This member of the cuckoo family thrives in semiarid, open country with scattered brush from the southwestern United States to Mexico. Listen for its call, which sounds like a whimpering dog, around refuge headquarters.

HIKING

BUTTERFLY TRAIL (about a 0.5-mile loop) begins at refuge headquarters and includes a spur to a viewing platform near a spring. Signs identify plants that attract such butterflies as Painted Ladies, sulphurs, and Monarchs.

OXBOW TRAIL (0.3-mile loop) takes off between stops 3 and 4 on the auto tour and offers good birdwatching in a wetlands area.

BITTER LAKE BIKE TRAIL (2 miles one way) starts at headquarters and is good for hiking.

CAMPING

Camping is not permitted at the refuge. However, Bottomless Lakes State Park (see Other New Mexico Sites, p. 282) offers unusually attractive campsites.

BEST TIMES TO VISIT

Sandhill Crane and Snow Geese numbers peak between November and mid-February, and shorebirds migrate through in April. Interior Least Terns and other shorebirds nest in summer, and Barking Frogs chorus in July and August. The greatest dragonfly diversity occurs in August, and the rare Pecos Puzzle Sunflowers, adapted to alkaline wetlands, bloom from late August into September.

INFORMATION

BITTER LAKE NATIONAL WILDLIFE REFUGE, 4065 Bitter Lakes Road, Roswell, NM 88201; 505-6622-6755.

Take US 380 east from Roswell about 3 miles to refuge signs at Red Bridge Road, or take US 285 north to Pine Lodge Road and follow signs another 7 miles to refuge.

BITTER LAKE NATIONAL WILDLIFE REFUGE

WEATHER
MEAN TEMPERATURES AND PRECIPITATION

MONTH	HIGH (°F)	LOW (°F)	PRECIP.	SNOW
January	54	25	0.4"	2.8"
April	77	45	0.5"	0.3"
July	95	67	1.7"	0.0"
October	77	47	1.1"	0.2"

Mean annual precipitation is 12.7 inches. Most moisture falls from May through October. Summers are hot, but relative humidities remain low until the August monsoon season. Data are for Roswell, New Mexico.

SELECTED WILDLIFE OF SPECIAL INTEREST

MAMMALS: Brazilian Free-tailed Bat, Spotted Ground Squirrel, Black-tailed Prairie Dog, Silky Pocket Mouse, Ord's Kangaroo Rat, Pecos River Muskrat (a rare subspecies), Coyote, Kit Fox, Badger, Mule Deer, Pronghorn.

BIRDS: Snow Goose (m), Ross's Goose (m), Osprey, Peregrine Falcon, Scaled Quail, Sandhill Crane (m), Snowy Plover, Black-necked Stilt, Interior Least Tern, Yellow-billed Cuckoo, Greater Roadrunner, Burrowing Owl, Long-eared Owl.

AMPHIBIANS AND REPTILES: Barking Frog, Plains Leopard Frog, Plains Spadefoot, Eastern Collared Lizard, Great Plains Skink, Texas Horned Lizard, Western Diamond-backed Rattlesnake, Western Rattlesnake, Arid Land Ribbonsnake (state endangered subspecies of Western Ribbonsnake), Spiny Softshell, Ornate Box Turtle.

CAPULIN VOLCANO NATIONAL MONUMENT

Between 56,000 and 62,000 years ago, a volcanic eruption created a 1,300-foot-high cinder cone and spewed rivers of lava onto the surrounding plains. Capulin Mountain is one of several cinder cones scattered across northeastern New Mexico, products of a period of volcanic activity that spanned 9 million years. Although Capulin Volcano is extinct, the surrounding Raton-Clayton volcanic field is considered dormant, meaning that future eruptions are possible.

Cinder cones are created by the accumulation of loose cinders, ash, and other debris ejected from a volcano's main vent. Four lava flows surround Capulin Mountain and cover 16 square miles. Older tongues of lava to the north have created a network of conifer-studded mesas, including 50-mile-long Mesa de Maya (known in Oklahoma as Black Mesa), which extends from southeastern Colorado into northwestern Oklahoma.

The word *capulin* means "wild cherry" in Spanish, and fruiting shrubs thrive in the pine-juniper-oak woodlands that grow on the volcano and adjacent lava fields. Shortgrass prairie dominates the surrounding plains. Tallgrasses, including Big Bluestem, Indian Grass, and Switchgrass, sprout from rocky soils in and around the lava fields.

Above: Capulin Volcano and surrounding shortgrass prairie.

One of the most celebrated archaeological sites in North America lies nine miles north of the national monument along the Dry Cimarron River. In September 1908, the foreman of the Crowfoot Ranch found a large bone protruding from the side of a shallow ravine. Eighteen years later scientists at the Colorado Museum of Natural History determined that this bone and others in the ravine were those of an extinct giant bison. When Raton blacksmith Carl Schwachleim returned to the site in 1927, he found several distinctive spear points embedded among the bones.

Radiocarbon tests dated the site at more than 10,000 years before the present, fully 7,000 years older than any previously discovered human site in North America. Its inhabitants were named Folsom Man after the nearby hamlet of Folsom. The archaeological site is not open to the public, but a small museum in Folsom houses displays on local history and culture.

TREES ON LAVA

From the top of Capulin Mountain it's easy to discern where the lava flows oozed out from the base of the cone. Near the mountain, these flows are covered with a dense woodland of pines, junipers, and scrub oaks whose dark green color contrasts with the pale hues of the surrounding shortgrass prairie.

The tenacious, spreading root systems of these trees and shrubs enable them to cling to and extract moisture from the hard black lava. Some tallgrasses also thrive on these lava flows, using their deep root systems to tap water-filled fissures in the rock.

The dominant trees and shrubs in these complex woodlands include Piñon Pine, Ponderosa Pine, Rocky Mountain Juniper, One-Seeded Juniper, Gambel Oak, and Wavy-Leaf Oak. Most of these species periodically produce bountiful seed or acorn crops that attract a diversity of birds and mammals, including Rock Squirrels, Colorado Chipmunks, Mexican Woodrats, Mule Deer, Wild Turkeys, and Western Scrub-Jays.

During years of abundant Piñon Pine seed crops, Pinyon Jays and Clark's Nutcrackers flock to the pines to harvest the large protein-rich seeds. The nutcrackers store two dozen or more seeds in a sublingual pouch and carry them as far as 20 miles to caching areas where they bury the seeds in the ground. Each nutcracker may cache up to 100,000 seeds per year in hundreds of different locations, using visual clues (rocks, trees, and other landmarks) to find its way back to these caches. The jays also cache seeds. Some seeds are inevitably left in the ground to germinate, enabling the pines to colonize new areas and creating expanded foraging habitat for the jays and nutcrackers.

While Piñon Pines benefit from the harvesting of some of their seeds, they can be damaged by over-harvest of their needles and bark by Porcupines, Mule Deer, and squirrels. The pungent, turpentine-like aromas produced by Piñon Pines result from volatilization of ethyl caprylates. These naturally occurring toxins protect the trees' foliage from browsing mammals and may also limit growth of competing grasses and shrubs. Juniper berries also contain toxins, called terpenes, that protect their fruits from over-harvest by birds and mammals.

PORCUPINES

Some of the Piñon Pines and junipers along the Crater Rim Trail show signs of Porcupine damage where these bark-eating rodents have gnawed on branches and trunks. Porcupines have an amazing capacity to thrive in isolated habitats. Throughout the Great Plains, Porcupines live on islands of conifers or deciduous trees that are encircled by miles of treeless grasslands.

Although the cambium, or inner bark, of conifers and deciduous trees makes up a major portion of their diet, Porcupines cannot survive on bark alone. In spring and summer they munch on wildflowers, fresh buds, mushrooms, and other delicacies, acquiring the fat they need to see them through winter.

Young (usually one per female) are born in the spring, typically in a den under a log, shrub, or rock. Within a few hours baby Porcupines can move around on their own, following their mother on her foraging rounds. During their first few weeks of life they feed on their mother's milk and on easily digested items, including flowers, willow catkins, mushrooms, and pond lilies. They learn to climb trees at an early age, using long claws and padded feet for gripping and stout tails for anchoring.

As Porcupines quietly make their evening rounds, they often seem oblivious to discreet human observers. (Photo by Glenn Cushman)

At dusk look for Porcupines as they waddle purposely through the woodlands, sniffing their way from tree to tree. At night listen for their soft grunts and childlike wails. During the day you might see a ball of prickly fur perched near the top of a Ponderosa or Piñon Pine.

CONVERGENT LADYBUGS

In early summer, thousands of Convergent Ladybird Beetles gather on shrubs, trees, and rocks around the crater rim. From a distance some of the the rock and tree trunk surfaces appear solid orange. By October many of these beetles will have crawled into cracks and crevices in the bark of junipers and Piñon Pines to overwinter. Others will have died, their desiccated exoskeletons scattered among the rocks.

Biologists don't fully understand why some ladybugs aggregate on mountain peaks. The same phenomenon occurs in the Colorado Rockies, the Sierra Nevada, and the Swiss Alps. Assuming natural selection determines where the largest aggregations occur, ladybugs wintering on mountaintops must enjoy a degree of success. Perhaps a relative lack of predators in these locations compensates for the effects of more severe weather conditions. Winter aggregation may help the beetles to conserve moisture and must make it easier for them to find mates when they emerge from hibernation in spring.

The Convergent Ladybird Beetle (*Hippodamia convergens*), one of hundreds of North American ladybug species, gets its name from the converging white lines on its thorax. Females lay several hundred eggs on leaves and twigs. Larvae and adults feed on aphids, scale insects, and mites. As spring and summer progress,

Convergent Ladybird Beetles gather by the thousands on Capulin Volcano's crater rim in summer.

adults may follow emerging aphid populations upslope toward mountain hibernation sites.

Some ladybug overwintering sites have been compromised by people who collect handfuls of beetles for use in their gardens. This practice disrupts the ladybugs' life cycle and offers no particular benefit to gardeners, since the relocated beetles usually disperse or head back up toward the mountaintops.

HIKING

CRATER TRAIL (0.2 miles) drops down to the plugged vent in the center of the crater.

CRATER RIM TRAIL (1 mile) starts at the crater rim parking area and encircles the crater. Look for ladybugs in summer and Porcupines and Golden Eagles year-round.

LAVA FLOW TRAIL (1 mile) starts at the visitor center and crosses lava flows to the picnic area.

There is a short nature trail behind the visitor center.

CAMPING

The closest public campgrounds are at Sugarite Canyon State Park, 30 miles northwest on SR 72, Maxwell National Wildlife Refuge, 50 miles southwest on I-25, and Clayton Lake State Park, 50 miles east off US 64/87.

BEST TIMES TO VISIT

Lupines, milk vetches, and paintbrushes bloom and ladybird beetles gather on the crater rim in late May and early June. Flocks of Mountain Bluebirds pass through in midspring and early fall. In October the oak and piñon-juniper woodlands come alive with sound and activity as Rock Squirrels, Colorado Chipmunks, and flocks of jays harvest acorns and pine nuts.

INFORMATION

CAPULIN VOLCANO NATIONAL MONUMENT, Box 40, Capulin, NM 88414; 505-278-2201. The road from the visitor center to the summit is open during daylight hours only.

HOW TO GET THERE

From Raton, New Mexico, take US 64 east for 27 miles and then go north for 2 miles on SR 325.

CAPULIN VOLCANO NATIONAL MONUMENT

WEATHER
MEAN TEMPERATURE AND PRECIPITATION

MONTH	HIGH (°F)	LOW (°F)	PRECIP.	SNOW
January	45	12	0.3"	6.0"
April	63	30	0.9"	2.4"
July	85	54	2.5"	0.0"
October	69	33	1.2"	1.1"

Mean annual precipitation is 13.47 inches. Severe thunderstorms can occur during July and August. Winters are dry and mild. Data are for Raton, New Mexico, which is 25 miles west of the national monument.

SELECTED WILDLIFE OF SPECIAL INTEREST

MAMMALS: Colorado Chipmunk, Rock Squirrel, Porcupine, Coyote, Black Bear, Bobcat, Mule Deer.

BIRDS: Golden Eagle, Prairie Falcon, Wild Turkey, Common Nighthawk, Black-chinned Hummingbird, Broad-tailed Hummingbird, Cassin's Kingbird, Western Scrub-Jay, Pinyon Jay, Chihuahuan Raven, Juniper Titmouse, Blue-gray Gnatcatcher, Mountain Bluebird, Virginia's Warbler, Western Tanager, Canyon Towhee, Black-headed Grosbeak.

AMPHIBIANS AND REPTILES: Eastern Fence Lizard, Eastern Collared Lizard, Greater Short-horned Lizard, Western Rattlesnake, Bullsnake.

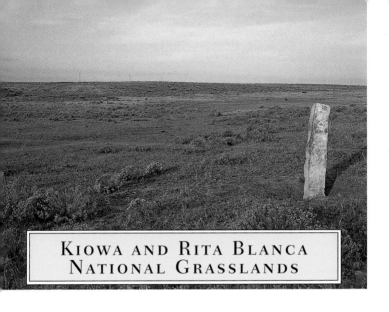

KIOWA AND RITA BLANCA NATIONAL GRASSLANDS

Cholla cactus and old-growth Ponderosa Pine, North American Pronghorn and Barbary Sheep, gaping canyons and some of the flattest land on earth—these jointly managed national grasslands offer a bit of everything.

Rita Blanca National Grassland and the eastern section of Kiowa National Grassland straddle the New Mexico–Texas border just north of the *Llano Estacado* (Staked Plains). Today these lands, which were devastated during the Dust Bowl droughts, are devoted to cattle ranching. But native mixed-grass prairie has slowly come back, along with Black-tailed Prairie Dogs, Long-billed Curlews, and Burrowing Owls. North of Clayton, New Mexico, you can hike in swales worn by wagons traveling the Santa Fe Trail or observe dinosaur footprints made 100 million years ago.

The western section of Kiowa National Grassland encompasses the 800-foot-deep Canadian River canyon (Mills Canyon) and adjacent tablelands in east-central New Mexico. Mills Canyon and a dozen rugged side canyons contain red sandstone cliffs, dripping springs, homestead ruins, and yawning rock shelters marked with pictographs. The jade green Canadian River meanders through thickets of cottonwood, willow, and tamarisk. Piñon Pines grow in

Above: Santa Fe Trail marker north of Clayton.

the canyon bottom, and statuesque Ponderosa Pines cling to rock outcrops on the canyon rim. Up on the juniper-studded mesa tops, a carpet of Buffalo Grass and Blue Grama extends westward 30 miles toward the snowcapped Sangre de Cristo Mountains.

MILLS CANYON

In 1881 Melvin Mills, a rancher, attorney, and territorial legislator, built a two-story rock house/hotel in this steep-walled canyon. During his 35 years of farming and ranching in the canyon, Mills planted extensive orchards of peach, apricot, quince, pear, apple, and a half-dozen other fruits.

The orchards and part of the house were washed away by a 1904 flood that also destroyed farmland and homesteads up and down the river. Mills lost not only his canyon home, but also a 20-room mansion in the nearby town of Springer when the bank foreclosed on his holdings. He founded the town of Mills a few years later, but the orchards and canyon ranch never returned to their former glory.

Today Mills Canyon is home to Wild Turkeys, Western Screech-Owls, Elk, Mountain Lions, and an occasional Black Bear, along with Barbary Sheep that were introduced by hunters during the 1950s. Melvin Mills died in 1925, but the ruins of his once stately home still bake in the New Mexico sun a half-mile east of the Mills Canyon campground.

Mills Canyon, carved by the Canadian River, is rich with wildlife and historic artifacts.

"Far away from my wife and child, and six hundred miles of constant danger in an uninhabited region was not a pleasant prospect for contemplation. But I laughed with the rest, joked about roasting our bacon with buffalo chips, and the enjoyment we would derive from the company of skeletons that would strew our pathway." —Hezekiah Brake, 1858

From 1821 until after the Civil War, the Santa Fe Trail linked the United States to Spanish and Indian settlements in the Southwest. American trade goods, Mexican silver and mules, immigrants and explorers all inched their way along this ribbon of wagon ruts and denuded prairie that traversed the southern plains from Missouri to Santa Fe.

Near Cimmaron, Kansas, the trail westward split in two. The original trail, known as the Cimmaron Route, followed the Cimmaron River through what is now southwestern Kansas, the Oklahoma Panhandle, and northeastern New Mexico. The Mountain Route followed the Arkansas River into present-day Colorado and then veered south across Raton Pass.

Cimmaron, Comanche, and Kiowa National Grasslands contain more than 30 miles of trail segments. In many places wagon ruts and swales created by years of travel are still visible. The trail route is marked with stone pillars, and in some areas grasses have been mown to accommodate hikers.

CLIFF-NESTING RAPTORS

Golden Eagles and Prairie Falcons nest on cliff faces in the Canadian River canyon and along the Cimmaron River north of Clayton. Throughout the year these and other raptors glide over the grasslands searching for prey.

During courtship in late winter and early spring, male eagles perform a roller-coaster flight, swooping and soaring over their mates. Pairs sometimes lock talons in midair, tumbling eagle over eagle toward the ground. These aerial antics constitute part of an "audition" during which the male proves his fitness as a hunter and territorial defender.

In late February or early March, females lay 2 or 3 eggs in a bulky stick nest, usually placed on a ledge or hollow of a sheer cliff. A pair of eagles may construct several nests on a single cliff face, rotating from one nest to another from year to year. Some nests are used off and on by various pairs for centuries. The young hatch out in April or May and leave the nest in early summer. On average one fledgling survives its first few months of life.

A young Golden Eagle calls from its nest high on a cliff face.

Prairie Falcons return to nesting cliffs in early spring. They usually lay their eggs right on the rock, either on a ledge or in a small cave or pothole. These easily visible nests are vulnerable to predation by ravens and Great Horned Owls, so Prairie Falcons spend much of the nesting season swooping over their territories while emitting piercing screams. The screams are audible from a mile or more away, and conspicuous splotches of whitewash (excrement) mark areas where the adults nest or perch.

Breeding populations of Golden Eagles and Prairie Falcons appear to be stable on the western plains. However, numbers have declined near urban areas, where recreationists have disturbed nest sites and urban sprawl has eliminated hunting areas. Many young eagles die from electrocution on power lines or collisions with automobiles.

ROVING TARANTULAS

On warm August and September evenings it isn't unusual to see multitudes of Texas Brown Tarantulas crossing highways throughout eastern New Mexico, southeastern Colorado, and the Texas Panhandle. Most of these hairy, saucer-sized spiders are males out searching for mates. These males are so single-minded

In late summer and early fall male Texas Brown Tarantulas searching for mates plod across highways in northern Texas, New Mexico, and southeastern Colorado.

in their quest that virtually nothing will stop them, including your boot or even your hand. They pose no great danger to humans; this species is docile by nature and its poison not much stronger than that of a wasp.

Tarantulas typically live in burrows, emerging to hunt small insects. When the adults are not out hunting or cruising for mates, you can sometimes see them resting in dark places such as the eaves and inside walls of barns and deserted buildings. In fall the female lays several hundred eggs in a sack woven from web silk. Each hatchling tarantula is no larger than the head of a pin.

HIKING

There are no designated hiking trails, but the mesa tops and flat-bottomed canyons invite cross-country travel.

SANTA FE NATIONAL HISTORIC TRAIL. You can walk several miles along the old trail route, navigating from one stone trail marker to another. From 3 miles east of Clayton on US 56/64, drive 12 miles north on SR 406 and turn left where the highway jogs to the east. Go 3 miles west, then 1 mile north to the picnic area.

MILLS CANYON. From the campground, you can bushwhack upstream or downstream for miles, following grassy benches on either side of the river. See directions, below, under Camping.

CAMPING

Dispersed camping is permitted throughout both national grasslands.

MILLS CANYON CAMPGROUND. This primitive campground lies at the bottom of the canyon along the river and is shaded by cottonwoods. From SR 39 at Mills turn west on Mills Canyon Road and continue for 9 miles. The last 3 miles require a high-clearance vehicle.

THOMPSON GROVE PICNIC AREA. Located on the Texas side in Rita Blanca, this picnic area lies in a grove of Siberian Elms within a relatively large block of recovering grasslands. From Texline, Texas, go 14 miles northeast on SR 296.

CLAYTON LAKE STATE PARK. Located 15 miles northwest of Clayton on SR 370, this lakeside park has developed campgrounds and a short trail leading to a 100-million-year-old dinosaur trackway.

BEST TIMES TO VISIT

Temperatures are usually pleasant and the grasslands nearly deserted in late fall and late winter. Migrating warblers, tanagers, and flycatchers flock to the riparian vegetation along the Canadian River in May. Pronghorn fawns are born in late May and early June. The Texas Panhandle region can be hot and windy during the summer months, but frequent thunderstorms in July and August create mesmerizing cloud and light effects. Tarantulas wander across the highways looking for mates from late August through early October.

INFORMATION

KIOWA AND RITA BLANCA NATIONAL GRASSLANDS, 714 Main Street, Clayton, NM 88415; 505-374-9652.

HOW TO GET THERE

From Clayton, New Mexico, go north on SR 406 or east on US 56 or 87 and explore on county roads. To reach the western parcel of Kiowa National Grassland, drive west 63 miles on US 56 and south 15 miles on SR 39 to Mills, and explore on county roads. **NOTE:** Because protected grassland parcels are widely dispersed, you will need a Kiowa and Rita Blanca National Grasslands map, available at the Clayton office, to find your way around.

KIOWA AND RITA BLANCA NATIONAL GRASSLANDS

WEATHER
MEAN TEMPERATURE AND PRECIPITATION

MONTH	HIGH (°F)	LOW (°F)	PRECIP.	SNOW
January	47	19	0.2"	3.8
April	66	37	0.9"	1.9"
July	88	61	2.7"	0.0"
October	69	41	0.9"	0.7"

Mean annual precipitation is 15.3 inches. The record high is 105°F, the record low −21°F. July and August thunderstorms can make primitive roads impassable. Data are for Clayton, New Mexico; the Mills Canyon area is slightly cooler and wetter.

SELECTED WILDLIFE OF SPECIAL INTEREST

MAMMALS: Black-tailed Jackrabbit, Coyote, Swift Fox, *Black Bear, Badger, *Mountain Lion, *Elk, Mule Deer, Pronghorn, *Barbary Sheep.

BIRDS: Swainson's Hawk, Ferruginous Hawk, Golden Eagle, Prairie Falcon, Wild Turkey, Scaled Quail, Long-billed Curlew, Greater Roadrunner, Western Screech-Owl, Burrowing Owl, Ladder-backed Woodpecker, Vermilion Flycatcher, Canyon Wren, *Hepatic Tanager, Lark Bunting, Blue Grosbeak.

AMPHIBIANS AND REPTILES: Eastern Collared Lizard, Texas Horned Lizard, Western Rattlesnake, Bullsnake, Western Ribbonsnake.

*Mills Canyon area only

BOTTOMLESS LAKES STATE PARK (HC 12, Box 1200, Roswell, NM 88201; 505-624-6058). Seven sinkholes filled with deep blue-green water are the main attractions of this park that also has orange-red bluffs, salt flats, and prairie grasses. Swimming and scuba diving are permitted in Lea Lake, largest of the sinkholes. Camping, hiking. Located 12 miles east of Roswell on US 380, then a short distance south on SR 409.

CLAYTON LAKE STATE PARK (Rural Route, Box 20, Seneca, NM 88437; 505-374-8808). More than 500 dinosaur footprints made by 8 different species are visible on an ancient mudflat. The park includes rolling grasslands, volcanic rocks, and sandstone bluffs. Camping, hiking, swimming, and boating. Fifteen miles northwest of Clayton on SR 370.

FORT UNION NATIONAL MONUMENT (Watrous, NM 87753; 505-425-8025). Erected in 1851 to protect travelers along the Cimarron Cutoff of the Santa Fe Trail, this fort was the largest in New Mexico territory. Trail ruts are still visible. Located 26 miles north of Las Vegas on SR 161.

LAS VEGAS NATIONAL WILDLIFE REFUGE (Route 1, Box 399, Las Vegas, NM 87701; 505-425-3581). This 8,672-acre conifer-savanna (*las vegas* means "meadows" or "fields" in Spanish) protects winter and migration habitat for ducks, geese, Sandhill Cranes, and other birds. Hiking trails. From I-25 Exit 345, go east on SR 104 for 1.5 miles, then south on SR 281 for 4 miles.

MAXWELL NATIONAL WILDLIFE REFUGE (Box 276, Maxwell, NM 87728; 505-375-2331). Three water storage impoundments surrounded by 2,800 acres of mixed-grass prairie and farmland attract migrating waterfowl and raptors, including American White Pelicans, Trumpeter Swans, Snow Geese, and Bald Eagles. Camping and boating. Located 28 miles south of Raton off I-25.

Bottomless Lakes State Park offers delightful camping around several sinkholes, including the Devils's Inkwell. (Photo by Glenn Cushman)

NORTH DAKOTA

Des Lacs
Kenmare
Little Missouri NG Lostwood
Williston
Minot
Watford City Lake Sakakawea
Theodore Roosevelt National Park
Cross Ranch
Medora
Belfield
Mandan Bismarck
Cannonball R.
Cedar R.
Little Missouri
Souris (Mouse) R.
Denhoff
Medina
Sheyenne R.
James R.
Sheyenne NG
Lisbon McLeod
Cayuga
Missouri R.

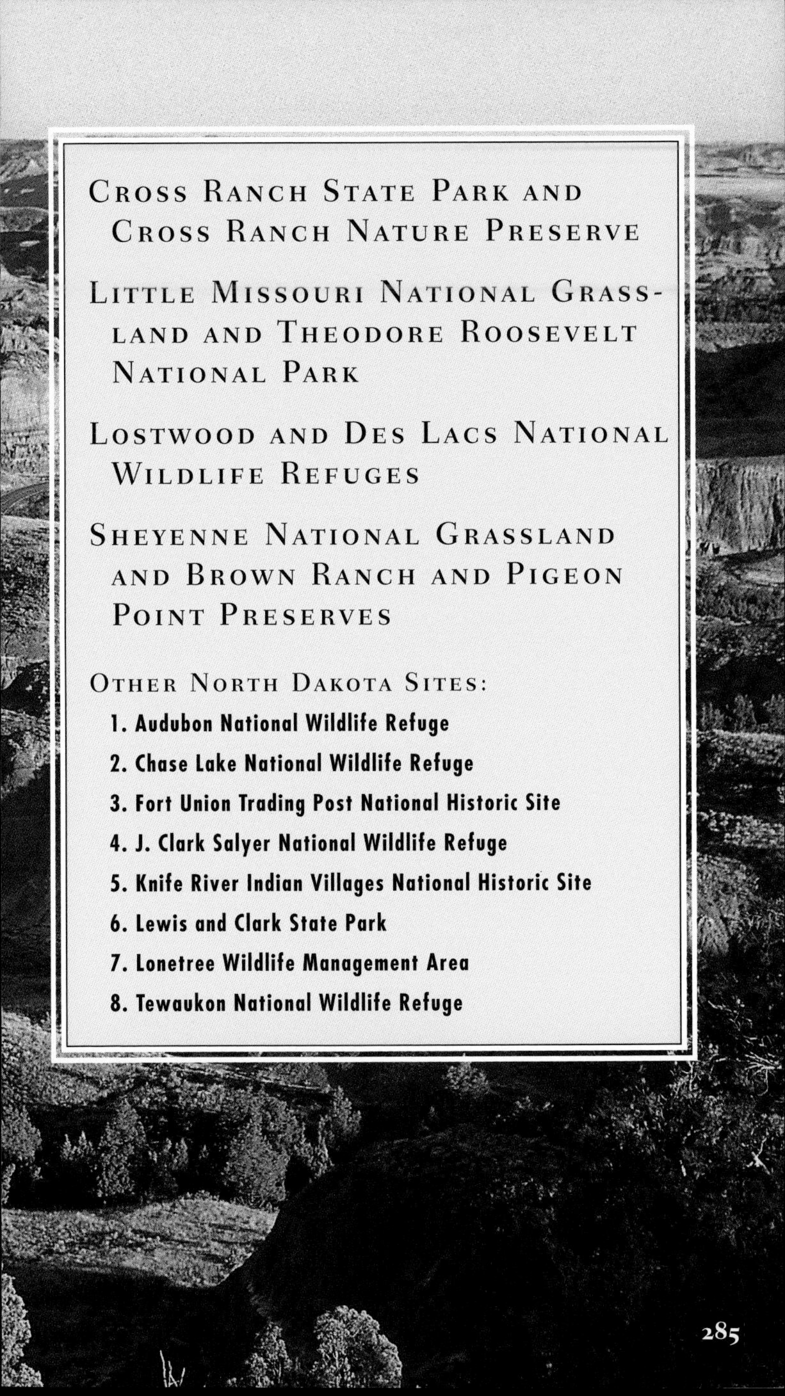

CROSS RANCH STATE PARK AND
  CROSS RANCH NATURE PRESERVE

LITTLE MISSOURI NATIONAL GRASS-
  LAND AND THEODORE ROOSEVELT
  NATIONAL PARK

LOSTWOOD AND DES LACS NATIONAL
  WILDLIFE REFUGES

SHEYENNE NATIONAL GRASSLAND
  AND BROWN RANCH AND PIGEON
  POINT PRESERVES

OTHER NORTH DAKOTA SITES:
  1. Audubon National Wildlife Refuge
  2. Chase Lake National Wildlife Refuge
  3. Fort Union Trading Post National Historic Site
  4. J. Clark Salyer National Wildlife Refuge
  5. Knife River Indian Villages National Historic Site
  6. Lewis and Clark State Park
  7. Lonetree Wildlife Management Area
  8. Tewaukon National Wildlife Refuge

CROSS RANCH STATE PARK AND CROSS RANCH NATURE PRESERVE

From the wide Missouri River to floodplain forests to the crest of grass-covered hills, the Cross Ranch area inspires peace. As we listened to owls and Coyotes and watched sunset reflections in the river on September 12, 2001, it was hard to imagine how such horror could have happened the previous day. September 11 is seared into our national memory, but nature can help heal. The Mandan and Hidatsa people, who lived in this area, were nearly exterminated by smallpox during the nineteenth century. Their three-word poem offers solace:

Earth

Always

Endures

The Nature Conservancy, committed to global preservation of natural diversity, purchased the Cross Ranch in 1982 and later donated part of it to North Dakota for a state park. The 6,000-

Above: Mixed-grass prairie and dense shrublands cover glacial moraines at Cross Ranch Nature Preserve.

acre nature preserve and the 589-acre park are connected by hiking trails.

The Missouri River, focal point of the park, shaped the landscape. When glaciers blocked the flow of the river to Hudson Bay, it cut a new route to the south. Over time, floodplain terraces formed, some of which now rise 50 feet above the river. Willows, Plains Cottonwoods, Green Ashes, Box Elders, American Elms, and Bur Oaks cover these terraces, providing winter roosting places for Bald Eagles, as well as cover for Wild Turkeys and White-tailed Deer. Migrating Whooping and Sandhill Cranes, Least Terns, Piping Plovers, and Canada Geese rest and forage on the sandbars.

Big and Little Bluestem, Blue Grama, wheatgrasses, and needlegrasses create a mosaic of colors and textures that Meriwether Lewis called a "handsome high prairie." Ephemeral streams cut through the hills, providing moist microhabitats where deciduous trees and shrubs thrive.

BERRIES OF THE PRAIRIE

The woody draws of Cross Ranch support many different shrubs whose berries attract wildlife. Silver Buffaloberry and snowberry are common throughout the northern Great Plains and grow abundantly at both the nature preserve and the state park.

The brilliant, crimson Buffaloberry fruit is almost translucent and resembles rubies when backlit, contrasting with the gray-green leaves covered in silvery scales. Also called Bullberry and *graise de boeuf*, the berries were formerly relished by Bison, bears, and wolves. Other mammals, birds, and people also like this sweet-sour treat that makes tasty jams, jellies, and pies. After the first frost, the berries become sweeter and are good eaten fresh.

Ethnobotanist Kelly Kindscher reports widespread use of these berries by various Plains Indian tribes. The Blackfoot sometimes mashed them in a buffalo horn and drank the juice, the Assiniboin sometimes added them to a meat broth, and many tribes dried them for winter use. The Dakota used them, along with Chokecherries, in ceremonies honoring a girl reaching puberty.

Painter George Catlin enjoyed a pudding made by the Mandans from Prairie Turnip flour and flavored with Buffaloberries. In his journals he described the shrub as "the most beautiful ornament that decks out the wild prairies." He and his traveling friends even made Buffaloberry wine. Using the same method employed by Plains Indians, they placed a blanket under the bushes and struck the shrub with a club, sometimes getting an eighth of a bushel of berries at a blow.

Buffaloberries (Shepherdia argentea) *turn translucent red in August.*

Snowberry, also called buckbrush, ranges from the prairies to the mountains and is sometimes used as an ornamental in landscaping. The pinkish bell-shaped flowers are followed by white berries that remain on the branches through winter. Some birds and mammals eat the fruit and seek cover under the canopy. Dakota Indians used the stems and roots as a survival food, the fruit as a cathartic and laxative and the roots for a tea to treat colds and stomachaches. Several American Indian tribes used the wood for bows and arrows.

Other attractive fruit-bearing plants that flourish on the prairie include Skunkbrush, Saskatoon Serviceberry, Prairie Rose, Chokecherry, hawthorn, and Wild Plum. Poison ivy, with flaming scarlet and orange leaves in autumn and rather dull yellowish berries, also grows profusely in the draws.

MOUNDS, EARTHLODGES, AND HOMESTEADS

Mandan, Hidatsa, and Arikara village sites, found in both the preserve and the park, contain vestiges of rectilinear lodges thought to date back to the twelfth century and round earthlodges similar to the ones in use when Lewis and Clark overwintered at Fort Mandan in 1804. A reconstructed earthlodge, numerous depressions showing where a village once stood, and excellent exhibits can be seen at nearby Knife River Indian Villages on the Fort Berthold Reservation.

In 1882 the Bagnell Family homesteaded in the Missouri River Valley. A. D. Gaines, a land agent for the Northern Pacific Railroad, began ranching in the 1890s and later absorbed the Bagnell homestead and others to form one of the largest ranches in the state. Gaines later purchased Teddy Roosevelt's Maltese cross brand, and subsequent owners Robert and Gladys Levis named the place Cross Ranch in honor of that brand. The nature trail at the preserve passes two old cemeteries and the foundations of the Bagnell house and outbuildings.

HIKING AND BOATING

Cross Ranch Nature Preserve:

WOODY DRAW TRAIL (0.75-mile loop) and River View Trail (2-mile loop) wind through prairies, woody draws, and Bison pastures. The longer loop offers panoramic views of the Missouri River. These two intersecting loops start at a trailhead about a mile north of the park entrance, where you can pick up a brochure.

Cross Ranch State Park:

MATAH ("RIVER") TRAIL (2.6 miles for outer loop; 2.1 miles for inner loop) begins at the park visitor center and follows the river shoreline.

MA-AK-OTI ("OLD VILLAGE") TRAIL (3-mile loop) connects the visitor center to the Sanger picnic shelter. The upper section traverses river bluffs with views of the abandoned town of Sanger, and the lower section follows the floodplain. A short spur from the shelter goes to the boat ramp.

COTTONWOOD TRAIL (3-mile loop); Bison Trail (2.1-mile loop); and Bob Levis Trail (2.3-mile loop) extend north from the end of the Matah Trail and wind through bottomland forests.

All types of boating are popular on the Missouri River.

CAMPING

Camping is not permitted at the Cross Ranch Nature Preserve. However, Cross Ranch State Park offers shaded campsites along the banks of the Missouri River. In addition to sites for recreational vehicles, tent-only and hike-in sites offer privacy. Log cabins are available for rent.

BEST TIMES TO VISIT

Sharp-tailed Grouse dance on leks scattered throughout the preserve in early spring. Bison calves are born in the nature preserve from May through July. Berries start ripening in July and continue through September, when cottonwoods, ashes, elms, and understory shrubs flame into shades of gold and scarlet. Ten miles of park trails are groomed for ski touring, and snow lovers can find solitude in winter.

INFORMATION

CROSS RANCH NATURE PRESERVE, The Nature Conservancy, 1401 River Road, Center, ND 58530; 701-795-8741.

CROSS RANCH STATE PARK, 1403 River Road, Center, ND 58530; 701-794-3731; Reservations 1-800-807-4723. River Peoples Visitor Center, near the park entrance, has exhibits and information on both the nature preserve and the park.

HOW TO GET THERE

Cross Ranch State Park is 35 miles north of Mandan. Five miles west of Mandan, turn north off I-94 onto SR 25 and follow the brown state park signs. The Nature Conservancy headquarters are a half-mile south of the park on the west side of the road. Watch for yellow TNC signs.

Gaines family cemetery on hilltop overlooking the Missouri River. (Photo by Glenn Cushman)

CROSS RANCH STATE PARK AND
CROSS RANCH NATURE PRESERVE

WEATHER
MEAN TEMPERATURE AND PRECIPITATION

MONTH	HIGH (°F)	LOW (°F)	PRECIP.	SNOW
January	20	-2	0.5"	7.6"
April	55	31	1.7"	4.0"
July	84	56	2.1"	0.0"
October	59	33	0.9"	1.8"

Mean annual precipitation is 15.5 inches. Record high and low temperatures range from 109°F to -44°F. Spring cold fronts create windy conditions from February through May. Data are for Bismarck, North Dakota.

SELECTED WILDLIFE OF SPECIAL INTEREST

MAMMALS: White-tailed Jackrabbit, Wyoming Ground Squirrel, Thirteen-lined Ground Squirrel, Northern Grasshopper Mouse, Southern Red-backed Vole, Coyote, Long-tailed Weasel, Least Weasel, Mink, Badger, Mule Deer, White-tailed Deer, Pronghorn, Bison.

BIRDS: Wood Duck, Sharp-tailed Grouse, Wild Turkey, Upland Sandpiper, Red-headed Woodpecker, Western Kingbird, Eastern Kingbird, Eastern Bluebird, Gray Catbird, Brown Thrasher, Sprague's Pipit, Field Sparrow, Lark Sparrow, Baird's Sparrow, Black-headed Grosbeak, Bobolink.

AMPHIBIANS AND REPTILES: Northern Leopard Frog, Tiger Salamander, Smooth Green Snake, Bullsnake, Snapping Turtle.

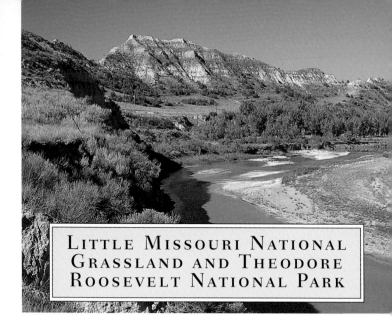

LITTLE MISSOURI NATIONAL GRASSLAND AND THEODORE ROOSEVELT NATIONAL PARK

Hundreds of buffalo once again roam in Theodore Roosevelt National Park, where the Little Missouri River cuts through colorful, eroded badlands and mixed-grass prairies. Established in honor of one of our most conservation-minded presidents, this park forms the heart of the million-acre Little Missouri National Grassland —largest of all the national grasslands.

Theodore Roosevelt created the United States Forest Service, which oversees the national grasslands, and also signed the Antiquities Act, allowing him to create 18 National Monuments. "There are no words that can tell the hidden spirit of the wilderness, that can reveal its mystery, its melancholy, and its charm," he said of this rugged land he loved so much.

The park is divided into a north unit, a south unit, and the Elkhorn Ranch unit containing the undeveloped site of Roosevelt's ranch. Almost 30,000 acres of designated wilderness, a network of hiking trails, and scenic drives with views of the river, the badlands, and wildlife are prime attractions.

Little Missouri National Grassland includes a 58-mile Wildlife and Scenic Tour of the Medora District (the southern portion of the grassland) keyed to a brochure available at the Medora Visitor

Above: Little Missouri River.

Center. Sharp-tailed Grouse leks, a plateau where Bighorn Sheep often graze, Golden Eagle nests, prairie dog colonies, petrified tree stumps, and the historic Custer Trail are featured on the drive. Bullion Butte, a 3,358-foot sandstone hill seen from the road, dominates an area being considered for wilderness designation.

In the northern half of the grassland, the McKenzie District includes Sather Lake and many buttes and badlands. Two parcels border Lake Sakakawea and the Fort Berthold Indian Reservation.

MEGAFAUNA

Bison returned to Theodore Roosevelt National Park in 1956 when 29 animals from Fort Niobrara National Wildlife Refuge were released. Now about 500 graze in the park. (See Custer State Park, South Dakota, for more information about Bison.)

Audubon Bighorn Sheep were common in the area until the late 1800s, when hunting and settlement drastically reduced their numbers and caused their extinction by 1905. In 1956 California Bighorn Sheep from British Columbia were introduced. The Bighorn population now numbers around 250. One of the best viewing sites is Moody Plateau, along the Wildlife and Scenic Tour in the Medora District of the grassland.

Wild horses in the badlands probably descended from animals turned loose in the 1930s and 1940s by ranchers who could no longer afford to feed them. The park now maintains a herd of 70 to 140. To prevent overgrazing, excess horses are rounded up every few years and sold at public auction. Good viewing points are from Painted Canyon Overlook or from the top of Buck Hill in the

By early June, Bison calves begin to show signs of independence.

south unit of the park. (See Bighorn Canyon National Recreation Area, Montana, for more information about wild horses.)

Deer and Elk are abundant in both the park and the grassland. In addition to the wild ungulates, some 54,000 cattle graze the national grassland.

PETRIFIED WOOD, FOSSILS, SCORIA, AND MORE

The Rocky Mountain uplift and the subsequent washing down of sediments to form an alluvial plain set the stage for the dramatic scenery of today's badlands, which are primarily sedimentary rock eroded into strange and wonderful formations. The bands of beige, salmon, maroon, and gray indicate different eras when various sediments were deposited.

The climate was subtropical 55 million years ago, and the area that is now the Little Missouri National Grassland was a swampy floodplain where turtles, crocodiles, alligators, and Champsosaurs (similar to crocodiles) lived. More than 200 sites, mostly in the Sentinel Butte and Bullion Creek Formations, also contain fossilized fish, snails, and clams.

Forests thrived in this moist environment, and many fallen trees were covered with flood deposits or volcanic ash that slowed decay. Eventually, silica-rich volcanic ash soaked into the trees, replacing the organic material with small quartz crystals. Some petrified stumps are 7 to 8 feet in diameter and are so well preserved that growth rings are still visible. Paleontologists have identified redwood, cypress, sycamore, ginkgo, and magnolia trees.

Other fallen trees were subjected to pressure from overlying sediments that converted the wood into soft coal or lignite. Lignite lends colors and shapes to the landscape when lightning or spontaneous combustion sparks a fire that can burn underground for many years. The Burning Coal Vein in the Medora District of the grassland has been smoldering at least since the mid-1800s. Lack of oxygen slows the burn to 10 feet or so per year.

The fires bake the overlying sediments into "clinker," locally called "scoria," a brick red rock resistant to erosion, that caps many formations in the badlands. Scoria knobs, colored red by iron oxide, are often pocked with holes where rattlesnakes and other animals den.

At about the same time the coal was formed, some organic material was covered by marine sediments and decayed into a material rich in carbon and hydrogen. Hydrocarbons flowed into porous rocks and became concentrated into oil and gas reserves. Oil and gas drilling are important activities on the grassland, with some 600 wells producing about 30,000 barrels a day.

The Little Missouri River is the chief architect of today's landscape. About 2 million years ago the continental ice sheets began to advance, blocking the course of the river. As it sought a new route, the river cut through sedimentary layers, sculpting the badlands. It also turned south, joining the Missouri River to find a new outlet in the Gulf of Mexico instead of Hudson Bay.

Drivers who swear at slick bentonite roads might enjoy the Bentonitic Clay Overlook along the north unit's scenic drive. Ash from Cretaceous period volcanoes formed the bentonite clay that is used in hundreds of products, including crayons, candy bar fillers, face cream, feed supplements, glue, laxatives, paint, toothpaste, and scouring soaps, as well as in oil drilling operations.

COLUMNAR AND CREEPING JUNIPERS

Near veins of burning coal, Rocky Mountain Junipers grow into slender columns instead of their typical globular pattern. Fumes from the burning coal are the suspected cause since the junipers revert to their usual shape when transplanted to other environments. This type of growth has also been noted near industrial sites. The best place to view the phenomenon is the Burning Coal Vein and the Columnar Juniper Overlook, about 30 miles south of Medora on FS 3. A short trail leads to the white castlelike formation seen from the overlook.

Creeping Juniper, common in both the grassland and the park, also has an interesting growth pattern. Its prostrate form is like a dense carpet, and occasionally it drips like a waterfall down a small overhang. Several cultivars of *Juniperus horizontalis*, such as 'Blue Chip' and 'Wiltonii', are popular in landscaping.

Junipers were a pharmacopoeia for many American Indian

Castlelike formations loom over columnar junipers above the Burning Coal Site at Little Missouri National Grassland. (Photo by Glenn Cushman)

tribes, according to ethnobotanist Kelly Kindscher. They used twigs, leaves, and berries in various decoctions and salves to ease stomachaches, colds, sore throats, toothaches, fevers, and even hiccoughs. Juniper was also used for birth control and to treat venereal disease. Poultices made from the berries or twigs helped arthritis, and a salve made from boiled twigs was used for measles and smallpox. Lakota Chief Red Cloud was reputed to have saved many lives with a juniper decoction during the cholera epidemic of 1849–50.

Many people burned the wood in sweat lodges during purification rites. Pawnees inhaled the smoke to cure bad dreams, and Kiowas made "love flutes" from the aromatic, blood red heartwood. Berries were widely used for flavoring, but American Indians never learned to turn them into gin. In Osage folklore junipers were called the tree of life and were said to be the home of Thunderbirds who brought storms to the prairies. The Lakota tied twigs to tepee poles to ward off lightning and said that if you stood under a juniper, lightning would never strike you.

Waxwings, robins, and other birds relish the berries of all juniper species and benefit from the prickly protective cover.

FRAGMENTS OF HISTORY

Projectile points suggest that Paleoindians hunted in the Little Missouri Badlands about 10,000 years ago. Buffalo jumps, campsites, and pits to trap eagles give evidence of later use of the area. Archaeologists think most of the sites were temporary field camps rather than permanent settlements.

General George Custer marched through the badlands on his way to defeat at the Battle of Little Bighorn. Three of his camps and remnants of the trail are still visible south of I-94. Initial Rock bears the initials that two of his men carved on May 28, 1876. The route was also used by Generals Sully and Crook and by emigrants and gold seekers.

An occasional cabin ruin still stands from homesteading days, and Roosevelt's Maltese Cross cabin, behind the Medora Visitor Center, has been restored. His Elkhorn Ranch site is 35 miles north of this visitor center, but check on road conditions before driving there.

HIKING AND CANOEING

The trails listed here are just a sampling of the many trails winding through the grassland and the park. The trails can be connected to make various loops and permutations, and most are open for horseback riding.

MAAH-DAAH-HEY TRAIL (100 miles) starts at Sully Creek State Park and terminates at the CCC Campground, connecting the two units of Theodore Roosevelt National Park. The name is a Mandan Indian phrase meaning "an area that has been or will be around for a long time." Check with one of the grassland or park offices for regulations and conditions.

JONES CREEK TRAIL (3.7 miles) crosses the heart of the badlands in the south unit of the park, connecting two trailheads on the Scenic Loop Drive.

PETRIFIED FOREST LOOP (15.3 miles) begins at Peaceful Valley Ranch Trailhead and winds through the largest collection of petrified wood in the park.

ACHENBACH LOOP (16 miles) begins at Juniper Campground, climbs from the river bottom through the Achenbach Hills to Sperati Point and Oxbow Overlook and returns to camp via the river bottom. This trail involves river crossings, so check with a ranger about conditions.

SPERATI POINT (1.5 miles round trip) starts at the Oxbow Overlook on the Scenic Drive. It goes to a "gateway" where the river found a new passage when the original course was blocked during the Ice Age.

Canoeing on the Little Missouri River is seasonal, usually limited to April through June. Check with rangers regarding permits and conditions.

CAMPING

Little Missouri National Grassland:

SATHER CAMPGROUND, 26 miles southwest of Watford City on SR 68.

SUMMIT CAMPGROUND, 18.5 miles south of Watford City on US 85.

CCC CAMPGROUND, 15 miles south of Watford City off US 85. Follow signs.

BUFFALO GAP CAMPGROUND, 7 miles west of Medora on I-94.

BURNING COAL VEIN AND COLUMNAR JUNIPER PRIMITIVE CAMPGROUND, 30 miles south of Medora on FS 3.

There are also campgrounds along the Maah-Daah-Hey Trail, and dispersed camping is permitted anywhere on the grassland.

Theodore Roosevelt National Park:

COTTONWOOD CAMPGROUND, along the Little Missouri River 5 miles north of the Medora Visitor Center.

JUNIPER CAMPGROUND, along the Little Missouri River 5 miles from the north unit park entrance.

BEST TIMES TO VISIT

Late March through mid-May are the best times to see dancing Sharp-tailed Grouse. Golden Eagles nest in March, and their young fledge in early to midsummer. Canoeing is usually best from April through June when water levels run high. Grasses and shrubs turn autumnal colors in September and October. Snow adds a special magic to colorful rock formations, and sometimes there's enough for cross-country skiing. However, some roads may be closed in winter.

INFORMATION

LITTLE MISSOURI NATIONAL GRASSLAND has two district offices: Medora District, 161 21st Street W., Dickinson, ND 58601; 701-225-5151 and McKenzie District, US 85, Watford City, ND 58854; 701-842-2393.

THEODORE ROOSEVELT NATIONAL PARK, Box 7, Medora, ND 58645-0007; 701-623-4466. Three visitor centers contain exhibits, books, and brochures. The Medora Visitor Center, just off I-94 at the park entrance in Medora, also contains Theodore Roosevelt exhibits. Painted Canyon Visitor Center is just off I-94 a few miles east of Medora. The North Unit Visitor Center is just off US 85.

HOW TO GET THERE

I-94 cuts through the center of the Little Missouri Grassland and skirts the southern border of Theodore Roosevelt National Park. From the historic town of Medora take the Park Road north into the south unit. To reach the park's north unit, continue on I-94 to US 85. Turn north at Belfield and continue about 50 miles to the North Unit Visitor Center. Or, from Watford City, go south on US 85 for 15 miles.

Many state and county roads shown on the grassland map also access Little Missouri Grassland, which surrounds the park. **NOTE:** A Little Missouri National Grassland map, available at either of the above offices, is essential for exploring this grassland.

LITTLE MISSOURI NATIONAL GRASSLAND AND

THEODORE ROOSEVELT NATIONAL PARK

WEATHER
MEAN TEMPERATURE AND PRECIPITATION

MONTH	HIGH (°F)	LOW (°F)	PRECIP.	SNOW
January	21	1	0.4"	8.0"
April	54	30	1.9"	4.0"
July	83	55	2.1"	0.0"
October	58	33	1.0"	1.5"

Mean annual precipitation is 15.9 inches. Midsummer temperatures can reach into the low 100s. Snow can fall during every month except July. Data are for Dickinson, North Dakota.

SELECTED WILDLIFE OF SPECIAL INTEREST

MAMMALS: Black-tailed Prairie Dog, Red Fox, Badger, Bobcat, Elk, Mule Deer, White-tailed Deer, Pronghorn, Bison, Bighorn Sheep, feral horse.

BIRDS: Northern Goshawk, Golden Eagle, Peregrine Falcon, Prairie Falcon, Sharp-tailed Grouse, Wild Turkey, Long-billed Curlew, Burrowing Owl, Short-eared Owl, Northern Saw-whet Owl, Red-headed Woodpecker, Ovenbird.

AMPHIBIANS AND REPTILES: Great Plains Toad, Woodhouse's Toad, Plains Spadefoot, Greater Short-horned Lizard, Common Sagebrush Lizard, Western Rattlesnake, Red-sided Gartersnake (Common Gartersnake).

LOSTWOOD AND DES LACS NATIONAL WILDLIFE REFUGES

In a 1915 letter, biologist Remington Kellogg lamented the loss of bird life in the Lostwood area "due to the fact that the marshes are drying up and are being turned into hay meadows.... Early Homesteaders here tell me that the ducks on some of the marshes formerly made so much noise at night that they had to get up and shoot to scare them away."

Kellogg would rejoice over the way Lostwood National Wildlife Refuge looks today. Located in the northwestern corner of North Dakota, this 26,900-acre refuge contains the largest contiguous block of northern mixed-grass prairie under federal ownership. It is crammed with potholes, prairies, and wildlife. Almost 100 types of grass can be found here, with needlegrasses and wheatgrasses tending to dominate. One of the largest populations of Sharp-tailed Grouse in the United States nests here along with Piping Plovers, Marbled Godwits, and Baird's Sparrows.

A 7-mile auto tour, keyed to a brochure available from refuge headquarters, winds past native prairie, restoration plots, aspen copses, leks, lakes, and alkali wetlands. The 5,577-acre Lostwood Wilderness Area stretches north from station 2, and a blind for viewing dancing Sharp-tailed Grouse is at station 9.

Des Lacs National Wildlife Refuge, only 16 miles to the north-

Above: Lower Des Lacs Lake in September. (Photo by Glenn Cushman)

cast, stretches south from the Canadian border for 26 miles along the Des Lacs River and encompasses 19,500 acres of prairie, natural lakes, and managed wetlands. Early French trappers in the glacial valley called the area *Rivière des Lacs*. It is, indeed, a "river of lakes" that sparkle like jewels strung on a necklace.

Des Lacs saw more human settlement and use than did Lostwood. The Blackfeet inhabited the area from about 1000 to 1500 A.D. and were followed by the Hidatsa and then by the Southern Assiniboin. These people built ceremonial effigy mounds, some shaped like turtles, and left tepee rings up to 30 feet in diameter. In the late 1800s settlers farmed, ranched, and mined for coal. Nowadays the refuge is a major migration stopover for Lesser Snow Geese, Tundra Swans, and many duck species; Giant Canada Geese produce 150 to 200 young each year; and Moose sometimes mosey down the wooded coulees. A 14-mile scenic drive curves around the lower and middle lakes and along the river.

Franklin Delano Roosevelt created both wildlife refuges in 1935. Des Lacs lies on the western edge of the "drift prairie," flat, glaciated plains dotted with shallow wetlands. In contrast, Lostwood lies in the knob-and-kettle country of the Missouri Coteau in the heart of the Northern Coteau Project Area. The goal of this project is to restore wetlands and grasslands on both public and private lands using rotational grazing of livestock to mimic bison grazing, prescribed burning to control aspen and other encroaching brush, conservation tillage, and reseeding of native grasses.

Upper Souris and Shell Lake National Wildlife Refuges, located nearby, are also part of the Northern Coteau Project Area. In addition, the U.S. Fish and Wildlife Service manages more than 175 small tracts (nearly 35,000 acres) called "Waterfowl Production Areas" that are open to the public.

PRAIRIE POTHOLES

Coteau, a French word meaning "little hill," describes the glacier-sculpted land stretching from northwest Iowa to central Alberta. As the Wisconsin Glacier retreated some 12,000 years ago, it left behind moraines of rubble and depressions filled with ice that became today's rounded, grassy hills and prairie potholes.

This knob-and-kettle country was once a vast expanse teeming with birds that fed and nested around 25 million potholes, 83 per square mile. Over the past century many potholes have been drained for agriculture and development; many other ponds come and go with the climate cycle. Surveys made between 1955 and 1985 showed pothole numbers ranging from a low of 2 million to more than 7 million. North Dakota alone has lost 49 percent of its original wetlands.

Potholes vary from 500-acre lakes to small pools only a few feet across and a few inches deep. They also vary greatly in character, ranging from freshwater to alkaline, from ephemeral ponds to year-round lakes. Rainfall and melting snow trapped above the dense clay and silt bottoms recharge most potholes. Low-lying alkaline pools, however, are also recharged by groundwater, which increases in salinity as it percolates through the soil. Fish do not thrive in these shallow potholes because of the salinity and winter freezing.

Vegetation around the ponds forms concentric rings, grading from marshes near open water through wet meadows to low-lying prairie. Algae, pondweeds, reeds, bulrushes, cattails, and other wetland species provide food and cover for wildlife that live in the varied habitats created by the "edge effect." Look for ducks feeding on Sago Pondweed, Muskrats building cattail lodges, Mink slinking along a half-submerged log, and shorebirds nesting on the alkaline flats.

PIPING PLOVERS: ENDANGERED AND THREATENED

Fairly abundant during John James Audubon's time, Piping Plovers were hunted almost to extinction by the end of the nineteenth century. Although hunting is no longer permitted, habitat destruction now threatens this pale, plump shorebird. Only 1,291 breeding pairs remained in the United States and Canada in 2001. They are listed as endangered in Canada and the Great Lakes region and threatened in the rest of their range. Piping Plover recovery biologist Jake Ivans reports an annual decline of 5 to 12 percent on the northern Great Plains and warns the birds could disappear from the region within 50 to 100 years.

One of the largest breeding populations in the United States nests at the John E. Williams Memorial Nature Conservancy Preserve near Turtle Lake in North Dakota. Additional populations breed on such refuges as Lostwood and Des Lacs, where they favor shallow alkali ponds or wetlands with little or no vegetation. Coyotes, foxes, small mammals, and other birds prey on these nests, and during the 1990s rising water tables and several years of above-normal precipitation also interfered with nesting success.

Recovery teams have been monitoring the birds since the mid-1980s and are working to increase fledgling survival. Crews build predator exclosures (wire mesh cages topped with bird netting) and sometimes electric fences to protect nests. Fires and cattle

Piping Plover nests are vulnerable to a variety of disturbances, including human recreational activities and fluctuating water levels. (Photo by Michael Forsberg)

grazing help reduce vegetation on some beaches, and the crews also create new habitat by building islands and reducing water behind impoundments.

Aptly named Piping Plovers resemble Killdeer with only one neck band, and their *peep-lo* whistle lacks the Killdeer's hysteric quality. Ornithologist Arthur Cleveland Bent described the call as "a soft, musical moan" and their color as "pale ecru drab." They feed in typical plover fashion, running in starts and stops on beaches or upland gravel areas where they probe for worms and other invertebrates. Sometimes they vibrate one foot against wet sand, perhaps to lure a potential snack to the surface.

During courtship, males perform aerial flights, tilting their stocky bodies from side to side. They also engage in nest scraping displays, tossing aside pebbles or shell fragments and squirming around in the sand to make shallow scrapes. When one of the scrapes is chosen by a bonded pair, they continue ritual stone tossing to line the nest. Later, they use a "broken wing" act to lure predators away from the well-camouflaged nest. Adults without chicks also feign injury to distract predators from other plover nests.

SNOW GEESE: EXPLODING POPULATIONS

A completely different dilemma is posed by Lesser Snow Geese. Instead of being endangered themselves, their exploding numbers are endangering their arctic breeding grounds. One of the most abundant waterfowl species in the world, Snow Geese forage on new shoots and grub for underground rhizomes and roots. In the process, crowded populations can create barren mudflats inhospitable to other species. Many scientists fear that if Snow Goose numbers aren't reduced, denuded arctic breeding grounds will lead to eventual population crashes of the geese and of other species. Already, some females starve to death each summer while incubating eggs.

Part of the problem is that some waterfowl conservation measures have worked too well. Conservation-minded legislators outlawed spring and summer hunting of migratory waterfowl in 1918. At the same time, prairies were being turned into grain fields—a smorgasbord for Snow Geese who fatten up on leftover grain during winter and gain up to 2 pounds during their three-month spring migration. West of Hudson Bay more than 7,000 nests have been found in one square mile, and the total population has grown by almost 300 percent since the 1960s. It is now estimated at between 5 million and 6 million. (See photo p. 374.)

To protect the arctic habitat and prevent an ecological catastrophe, the U.S. Fish and Wildlife Service, the National Audubon Society, and Ducks Unlimited all recommend expanded hunting.

Even though Snow Geese have become an environmental problem on their breeding grounds, most birdwatchers continue to gasp in delight on looking up to see thousands of geese at once—like a blizzard obliterating the sky. They migrate through North Dakota refuges in both spring and fall, and the town of Kenmare holds an annual "Goosefest" to celebrate their return in October.

TIGER SALAMANDERS

Tiger Salamanders are abundant, but adults are seldom seen because they live underground most of the time. During fall and spring rains, however, they seem possessed with a mania for crossing roads and open areas. Why does a salamander cross the road? To reach or return from overwintering sites. In fall they crawl into burrows or piles of debris or dig their own burrows to ensure optimal temperature and humidity levels for the upcoming cold season.

In spring they return to ponds or wetlands to mate. After a bit of mutual nudging, the male deposits a spermatophore that the female maneuvers into her cloaca. Eggs, deposited on strands of vegetation or on the floor of a pond, hatch into larvae that usually metamorphose into adults in late summer. Adults, ranging from 6 to 13 inches long, are marked with blotches or bands against a dark background. Many have a clownish appearance with yellow spots against a black background.

If a permanent pond brims with food (almost anything smaller than a salamander) some larvae may become sexually mature

Tiger Salamanders grow up to 6.5 inches long. Among subspecies the marking pattern varies from cream-colored dots to yellow stripes. (Photo by W. Perry Conway)

without metamorphosing into terrestrial adults. A few larvae may grow into huge-headed cannibals with an extra row of teeth.

Normally, many thousands of salamanders inhabit North Dakota's wetlands. But in the summer of 2000 an enormous, unprecedented die-off began at Cottonwood Lake Study Area near Jamestown. In wetlands where researchers had caught 100 to 150 salamanders per trap, they caught a total of only 8 in July 2000. Wildlife pathologist D. Earl Green attributes most of the deaths to an iridovirus infection, the same virus suspected in many other amphibian die-offs across North America.

Although disease appears to be the major cause of amphibian deaths, their worldwide decline remains a mystery. Biologists continue to investigate such possible causes as global warming, ozone depletion with an increase in ultraviolet radiation, pesticides, heavy-metal pollution, acid rain, destruction of wetlands, habitat fragmentation, bacterial disease, or a combination of factors.

Hiking and Canoeing

LOSTWOOD: A 5-mile trail through prairie and past wetlands begins at station 7 on the auto tour. Hiking, ski touring, and snowshoeing are also permitted in the Lostwood Wilderness Area.

DES LACS: Munch's Coulee (1 mile) is a self-guided nature trail on the east side of Lower Des Lacs Lake. It leads up a woody draw and through prairie to a spectacular viewpoint. Trasker's Coulee, a wooded area on Middle Des Lacs Lake accessed by CR 1A, also has trails. Canoeing is good on any of the lakes or on the river.

Camping

No camping is permitted on the refuges, but there are campgrounds in the nearby towns of Kenmare and Stanley.

Best Times to Visit

Sharp-tailed Grouse dance in late April and May and can be viewed from blinds at both refuges. At Des Lacs, Western Grebes dance across the water in May. In late summer thousands of ducks, grebes, and coots gather to rest and refuel during migration. In October Snow Geese and Tundra Swans return. Ski touring and snowshoeing are enjoyable in winter.

Information

LOSTWOOD NATIONAL WILDLIFE REFUGE, Box 98, Kenmare, ND 58746; 701-848-2722. Refuge headquarters is on Thompson Lake near the start of the auto tour.

DES LACS NATIONAL WILDLIFE REFUGE, Box 578, Kenmare, ND 58746; 701-385-4046. Refuge headquarters is a half-mile west of Kenmare on CR 1A.

How to Get There

LOSTWOOD: 12 miles west of Kenmare on CR 2 and 4 miles south on SR 8.

DES LACS: adjacent to Kenmare; can be accessed by US 52, CR 2, and CR 1A.

WEATHER
MEAN TEMPERATURE AND PRECIPITATION

MONTH	HIGH (°F)	LOW (°F)	PRECIP.	SNOW
January	18	0	0.8"	8.1"
April	53	32	2.0"	4.3"
July	82	58	2.5"	0.0"
October	56	35	1.0"	1.7"

Mean annual precipitation is 18.7 inches. Winter temperatures (December through February) range from 66°F to -36°F; summer temperatures (June through August), from 107°F to 32°F. Data are for Minot, North Dakota (temperatures and precipitation) and Williston, North Dakota (snow).

SELECTED WILDLIFE OF SPECIAL INTEREST

MAMMALS: White-tailed Jackrabbit, Thirteen-lined Ground Squirrel, Meadow Jumping Mouse, Porcupine, Mink, Badger, White-tailed Deer, Moose.

BIRDS: American White Pelican, Snow Goose (m), Tundra Swan (m), Sharp-tailed Grouse, Sandhill Crane (m), Piping Plover, Upland Sandpiper, Marbled Godwit, Long-eared Owl, Short-eared Owl, Sprague's Pipit, Baird's Sparrow, Bobolink.

AMPHIBIANS AND REPTILES: Northern Leopard Frog, Wood Frog, Tiger Salamander, Smooth Green Snake, Plains Gartersnake.

SHEYENNE NATIONAL GRASSLAND AND BROWN RANCH AND PIGEON POINT PRESERVES

A wildflower oasis is how some people describe Sheyenne National Grassland. Out of 1,250 species of flowering plants statewide, 850 occur in the Sheyenne delta. The sandy soil, originally deposited at the end of the Ice Age when Lake Agassiz (see Bluestem Prairie, Minnesota) covered much of what is now eastern North Dakota and northern Minnesota, supports about 36 rare or sensitive plant species.

The many flowering plants attract rare butterflies such as Dakota Skippers and Regal Fritillaries. American Elm and Bass-

Above: Nodding Ladies'-Tresses (Spiranthes cernua) *at Brown Ranch in September. (Photo by Glenn Cushman)*

wood forests reach their westernmost extension along the Sheyenne River. A remnant population of Greater Prairie-Chickens and large numbers of Sharp-tailed Grouse nest on the prairies, and Beaver and an occasional Moose or Elk wander along the river.

More than 70,000 acres of protected tallgrass meadows, fens, sandhills, and Bur Oak savannas are interspersed with an equal amount of private agricultural land in southeastern North Dakota to form the only national grassland in the northern tallgrass prairie region. The Sheyenne River, designated a state wild and scenic river, meanders along the northern side of the grassland, and numerous small streams and springs bubble up from a water table so near the surface that in wet years it wells above the ground.

Much of the prairie within this grassland has been seriously degraded by cattle grazing and is dominated by cool-season grasses and annual weedy forbs. Sheyenne National Grassland staff are working with the Nature Conservancy and local ranchers to improve range management throughout the region.

The Nature Conservancy owns two preserves, Brown Ranch and Pigeon Point, within the boundaries of the grassland. These preserves are open to the public for passive uses such as hiking and wildflower photography and include remnant native prairie as well as reconstructed prairie and wetlands. Land steward Robert Self calls Pigeon Point a unique ecoregion and says it has the highest species diversity of any place in the state. Plant rarities in these preserves include Spinulose Wood Fern, Marsh Fern, Prairie Blazing Star, Wood Lily, Closed Gentian, and Western Prairie Fringed Orchid.

WESTERN PRAIRIE FRINGED ORCHIDS

It's a midsummer night and some two dozen white blossoms flutter from a single erect plant. Blooming continues for about 3 weeks with individual flowers lasting up to 10 days. Edged with delicate fringe, the showy flowers are about 1 ½ inches long, and the stalk can reach 4 feet high. Hundreds of the plants grow in wet swales at Sheyenne National Grassland, which harbors one of the last viable populations of Western Prairie Fringed Orchids (*Platanthera praeclara*) in the world.

Once fairly abundant on the Great Plains, this orchid is now on the U.S. Fish and Wildlife Service's federal threatened species list and lives only in scattered remnants on tallgrass sand prairies and hay meadows. It needs a moist habitat with full exposure to sunlight. In 1996 there were 175 known populations in just six states

Western Prairie Fringed Orchids bloom for only a couple of weeks in late June and early July. (Photo by Michael Forsberg)

and one province, and many of these populations may be too small to perpetuate themselves over time.

This orchid's continuing survival depends on one type of insect —long-tongued hawkmoths. At night the orchid emits a delectable scent to lure the moths to its flowers. White fringed petals guide the moths to nectar in the spur, the longest spur of any North American orchid. Specialized structures brush pollen onto the moth's eyes; when the moth visits other blooms, its eyes touch that orchid's stigma, transferring the pollen. Only hawkmoths with suitably long tongues and properly spaced eyes can serve as pollinators.

Both orchid and moth face disaster as prairies are plowed. Often the moths are killed by pesticides or cannot find isolated stands of orchids because they are surrounded by croplands. The orchids also suffer from loss of habitat due to overgrazing and intensive mowing and are encroached upon by trees, shrubs, and exotic weeds such as Leafy Spurge, which now infests some 11,000 acres of the grassland.

Although established orchid populations can spread slowly through root regeneration, moths are indispensable for sexual reproduction of the orchid, which ensures genetic diversity. Land managers are attempting to provide hawkmoth "corridors" of native prairie between fragmented orchid stands to help the moths find the route, and in some cases, biologists even pollinate the flowers by hand. When pollinated seeds mature, they are dispersed by the wind (see Manitoba Tallgrass Prairie Preserve for more information).

Look for these orchids in early July. They are often associated with cordgrass and sedges. Other orchids in the Sheyenne delta include Small White Lady's-Slipper, Yellow Lady's-Slipper, Showy Lady's-Slipper, Northern Green Orchid, Nodding Ladies'-Tresses, and Loesel's Twayblade.

BUR OAK SAVANNAS

The sand dunes of Lake Agassiz are mostly covered now with grasses, shrubs, and wildflowers—and with Bur Oaks, which provide shelter for such diverse understory plants as Snowberry, Smooth Sumac, and poison ivy. In autumn when the oak leaves turn a rich, cinnamony brown, the trees bear nutritious acorns for

Sunflowers and oak woodlands catch the morning light at Sheyenne National Grassland.

Sharp-tailed Grouse, Wild Turkeys, songbirds, deer, foxes, squirrels, and many other animals.

Savannas are parklike areas with expanses of prairie interspersed with open groves of trees. Thirty million acres of oak savanna once covered areas of the Midwest and Great Plains, but less than 1 percent remain in a relatively unaltered state. Sheyenne is one of the few tallgrass preserves where oak savannas still thrive.

In *Where the Sky Began,* John Madson writes of Bur Oak: "If there is a tree designed to invade prairie sod, it's this tough oak with its deeply lobed leaves and huge-capped acorns. It succeeds by growing deep and fast before it ever puts on much growth above-ground." A seedling may develop a 9-inch taproot before any leaves unfurl. By its third year the sapling may be only 3 feet high, but its root system may stretch 6 feet deep and 4 feet outward.

Deep roots and thick bark enable Bur Oaks to withstand fire better than most trees. They can reach 70 to 80 feet in height, with spreading branches that provide welcome shade on the sundrenched prairie. The acorn caps have a burred or mossy fringe of scales around the edge, leading to the name "Bur" or "Mossy-capped" Oak.

NORTHERN LEOPARD FROGS

The call of the Northern Leopard Frog signals spring in ponds and shallow bodies of water throughout the northern plains. After spending the winter hibernating at the bottom of ponds, males start sounding off in March or April. They inflate vocal sacs on the sides of their heads to produce a prolonged "snore" followed by stuttering croaks.

The female deposits 600 to 6,000 eggs in a gelatinous mass that the male fertilizes externally. Tadpoles hatch in 4 to 15 days and metamorphose into froglets about 3 months later. Hundreds of frogs can be seen hopping across roads in summer as they disperse from the breeding ponds and again in fall as they head for overwintering sites. They cover up to 6 feet in a hop and travel in a zigzag course, but are no match for a lethal car.

Once the most widespread frog species in North America, Northern Leopard Frogs are declining throughout the country along with other amphibian species. Leopard frogs have been especially susceptible to a fungal disease called chytridiomycosis. Their numbers have increased recently at Sheyenne, however, perhaps because of increased rainfall in the late 1990s. Gartersnakes, which prey on the frogs, have also increased in numbers.

Northern Leopard Frog adults prey on insects, worms, and occasionally other frogs. They are most active at dusk and dawn and like to bask along the shores of ponds during the day. Sometimes called meadow frogs, they often forage in wet meadows far from open water, possibly absorbing dew to keep themselves moist. Large dark spots against a green, gray, or brown background led to their apt name.

HIKING

As in all national grasslands, hiking is permitted anywhere. In addition, a 29-mile stretch of the North Country National Scenic Trail crosses Sheyenne National Grassland. The gravel trail passes Greater Prairie-Chicken leks, Iron Spring Creek (the only known location for the Rosy-faced Shiner, a small minnow), an oxbow lake called Mirror Pool, and a vista point with a view of the Sheyenne River Valley. When completed, the trail will stretch from Lake Champlain in New York to Lake Sakakawea in North Dakota and will be the longest continuous foot path in the country. Sheyenne's northern trailhead is on Richland CR 23 seven miles north of SR 27; the southern trailhead is on Ransom CR 54, 3 miles south of SR 27.

Some stretches of the Sheyenne River are canoeable.

CAMPING

Dispersed camping is permitted anywhere on the grassland except at trailheads but is not permitted on the Nature Conservancy preserves. Developed campgrounds are located in the nearby town of Lisbon, at Fort Ransom State Park, and at Dead Colt Creek Recreation Area.

BEST TIMES TO VISIT

Prairie-chickens and Sharp-tailed Grouse dance from mid-March to the first of May. The wildflower show stretches from early April, when Pasque Flowers blossom, into September, when Nodding Ladies'-Tresses and Closed Gentians bloom. Penstemons bloom in May and June, Western Prairie Fringed Orchids and Wood Lilies in July. In August Prairie Blazing Stars arise from green meadows like giant magenta candles. Sumacs flame into brilliant scarlet, a few stands of aspen and elm turn gold, and Big and Little Bluestem turn shades of rosy mauve in September. Leopard frogs are active from spring to fall.

SHEYENNE NATIONAL GRASSLAND, 701 Main Street, Box 946, Lisbon, ND 58054; 701-683-4342.

THE NATURE CONSERVANCY, Sheyenne Delta Office, 7290 146th Avenue SE, Milnor, ND 58060; 701-439-0841.

How to Get There

From Lisbon drive east on SR 27, which cuts through the center of the grassland. To reach one of the prettiest parts of the grassland and the North Country National Scenic Trail, continue on SR 27 to FS 263 (CR 23). This turn-off is about 21 miles east of Lisbon. Go north for about 4 miles through private property. At this point several gravel roads diverge; follow the signs. Numerous county and Forest Service roads, some requiring four-wheel drive, also provide access to the grassland.

To reach Brown Ranch, the Nature Conservancy headquarters, go to the small town of McLeod, about 3 miles south of SR 27 on CR 618. Take the unnamed gravel road west and south 3.5 miles to the first four-way intersection; the road winds around, but no other roads intersect with it. At the intersection, turn west and go 2 miles; turn north and go a short distance to the driveway of the house/office. Watch for small yellow TNC signs.

To reach Pigeon Point, which is on the Sheyenne River, take SR 27 east from Lisbon for 16 miles. Turn north on CR 53 and go 4 miles north and 2 miles west to the preserve gate. Watch for small yellow TNC signs. **NOTE:** A Sheyenne National Grassland map, available at the Lisbon office, is essential to explore this grassland and to avoid trespassing on the private inholdings.

SHEYENNE NATIONAL GRASSLAND AND BROWN RANCH AND PIGEON POINT PRESERVES

WEATHER
MEAN TEMPERATURE AND PRECIPITATION

MONTH	HIGH (°F)	LOW (°F)	PRECIP.	SNOW
January	15	-4	0.7"	9.6"
April	54	32	1.8"	3.2"
July	83	59	2.7"	0.0"
October	57	35	1.7"	0.6"

Mean annual precipitation is 19.45 inches. Summers are humid with occasional thunderstorms. Blizzards can occur in March and April. Data are for Fargo, North Dakota.

SELECTED WILDLIFE OF SPECIAL INTEREST

MAMMALS: White-tailed Jackrabbit, Richardson's Ground Squirrel, Thirteen-lined Ground Squirrel, Beaver, Porcupine, Coyote, Mink, Striped Skunk, White-tailed Deer, Moose.

BIRDS: Wood Duck, Sharp-tailed Grouse, Greater Prairie-Chicken, Wild Turkey, Yellow Rail (sporadic), Upland Sandpiper, Marbled Godwit, American Woodcock, Clay-colored Sparrow, Savannah Sparrow, Grasshopper Sparrow, Indigo Bunting, Bobolink.

AMPHIBIANS AND REPTILES: Northern Leopard Frog, Wood Frog, Tiger Salamander, Prairie Skink, Western Hog-nosed Snake, Red-bellied Snake, Snapping Turtle.

North Dakota contains 63 National Wildlife Refuges encompassing more than 290,000 acres—more than any other state. In addition, 11 Wetland Management Districts protect more than 254,000 acres. All of these places contain native prairie, wetlands, and a variety of wildlife. They are all worth visiting. A sampling of some of the best are included here.

AUDUBON NATIONAL WILDLIFE REFUGE. (RR1, Box 16, Coleharbor, ND 58531; 701-442-5474). Many migrating birds, including Whooping Cranes, pass through, and many water and shorebirds, including endangered Piping Plovers, nest on this 14,735-acre refuge that includes more than 100 natural islands. An 8-mile auto tour, a 1-mile nature trail, and barge tours to nesting islands are special attractions. Located east of SR 83 about 39 miles south of Minot; follow signs.

CHASE LAKE NATIONAL WILDLIFE REFUGE (5924 19th Street SE, Woodworth, ND 58496; 701-752-4218). One of the largest breeding colonies of American White Pelicans in North America plus Piping Plovers nest on this 4,385-acre refuge. Native prairie and the Chase Lake Wilderness Area are additional features. About 23 miles northwest of Medina (I-94 Exit 230). Go 10 miles north on CR 68; 7 miles west on an un-numbered township road; 1 mile south on another un-numbered road.

FORT UNION TRADING POST NATIONAL HISTORIC SITE (15550 SR 1804, Williston, ND 58801; 701-572-9083). Located at the confluence of the Yellowstone and Missouri Rivers and lying partly in Montana, this reconstructed fort and trading post sits in the midst of 443 acres of shortgrass prairie. On SR 1804, 25 miles southwest of Williston.

J. CLARK SALYER NATIONAL WILDLIFE REFUGE (Box 66, Upham, ND; 701-768-2548). The largest national wildlife refuge in the state and the most diverse in habitat stretches for 50 miles along the Souris River and covers 58,700 acres. There are more than 300 bird species as well as Moose and Mink. From Upham, 50 miles northeast of Minot, go 2 miles north on SR 14.

KNIFE RIVER INDIAN VILLAGES NATIONAL HISTORIC SITE (Box 9, Stanton, ND 58571; 701-745-3309). This 1,758-acre site includes a reconstructed earthlodge and museum exhibits on the lives of the Mandan, Hidatsa, and Arikara. Nature trails wind through prairie, passing by depressions where earthlodges once stood on the banks of the Knife River. Sixty miles north of Bismarck. From I-94 Exit 159, take US 83 north 40 miles to SR 200, and go west 19 miles to Stanton.

LEWIS AND CLARK STATE PARK (Rt. 1, Box 13A, Epping, ND 58843; 701-859-3071). Located on a western bay of Lake Sakakawea, the park includes one of the largest intact native prairies in the state park system as well as bluffs, badlands, coulees, and trails. Paddlefish and the endangered Pallid Sturgeon live in the bay. Camping, hiking. Nineteen miles east of Williston on SR 1804.

LONETREE WILDLIFE MANAGEMENT AREA (North Dakota Game and Fish Department, RR2, Box 32, Harvey, ND 58341; 701-324-2211). This 3,200-acre preserve was created to mitigate habitat lost to the Garrison Diversion Unit Irrigation Project. It includes 6,611 acres of native prairie, 9,135 acres of restored prairie, the Sheyenne Lake National Wildlife Refuge, wetlands, numerous plantings for wildlife, and a self-guided auto tour. Camping. On SR 14 about 12 miles north of SR 200 and the town of Denhoff; follow signs to headquarters.

TEWAUKON NATIONAL WILDLIFE REFUGE (9754 143½ Avenue SE, Cayuga, ND 58013; 701-724-3598). An auto tour circles 1,000-acre Lake Tewaukon, passing through native tallgrass and restored prairies. The refuge lies within both the Central and Mississippi Flyways. Five miles south of Cayuga on CR 12. Cayuga is 27 miles west of I-29 Exit 8, on SR 11.

Native grasses grow on this reconstructed earthlodge at Knife River Indian Villages National Historic Site. (Photo by Glenn Cushman)

OKLAHOMA

Tallgrass Prairie Preserve

2 Boise City

325

64

8

11

4 Jet

60

Bartlesville

60

Rawhuska

Cimarron R.

35

Tulsa

44

Arkansas R.

3

283

1

47

Cheyenne

Oklahoma City ☆

40

75

Indian Nation Tpk.

40

Canadian R.

Wichita Mountains
National Wildlife ▲
Refuge   • Lawton

44

Ada

35

3

377

TALLGRASS PRAIRIE PRESERVE

WICHITA MOUNTAINS NATIONAL
  WILDLIFE REFUGE

OTHER OKLAHOMA SITES:
  1. Black Kettle National Grassland
  2. Black Mesa State Park
  3. Pontotoc Ridge Preserve
  4. Salt Plains National Wildlife Refuge

TALLGRASS PRAIRIE PRESERVE

Bison graze amidst oil and gas wells at this nearly 40,000-acre Nature Conservancy preserve in northeastern Oklahoma's Osage Hills. Coyotes nose around in fire-blackened meadows. Down in the shallow canyons that run through these low hills, Painted Buntings chatter and Wild Turkeys gobble in tangled oak thickets.

The Nature Conservancy bought the 29,000-acre Barnard Ranch, the cornerstone of the preserve, in 1989. This 85-year-old ranch lies in the heart of Osage County, a culturally complex region where Big Oil, cattle ranching, and Osage tribal politics mix as unpredictably as grass and wind.

During the late 1980s, Oklahoma congressional representatives introduced legislation to create a tallgrass prairie national park in the region. A fragile coalition of environmentalists, ranchers, oil industry executives, and local political leaders reached a tentative agreement that would have limited the park to 50,000 acres and retained oil wells and grazing leases within its boundaries. This agreement fell apart when national environmental groups objected to these conditions.

At this point the Nature Conservancy decided to move ahead with acquisition of the Barnard Ranch. They raised $15 million to

Above: Bison graze on recently burned prairie at Oklahoma's Tallgrass Prairie Preserve.

purchase the ranch and establish an endowment to cover operational expenses. Since the 1989 acquisition, an additional 9,600 acres of surrounding lands have been added to the preserve.

The conservancy's goal at the preserve is "to re-create a functioning tallgrass prairie ecosystem . . . an entire natural process embracing climate, size, and interactions of fire and grazing bison." Three hundred Bison were reintroduced in 1993. By 2002 the herd numbered 1,500 and was projected to expand eventually to 3,000. Preserve biologists use prescribed fire to create a "fenceless rotation." Randomly selected patches constituting about a third of the Bison range are burned at different times of the year, and the herds are allowed to wander over the entire range. The Bison know that recently burned areas produce succulent grasses, and you can see them kicking up clouds of soot and ash as they file through patches of charred prairie.

This image of robust life in the midst of fire and death is typical of the shifting viewscapes of the Osage Hills. In late summer, when a haze of smoke and humidity often hangs over the heat-seared grasslands, the hills can feel drab and unwelcoming. But catch them in fall when golden sunflowers glow in the clear light, or in late spring when the countryside turns every shade of green, and they're like a slice of heaven.

"England in May is no more inspiring than my country during this time," writes Osage naturalist John Joseph Mathews in *Talking to the Moon*. "The rain comes not in great crazy storms but gently. The prairie undulates in the green velvet of the bluestem, and cattle dot the hills, while mauve cloud shadows move indolently over them and across the canyons."

OSAGE HILLS

The limestone and sandstone hills that extend southward from Kansas into northeastern Oklahoma are known both as the southern Flint Hills and the Osage Hills. The latter name honors the powerful tribe that hunted in the region for more than 100 years and settled here in 1872. Pawhuska, the Osage County Seat, is named after the nineteenth-century Osage chief, Paw Hue Skah.

When Lewis and Clark sailed up the Missouri River in 1804, the Osage were living in villages west of present-day St. Louis and hunting westward from the Mississippi River into present-day Kansas and Oklahoma. The tribe numbered more than 5,000. Their young men were known as fierce warriors, their women as skilled farmers, their elders as shrewd negotiators.

As European-American settlers pushed west, the Osage sold off portions of their lands until only an 8-million-acre reservation in southeastern Kansas remained. When westering Kansans began to overrun these lands during the 1860s, the tribe sold the entire reservation to the federal government for $1.25 an acre and purchased 1.5 million acres of virtually untillable grassland in northeastern Oklahoma. Osage leader Wah Ti An Kah reputedly said, "The white man will not come to this land. The white man cannot put that iron thing in the ground here."

For a while his prophecy proved true. The hardscrabble hills of the reservation were much better suited for grazing than for farming. However, when oil was discovered in the region during the 1890s, white men leased mineral rights on the reservation and thrust hundreds of oil wells into the ground.

Income from the mineral leases made the Osage the richest native people per capita in the United States. In 1906 the federal government coerced the Osage into dividing their reservation into individual allotments, but the tribe retained communal ownership of mineral rights. Some tribal members became millionaires, and oil annuities have continued to flow to this day, though in diminishing amounts.

During the 1980s Osage leaders, suspicious of further federal incursions into their historic lands, resisted efforts to establish a tallgrass prairie national park in the region. Since then the privately owned Tallgrass Prairie Preserve has won the acceptance and even admiration of some tribal leaders and many other Osage County residents. In a relatively nonintrusive way, the preserve protects lands that the Osage long ago identified as a last refuge from European-American exploitation.

CROSS-TIMBERS

When author Washington Irving traversed present-day eastern Oklahoma in 1832, he wrote that "it was like struggling through forests of cast iron." The cross-timbers region, a prairie landscape interrupted by mazelike belts of oak and other deciduous trees, extended from east-central Kansas through Oklahoma into north-central Texas. These complex upland forests contained several species of oak, along with hickories, mulberries, persimmons, walnuts, cottonwoods, sycamores, and a wealth of wildlife. Most of this diversity was lost when farmers cleared the land.

The intended meaning of the term "cross-timbers" remains unclear. Some historians believe it referred to the fact that homesteaders had to cross these belts of forest to reach available lands farther west. Others assert the term alluded to the impenetrable nature of these forests or the way the strips of forest crossed the open prairie from north to south.

At the Tallgrass Prairie Preserve, cross-timbers occur on rocky

Cross-timbers in the Sand Creek drainage provide shelter for Bobcats, White-tailed Deer, and Wild Turkeys.

hillsides with sandy soils. Groundwater reserves beneath the underlying sandstones enable these areas of luxuriant vegetation to thrive and resist drought. The two dominant trees, Post Oak and Blackjack Oak, have tenacious root systems that help them compete with grasses and draw water in rocky soils.

The density and extent of the forests depends on the frequency of fire. Though the deep-rooted, thick-barked Post Oaks and Blackjack Oaks are more fire resistant than many other trees, they recover less quickly from frequent fires than do the dominant tallgrasses.

The two nature trails at the preserve cut through small stands of cross-timbers in the Sand Creek drainage. Early in the morning listen for Wild Turkeys and Tufted Titmice, and watch for White-tailed Deer. The Oklahoma state tree, the Eastern Redbud, displays a profusion of bright pink blossoms in April and can be identified at other times by its dark green heart-shaped leaves.

Bobcats

These 12- to 35-pound carnivores are most often seen at night slinking across refuge roads or at dusk skulking through riparian woodlands and brushy ravines. They hunt primarily by ambush, and their preferred prey include jackrabbits, cottontails, and other small mammals.

During periods of peak activity, adults may consume more than half their weight daily in prey. Males and females remain solitary except during the breeding season, usually late winter and early spring, and when females are rearing young in late spring or early summer.

Because their nocturnal, secretive habits enable them to sur-

Bobcats take prey ranging in size from mice and Kangaroo Rats (shown here) to White-tailed Deer fawns. (Photo by W. Perry Conway)

vive around farms and towns, Bobcats continue to range throughout most of Mexico, the United States, and southern Canada. Preserve biologists frequently encounter Bobcat tracks in the Sand Creek drainage and occasionally surprise individuals prowling around the old headquarters ranch house.

HIKING

A 1-mile interpretive trail and a 3-mile hiking trail take off from the parking area 0.3 miles west of the preserve headquarters. The trails pass through riparian woodlands and cross-timbers along Sand Creek and traverse gentle hills covered with tallgrass prairie.

CAMPING

Camping is not permitted. Osage Hills State Park, 12 miles east of Pawhuska on US 60, has a developed campground.

Best Times to Visit

The prairie begins to green up, Eastern Redbuds bloom, Greater Prairie-Chickens dance, and Bison calve in April and May. Spiderworts, Showy White Evening-Primroses, Spider Milkweeds, and Prairie Larkspurs carpet the grasslands in late spring; Pale Purple Coneflowers, blazing stars, and blanket flowers bloom in early summer. During relatively wet years, the tallgrasses bloom in August, but summer droughts accompanied by 100°F temperatures may wilt the grasses before they flower. Colors intensify in late October, when skies turn bluest.

Information

TALLGRASS PRAIRIE PRESERVE, Box 458, Pawhuska, OK 74056; 918-287-4803. A visitor center at the preserve headquarters is open limited hours during most days. The preserve is open dawn to dusk, mid-March through November; roads through the preserve are open year-round.

How to Get There

From US 60 in downtown Pawhuska, drive north on Kihekah Street. Continue northwest for 17 miles, following frequent directional signs to the preserve headquarters. The last 9 miles are a loose gravel road with heavy truck traffic and few pullouts.

TALLGRASS PRAIRIE PRESERVE

WEATHER
MEAN TEMPERATURES AND PRECIPITATION

MONTH	HIGH (°F)	LOW (°F)	PRECIP.	SNOW
January	47	24	1.5"	3.0"
April	73	48	3.8"	0.1"
July	94	69	3.3"	0.0"
October	75	48	3.2"	0.1"

Mean annual precipitation is 37.04 inches. Violent thunderstorms and tornadoes are possible April through September. Annual temperature range (from the year's high to the year's low) can exceed 140°F. Data are for Bartlesville, Oklahoma.

SELECTED WILDLIFE OF SPECIAL INTEREST

MAMMALS: Virginia Opossum, Nine-banded Armadillo, Woodchuck, Beaver, Coyote, Bobcat, Mule Deer, White-tailed Deer, Bison.

BIRDS: Bald Eagle (w), Northern Harrier, Greater Prairie-Chicken, Wild Turkey, Northern Bobwhite, Upland Sandpiper, Barred Owl, Chuck-will's-widow, Whip-poor-will, Pileated Woodpecker, Scissor-tailed Flycatcher, Carolina Chickadee, Tufted Titmouse, Northern Mockingbird, Blue Grosbeak, Indigo Bunting, Painted Bunting, Dickcissel.

AMPHIBIANS AND REPTILES: Common Five-Lined Skink, Timber Rattlesnake, Spiny Softshell Turtle, False Map Turtle, Eastern Box Turtle.

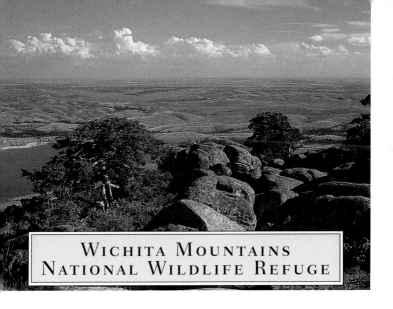

WICHITA MOUNTAINS NATIONAL WILDLIFE REFUGE

These dark granitic mountains, which rise 1,500 feet above the surrounding plains, harbor a wealth of native plant and animal species. Bison and Elk graze in mixed-grass prairies. Bobcats and Barred Owls haunt dense groves of oak and juniper. Armadillos and opossums waddle through brushy canyons. In all, this 100-square-mile island of protected grasslands and woodlands supports 50 species of mammals, more than 300 birds, 64 reptiles and amphibians, and 36 fishes.

For centuries, Native American peoples came to these mountains to hunt and worship. A Wichita story tells of a man who discovered a mountainside cave where thousands of buffalo lived; periodically, a large boulder blocking the cave entrance would shift, and the buffalo would come streaming out onto the prairie. According to a Kiowa story, when remaining buffalo in the Wichita Mountains area realized they were doomed to extinction during the late nineteenth century, they all walked single file into the depths of Mount Scott. They're still there, waiting to emerge when conditions improve.

These stories proved prophetic, for this refuge helped save Bi-

Above: These red boulders on Mount Scott were formed more than 500 million years ago when hot granitic magma oozed up through volcanic vents.

son from extinction. Under encouragement from big game conservationists, Theodore Roosevelt established the 60,000-acre Wichita Forest and Game Preserve by presidential decree in 1905. At the time, fewer than 1,000 Bison remained in North America, and populations of many other game animals were threatened.

In 1907 volunteers from the American Bison Society and the New York Zoological Society packed 15 Bison into individual crates and shipped them by rail from New York City to Oklahoma. A cheering crowd of cowboys, ranchers, soldiers, and local Plains Indians in ceremonial dress met the Bison at the station in Cache and escorted them to the refuge. Elk, Pronghorns, and Wild Turkeys were reintroduced a few years later.

Today more than 500 Bison roam the refuge, along with 600 to 700 Elk and about 300 Texas longhorn cattle. Each fall Bison and longhorns are culled from the herds and sold at auction. Limited hunting controls the size of the Elk herd. Refuge staff use prescribed burns to restore and maintain native mixed-grass prairie and to limit encroachment of oak and juniper woodlands.

In spring when greening meadows are carpeted with coreopsis and blanket flowers, and in fall when the calls of bugling Elk echo through granite canyons, the Wichita Mountains feel a little like a mountain wilderness. But the periodic roar of jet planes overhead and the thunder of heavy artillery on the adjacent Fort Sill Military Reservation remind visitors that this refuge, like all remaining prairie fragments on the southern Great Plains, is surrounded by altered lands.

Lava and Granite

The darker volcanic rocks of Oklahoma's Wichita Mountains formed 550 million to 600 million years ago when lava flows invaded sedimentary strata deposited on the bed of an ancient sea. The lava cooled into a gray-black igneous rock known as gabbro. After the gabbro solidified, the area was uplifted thousands of feet. Subsequent erosion washed away the overlying sediments, exposing the volcanic rock.

Between 500 million and 550 million years ago, a hot granitic magma pushed upward into the overlying gabbro, oozing to the surface through volcanic vents. This red granite, now the most widespread rock in the refuge, has weathered to form loaf-shaped boulders and narrow slot canyons.

During the ensuing 200 million years, the land sank and was covered at times by seawater. A second major uplift occurred about 300 million years ago, forming the present mountain range.

Once again wind and water eroded away the overlying sediments, exposing the harder gabbro and granite. Some of the most spectacular formations occur in the refuge's Charons Garden Wilderness Area, where mazes of giant granite boulders challenge cross-country travelers and entice technical rock climbers.

BLACK-CAPPED VIREOS

About 100 pairs of endangered Black-capped Vireos, the largest remaining nesting population in Oklahoma, breed in the refuge's oak woodlands. These dark-headed, white-spectacled songbirds require good-sized stands of oaks or shrubbery, where they suspend their delicate nests amid dense foliage. Their territorial song, a series of twittering 2- or 3-note phrases, distinguishes them from other vireos.

During the late 1980s biologists suddenly realized that these small reclusive insectivores were rapidly disappearing from their historic breeding range on the southern plains and in northern Mexico. By 1990 Black-capped Vireos had been extirpated from Kansas and from large areas of Oklahoma and Texas. Experts feared they would become extinct by the end of the century.

Disturbance and fragmentation of nesting habitat by farming and ranching, accompanied by increased nest parasitism by Brown-headed Cowbirds, have contributed to the species' decline. In some areas 100 percent of Black-capped Vireo nests contain cowbird eggs. By the time the vireo eggs hatch, the cowbird chicks weigh 10 times as much as the vireo chicks, and no vireo nestlings survive.

Refuge staff monitor nests, trap and remove cowbirds, and use prescribed burns to enhance nesting habitat. Refuge populations now appear to be stable, and biologists are hopeful that this sweet-singing vireo can be saved from extinction.

OWL CONVERGENCE

On summer and autumn nights at the refuge's Doris Lake Campground, the ghostlike wails, warbles, and whinnies of Eastern Screech-Owls mingle with the hoots and barks of Great Horned Owls and Barred Owls. The chorus generally peaks just before dawn as the owls court and proclaim their territorial dominance after a night of hunting.

In nearby canyons you might hear the loud hiss-scream of a Barn Owl. Burrowing Owls occasionally poke their heads out of prairie dog holes in meadows beside the main refuge road. In winter reclusive Long-eared Owls roost communally in oak thickets.

A young Eastern Screech-Owl gazes out from its nest cavity in an Eastern Red Cedar.

The variety of ecosystems found within the Wichita Mountains helps to explain this diversity of owl species. The refuge's geographic location, where western mixed-grass prairie intermingles with eastern deciduous forest, also contributes to species diversity.

Burrowing Owls nest in grasslands throughout much of the Western Hemisphere, but their breeding range on the Great Plains is limited by the availability of rodent burrows, primarily those of Black-tailed Prairie Dogs. They also shun tallgrass prairies, where their views of terrestrial predators are restricted. Barred Owls and Eastern Screech-Owls frequent deciduous forests throughout eastern North America. Oak woodlands and cottonwood groves within the refuge provide nesting habitat and camouflaging cover for these owls.

Wood Ducks

Wood Ducks seem out of place on the prairie, but they nest in prairie preserves from Manitoba to New Mexico. Their primary breeding requirements are a large tree cavity or artificial nest box, along with water and undergrowth for resting, foraging, and hiding from predators.

These brilliantly colored woodland ducks have expanded west onto the Great Plains as gallery forests developed along prairie rivers and streams. In the East, where Wood Ducks were nearly extirpated because of overhunting and habitat destruction 100 years ago, populations have recovered dramatically. Today Wood Duck populations are increasing or stable throughout most of their North American range.

Male Wood Ducks assume full breeding plumage by late November, and courtship begins long before pairs migrate north to summer nesting sites.

A young Wood Duck's life begins with a splash, or a thud. About 24 hours after her eggs hatch, the female flies down to the ground or water surface below the nest and begins calling softly: *kuk, kuk, kuk.* One by one, the ducklings step up to the edge of the nest cavity and push off. Though hardly aerodynamic, the lightweight, fluffy young can survive falls of up to 300 feet.

Clutches may number as many as 15 ducklings, since female Wood Ducks often dump their eggs in other females' nests. Hooded Mergansers also parasitize Wood Duck nests. European Starlings commonly raid or take over nests.

Biologists in Missouri struggled for years to protect nesting Wood Ducks from marauding starlings before they hit upon an ingenious strategy. After a starling lays her eggs in a Wood Duck nest box, the scientists replace them with a clutch of eggs coated with clear varnish. Then they erect a second nest box above the first. The female starling sits there most of the spring attempting to incubate her eggs, while the Wood Ducks nest peacefully right above her.

HIKING

Fifteen miles of hiking trails are accessible from the main refuge road. Trails are closed from sunset to 9 A.M., to benefit wildlife.

ELK MOUNTAIN (1 mile) and Charons Garden Wilderness Area trails (2 miles) take off from the Sunset Picnic Area 0.5 miles west of refuge headquarters.

DOG RUN HOLLOW TRAILS SYSTEM (1–6 miles round-trip), a part of the National Recreation Trails System, has trailheads at several parking areas south and east of refuge headquarters. These trails pass through oak woodlands, grasslands, and narrow granite canyons.

CAMPING

DORIS LAKE CAMPGROUND, on SR 49 halfway between the east and west refuge entrances, has walk-in sites and drive-in sites with or without electrical hookups.

CHARONS GARDEN WILDERNESS AREA. A limited number of backcountry permits are available each day at the park visitor center.

BEST TIMES TO VISIT

In late April and early May blooming wildflowers paint the grasslands crimson and gold; Bison calve and Wood Ducks and Wild Turkeys nest. Barred Owls and Eastern Screech-Owls call actively in early summer, after their chicks fledge, and again in late fall. Refuge staff lead bugling Elk tours in September and October. Crowds are sparse and temperatures usually comfortable throughout the winter.

INFORMATION

WICHITA MOUNTAINS NATIONAL WILDLIFE REFUGE, Route 1, Box 448, Indiahoma, OK 73552; 580-429-3221. The state-of-the-art visitor center has exhibits, interpretive videos, and a bookstore.

HOW TO GET THERE

From Lawton, Oklahoma, go 6 miles north on I-44 to Exit 45. Go west 6 miles through Medicine Park to the refuge entrance.

WICHITA MOUNTAINS NATIONAL WILDLIFE REFUGE

WEATHER
MEAN TEMPERATURES AND PRECIPITATION

MONTH	HIGH (°F)	LOW (°F)	PRECIP.	SNOW
January	52	27	1.3"	2.4"
April	75	49	2.7"	0.0"
July	96	71	2.3"	0.0"
October	78	51	3.1"	0.0"

Mean annual precipitation is 30.87 inches. Severe thunderstorms occur from April through September. Long stretches of 100°F weather are common in July and August. Data are for Lawton, Oklahoma.

SELECTED WILDLIFE OF SPECIAL INTEREST

MAMMALS: Virginia Opossum, Nine-banded Armadillo, Black-tailed Jackrabbit, Black-tailed Prairie Dog, Coyote, Gray Fox, Ringtail, Bobcat, Elk, White-tailed Deer, Bison.

BIRDS: Green Heron, Wood Duck, Mississippi Kite, Wild Turkey, Greater Roadrunner, Eastern Screech-Owl, Barred Owl, Chuck-will's-widow, Black-chinned Hummingbird, Scissor-tailed Flycatcher, Black-capped Vireo, Tufted Titmouse, Carolina Wren, Bewick's Wren, Northern Cardinal, Painted Bunting.

AMPHIBIANS AND REPTILES: Plains Leopard Frog, Eastern Collared Lizard, Texas Horned Lizard, Western Diamond-backed Rattlesnake, Western Rattlesnake, Massasauga, Ornate Box Turtle, Pond Slider.

OTHER OKLAHOMA SITES

BLACK KETTLE NATIONAL GRASSLAND (Route 1 Box 55 B, Cheyenne, OK 73628; 580-497-2143). The 34,000 acres of mixed-grass prairie in scattered parcels include Washita Battlefield National Historic Site. Camping areas around three lakes offer fishing, swimming, and boating. West of Cheyenne on either side of SR 47, and north of Cheyenne on either side of US 283.

BLACK MESA STATE PARK AND NATURE PRESERVE (HCR 1, Box 8, Kenton, OK 73946; 580-426-2222). This tranquil park in the Oklahoma Panhandle features high-quality shortgrass prairie, dinosaur tracks, a fishing lake, and a 4.2-mile hiking trail to the top of Black Mesa. Camping, hiking, and boating. From Boise City go west then north 20 miles on SR 325.

PONTOTOC RIDGE PRESERVE (The Nature Conservancy, Route 2, Box 72B, Stonewall, OK 74871; 580-777-2224). This 2,900-acre preserve on the Arbuckle Uplift contains limestone outcrops, springs and streams, moist hardwood forests, and tallgrass prairie. Hiking trail. From 2 miles east of Ada take US 377 south 16 miles to Pontotoc-Johnson County line. Go east on Pontotoc Road until it turns north (about 1 mile). Continue north a short distance and look for the double-gated preserve entrance on your right.

SALT PLAINS NATIONAL WILDLIFE REFUGE (Route 1, Box 76, Jet, OK 73749; 580-626-4794). The 32,000 acres of salt flats, open water, woodlands, and croplands provide habitat for migrating Whooping Cranes and shorebirds. Bald Eagles and Peregrine Falcons overwinter. Hiking. From Jet, drive north 13 miles on SR 38, then 1 mile west to refuge headquarters.

Bigflower Coreopsis (Coreopsis grandiflora), *Larkspur (*Delphinium spp.*), and Common Spiderwort* (Tradescantia ohiensis) *bloom throughout northeastern Oklahoma's tallgrass prairie region in May and early June.*

SOUTH DAKOTA

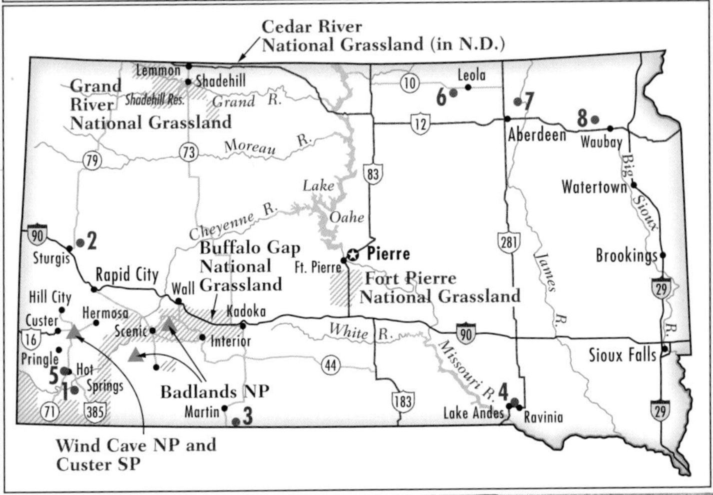

Cedar River
National Grassland (in N.D.)

Grand
River
National Grassland

Lemmon
Shadehill
Shadehill Res.
Grand R.

Moreau R.

79
73

Leola
10
6
7
12
Aberdeen
Waubay
8

83
Watertown

Lake
Oahe

Cheyenne R.

90
2
Sturgis
Rapid City

Buffalo Gap
National
Grassland
Wall
Kadoka

Pierre
Ft. Pierre
Fort Pierre
National Grassland

281
Brookings

29

Hill City
Custer
16
Hermosa
Scenic
Interior

White R.
90

Missouri R.
Sioux Falls

Pringle
5
1
Hot
Springs
71
385

Badlands NP

Martin
3
44

183

Lake Andes
4
Ravinia

29

Wind Cave NP and
Custer SP

BADLANDS NATIONAL PARK

BUFFALO GAP NATIONAL GRASSLAND

FORT PIERRE NATIONAL GRASSLAND

GRAND RIVER AND CEDAR RIVER
    NATIONAL GRASSLANDS

WIND CAVE NATIONAL PARK AND
    CUSTER STATE PARK

OTHER SOUTH DAKOTA SITES:
1. Angostura Recreation Area
2. Bear Butte State Park
3. Lacreek National Wildlife Refuge
4. Lake Andes National Wildlife Refuge Complex
5. Mammoth Site
6. Samuel H. Ordway Jr. Memorial Preserve
7. Sand Lake National Wildlife Refuge
8. Waubay National Wildlife Refuge

BADLANDS NATIONAL PARK

Purple and gold mounds, pink pyramids and pillars, creamy buff cliffs striated in maroon—the Badlands delight the imagination. But there's more to this 240,000-acre fantasyland than pretty, eroded rocks. Bison graze on Blue Grama and Buffalo Grass, and Pronghorns browse on the low shrubs of the mixed-grass prairie. Endangered Black-footed Ferrets hunt in prairie dog colonies, and Burrowing Owls sit watchfully on the mounds. Orange-colored Painted Lady and fritillary butterflies flit over the unexpectedly profuse wildflowers. Fossils poke out from mud-gray shales.

The Lakota called it *mako sica*. French trappers called it les *mauvaise terres à traverser*. Both phrases mean badlands. Bad to travel across, but beautiful to look at. Conservationist Freeman Tilden felt that beauty when he wrote of "peaks and valleys of delicately banded colors—colors that shift in the sunshine. . . . In the early morning and evening, when shadows are cast upon the infinite peaks or on a bright moonlit night when the whole region seems a part of another world, the Badlands will be an experience not easily forgotten."

Most visitors see only the developed portion of the north unit of the park, including the 30-mile Loop Road with scenic overlooks, hiking trailheads, a visitor center, and lodging. However,

Above: White River Badlands.

the north unit also includes the 64,000-acre Badlands Wilderness Area, skirted on the north by the Loop Road. Divided into the Sage Creek unit and the Conata Basin, this wilderness is about one-third badlands; the remainder makes up the largest prairie wilderness in the United States. There are no established trails, so many hikers simply follow the Bison tracks. No permits are needed, but a good map and plenty of water are essential.

The two south units, Stronghold and Palmer Creek, also appeal to seekers of solitude. Located on the Pine Ridge Indian Reservation, they are managed by the National Park Service in cooperation with the Oglala Sioux tribe.

STRONGHOLD

Stronghold Table, a grassy mesa surrounded by steep bluffs, may have been the site of the last Ghost Dance of the nineteenth century. Devotees of the Ghost Dance religion believed that impassioned dancing would bring back the buffalo and a world without whites. Instead, the practice frightened whites, already inflamed by newspaper articles, and helped precipitate the tragedy at Wounded Knee where at least 200 members of the Minneconjou Lakota were shot down by the 7th Cavalry on December 29, 1890. Many were women and children trying to escape. The Wounded Knee Massacre Site (not a part of Badlands National Park) lies 42 miles south of the White River Visitor Center on BIA Route 27.

Both Stronghold Table and Sheep Mountain Table are sacred places where young Lakota men go to fast and pray. Prayer sticks, "tobacco ties" (bundles of tobacco left as offerings), and strips of brightly colored cloth tied to trees are evidence of vision quests or other religious rites and should not be disturbed. The rough 7-mile Sheep Mountain Table Road, which heads west from BIA 27, is the only road (other than private "two-tracks") into the Stronghold Unit. It leads to an overlook where the prairie suddenly drops off to reveal a basin of pink obelisks—as though a hidden secret has been bared.

During World War II, parts of this area were used as a gunnery range by the Army Air Corps. To accommodate the bombing exercises, 125 families were relocated, and many never returned. There were no civilian casualties, but members of flight crews were killed in crashes, and several buildings in the area were hit by shells. The bright white fossils of *Titanotheres*, a rhinoceros-like creature, were favorite targets. Unexploded ordnance still remains in the area and should be reported if found.

The undeveloped Palmer Unit, southeast of the main Stronghold Unit, has no vehicle access. Hikers into this remote area must obtain permission from adjacent landowners to cross their property. Maps are essential.

BURROWING OWLS

In Zuñi folklore, Burrowing Owls acted as high priests who looked out for prairie dogs by controlling the weather and the growth of plants. In exchange, the prairie dogs provided comfortable homes for the owls. Some Lakota warriors thought that a man who carried a Burrowing Owl into battle could not be wounded.

From May through August these little owls perch on prairie dog mounds, occasionally twisting their heads nearly upside down to discern a distant object in the sky. They nest in grasslands throughout the western plains, and they range from southern Canada to Tierra del Fuego. Although Burrowing Owls are capable of digging their own nest chambers, most depend on previously excavated rodent burrows.

Females typically lay 6 to 11 eggs in late spring, and it's not unusual to see 5 or 6 young beside a prairie dog burrow in early summer. The parents keep busy throughout the day bringing insects and small rodents to their hungry young. Golden Eagles, Prairie Falcons, Great Horned Owls, Swift Foxes, and Coyotes kill many young owls, and many more succumb to hazards encountered as they migrate south to Arizona, Texas, and Mexico.

Burrowing Owl populations have declined precipitously throughout the plains. These owls are listed as endangered in British Columbia, Alberta, Manitoba, Saskatchewan, Iowa, and

By 2 months of age Burrowing Owls have begun to take active interest in creatures, including nature photographers, who approach their burrow. (Photo by Richard W. Holmes)

Minnesota; threatened in Mexico; and of special concern (declining) in a dozen western states. Automobile collisions and poisoning of insect prey on Mexican wintering grounds may contribute to this decline, but fragmentation of native grasslands and elimination of prairie dog colonies probably have taken the greatest toll.

WHITE RIVER BADLANDS

About 70 million years ago, a shallow sea covered the area of central North America where the Badlands now lie. As the Rocky Mountains rose up to the west and the sea drained away, the mud sea bottom hardened into shales embedded with many clam and ammonite fossils. The upper layers weathered into a fossil soil or "paleosol" seen in the Yellow Mounds at Badlands.

As millions of years passed, subtropical forests covered the land, and floods deposited additional sediments. The White River Group of sedimentary rock contains fossils of alligators, land tortoises, and *Titanotheres*. Over millions of years, stream deposits and volcanic ash formed layers of soft sediments. Wind and water sculpted these layers into spires, windows, serrated cliffs, and canyons. The Cheyenne and White Rivers cut through sediments to form the Badlands Wall. As eons passed, the wall (which gave the town of Wall its name) eroded away from the river and marks the present-day route of the Loop Road.

Since 1847 when the first Badlands fossil was documented, the area has been renowned as one of the richest mammal fossil sites in the world, and the research continues. In 1993 two visitors found a large backbone jutting up from the ground near the

Bison graze on lush mixed-grass prairie beneath the backdrop of the White River Badlands.

Conata Picnic Area. The bone belonged to a piglike mammal called *Archaeotherium,* and its discovery led to an ongoing excavation affectionately called the "Big Pig Dig." Ancient rhinoceroses, horses, and deerlike creatures have since been uncovered at this important site, which is open to the public during the summer.

The Fossil Exhibit Trail (a quarter-mile loop) is keyed to a pamphlet and showcases replicas of a few of the many Badlands fossils, such as *Merycoidodon* (related to camels), *Mesohippus* (an early 3-toed horse), and *Hyracodon* (related to rhinoceroses). Fossils are also displayed at the visitor center.

EARLY INHABITANTS

An 11,000-year-old hunting camp is the oldest human site found in the Badlands. More than 300 additional sites consist of worked Bison bones, quarries, hearths, and fire pits—evidence that people used the Badlands more as a hunting ground than as a permanent living place. Archaeologists think large charcoal accumulations indicate that hunters set prairie fires to flush game.

A few homestead ruins slowly decay in the Sage Creek area, which was settled between 1920 and 1940. For the most part, the Badlands were an inhospitable home.

HIKING

All trailheads are on the Loop Road within a mile or so of the visitor center. Here is a sampling of the park's trails:

CASTLE TRAIL (5 miles one-way) connects the Fossil Exhibit Trail and the Door/Window parking area and features overlooks, pink-red sandstone formations, and prairie vistas.

SADDLE PASS TRAIL (0.25 miles) is very steep and impassable when wet. It provides access to the middle of Castle Trail.

MEDICINE ROOT TRAIL (about 5 miles) makes a loop within Castle Trail and is a good place to find wildflowers.

NOTCH TRAIL (1.5 miles and treacherous when wet) goes through a canyon, up a 45° angle cable and a ladder, and along a ledge to "the Notch" with spectacular views.

CLIFF SHELF NATURE TRAIL (0.5 mile loop) is keyed to a guide and passes through a "slump" area, where part of a formation has collapsed, to an oasis surrounded by badlands.

Camping

CEDAR PASS is a developed campground just south of the Ben Reifel Visitor Center near the southern entrance to the park.

SAGE CREEK, 13.5 miles northeast of Scenic on CR 590, is a primitive campsite with no water.

Best Times to Visit

In May and June the prairie turns a lush green, wildflowers bloom profusely, Bison and Pronghorn calves nurse greedily, and mild temperatures prevail. Summer can be very hot. In September and October temperatures turn mild again, and prairie grasses glow russet and gold. In winter when snow dusts the junipers, the contrast with barren badlands delights the few visitors. At all seasons rock formations glow in early morning or late afternoon light.

Information

BADLANDS NATIONAL PARK, Box 6, Interior, SD 57750; 605-433-5361. The Ben Reifel Visitor Center near Cedar Pass provides interpretive exhibits, videos, books, and brochures.

THE WHITE RIVER VISITOR CENTER, 20 miles south of Scenic on BIA 27, has exhibits, videos, and brochures on the Stronghold District and on the Lakota people. This center is open seasonally, usually from June through August.

How to Get There

From I-90 at Wall, take SR 240 (the Badlands Loop Road) to the Pinnacles Entrance. From I-90 at Cactus Flat, take the other end of SR 240 to the Northeast Entrance. From the town of Interior, take SR 377 to the Interior Entrance. From the town of Scenic, take SR 44; turn north on SR 590, which becomes the Sage Creek Rim Road, and then the Badlands Loop Road that goes past the Pinnacles Entrance.

To get to the Stronghold District, go south from Scenic on CR 589, which becomes BIA 27, to the White River Visitor Center. Four miles south of Scenic, the dirt road to Sheep Mountain Table (impassible when wet) heads west.

BADLANDS NATIONAL PARK

WEATHER
MEAN TEMPERATURES AND PRECIPITATION

MONTH	HIGH (°F)	LOW (°F)	PRECIP.	SNOW
January	34	11	0.3"	5.2"
April	62	36	1.8"	6.5"
July	92	62	1.9"	0.0"
October	68	39	0.9"	1.7"

Violent winds can blast through at any time of year. Temperatures can top 100°F in summer and drop below zero in winter. From spring to late summer dramatic thunderstorms with vivid bolts of lightning bring drenching rains that continue the age-old work of eroding the Badlands.

SELECTED WILDLIFE OF SPECIAL INTEREST

MAMMALS: Black-tailed Prairie Dog, Porcupine, Coyote, Swift Fox, Red Fox, Black-footed Ferret, Badger, Pronghorn, Bison, Bighorn Sheep.

BIRDS: Trumpeter Swan (m), Bald Eagle (w), Ferruginous Hawk, Ring-necked Pheasant, Sharp-tailed Grouse, Sandhill Crane, Upland Sandpiper, Long-billed Curlew, Burrowing Owl, Long-eared Owl, Short-eared Owl, Blue Grosbeak.

AMPHIBIANS AND REPTILES: Woodhouse's Toad, Plains Spadefoot, Greater Short-horned Lizard, Western Rattlesnake, Western Hog-nosed Snake.

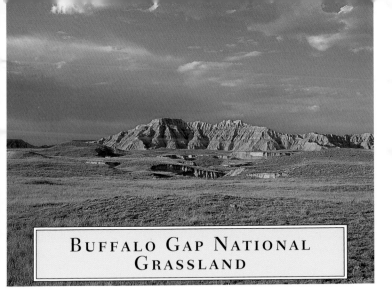

BUFFALO GAP NATIONAL GRASSLAND

Green Needlegrass stretches away to broken badlands the color of sunsets. Golden Pea, locoweeds, penstemons, and Scarlet Globemallows add yellow, purple, magenta, blue, and orange to the palette. A leaflet says, "Time needed depends on your tolerance for nothingness . . . Watching grass grow can be exciting." Here there is world enough, and time.

The opportunity to absorb the nuances of nature draws lovers of solitude to Buffalo Gap National Grassland, adjacent to Badlands National Park and the Pine Ridge Indian Reservation. At 591,000 acres, it's the nation's second-largest national grassland, and, like the others, it is composed of a checkerboard of public and private land. Conservationists have recommended two areas for wilderness designation: Red Shirt, northwest of the town of Red Shirt, and Indian Creek, west of the town of Scenic.

Mixed-grass prairie predominates, but some shortgrass prairie grows in the southwest and some tallgrass prairie, in the wetter areas. Eroding badlands punctuate the prairie here and there, providing niches for a wealth of plant and wildlife species, including Bighorn Sheep. Woody draws occupy less than one percent of the grassland but provide critical habitat for many species, such

This area south of Scenic is one of several Black-footed Ferret reintroduction sites in Buffalo Gap National Grassland.

as Porcupine and White-footed Mouse. The Cheyenne River divides Buffalo Gap into an eastern and a western district.

Cattle graze on the rich native grasses, and, as in all western prairies, Black-tailed Prairie Dogs provide the food base for raptors, Coyotes, Badgers, and Black-footed Ferrets. It's because of the numerous prairie dogs that this is one of the few places where the most endangered mammal in North America has been successfully reintroduced. Just knowing a Black-footed Ferret may be sleeping underground in a burrow adds magic to Buffalo Gap.

BLACK-FOOTED FERRETS

This slim, sinuous member of the weasel family matches the coloring of the prairie with yellowish buff fur, black mask and feet, and a black-tipped tail. Even before Black-footed Ferrets were declared endangered in 1967, they were seldom seen, as they hunt by night, mostly underground.

They were thought to be extinct by the mid-1970s. Then in 1981, a ranch dog killed one, leading to the discovery of a small population near Meeteetse, Wyoming. Hopes for the species' recovery were dashed in 1985 when canine distemper and sylvatic plague decimated the colony and also killed off the prairie dogs, the main source of food and burrows. To save the species, biologists trapped the remaining 18 ferrets and moved them to a captive breeding facility. The first reintroduction was at a White-tailed Prairie Dog colony in Shirley Basin, Wyoming, in 1991. The ferrets thrived until disease struck again in 1994. Only about 15 still inhabit Shirley Basin.

Ferrets were successfully returned to the wild in several different locales as researchers learned to identify good sites and improved their reintroduction techniques. Buffalo Gap now has the most successful reintroduction program in North America. A "ferret crew," including biologists Doug Sargent and Travis Livieri, counted 207 ferrets on three Buffalo Gap release sites by the end of the year 2000. Sargent estimates the total number of wild ferrets throughout the country at 350 to 400; the goal is to have 1,500 ferrets established in 10 or more populations by 2010.

Because all known wild ferrets are descended from the 18 Meeteetse captives, there is some concern about inbreeding. Captive inbred ferrets sometimes have kinked tails and shortened ears; however, Sargent says defects caused by inbreeding have not been detected in the wild.

One of the reasons for the success of the Buffalo Gap program is that the biologists require a Black-tailed Prairie Dog colony of at least 5,000 acres, with an optimum 16 to 24 prairie dogs per hectare (2.471 acres), before considering a release. A Black-tailed Prairie Dog colony is preferable to a White-tailed colony such as the one at Shirley Basin, Wyoming, because the smaller, more social Black-tails are easier prey, and their more densely populated colonies facilitate hunting.

Seven captive breeding facilities in the United States and Canada provide kits to be released. Young ferrets are kept in preconditioning pens, which are placed over a prairie dog colony at the release site, for about 45 days. The ferrets are fed "processed prairie dog" for a few weeks, then small live ones; eventually they learn to catch their own. Doug Sargent says this technique has doubled the survival rate over a "soft release," where ferrets are kept in small pens for only 10 days. The kits are vaccinated for canine distemper, given antibiotics, and implanted with two microchips for identification. In late summer biologists use transponders and spotlights to find dens with wild-born kits, which are trapped, medicated, and implanted with microchips before being released back into their original burrow.

The ferrets do not appear to be disturbed by human interaction. In 1998 "Number 49" was released in Badlands National Park and traveled 10 miles to a site on Buffalo Gap. This friendly male was seen over a period of about three years. "He'd jump on your leg as though saying ,'Good to see you again,'" said Sargent. In captivity a ferret's life span is five to seven years; in the wild, it is two to four years. Their enemies include Coyotes, Badgers, Bobcats, Foxes, and Great Horned Owls. But the greatest enemy is loss of habitat and prey.

The Black-footed Ferret population at Buffalo Gap is currently thought to be self-sustaining. With such a small, isolated group, however, there is always fear that a catastrophic event could eliminate the entire population.

BADGERS

Short, squat Badgers with heavy claws up to 2 inches long, powerful jaws and teeth, and muscular front legs can vanish below ground after only three minutes of digging. They dig new dens with several openings for themselves almost daily and easily excavate burrows of prairie dogs, ground squirrels, and mice. Cunning hunters, they sometimes plug up secondary escape holes before digging into the main entrance of a burrow.

Despite their irascible reputation, Badgers sometimes collaborate with Coyotes, who have more acute eyesight and hearing for locating prey. Coyotes sometimes wait at secondary ground squirrel holes while Badgers dig out the main entrance. By hunting together and covering more escape routes, both species catch more rodents and use less energy than either would alone. Writer John Madson calls them "two of the great common denominators of our original grassland biome, together with Bison, antelope, and buffalo wolf . . . ."

The Aztecs called the American Badger *tlalCoyotl*, meaning "Earth Coyote," and American Indians often paired the two in folk tales. In one story, Badger methodically positions stars into constellations until impatient Coyote trots up. Coyote flings the remaining stars at random into the sky, forming the Milky Way. In another story, Badger pities Coyote when Coyote loses his skin and gives him an old one of his own—which is why Coyote has rough, grizzled fur.

Badgers, primarily nocturnal, are most likely to be seen in late afternoon or at dawn in prairie dog towns. Although Badger and prairie dog dens appear similar, a prairie dog mound is higher and more uniform, whereas a Badger den is fanned out with a more elliptical opening—the better to accommodate what Madson describes as "a bowlegged, pigeon-toed doormat that sweeps the ground with its trailing end."

DON COYOTE

The tawny-gray coyote materializes like a ghost at dusk and dawn and sends its unearthly howl ringing through the prairie night. Had western settlers' efforts to eradicate all "bad" predators succeeded, this species might have become a ghost. Instead, the adaptable Coyote multiplies in the face of concerted efforts to eradicate it and lives up to its reputation as the Trickster/Hero.

Coyotes have spread to all Canadian provinces, to all states except Hawaii, and even into the suburbs of New York City and Los Angeles. They are probably more numerous now than before the West was settled, in spite of the fact that approximately 400,000 are killed each year. They learn to stay just out of range of guns and to avoid traps, and they teach this wary behavior to their pups. Observers have reported that some previously trapped Coyotes will deliberately spring traps while staying out of range of the steel jaws.

Perhaps their greatest survival trick is the ability to produce larger litters when their population drops. More females breed and more pups survive to fill the vacuum. This trait, called "density dependent reproduction," plus the fact that wolves and other competing predators have been extirpated, helps Coyotes prosper.

Weighing about 35 pounds, Coyotes prey chiefly on rodents and even on grasshoppers, performing a valuable pest control ser-

Opportunistic Coyotes feed on grasshoppers, mice, prairie dogs, carrion, and a variety of wild fruits, including chokecherries and prickly pears. (Photo by John B. Weller)

vice for farmers. In fact, when Coyotes are removed from an area, rodents and smaller predators proliferate. They also help clean the prairie of carrion. Coyotes usually hunt individually or in family groups, but in areas where large prey abounds, they sometimes hunt in packs and occasionally take fully grown sheep or deer. However, they are more likely to kill unguarded young and injured or sick animals.

Coyote family life is notable for the affection shown by adults and pups. Pairs often mate for life and greet each other with tail wagging, wriggling, and muzzle licking. "Nannies" (pups from the previous year's litter) often babysit, play with the pups, and help protect the den site. Skirmishes usually end amicably when a subordinate Coyote rolls over to expose its belly or kneels submissively. Coyotes communicate through body language, face grimacing, and a variety of vocalizations, including the spine-tingling yip-howls, antiphonal yodels that inspire such affectionate names as "Song Dog" and "God's Dog."

ROCK HOUNDING

Fairburn Agate, the state gemstone, is a brightly banded semiprecious stone used in jewelry and prized by collectors. Other stones from alluvial deposits at Buffalo Gap include Bubble Gum, Prairie, and Moss Agate; Jasper; Rose Quartz; Red Carnelian; Blue Chalcedony; and Puddingstone Conglomerate. Collecting rocks and invertebrate fossils is permitted on the grassland as long as the site is not disturbed, but is prohibited in Badlands National Park. Maps identifying rock hounding areas are available at the visitor center.

Cretaceous and Oligocene Era fossils also abound in the eroded clay. However, collecting vertebrate fossils or cultural artifacts is illegal. For more information on the geology and paleontology of the area, see the section on Badlands National Park.

HIKING

PRAIRIE BIKE TRAIL (14 miles), the only official trail on the grassland, provides views of the Badlands Wall and various prairie features. It begins about 1 mile south of Wall on the east side of US 240 and makes a large, or a small, loop connecting to FS 7116. Many two-track roads also offer easy, mostly level, hiking, and Badlands National Park contains many good trails.

CAMPING

THE FRENCH CREEK PICNIC AREA, on CR 18 about 10 miles east of Fairburn, is the only developed camping or picnicking site. However, primitive camping is permitted anywhere on the grassland.

BEST TIMES TO VISIT

Golden Peas and White Penstemons bloom in May and June as prairie dog pups emerge above ground and deer and Pronghorn fawns appear. Summers are hot, but mild weather returns in September and October when prairie grasses turn to shades of rose and gold. Winter is a time of enhanced solitude, occasionally broken by a Coyote's howl.

INFORMATION

NATIONAL GRASSLANDS VISITOR CENTER (708 Main Street, Wall, SD 57790; 605-279-2125) administers the eastern district. This center, containing exhibits, videos, and a bookstore, is one of the best sources in the country for information on prairie ecology and on all the national grasslands.

FALL RIVER RANGER DISTRICT (209 N. River Street, Hot Springs, SD; 605-745-4107) administers the western district.

HOW TO GET THERE

The eastern district extends roughly from Kadoka on the east to the Cheyenne River on the west; from US 44 on the north to the

Pine Ridge Indian Reservation on the south. The western district extends from the Cheyenne River on the east to the Wyoming and Nebraska borders on the west and south, with US 18 cutting through the center. Numerous roads access both districts. **NOTE:** A Buffalo Gap National Grassland map, available at either of the above visitor centers, is essential for exploring this grassland.

BUFFALO GAP NATIONAL GRASSLAND

WEATHER
MEAN TEMPERATURES AND PRECIPITATION

MONTH	HIGH (°F)	LOW (°F)	PRECIP.	SNOW
January	34	11	0.3"	5.2"
April	62	36	1.8"	6.5"
July	92	62	1.9"	0.0"
October	68	39	0.9"	1.7"

Mean annual precipitation is 15 inches, but annual amounts have ranged from 7.13 inches to 26.36 inches. Historic temperatures have ranged from -42°F to 116°F. Long periods of drought are common, but so are blizzards and thunderstorms. Over 5 inches of rain fell on August 17, 1930, and 18 inches of snow accumulated on April 14, 1927.

SELECTED WILDLIFE OF SPECIAL INTEREST

MAMMALS: Black-tailed Prairie Dog, Coyote, Swift Fox, Black-footed Ferret, Badger, Mink, Eastern Spotted Skunk, Mule Deer, White-tailed Deer, Pronghorn, Bison, Bighorn Sheep.

BIRDS: Trumpeter Swan, Bald Eagle (w), Golden Eagle, Ring-necked Pheasant, Sharp-tailed Grouse, Upland Sandpiper, Long-billed Curlew, Burrowing Owl, McCown's Longspur, Chestnut-collared Longspur, Blue Grosbeak.

AMPHIBIANS AND REPTILES: Woodhouse's Toad, Plains Spadefoot, Greater Short-horned Lizard, Western Rattlesnake, Western Hog-nosed Snake, Snapping Turtle.

FORT PIERRE NATIONAL GRASSLAND

As Lewis and Clark's Corps of Discovery worked its way up the Missouri River in late September 1804, the explorers passed through a country of bluffs and upland prairies teeming with wildlife. They saw Elk, White-tailed Deer, Mule Deer, Bighorn Sheep, Pronghorns, and herds of Bison that, wrote Meriwether Lewis, "were in such multitudes that we cannot exaggerate in saying that in a single glance we saw 3000 of them before us." Wild Plums and Chokecherries crowded the banks of the Missouri, and the uplands hosted "multitudes of barking squirrels [prairie dogs], who entice hither the wolves of the small kind [Coyotes], hawks, and polecats."

Within 115 years, most of this prairie was gone, along with the Bison, Elk, Bighorn Sheep, Grizzly Bears, and wolves. Dryland farms had replaced the lush grasslands. When the 1930s drought hit, many farmers abandoned these lands or sold out to the federal government. In 1937 the Soil Conservation Service assumed control of about 100,000 acres of deserted farmlands in central South Dakota just upstream from the Great Bend of the Missouri.

Today the Fort Pierre National Grassland is a patchwork of

Above: Small reservoirs throughout Fort Pierre National Grassland attract migrating waterfowl and nesting songbirds.

116,078 acres of public land interspersed with private farmlands and again abounds with wildlife. Greater Prairie-Chickens and Sharp-tailed Grouse dance each spring on more than 200 leks. Northern Harriers and Short-eared Owls skim over knee-high grasses. An Upland Sandpiper seems to stand on every fifth fence post. There are small herds of Pronghorns and deer, as well as 300 head of Bison.

Several small reservoirs surrounded by woody vegetation attract birdwatchers and campers. Intermittent streams running through U-shaped coulees create natural pathways for hikers and hunters. Two small blinds may be reserved for observing and photographing dancing grouse and prairie-chickens in April and May.

CHOKECHERRIES

During the Moon of Black Cherries Ripening, halfway between the summer solstice and the autumnal equinox, Plains Indian women and children would scour the hills and valleys for Chokecherries (*Prunus virginiana*). Most of the tart, astringent cherries were crushed and mixed with Bison fat to make pemmican, a staple of the winter diet. Others were boiled up into stews or festive drinks, while some were reserved for important ceremonies.

The Lakota name for this member of the rose family is *canpa'-hu* ("bitter-wood stem"). The Lakota used the blood red fruits and their juices in rites honoring a young woman's first menstruation. The sun dance typically began on the day of the full moon during the month when Chokecherries were ripe.

Plains Indians may have extended the range of Chokecherries

An Eastern Kingbird perches near its nest in a Chokecherry bush at Fort Pierre's Richland Wildlife Area.

by planting the seeds around their villages, but these hardy shrubs grow naturally from Saskatchewan to Newfoundland and south to New Mexico, Tennessee, and North Carolina. On the Great Plains they bloom in April and May. Although the berries usually ripen by mid-August, they are sweeter and less astringent after they have been touched by the first frost.

Some plains residents still gather Chokecherries each summer to use in jellies or pies. When mixed with sugar, they make a wonderful syrup for ice cream. Many wildlife enthusiasts prefer to leave the berries on the bush for the bears, Coyotes, Red Foxes, Porcupines, squirrels, and songbirds.

GREATER PRAIRIE-CHICKENS

In April and May, Greater Prairie-Chickens strut on more than 150 booming grounds scattered throughout this national grassland. Most booming grounds are located on hilltops or sparsely vegetated flats where dancing males have an unobscured view of potential predators.

The spectacle generally begins as the first colors of dawn warm the eastern sky. Several males plop down onto the lek. Gradually, as the strengthening light fuels their sexual fervor, they fan their tails, lower their heads, and raise the stiff pinnate feathers on their necks. Then they inflate the saffron sacs on each side of their necks, emitting a low *whoom* or *ooh den doooo,* a sort of moaning, whining version of the sound made by blowing across the opening of an empty cider jug.

The males stomp their feet or skitter across the lek with wings dragging and tail feathers fully fanned out. Two males may square off head-to-head, cackling and leaping into the air. The performance continues until after sunrise, when the males and watching females disperse into the surrounding grasslands.

All this expenditure of energy is futile for most of the dancers, since only one or two males, generally those occupying the center of the lek, will actually mate. The process ensures that the fittest genes are passed on to succeeding generations. This complex, ritualized behavior evolved over millions of years. It was nearly snuffed out during less than a century.

An August 1863 article in the Sioux City, Iowa, *Register* boasted that "never . . . have prairie-chickens been as numerous as the present season." During a single day, marveled the writer, 36 men had killed 1,269. By 1900 Greater Prairie-Chickens had been extirpated from most of their historic range. Overhunting was a driving force, as was cultivation of tallgrass prairies and clearing of oak woodlands.

Today scattered populations hold on in portions of Wisconsin and Illinois west to the Dakotas, northeastern Colorado, and south Texas. In some areas cultivated grains have replaced the acorns and other wild seeds and fruits that made up a major portion of prairie-chicken diets, enabling these grouse to expand their range westward. But throughout much of the heart of their historic range in the Ohio, Mississippi, and Missouri River Valleys, they remain threatened.

One major threat is inbreeding within isolated flocks. During the early 1990s, Illinois biologists began mixing prairie-chickens captured in adjacent states into dwindling Illinois flocks, and the flocks began to recover. However, remaining populations in Illinois began to decline sharply again during the late 1990s. Some scientists believe that nesting habitat in midwestern states is simply too fragmented to support viable populations.

At Fort Pierre National Grassland, numbers of Greater Prairie-Chickens observed on booming grounds increased throughout the 1990s, while numbers of dancing Sharp-tailed Grouse decreased. No one fully understands the causes of these population fluctuations, but they could be driven by weather, grazing intensity, availability of fruits and insects, episodes of disease, or patterns of predation. Reduced cattle stocking levels and above-average precipitation during the 1990s may have benefited Greater Prairie-Chickens by increasing overall grass cover.

UPLAND SANDPIPERS

Where mixed-grass and tallgrass prairies remain relatively natural, these long-necked shorebirds perch placidly on fence posts or sail overhead bleating out sweet, rolling trills. They lay their eggs in loose, cup-shaped nests concealed by overarching grasses. They defend their nests and fledglings heroically, swooping down on anyone who gets too close.

Upland Sandpipers, formerly called Upland Plovers, nest from Alaska and Nova Scotia to Oklahoma and Virginia, and they winter as far south as Argentina. They once numbered in the millions, and their annual northward flight marked the passing of winter and the greening of prairie grasses. Their fate was nearly that of the Passenger Pigeon as overhunting and habitat destruction decimated their numbers.

Today, populations are fairly stable, though a small fraction of historic numbers. On cold spring nights, prairie dwellers again listen for the lonesome, liquid calls of birds heading north, a sure sign of spring.

In A. C. Bent's *Life Histories of North American Shore Birds*, explorer William Henry Hudson writes in awe of the feelings evoked by this migratory flight:

Lying awake in bed, I would listen by the hour to that sound coming to me from the sky, mellowed and made beautiful by distance and the profound silence of the moonlit world . . . that delicate, frail, beautiful being, traveling in the sky, alone, day and night, crying aloud at intervals as if moved by some powerful emotion, beating the air with its wings, its beak pointing like the needle of the compass to the north, flying, speeding on its 7,000-mile flight to its nesting home in another hemisphere.

HIKING

There are 40 miles of two-track roads suitable for hiking. Overland travel is fairly easy, but watch for rattlesnakes.

CAMPING

Camping is permitted on Federal lands throughout this national grassland, but off-road travel is restricted during the fall months and year-round in the Richland Wildlife Area. Check with the Fort Pierre National Grassland office in Pierre concerning regulations.

BEST TIMES TO VISIT

Sharp-tailed Grouse and Greater Prairie-Chickens dance in April and May. Call ahead to reserve a blind for dawn viewing. Young Black-tailed Prairie Dogs begin to emerge from their burrows in early May. Upland Sandpipers and Marbled Godwits begin displaying and nesting a couple of weeks later. In autumn, large flocks of migrating ducks sweep through, while migrating Northern Harriers, Swainson's Hawks, and Ferruginous Hawks glide over amber and burgundy grasses.

INFORMATION

FORT PIERRE NATIONAL GRASSLAND, 124 S. Euclid Avenue, Box 417, Pierre, SD 57501-0417; 605-224-5517.

HOW TO GET THERE

From Fort Pierre take US 83 south for about 8 miles. Explore on county roads. **NOTE:** Because federal lands are scattered, you will need a Fort Pierre National Grassland map, available at the Pierre office, to find your way around.

FORT PIERRE NATIONAL GRASSLAND

WEATHER
MEAN TEMPERATURES AND PRECIPITATION

MONTH	HIGH (°F)	LOW (°F)	PRECIP.	SNOW
January	27	7	0.5"	5.5"
April	59	35	1.8"	2.6"
July	90	63	2.3"	0.0"
October	64	38	1.3"	0.9"

Mean annual precipitation is 18.00 inches. Severe thunderstorms and heat indexes of more than 105°F commonly occur during the summer months. Data are for Pierre, South Dakota.

SELECTED WILDLIFE OF SPECIAL INTEREST

MAMMALS: White-tailed Jackrabbit, Black-tailed Prairie Dog, Coyote, Badger, Long-tailed Weasel, Mink, White-tailed Deer, Pronghorn.

BIRDS: Northern Shoveler, Northern Harrier, Swainson's Hawk, Ferruginous Hawk, Greater Prairie-Chicken, Sharp-tailed Grouse, Marbled Godwit, Upland Sandpiper, Burrowing Owl, Short-eared Owl, Grasshopper Sparrow, Lark Bunting, Chestnut-collared Longspur, Blue Grosbeak, Dickcissel, Orchard Oriole.

AMPHIBIANS AND REPTILES: Great Plains Toad, Woodhouse's Toad, Northern Leopard Frog, Eastern Racer, Western Rattlesnake.

GRAND RIVER AND CEDAR RIVER NATIONAL GRASSLANDS

Mixed-grass prairie, dotted with prairie potholes and punctuated by buttes, rolls across the Missouri Plateau in the Grand River and Cedar River National Grasslands. Grand River, the larger of the two, spreads across northwestern South Dakota. Cedar River lies just over the border in southwestern North Dakota and consists of only a few widely scattered parcels. Together these grasslands total 161,000 acres.

Billowing stands of Needle-and-Thread, Blue Grama, Western Wheatgrass, and introduced Crested Wheatgrass are enlivened by various species of penstemon, phlox, sunflower, and mustard. Cottonwoods, Green Ash, American Elm, Box Elder, Buffaloberry, Snowberry, and Chokecherry grow in the woody draws.

Above: Hay meadow above Shadehill Reservoir, Grand River National Grassland. (Photo by Glenn Cushman)

Views from the Hugh Glass Memorial looking across Shadehill Reservoir, Grand River National Grassland. (Photo by Glenn Cushman)

During the late Cretaceous Period, *Triceratops* and *Edmontosaurus* dinosaurs lumbered where Bison and Elk later roamed and where cattle now graze. Petrified wood and calcite crystals frequently sparkle on the surface of the ground, and many fossilized bones and skeletons have been excavated in the region.

Private lands, state lands, and the Standing Rock Indian Reservation are intermixed with the grasslands. The two branches of Grand River were dammed to form a 5,000-acre lake at Shadehill Reservoir State Recreation Area, managed by the Bureau of Reclamation. Both Grand and Cedar Rivers flow east to join the Missouri River near Mobridge, South Dakota. Other noteworthy features include White Butte, the tallest point in the area, and the Little Egypt Badlands east of SR 73.

The 11-mile Grand River Scenic Route, keyed to a brochure available at the grassland office, provides an overview of grasslands management. Starting from SR 73 about 16 miles south of Lemmon, the loop has viewing points for livestock corrals, small reservoirs, woody draws, prairie dog colonies, a Golden Eagle nest, and possible turkey sightings. As you drive the route watch for the heart-shaped white rumps of Pronghorns.

FLASHING PRONGHORNS

Often mistakenly called "antelope," Pronghorns are unique. They warrant a family all their own, the Antilocapridae or "goat-antelope." Fossils show the family evolved in western North America during the Pleistocene. Today, *Antilocapra americana* is the sole surviving species and has changed little over the millennia.

Its common name comes from a pair of curved horns with a

prong jutting out from the side. A black outer sheath made of modified skin cells is shed each year and covers a bony core that is permanent. Another unique feature is the large white rump patch that is flared when the animal is alarmed. Other ungulates, such as White-tailed Deer, use a similar alarm signal, but only Pronghorns can actually erect and spread the rump hairs, which sometimes stick out 3 inches from the body. The white flash can be seen for up to 3 miles on the open grasslands.

Pronghorns have exceptional eyesight that has been compared to a person with 8-power binoculars. The huge eyes set far back on the side of the face give Pronghorns a wide field of view, enabling them to detect predators, such as Coyotes and hunters, from a long distance. Second only to the Cheetah in world speed records, they can run up to 60 miles per hour and cover 27 feet in a leap.

Fifty million Pronghorns may have browsed the sagebrush and grazed the grasses and forbs of North American prairies prior to European settlement. In 1859 one hunter alone killed 5,000, taking only hides. By 1924 unlimited hunting had caused the population to drop to 26,600. Hunting restrictions allowed the population to recover, and today about one million once again flash across the plains and high desert.

PASQUE FLOWER

The Pasque Flower (*Anemone patens,* see photos pp. 33, 409) blooms before the grass greens up, sometimes even before the snow melts. Hunting for the first pale purple harbinger of spring is an adult's equivalent of an Easter egg hunt. In *Sand County Almanac*, Aldo Leopold wrote, "For those of us in the minority, the opportunity to see geese is more important than television, and the chance to find a pasque-flower is a right as inalienable as free speech."

Although they look fragile, Pasque Flowers (the official flowers of South Dakota and Manitoba) thrive in gravelly soil, such as glacial moraines, from 4,000 to 10,000 feet and even at treeline. Their preferred habitats include hillsides that have been heavily grazed or burned.

The flower's popularity is proven by its many names, both scientific and common. At various times botanists have classified it as *Anemone patens, Pulsatilla patens, P. hirsutissima,* and *P. ludoviciana.* Among the many Plains Indians names are *hoksi' cekpa,* meaning "child's navel," because of the resemblance of the bud to an infant's navel (Lakota), and *napi,* meaning "old man," because of the hairy gray seed heads (Blackfoot).

Also called Prairie Smoke, Blue Tulip, Hartshorn, Windflower, Goslin Wing, and Easter Flower, this member of the buttercup family has been widely known since John Gerard's *The Herbal or General History of Plants* was published in England in 1597.

Lavender flowers are the norm, but on occasion pure white or deep purple blooms occur. Later, the styles lengthen into a feathery cluster resembling an unruly head of hair. The silky gray hairs covering the buds and stems protect the plant from dehydration by reducing wind velocity and may also deflect the sun's rays.

The Blackfeet and the Omaha used the crushed leaves in a poultice as a counter-irritant for injuries and arthritis, according to ethnobotanist Kelly Kindscher. The Blackfeet also made a tea to aid childbirth. Closely related *Anemone* species were used by various tribes to induce abortions and to cure sores, and the smoke from the seed heads was inhaled to relieve headaches. Because the plant contains some toxic substances, its use was primarily external, and some tribes limited its use to medicine men.

SIGNS OF THE PAST

Tepee rings, arrowheads, buffalo jumps, and petroglyphs attest to frequent use of these grasslands by prehistoric nomadic Indians who hunted the huge herds of Bison. By the time Europeans arrived, both Arikara and Lakota occupied the area. During the latter half of the nineteenth century, Standing Rock was the home of Sitting Bull, one of the most famous Lakota chiefs.

In the early 1800s trappers and explorers such as Jim Bridger and Hugh Glass, a local folk hero, roamed the area. Glass signed on with a trapping and hunting party in 1823. Near the Grand

Tepee rings show where Plains Indians once camped. (Photo by Glenn Cushman)

River he surprised a female Grizzly with cubs and was mauled so badly he was not expected to live. The main party continued on toward Yellowstone, but Bridger and another hunter were left behind to bury his body. When they heard rumors regarding a band of hostile Indians, the two men decamped with all the group's equipment, leaving Glass for dead.

He regained consciousness to find himself alone and unarmed with a broken leg and festering wounds — 200 miles from the nearest settlement. It took him more than two months to crawl 100 miles to the Cheyenne River, where he made a dugout and floated down to Fort Kiowa. A monument made from petrified wood commemorates Glass's ordeal and stands on a bluff with spectacular views of the reservoir, distant buttes, and woody draws. Look and listen for Wild Turkeys.

In July 1874, General George Custer led the 7th Calvary through what later became part of the grasslands en route to the Black Hills. The faint markings that look like *U S 7* on a bluff above Shadehill Dam may have been carved by some of his troops. After the discovery of gold in the Black Hills, the Bismarck-Deadwood Trail through the grassland became a busy route to the gold fields. White signs mark places where the trail crosses highways.

HIKING AND BOATING

Although there are no official trails, hiking is permitted anywhere on the grasslands, and the two-track roads make good trails. A pleasant walk follows the exposed shoreline of Shadehill Reservoir, where petrified wood lies scattered. Boating is popular on the reservoir and on both Cedar and Grand Rivers.

CAMPING

Camping is allowed anywhere on these national grasslands. In addition, several developed campgrounds dot the shore of Shadehill Reservoir.

BEST TIMES TO VISIT

These grasslands lie under the western edge of the Central Flyway, making spring and fall prime times to see migrating birds. Pronghorns give birth from late May through June; they mate and engage in territorial disputes in September and October. Pasque Flowers begin to bloom in April; asters and blazing stars bloom in September as cottonwoods, understory shrubs, and grasses turn yellow, red, and burgundy.

GRAND RIVER RANGER DISTRICT, 1005 5th Avenue, Box 390, Lemmon, SD 57638; 605-374-3592.

How to Get There

The various units of these two grasslands are widely scattered and are accessed by numerous county and Forest Service roads, making the map mentioned below even more necessary than usual. The Grand River sections are south of US 12, which passes through Lemmon. To reach Shadehill Reservoir, take SR 73 south from Lemmon 12 miles to the town of Shadehill, where a dirt road leads west to a campsite and boat launch. A few miles south of Shadehill, FS 5625 branches away from SR 73 and continues 3 miles to the Hugh Glass Monument and nearby Hugh Glass Campground. A short distance south of the campground, this road intersects the Grand River Scenic Loop on FS 5622, which loops back to SR 73.

The few parcels of Cedar National Grassland are accessed by various county roads north of US 12 and east of Lemmon. **NOTE:** A Grand River and Cedar River National Grassland map, available at the above office, is essential for exploring these grasslands.

GRAND RIVER AND CEDAR RIVER NATIONAL GRASSLANDS

WEATHER
MEAN TEMPERATURES AND PRECIPITATION

MONTH	HIGH (°F)	LOW (°F)	PRECIP.	SNOW
January	26	5	0.5"	7.6"
April	57	32	2.1"	4.0"
July	86	58	2.4"	0.0"
October	61	35	1.0"	1.8"

Mean annual precipitation is 18.5 inches. Summer (June–August) temperatures range from 32°F to 107°F with occasional severe thunderstorms. Data are for Lemmon, South Dakota (temperatures and precipitation), and Bismarck, North Dakota (snow).

SELECTED WILDLIFE OF SPECIAL INTEREST

MAMMALS: White-tailed Jackrabbit, Thirteen-lined Ground Squirrel, Black-tailed Prairie Dog, Coyote, Red Fox, Long-tailed Weasel, Badger, Bobcat, Mule Deer, White-tailed Deer, Pronghorn.

BIRDS: Ferruginous Hawk, Golden Eagle, Gray Partridge, Sharp-tailed Grouse, Wild Turkey, Upland Sandpiper, Marbled Godwit, Barn Owl, Burrowing Owl, Loggerhead Shrike, Sprague's Pipit, Lark Bunting, Grasshopper Sparrow, Baird's Sparrow, Chestnut-collared Longspur.

AMPHIBIANS AND REPTILES: Great Plains Toad, Woodhouse's Toad, Northern Leopard Frog, Plains Spadefoot, Tiger Salamander, Western Rattlesnake, Western Hog-nosed Snake, Bullsnake.

WIND CAVE NATIONAL PARK AND CUSTER STATE PARK

Bison amble by, amiable for the moment. White-tailed Deer leap up the hill. A woodpecker drums on a reverberating metal sign as a Black-headed Grosbeak carols overhead. That's what an awakening camper may experience in the Black Hills of southwestern South Dakota.

Wind Cave National Park (28,295 acres) and Custer State Park (73,000 acres) form a contiguous area of protected lands adjacent to the Black Hills National Forest. East meets West, and the plains meet the mountains in these unique parks where species from the west, the east, the prairies, and the mountains all intermingle.

The diversity of habitats includes mixed-grass prairie, woody draws, aspen groves, relict stands of Paper Birch, and the dark forests of Ponderosa Pine that prompted the Lakota to call the area *paha sapa,* meaning "the Black Hills." And, of course, there are the world-famous caverns.

LIMESTONE CAVES

Wind whistling from a hole in the ground in 1881 led Jesse and Tom Bingham to a cave filled with crystalline beauty, and it was

Above: Feral burros often beg for food along the Wildlife Loop at Custer State Park. (Photo by Glenn Cushman)

this wind that gave the cave its name. It's a living cave (features are still being formed) that breathes: When outside air pressure increases, air flows into the cave; when pressure drops, air flows out.

A few years after its discovery, Wind Cave was developed for tourism and called "the Great Freak of Nature." Guides led candlelit tours, and many cave features were broken off for souvenirs, but in 1903 it received protection as part of Wind Cave National Park.

The story of the cave goes back more than 300 million years to a time when inland seas were coming and going. Shells and other organic remains accumulated on the sea floor and eventually consolidated into limestone. Parts of the limestone dissolved to form passageways, which later filled with sediment. More sediment was deposited on top. Then about 60 million years ago the Black Hills, along with the Rocky Mountains, began a gradual uplift. The stress of the uplift produced fractures in the overlying limestone. Over millions of years, groundwater dissolved the limestone along the joints, and Wind Cave, one of the most complex caves in the world, was born.

In more modern times water levels within the cave dropped, draining additional passageways. In some places where older passages and newer ones intersect, rocks and mud from 320 million years ago are exposed. Wind Cave is multistoried in more ways than one.

Thin calcite plates arranged in a boxlike pattern have made Wind Cave famous for featuring more "boxwork" than any other cave in the world. Looking like honeycombs, these crystalline structures completely cover the walls in many places. Other cave features include frostwork, "popcorn" (rough clusters of calcium carbonate), helictites, flowstone, and a few stalactites and stalagmites.

Cavers continue to add new passages and rooms to the more than 100 miles that have been mapped. Based on wind velocities and barometric pressure gradients in the cave, scientists estimate that only about 5 percent of the cave has been discovered. Several guided tours, including one by candlelight, are offered. Reservations are recommended. Nearby Jewel Cave is also worth exploring.

BISON

A Lakota legend says that Bison came from the hole where the wind blows. The Plains Indians revered Bison and depended on them for food. They used every part of the animal, making hides

Bison like to roll on the ground, creating wallows. The wallows fill with water and then dry up, providing microhabitats for wetland plants in spring and drought-tolerant plants in late summer. (Photo by Glenn Cushman)

into robes, tepees, and canvasses for painting; horns into cups; shoulder blades into shovels; and tails into fly swatters. Children even tied jaw bones together with rawhide to make sleds.

French explorers called them *les boeufs,* meaning oxen, a word that evolved into *buffle, bufelo,* and eventually "buffalo." However, "buffalo" generally applies to African and Eurasian animals, which are quite different. "Bison" has become the correct common name for this herbivore that was instrumental in shaping the prairie landscape.

Bison were extirpated from the Black Hills region by the late 1880s. They were reintroduced at Wind Cave in 1913 when 14 were donated by the Bronx Zoo. That herd now numbers about 350. A year later, 36 Bison purchased from rancher Scotty Phillip were released in the game reserve that later became part of Custer State Park.

To avoid overgrazing, surplus Bison from Custer are sold three times a year, keeping the herd to about a thousand animals. About 90 percent of North America's current Bison population (around 300,000) are on private ranges and preserves, and most are descended from the Bison sold by Phillip to Custer State Park.

Male Bison are the largest mammals in North America. They weigh up to 2,000 pounds, stand 6 feet and more at the shoulder, and can run 35 miles per hour. They will win a confrontation, so visitors are urged to view them from a car. The main road through Wind Cave National Park and the 18-mile Wildlife Loop Road in Custer State Park are especially good places to see Bison and other wildlife up close.

Unbridled, Unbroken Ungulates

Because Elk and Pronghorn were also overhunted and eliminated by the late 1880s, an important mission for both parks has been to bring them back. Pronghorn are now common, and Elk can sometimes be seen, especially during the autumn rut.

Burros along the Wildlife Loop Road in Custer State Park often poke their heads into an open car window hoping for a snack. Please refrain from feeding these endearing animals. They are descended from Burros that formerly carried tourists to the summit of Harney Peak, the highest point in the United States east of the Rockies.

White-tailed and Mule Deer are common in both parks. Eight Rocky Mountain Bighorn Sheep replaced the extinct Audubon Bighorns in Custer State Park in 1922, and Mountain Goats that escaped from a fenced enclosure in 1924 can sometimes be seen near Harney Peak.

Private Lives of Prairie Dogs

During the first few years of a 15-year study of Black-tailed Prairie Dogs at Wind Cave National Park, ecologist John Hoogland wondered why roughly one-half of females who were observed copulating did not produce visible young (young seen above ground). After several more years of tedious, dawn to dusk observation, Hoogland and his fellow researchers arrived at an explanation that stunned the scientific community.

Black-tailed Prairie Dog colonies are divided into coteries, small groups of mostly related individuals. A coterie often consists of one dominant male, several mature females, and young of the year. Members of each coterie aggressively defend their turf. They maintain a network of interconnecting burrows, some extending 10 feet underground. Adults care cooperatively for the young, which are generally born in April or May.

While observing coterie interactions during the breeding season, Hoogland saw lactating females sneaking into their sisters' burrows. When they emerged, they often stopped to rub their faces in the dirt and lick their paws. Hoogland eventually determined that the burrows that had been visited by sisters were the ones producing no visible young. Later, he observed direct evidence of infanticide by females and, occasionally, males.

Infanticide is common among rodents, but infanticide among closely related individuals is rare. Since the function of procreation is to pass your genes along to succeeding generations, eating your own nieces and nephews seems counterproductive.

Black-tailed Prairie Dog pups engage in a variety of social activities, including chasing, wrestling, kissing, and mutual grooming.

Hoogland hypothesized that female prairie dogs raid their sisters' nests because these are the only nests available to them. In addition, raiding may reduce competition for scarce resources within coteries. He describes cannibalism among prairie dogs as a probable cost of colonial life. Presumably the benefits, including alertness to predators, outweigh this cost.

In Arizona another biologist has decoded the alarm barks used by Gunnison's Prairie Dogs. C. N. Slobodchikoff and his colleagues recorded alarm barks and noted the type of predator that had elicited the barking. They concluded that Gunnison's Prairie Dogs use distinct calls to identify humans, dogs, hawks, or other predators, and they use specific calls for specific individuals within a predator category. Prairie dogs apparently use body shape and color of clothing to distinguish one human from another. One alarm bark may designate "tall human," while another signifies "human red shirt."

The sociability of prairie dogs makes them fascinating subjects for casual, as well as scientific, study, especially in late spring when the young first appear above ground. The young roll and tumble in the grass, pile on top of their mothers, and touch lips in a ritualistic kiss. At intervals, colony members leap up on their hind legs and issue a nasal yip, a contact or "all clear" call that keeps individuals informed of others' whereabouts. When danger approaches, adults scurry into their burrows or sit up on their haunches and bark. The barks may all sound the same to us, but subtle differences in their acoustic structure convey life and death information to these sociable rodents.

Wind Cave has eight main trails plus three short nature trails, and Bison may be spotted on any of them. Several segments can be combined for a variety of loops. The following trails are especially good for prairie viewing.

WIND CAVE CANYON TRAIL (1.8 miles) begins on the east side of US 385, across from the natural cave entrance, and follows the canyon to a boundary fence. Woody draws and limestone cliffs attract a diversity of birds, including Wild Turkeys and Red-headed and Lewis's Woodpeckers.

EAST BISON FLATS TRAIL (3.7 miles) traverses prairie hills and offers panoramic views all the way to Buffalo Gap. It connects Wind Cave Canyon to US 385 near the south boundary of the park.

SANCTUARY TRAIL (3.6 miles) begins north of the Rankin Ridge fire tower on SR 87 and crosses a large prairie dog town before ending at the Highland Creek Trail.

BOLAND RIDGE TRAIL (2.7 miles), starting one mile north of the junction of park roads 5 and 6, climbs to a ridge with panoramic views.

Custer State Park has more than a dozen trails. Prairie and wildlife viewing are especially good on the following:

PRAIRIE TRAIL (3 miles), starting 4 miles south of the Wildlife Station Visitor Center, crosses open grasslands.

FRENCH CREEK (12 miles) cuts through the French Creek Natural Area, passing limestone cliffs and pools for some of the best scenery in the Black Hills. The west trailhead is 3.1 miles east of Blue Bell Campground on CSP 4; the east trailhead is 3.8 miles south of the State Game Lodge on the Wildlife Loop Road.

CAMPING

ELK MOUNTAIN CAMPGROUND, near the Wind Cave Visitor Center, is officially open April through October.

CUSTER STATE PARK has seven campgrounds. For reservations, call 1-800-710-2267. Walk-in camping is also allowed in the French Creek Natural Area; register at the trailhead.

BEST TIMES TO VISIT

The spectacular Bison rut occurs from mid-July to the end of August, and calves are born in April and May. At Custer State Park the annual Bison roundup is held in late September or early October, and about 350 animals are sold at the live auction on the third Saturday in November. In September prairie grasses, aspen, and birch turn to gold, and Elk bugle. For caving, any time of year is fine since cave temperatures stay constant at 53°F.

NFORMATION

CUSTER STATE PARK, HC 83, Box 70, Custer, SD 57730; 605-255-4515. Two visitor centers have excellent exhibits and brochures. The Peter Norbeck Visitor Center is on US 16A on the east side of the park, and the Wildlife Station is on the Wildlife Loop Road.

WIND CAVE NATIONAL PARK, RR1, Box 190, Hot Springs, SD 57747; 605-745-4600. The Wind Cave Visitor Center, where cave tours begin, has excellent exhibits, brochures, and information on caves. It is on US 385.

HOW TO GET THERE

CUSTER STATE PARK: The main east/west route is US 16A connecting Custer and Hermosa; the main north/south route is SR 87 connecting Wind Cave and Hill City.

WIND CAVE NATIONAL PARK: From Custer State Park, take SR 87 south; from Hot Springs, take US 385 north; from Pringle, take US 385 east.

WIND CAVE NATIONAL PARK AND CUSTER STATE PARK

WEATHER
MEAN TEMPERATURES AND PRECIPITATION

MONTH	HIGH (°F)	LOW (°F)	PRECIP.	SNOW
January	34	11	0.4"	5.2"
April	58	32	1.9"	6.5"
July	86	58	2.0"	0.0"
October	63	35	1.1"	1.7"

Mean annual precipitation is 16.6 inches. Spring blizzards and severe summer thunderstorms are likely. Fall temperatures are surprisingly mild, with November highs typically in the mid-50s. Data are for Rapid City, South Dakota.

SELECTED WILDLIFE OF SPECIAL INTEREST

MAMMALS: Least Chipmunk, Black-tailed Prairie Dog, Porcupine, Coyote, Mink, Mountain Lion, Bobcat, Elk, Pronghorn, Bison, Bighorn Sheep.

BIRDS: Bald Eagle, Golden Eagle, Prairie Falcon, Wild Turkey, Upland Sandpiper, Burrowing Owl, Lewis's Woodpecker, Plumbeous Vireo, Canyon Wren, Eastern Bluebird, Mountain Bluebird, Western Tanager, Red Crossbill.

AMPHIBIANS AND REPTILES: Great Plains Toad, Woodhouse's Toad, Tiger Salamander, Western Rattlesnake, Milk Snake.

ANGOSTURA RECREATION AREA (HC 52, Box 131-A, Hot Springs, SD 57747; 605-745-6996). About 4,500 acres of mixed-grass prairie and croplands surround a large reservoir 10 miles southeast of Hot Springs off US 385. Hiking, boating, camping. Nearby Cascade Falls, a thermal feature with turquoise water tumbling over travertine formations, is a few miles west of Angostura on US 71.

BEAR BUTTE STATE PARK (Box 688, Sturgis, SD 57785; 605-347-5240). This sentinel mountain of igneous rock, sacred to the Lakota and Cheyenne, looms up out of the mixed-grass prairie. This 1,945-acre park also contains a Bison herd and a small lake. Hiking, camping. Six miles northeast of Sturgis on SR 79.

LACREEK NATIONAL WILDLIFE REFUGE (HC 5, Box 114, Martin, SD 57551; 605-685-6508). American White Pelicans and Double-crested Cormorants nest at this 16,410-acre refuge containing shortgrass uplands, freshwater marshes, and sandhills. Trumpeter Swans overwinter and Bald Eagles and Whooping Cranes migrate through. Auto tour, hiking, boating. Nearby Little White River Recreation Area offers camping. About 13 miles southeast of Martin and east of US 73.

LAKE ANDES NATIONAL WILDLIFE REFUGE COMPLEX (291st Street, Lake Andes, SD 57356; 605-487-7603). This mix of protected wetlands and prairie includes the natural, shallow Lake Andes, the Lake Andes Wetland Management District, and the Karl E. Mundt Refuge where Bald Eagles roost in winter. Auto tour, hiking, boating. Located between the towns of Lake Andes and Ravinia, off US 281.

MAMMOTH SITE (Box 692, Hot Springs, SD 57747; 605-745-6017). The largest concentration of mammoth bones in the Western Hemisphere features in situ fossils of Woolly and Columbian Mammoths and other extinct mammals of the Great Plains. Interpretive tours, research, and educational programs. On US 18 Bypass in Hot Springs.

SAMUEL H. ORDWAY JR. MEMORIAL PRESERVE (The Nature Conservancy, 1000 West Avenue N., Suite 100, Sioux Falls, SD 57104; 605-331-0619). More than 300 plant species populate this 7,800-acre prairie, and thousands of shorebirds nest on the shores of its 400 potholes. A nature trail loops through swales and past ponds. Bison graze in a separate pasture closed to the public. From Leola, go 8 miles west on SR 10 and watch for the yellow TNC signs on the south side of the road.

SAND LAKE NATIONAL WILDLIFE REFUGE (39650 Sand Lake Drive, Columbia, SD 57433; 605-885-6320). The world's largest nesting colony of Franklin's Gulls and migrating Snow Geese (more than

1.2 million during spring migration) can be found in this 21,498-acre refuge in the heart of the prairie pothole region. A mix of marshes, woodlands, grasslands, and croplands provides habitat for ducks and shorebirds. Auto tour, hiking, boating. Located along the James River 27 miles northeast of Aberdeen via US 12 and CR 16.

WAUBAY NATIONAL WILDLIFE REFUGE (RR 1, Box 39, Waubay, SD 57273; 605-947-4521). *Waubay,* a Lakota word meaning "nesting place for birds," aptly describes these 4,650 acres of marsh, prairie, and forest where more than 100 bird species nest. Many eastern species, including Jack-in-the-Pulpit, trilliums, and Rose-breasted Grosbeaks, reach their westernmost extension here. Auto tour, hiking. From the town of Waubay take US 12 1 mile east and CR 1 7 miles north.

More than a million migrating Snow Geese stop off at Sand Lake National Wildlife Refuge in early spring.

Bear Butte State Park protects the place where Cheyenne culture hero Sweet Medicine received the tribe's Sacred Arrows and where generations of young men have gone to pray and receive visions.

Wildflowers and lush green grasses surround prairie potholes in midsummer at Samuel Ordway Jr. Memorial Preserve.

TEXAS

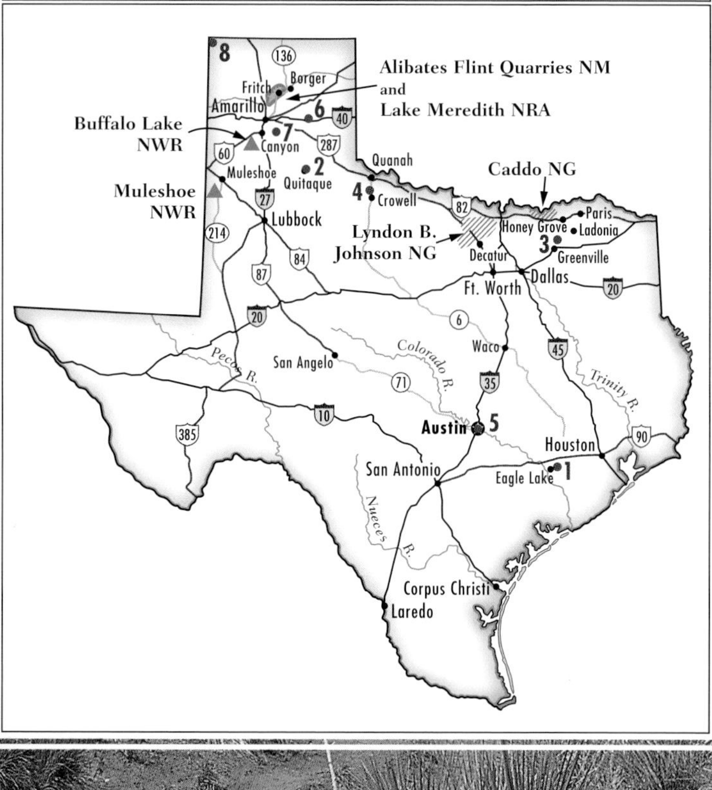

Buffalo Lake NWR

Muleshoe NWR

Alibates Flint Quarries NM
and
Lake Meredith NRA

Caddo NG

Lyndon B.
Johnson NG

8 (136) Børger
Fritch
Amarillo 6 (40)
Canyon 287
Muleshoe 60 Quanah
27 2 Quitaque
214 Lubbock 4 Crowell
84 Paris
82 Honey Grove Ladonia
Decatur 3 Greenville
Ft. Worth Dallas
20 87
20
Pecos R. San Angelo 6 Waco 45
Colorado R. 35 Trinity R.
71
10 Austin 5 Houston
385 San Antonio 90
Eagle Lake 1
Nueces R.
Corpus Christi
Laredo

Alibates Flint Quarries National Monument and Lake Meredith National Recreation Area

Caddo and Lyndon B. Johnson National Grasslands

Muleshoe and Buffalo Lake National Wildlife Refuges

Other Texas Sites:

1. Attwater Prairie Chicken National Wildlife Refuge
2. Caprock Canyons State Park
3. Clymer Meadow Preserve
4. Copper Breaks State Park
5. Lady Bird Johnson Wildflower Center
6. McClellan Creek National Grassland
7. Palo Duro Canyon State Park
8. Rita Blanca National Grassland

ALIBATES FLINT QUARRIES NATIONAL MONUMENT AND LAKE MEREDITH NATIONAL RECREATION AREA

Over eons of time the shortgrass prairie of the Llano Estacado has been cut into rugged canyons and breaks by the usually docile Canadian River. Many breaks are 200 feet deep and capped with white dolomite limestone, contrasting with orange-red walls. Grama grasses, Little Bluestem, Buffalo Grass, prickly pears, Honey Mesquite, and yuccas cover the mesa tops while willows, cottonwoods, and Soapberry trees grow in the draws.

For almost a century this area in the central section of the Texas Panhandle was heavily grazed by cattle. Today grazing is not permitted in the Alibates Flint Quarries National Monument and in some areas of the Lake Meredith National Recreation Area. The monument covers 1,279 acres, most of which is classified as prairie; the recreation area is about 44,994 acres, with about 21,000 acres in prairie.

In 1965 the Canadian River was dammed to create Lake Meredith, which also flooded many side canyons carved by tribu-

Above: Mixed-grass prairie at Alibates Flint Quarries. (Photo courtesy of Amarillo Convention and Visitors Center)

taries to the river. The Alibates Flint Quarries (accessible by guided tour with advance reservations) and Lake Meredith are adjacent National Park units.

ALIBATES FLINT

Rainbow-streaked Alibates flint is agatized dolomite formed when highly mineralized water seeped through the limestone caprock. It feels cool, hard, and smooth to the hand and has been prized by various cultures for at least 12,000 years. Clovis hunters used it for spear points to hunt mammoths, camels, and Bison. The frequent discovery of Alibates flint projectile points among skeletons of now extinct species has provided ammunition for scientists who contend that Clovis hunters helped bring on the mass extinctions of big game animals around 11,000 years ago.

Colorful flint outcroppings in the area contain stone that is too weathered to be worked for tools, so the people dug by hand or with sticks, antlers, or bone down to unweathered flint layers lying just below the surface of the ridges. About 735 pits, varying from 3 to 5 feet deep and from 5 to 25 feet in diameter, occur in a 10-square-mile area around Lake Meredith. The quarriers chipped out large chunks and took them away to flake into points, knives, and scrapers. Dirt and vegetation have accumulated in the quarries, making them almost invisible to the untrained eye, although shiny tailings still glint in the sun.

From 1000 to 1500 A.D. a farming culture, ancestors of the Pawnee and Wichita tribes, replaced the hunters and gatherers and built stone and adobe villages in the area. They also used Alibates flint and traded it for pottery from southwestern pueblos,

Colorful flint quarried at Alibates Flint Quarries National Monument was traded for such objects as seashells and Minnesota pipestone. (Photo by Glenn Cushman)

seashells from the Pacific Coast, and pipestone from Minnesota. Historic users of the flint included the Apache, Kiowa, Southern Cheyenne, and Comanche.

On the half-mile walk up to the ridgetop quarries, a ranger tells the story of the flint and the people who used it. A creek below the bluffs was named for cowboy Allie Bates (a clue to the proper pronunciation) and inspired the quarry's current name.

MESQUITE, BELOVED AND REVILED

The various species of mesquite (*Prosopis* spp.) have evolved strange and wonderful ways of coping with an arid environment. Before germinating, the hard seeds need to be scarified by passing through the digestive tract of an animal. Little above-ground growth occurs until the roots, which can reach depths of 65 feet, tap into water. Requiring less than 4 inches of preciptiation per year, this woody shrub or straggly tree out-competes native grasses.

Early explorers described this region as savanna, isolated stands of mesquite amid rolling grasslands, but the great cattle drives of the nineteenth century initiated a dramatic transformation. Cows ate mesquite fruit, a good source of protein and sugars, and excreted the seeds in nourishing dung piles. During the twentieth century, fires, which killed off young trees, were suppressed. Prairie dogs, consumers of tender mesquite seedlings, were killed off. And the proliferation of cattle set the stage for a mesquite takeover.

Mesquite, which has adapted too well to life on the range, now forms almost impenetrable brush over some 82 million acres in Texas, Oklahoma, Arizona, and New Mexico. Range managers consider it a noxious weed and use prescribed burns to control it.

However, rodents, deer, Raccoons, Coyotes, Wild Turkeys, Mallards, Mule Deer, Scaled Quail, and numerous other animals consume mesquite plant parts and rely on the dense scrub for cover and for shade. Collared Peccaries will even dig out woodrat nests to get stored mesquite beans. Among the many birds that nest in the thickets are Swainson's Hawks, Harris's Hawks, Greater Roadrunners, Scissor-tailed Flycatchers, Northern Mockingbirds, and Northern Cardinals.

This much-reviled plant is admired by many people, including Texas author J. Frank Dobie, who wrote, "It is as native as rattlesnakes and mocking birds, as characteristic as northers, and as blended into the life of the land as cornbread and tortillas." In other parts of the world it is used to combat erosion caused by poor farming practices. Like other legumes, it is important in fixing nitrogen in the soil. Southwestern Indians used mesquite for fuel, food, basket-making, and medicine, as well as in religious ceremonies. In *The Magnificent Mesquite*, Ken Rogers writes that the Coahuiltecan Indians made a flour from the beans, mixed it with the pulverized bones of dead warriors, and ate the concoction during ceremonies.

Wood carvers, furniture makers, and barbecue aficionados all prize the reddish, fragrant wood, while gourmands relish mesquite jelly, liquid smoke, honey, and the sugary raw pods. For many Texans the greening leaves and yellow blossoms are the official herald of spring. Perhaps with intelligent use of prescribed burning and other management techniques, both mesquite and grass can thrive in restored savannas.

HORNED LIZARDS

Looking like mini-dragons and affectionately called "horny toads," horned lizards bask in the sun and slurp up ants throughout the prairie region. Some 13 or 14 species (taxonomic shuffling is underway) range from southern Canada to Guatemala and west to the Pacific Coast. Loss of habitat has led to the decline of several species, including the Texas Horned Lizard. Collecting, use of insecticides, and predation by house cats exacerbate the problem, and in some areas the invasion of fire ants has reduced populations of native ant species, thus decreasing food supplies.

Named for the thornlike spikes on their head, horned lizards also have jagged scales on their backs, and most of them sport a sawtooth fringe along their sides. Their mottled colors match the prairie dirt or pebbles, making them difficult to see. When they flatten themselves against the ground, even their shadow disappears. To find them, herpetologist Robert Stebbins suggests walking in spirals around ant nests, where a small rounded lizard may lie in wait for dinner. When threatened, horned lizards can inflate themselves and jab with their horns. Some species spurt blood from a pore in the eyelid, aiming the stream at a predator, such as a Swift Fox or Coyote, up to 7 feet away.

Three species occur in Texas but only the Texas Horned Lizard is found at Alibates. Gary Lantz writes in *National Wildlife* that the Texas Horned Lizard was so common in the 1950s that a gas station paid kids a nickel apiece for them and then gave them away to customers. Since then they have disappeared from about 30 percent of their range, and Texas now prohibits collection. Although horned lizards do not live long in captivity, some pet stores still stock them.

HIKING AND BOATING

Lake Meredith was created to provide water for Panhandle cities and for water recreation. Many swimming areas, docks, and boat ramps are available, but water levels are often so low that the launches are left high and dry. Phone ahead for conditions.

MULLINAW TRAIL (4 miles) starts at the Mullinaw campground and winds through the canyon to the Rosita Motorcycle area.

PLUM CREEK/DEVILS CANYON TRAIL (4 miles) connects Plum Creek Campground to Devils Canyon.

CAMPING

Thirteen campgrounds are located on the caprock bluffs, in the canyons, and on the shoreline of Lake Meredith. The primitive campsites in McBride Canyon and at Mullinaw Creek, a few miles south of the flint quarries, are the most secluded. These sites are not on the lake but are shaded by large cottonwoods and Soapberry trees and are the closest ones to the quarries.

BEST TIMES TO VISIT

Temperatures in the summer can exceed 100°F, but it's a popular season for swimming and boating. Hiking is better during the off-season, when it's cooler. Wildflowers bloom, Wild Turkeys display, and courting birds, including Northern Cardinals and Bewick's Wrens, sing in April and May. Mesquite blooms from late May into June.

INFORMATION

ALIBATES FLINT QUARRIES NATIONAL MONUMENT, Box 1460, 419 E. Broadway, Fritch, TX 79036; 806-857-3151. Tours of the quarries available by reservation only.

LAKE MEREDITH NATIONAL RECREATION AREA, same address and phone.

HOW TO GET THERE

Several county and state roads access various points on Lake Meredith. To reach the headquarters, take Exit 71 from I-40 in Amarillo and head north on SR 136 for 37 miles to Fritch, or go 14 miles west from Borger. To reach the Alibates Quarries Contact Station, go 7 miles south of Fritch on SR 136; turn onto Cas Johnson Road and follow signs.

ALIBATES FLINT QUARRIES NATIONAL MONUMENT AND
LAKE MEREDITH NATIONAL RECREATION AREA

WEATHER
MEAN TEMPERATURES AND PRECIPITATION

MONTH	HIGH (°F)	LOW (°F)	PRECIP.	SNOW
January	49	21	0.5"	4.3"
April	72	42	1.0"	0.6"
July	92	66	2.6"	0.0"
October	73	45	1.4"	0.2"

Mean annual precipitation is 19.56 inches. Strong windstorms scour west Texas throughout winter and early spring. Frequent thunderstorms bring relief from summer heat in July and August. Data are for Amarillo, Texas.

SELECTED WILDLIFE OF SPECIAL INTEREST

MAMMALS: Spotted Ground Squirrel, Thirteen-lined Ground Squirrel, Beaver, Coyote, Badger, Mule Deer, White-tailed Deer.

BIRDS: Snow Goose (m), Mississippi Kite, Ring-necked Pheasant, Wild Turkey, Scaled Quail, Northern Bobwhite, Sandhill Crane (m), Snowy Plover, Semipalmated Plover (m), Black-necked Stilt, Upland Sandpiper (m), Greater Roadrunner, Burrowing Owl, Scissor-tailed Flycatcher, Bewick's Wren, Northern Mockingbird, Brown Thrasher, Northern Cardinal.

AMPHIBIANS AND REPTILES: Northern Cricket Frog, Tiger Salamander, Eastern Collared Lizard, Texas Horned Lizard, Eastern Fence Lizard, Western Diamond-backed Rattlesnake, Western Rattlesnake, Coachwhip.

CADDO AND LYNDON B. JOHNSON NATIONAL GRASSLANDS

Post Oak and Blackjack Oak savannas, stands of bluestem grasses, large freshwater lakes, and deciduous and pine forests intermingle with cropland on these two north Texas grasslands. Armadillos snuffle and scuffle through oak duff, and Northern Cardinals and Northern Mockingbirds sing from dogwood trees. It's not your typical prairie scene. However, these jointly managed national grasslands contain about 20,000 acres of mixed-grass and tallgrass prairie.

Caddo National Grassland is where the eastern deciduous forest and the blackland prairies meet. Located almost on the Oklahoma border, the 17,873-acre preserve is broken into three parcels. The largest section centers around Lake Davy Crockett and Coffee Mill Lake. The smaller western section centers around Lake Fannin, and the smallest southern section is 1 mile west of Ladonia.

Several mima mounds, rounded hillocks about 2 feet high, pockmark the Bois d'Arc Unit near the town of Honey Grove. Also called "pimple mounds" and "prairie blisters," these small hills of disturbed soil are intriguing because geologists do not fully un-

Above: Dogwoods and oaks form islands among grassland fragments at Caddo National Grassland. (Photo by Glenn Cushman)

Post Oaks (Quercus stellata) *bloom in April at Caddo National Grassland. (Photo by Glenn Cushman)*

derstand how they were formed. (See Wallace C. Dayton Conservation and Wildlife Area, Minnesota.)

Lyndon B. Johnson National Grassland, about 145 miles southwest of Caddo, lies in the cross-timbers ecosystem (see Tallgrass Prairie Preserve, Oklahoma, for more information on cross-timbers). Two major recreational lakes, Cottonwood and Black Creek, as well as the 50-mile LBJ Multi-use Trail system, are featured attractions. Although larger than Caddo, this 20,313-acre preserve is more checkerboarded with private land.

BLACKLAND PRAIRIE

Named for their rich, black, clayey soils, the blackland prairies once covered some 12 million acres in an arc running from San Antonio to the Red River. The fertile soils, which swell and shrink depending on weather conditions, formerly supported luxuriant grasses such as Big Bluestem, Little Bluestem, Indian Grass, Tall Dropseed, and Silveus Dropseed. However, about 98 percent of the Texas blackland prairie was plowed and planted to cotton, sorghum, corn, and wheat, and the depleted soil lost its productivity. Since the 1950s, about half of the cropland has reverted to pasture for livestock.

Some 4,000 acres of native blackland prairie persevere on the Ladonia Unit of Caddo National Grassland. Other good examples of blackland prairies have been preserved by the Nature Conservancy at Clymer Meadow and other small parcels (See Other Texas Sites, p. 397).

One of the most bizarre mammals in North America moved up to Texas from South America via Mexico starting around 1850 and has been slowly expanding its range ever since. Nine-banded Armadillos now range north into Kansas and east to Georgia and Florida. Texas currently supports between 30 million and 50 million armadillos and has declared them the state mammal.

About the size of a small dog, this cousin to anteaters and sloths is mostly encased in a bony carapace. Large plates made up of some 2,500 smaller platelets cover rump and shoulders, and 9 leathery bands encircle the midsection like a cummerbund. A reptilian face topped with mulelike ears peers out from the armor, a ratlike tail protrudes behind, yellowish hairs sprout incongruously here and there, and powerful claws scrabble into the earth. It's what a committee might create from a turtle, a mule, a rat, and a Badger. Imagine coming face to face with the 7-foot-long, 500-pound armadillo ancestor that roamed the southern plains 10,000 years ago!

The Armadillo's behavior is as singular as its appearance. Armadillos often gather around creeks and small ponds to indulge in mud baths. Because their heavy shields make swimming difficult, they usually simply walk underwater, staying submerged for up to six minutes. If one opts to swim, it swallows air, inflating its stomach to twice its usual size. Then, like a buoyant football, it dog-paddles across.

Armadillo reproduction is also unusual, beginning with a penis that is one-third of the male's body length (two-thirds in some species). After mating in the missionary position, usually in July,

Nine-banded Armadillos are common at Caddo National Grassland. (Photo by Rick and Nora Bowers)

implantation is delayed until November. Identical sets of quadruplets, each conceived from a single egg, are most often born in March. Under stressful conditions, implantation has been delayed up to two years.

Digging is what armadillos do best. They excavate numerous burrows, up to 15 per animal, and probe into the ground for grubs, worms, and insects — staples of their diet. They are the only mammal known to prey on ferocious fire ants. Although they do help control crop-eating insects, some gardeners dislike armadillos because of this propensity for digging.

Armadillos are often killed by automobiles. When frightened, they jump straight up in the air and into the grill of a car that might otherwise pass harmlessly over them. This defense behavior might be effective in scaring off a predator, but not a multiton vehicle.

Don't attempt to handle these slow-moving, docile creatures. Accidental cuts from the carapace and claws can become infected, and some armadillos carry Hansen's disease.

HIKING

Caddo National Grassland:

BOIS D'ARC TRAIL (25 miles) winds between Coffee Mill and Davy Crockett Lakes beginning at the trailhead just north of Coffee Mill Lake on CR 409.

Lyndon B. Johnson National Grassland:

LBJ MULTI-USE TRAIL SYSTEM (four loops totaling 50 miles) may be accessed at several places, including TADRA Point.

COTTONWOOD-BLACK CREEK TRAIL (4 miles) connects Cottonwood and Black Creek Lakes.

CAMPING

Camping is permitted anywhere on the grasslands and in the developed lakeshore campgrounds (see next page).

Caddo National Grassland:

LAKE COFFEE MILL CAMPGROUND, on the north shore of the lake, is on FS 919 about 16 miles from Honey Grove.

LAKE DAVY CROCKETT CAMPGROUND, on the northwest shore of the lake, is on FS 919 about 12 miles from Honey Grove.

Lyndon B. Johnson National Grassland:

BLACK CREEK LAKE CAMPGROUND, on the north shore of the lake, is on FS road 902.

TADRA POINT CAMPGROUND, the primary access point for the LBJ trail system, is on FS 900 about 9 miles north of Decatur.

BEST TIMES TO VISIT

Blue-eyed Grass, dogwoods, and May-Apples begin to bloom in April, and the wildflower show continues through June. Late-spring temperatures are pleasant, and cardinals and mockingbirds carol throughout the day. Horseback riding on the multiuse trails is popular from October through June. Summers are hot, but the many freshwater lakes remain cool.

INFORMATION

CADDO-LYNDON B. JOHNSON NATIONAL GRASSLANDS, Box 507, Decatur, TX 76234; 940-627-5475.

HOW TO GET THERE

CADDO NATIONAL GRASSLAND: To reach Lake Crockett and Coffee Mill Lake, go 17 miles west from Paris on US 82, take CR 100 north from Honey Grove for 5.5 miles to FS 919, and turn left. To reach Lake Fannin, take CR 273 west from Telephone and follow the signs. To see the blackland prairie, drive west from Ladonia on CR 34 for 1 mile.

LYNDON B. JOHNSON NATIONAL GRASSLAND: Numerous county and Forest Service roads access this grassland located a few miles north of Decatur and east of Alvord. **NOTE:** A grassland map, available at the above address, is essential for exploring these grasslands.

CADDO AND LYNDON B. JOHNSON NATIONAL GRASSLANDS

WEATHER
MEAN TEMPERATURES AND PRECIPITATION

MONTH	HIGH (°F)	LOW (°F)	PRECIP.	SNOW
January	51	30	2.5"	1.8"
April	75	53	4.0"	0.0"
July	94	73	3.6"	0.0"
October	77	53	4.6"	0.0"

The mean annual precipitation is 46.3 inches. Summers are hot and humid with frequent severe thunderstorms. May and September are the wettest months. Data are for Paris, Texas.

SELECTED WILDLIFE OF SPECIAL INTEREST

MAMMALS: Nine-banded Armadillo, Beaver, Coyote, Red Fox, Black Bear, Bobcat, Mule Deer, White-tailed Deer.

BIRDS: Wood Duck, Mississippi Kite, Wild Turkey, Northern Bobwhite, Sandhill Crane (m), Long-billed Curlew (m), Greater Roadrunner, Barn Owl, Barred Owl, Pileated Woodpecker, Scissor-tailed Flycatcher, Northern Mockingbird, Rufous-crowned Sparrow, Field Sparrow, Northern Cardinal, Painted Bunting, Dickcissel.

AMPHIBIANS AND REPTILES: Northern Cricket Frog, Woodhouse's Toad, Southern Leopard Frog, Prairie Skink, Copperhead, Eastern Racer, Coachwhip.

MULESHOE AND BUFFALO LAKE NATIONAL WILDLIFE REFUGES

Grama grasses, Buffalograss, Silver Bluestem, and yuccas spread across these two refuges on the Texas Panhandle. Northern Bobwhites whistle campers to sleep at night and wake them in the morning. Spectacular sunrises, sunsets, and apricot afterglows light up the sky above a seemingly unbroken flatness that the first Spanish explorers called the *Llano Estacado* or "Staked Plains." One explanation for that name is that the explorers had to drive stakes into the ground to find their way back. Another story says the men thought the yuccas, also called Spanish Bayonets, looked like stakes.

Muleshoe National Wildlife Refuge was established in 1935 as a 5,809-acre wintering area for Sandhill Cranes and migratory waterfowl. Several woody draws lead down to three large playa lakes that have no outlets and are periodically dry. When they are full, 600 surface acres of shallow, nutrient-rich water provides habitat for hundreds of thousands of birds and other wildlife.

Muleshoe staff also administer Grulla National Wildlife Refuge, 30 miles northwest of Muleshoe on New Mexico SR 88.

Above: Sandhill Cranes circle in for a landing at Muleshoe National Wildlife Refuge. (Photo by Michael Forsberg)

Most of this 3,236-acre shortgrass prairie refuge is covered by a huge saline lakebed that attracts wintering Sandhill Cranes. Grulla is unstaffed, but you can hike the half-mile access road or drive to a hilltop overlook.

Some of the least disturbed shortgrass prairie in the southern plains is found at nearby 7,664-acre Buffalo Lake National Wildlife Refuge, where a portion has been designated a National Natural Landmark. Shortgrasses flourish under a system of rotational cattle grazing designed to mimic Bison grazing patterns. To provide food and cover for wildlife, the normally dry lakebed is planted to winter wheat, milo, and hay, and one unit of the marsh is flooded each spring and fall. Interpretive signs mark a 5-mile auto tour.

For a few decades Buffalo Lake was full of water. Umbarger Dam, constructed in 1937, blocked the flow of Tierra Blanca Creek to form a large reservoir. However, in the 1970s, drought and water pumping dried it up. After a 1978 flood, the dam was condemned and the remaining water was drained.

WINTERING SANDHILL CRANES

From December to mid-February, one of the largest concentrations of Lesser Sandhill Cranes in North America fattens up on grain and grasses at the refuges and on nearby croplands. In February 1981, Muleshoe birders counted a record 250,000 cranes. In late September the cranes begin arriving from their breeding grounds in northern Canada, western Alaska, and Siberia. For about six months they roost on the shores of refuge playas and other nearby lakes, flying out at sunrise with a thunder of wings and a fanfare of trumpeting. (See Lillian Annette Rowe Sanctuary, Nebraska, and Wallace C. Dayton Conservation and Wildlife Area, Minnesota, for more information on Sandhill Cranes.)

PLAYAS

When rainfall is sufficient to fill them, these ephemeral pools turn the shortgrass prairies of the Texas Panhandle into a demi-paradise. During a wet spring, rainfall from frequent thunderstorms is caught and held in the impermeable clay bottoms of playa basins. The scorching summer sun sucks up most of this moisture, and by autumn many playas are bone dry.

Wetland plants growing around the playas create crucial habitat for wildlife and for millions of migrating birds. Some of the creatures nurtured by these oases are Great Blue Herons, Sandhill Cranes, Snow Geese, American Avocets, dragonflies, spade-foot toads—*and* mosquitoes! Playas also help replenish the High Plains (Ogallala) Aquifer and provide a source for crop irrigation and water storage. They delight and surprise the eye of the traveler grown accustomed to aridity, flatness, and monotony.

In 1541 Pedro de Castaneda, who chronicled explorer Francisco Vásquez de Coronado's search for the mystical city of Quivira, was probably the first to describe the playas (Spanish for "beaches"): "Occasionally there were found some ponds, round like plates, a stone's throw wider or larger. Some contained fresh water, others salt."

No one knows exactly how these hollows formed. The most likely theories are that they were carved by wind or are old sink-holes (see Bitter Lake National Wildlife Refuge, New Mexico, for information on sinkholes). The one constant about playas is their gone-today-here-tomorrow nature. In *Playas: Jewels of the Plains,* Jim Steiert writes, "Playa basins can be deceptively dry in one instant and, in the space of a few hours, be transformed into deep lakes when the fickle rainclouds unleash their torrents." He tells the story of a man driving his wagon across a dry basin in the morning and returning by the same route that night only to drown in deep water. He also writes of Buffalo Soldiers dying of thirst in 1877 while a rescue party rode through a full playa only a few miles away.

Human impact often degrades playas and adversely affects the birds that depend on them. When deeper pits are dug in the basins to catch irrigation runoff water for reuse, there is less surface water for wintering birds. When feedlots are located on temporarily dry playas, animal wastes are concentrated, exacerbating avian diseases. Poultry waste discarded near playas in the 1940s may have led to the introduction of avian cholera into North America. This disease, along with avian botulism, probably kills tens of thousands of birds each year.

Since 1990 the Playa Lakes Joint Venture (including government agencies, conservation organizations such as Ducks Unlimited, and commercial companies) has worked to improve and preserve playas. One of their projects is the Dimmitt Wildlife Management Area near Paducah, Texas.

Some 20,000 playas, ranging in size from 1 to 100 acres, dot the Texas Panhandle, and there may be an additional 5,000 of these life-giving bodies of water in eastern New Mexico, southeastern Colorado, southwestern Kansas, and the Oklahoma Panhandle.

Texans sometimes poke fun at their state, saying "Everything sticks, stings, or stinks!" Many plants typical of Texas prairies do their best to live up to that billing. Prickly pears, Chollas, mesquites, and yuccas thrive in poor soils and arid climates and bear wicked thorns, spines, or sharp bayonet-shaped leaves. In a sparsely vegetated land where every plant is a potential food source, barbs, bristles, and bayonets protect succulent plants from being eaten.

Large browsing animals avoid sharp, stickery plants, but other animals use the thorns to their advantage. In *Heralds of Spring in Texas*, Roland H. Wauer writes that 42 species of birds, including Greater Roadrunners, Northern Mockingbirds, and White-tailed Kites, nest within the protection of yucca leaves. Cholla has the reputation of "jumping" out and grabbing hold of anything that passes, but Cactus Wrens nest in its branches, and Bushy-tailed Woodrats ("pack rats") and ground squirrels feed on its fruits. Pack rats even pile up Cholla stems to defend their burrows from predators, and various woodrats build their nests in the middle of a prickly pear cactus. Other animals, including humans, have learned to thwart the thorns and enjoy eating such delectables as yucca flowers and prickly pear fruits.

Many Plains Indians ate the fruits, pads, buds, and flowers of the various species of prickly pear cactus (*Opuntia* spp.), often drying the pulp and cooking it in stews. Ethnobotanist Kelly Kindscher says that Cheyenne women made deerskin finger tips to protect themselves as they performed the job of "despining" the cactus.

Plains Indians ate the flowers and fruits of Yucca (Yucca glauca), rubbed the roots in water to make suds, and crafted thread and brooms from the fibrous leaves.

Remains of pads, pollen, and seeds have even been found in the coprolites (fossilized feces) of people living 6,000 years ago in southwest Texas. Today gourmet groceries sell the fruit, called *tunas,* and pads, called *nopales.* Peccaries, Black Bears, rabbits, deer, squirrels, and many birds also eat the fruit.

Yucca glauca, commonly called Soapweed or Spanish Bayonet, was even more widely used by Native Americans, who made sandals from leaf fibers and soap from the roots. The root was sometimes placed on cuts to stop bleeding and reduce inflamation and was used in various medicines, including a solution to kill head lice and prevent hair loss, according to Kindscher. The buds, immature fruits, and waxy white flower petals, which taste like asparagus, were eaten raw.

HIKING

Muleshoe National Wildlife Refuge:

GOURD VINE NATURE TRAIL (1-mile loop) starts at the campground and loops through a sycamore-maple grove, around wetlands, past prairie, and through a locust tree grove.

PAULS LAKE NATURE TRAIL (0.25 miles) starts 6 miles northeast of the refuge headquarters and winds through prairie to a viewpoint of the lake.

Buffalo Lake National Wildlife Refuge:

COTTONWOOD CANYON BIRDING TRAIL (0.5 miles) follows a tree-shaded canyon that crosses an unnamed spur road on the northwest shore of the lakebed.

FIRE LANE (9.5 mile loop) skirts the lakebed, passing through varied habitats. Start either on the spur road mentioned above or at Stewart Dike.

PRAIRIE DOG TOWN INTERPRETIVE TRAIL (about 0.5 miles) starts from CR 168 about 2 miles south of the turnoff for refuge headquarters.

CAMPING

MULESHOE CAMPGROUND AND PICNIC AREA, located near refuge headquarters, is adjacent to a locust grove and a sycamore-maple grove. Russian Olives have been planted around the perimeter.

BUFFALO LAKE CAMPGROUND AND PICNIC AREA, located near the headquarters, is shaded by elms and cottonwoods.

Best Times to Visit

Sandhill Crane numbers peak between December and mid-February. Great Horned Owls begin to nest in January and Burrowing Owls in late March. Courting birds begin to sing and wildflowers begin to bloom in April and continue into June. Greatest bird species diversity occurs during spring and fall migrations (April through May and September through October) when you might spot Ospreys, Bald Eagles, Ferruginous Hawks, Mountain Bluebirds, and Blue Grosbeaks.

Information

MULESHOE NATIONAL WILDLIFE REFUGE, Box 121, Muleshoe, TX 79347; 806-946-3341.
BUFFALO LAKE NATIONAL WILDLIFE REFUGE, Box 179, Umbarger, TX 79091; 806-499-3382.

How to Get There

MULESHOE NATIONAL WILDLIFE REFUGE: From the town of Muleshoe, 66 miles northwest of Lubbock on US 84, go south 20 miles on SR 214 to refuge signs.
BUFFALO LAKE NATIONAL WILDLIFE REFUGE: From Umbarger, 25 miles southwest of Amarillo on US 60, go south on CR 168 for 1.5 miles to refuge signs.

Blue-eyed Grass (Sisyrinchium *sp.*). *(Photo by Glenn Cushman)*

MULESHOE AND BUFFALO LAKE NATIONAL WILDLIFE REFUGES

WEATHER
MEAN TEMPERATURES AND PRECIPITATION

MONTH	HIGH (°F)	LOW (°F)	PRECIP.	SNOW
January	53	25	0.4"	2.4"
April	75	47	1.0"	0.2"
July	92	68	2.4"	0.0"
October	75	48	1.9"	0.0"

Mean annual precipitation is 17.9 inches. Winter temperatures have ranged from -17°F to more than 90°F. The record high is 114°F. Data are for Lubbock, Texas.

SELECTED WILDLIFE OF SPECIAL INTEREST

MAMMALS: Black-tailed Jackrabbit, Black-tailed Prairie Dog, Porcupine, Coyote, Red Fox, Badger, Bobcat, Mule Deer.

BIRDS: Ring-necked Pheasant, Scaled Quail, Northern Bobwhite, Sandhill Crane (m), Snowy Plover, Black-necked Stilt, Least Sandpiper (w, m), Baird's Sandpiper (m), Greater Roadrunner, Burrowing Owl, Scissor-tailed Flycatcher, Chihuahuan Raven (rare), Northern Mockingbird, Northern Cardinal.

AMPHIBIANS AND REPTILES: Plains Spadefoot, Western Spadefoot, Texas Horned Lizard, Western Rattlesnake, Western Hog-nosed Snake.

OTHER TEXAS SITES

ATTWATER PRAIRIE CHICKEN NATIONAL WILDLIFE REFUGE (Box 518, Eagle Lake, TX 77434; 979-234-3021). More than 1,000 acres of coastal prairie, much of it in native tallgrasses, has been preserved and restored for the endangered Attwater's Prairie-Chicken. Although prairie-chickens may stay out of sight, whistling-ducks, Roseate Spoonbills, Anhingas, armadillos, alligators, and Bison also inhabit the refuge. From Eagle Lake, 60 miles west of Houston on US 90, go 7 miles northeast on CR 3013. Aransas, Brazoria, and San Bernard National Wildlife Refuges also preserve Texas coastal prairie, now reduced to less than 1 percent of its former extent.

CAPROCK CANYONS STATE PARK (Box 204, Quitaque, TX 79255; 806-455-1492). Redrock canyons cut into mesa tops covered with mixed-grass prairie and mesquite in this 15,313-acre park. Includes the largest Bison herd in the state, Pronghorns, and a large lake. Hiking, boating, camping. From Quitaque, about 80 miles southeast of Amarillo, go 3.5 miles north on CR 1065.

CLYMER MEADOW PRESERVE (The Nature Conservancy, Box 26, Celeste, TX 75423; 903-568-4139). One thousand acres of virgin blackland prairie (named for the deep, dark clay soils) is pocked with "gilgais" or "hogwallows." These shallow basins often hold water and make honeycomb patterns on the humus-rich land that supports unusual plant communities and some 300 native plant species. Hunt County north of Greenville. Access to this and several other blackland prairies managed by the Nature Conservancy is by appointment only.

COPPER BREAKS STATE PARK (777 Park Road 62, Quanah, TX 79252; 940-839-4331). Mesas are covered with mixed-grass prairie, juniper, and mesquite in this nearly 2,000-acre park that also includes red-orange canyons and a large lake. Hiking, boating, camping. Between Quanah and Crowell off of SR 6.

LADY BIRD JOHNSON WILDFLOWER CENTER (4801 La Crosse Avenue, Austin, TX 78379; 512-292-4200). Although not a prairie preserve, this nonprofit research and educational center is an excellent source of information on native plants. Visitors can see the effects of different land management techniques, such as burning, on 42 acres of display gardens and research plots.

MCCLELLAN CREEK NATIONAL GRASSLAND (Black Kettle Ranger District, Box 266, Cheyenne, OK 73628; 580-497-2143). Mixed-grass prairie, marshes, woodlands, and Lake McClellan make this 1,449-acre grassland in the Texas panhandle a popular recreational area. Lake Marvin, northeast of McClellan, and Black Kettle National Grassland (see Oklahoma) are also administered by the Black Kettle Ranger District. Hiking, boating, camping. Just north of I-40, about 55 miles east of Amarillo.

PALO DURO CANYON STATE PARK (11450 Park Road 5, Canyon, TX 79015; 806-488-2227). Called the "Grand Canyon of Texas," this park covers about 18,000 acres. Junipers dot the canyon, about 1,000 feet deep and 120 miles long, and shortgrass prairie spreads across the Canoncita Range on the rim. Wild Turkeys roam the campsites, satin-spar gypsum intrudes into red claystone formations, and trails wind along streams. Hiking, camping. From the town of Canyon go about 12 miles east on SR 217 and Park Road 5. Also noteworthy is the Panhandle-Plains Historical Museum in Canyon.

RITA BLANCA NATIONAL GRASSLAND. See Kiowa and Rita Blanca National Grasslands, New Mexico.

The many ponds at Copper Breaks State Park attract a variety of birds and other animals. (Photo by Glenn Cushman)

Redrock formations at Caprock Canyons State Park glow in dawn light. (Photo by Glenn Cushman)

A Greater Short-horned Lizard perches on a prickly pear. (Photo by Glenn Cushman)

WISCONSIN

- 53
- Flambeau R.
- Jump R.
- Black R.
- Chippewa R.
- Eau Claire
- 94
- 12
- 51
- Wisconsin R.
- Wausau
- Peshtigo R.
- Petenwell Lake
- Castle Rock Lake
- 51
- Appleton
- Lake Winnebago
- Green Bay
- 43
- La Crosse
- Fond du Lac
- Sheboygan
- 27
- 14
- 23
- 12
- Spring Green
- 67
- 4
- Steuben
- 3
- Avoca
- 1
- 5
- Mt. Horeb
- 6
- Madison
- 94
- Milwaukee
- Prairie du Chien
- 61
- 151
- 14
- 90
- Eagle
- 2
- 43
- Chiwaukee Prairie
- Kenosha

Chiwaukee Prairie State Natural Area

Other Wisconsin Sites:

1. Avoca Prairie-Savanna
2. Kettle Moraine Fen and Low Prairie
3. Spring Green Preserve
4. The Hogback
5. Thomson Memorial Prairie
6. University of Wisconsin Arboretum

At first glance this 354-acre preserve on the western shore of Lake Michigan looks more like a forest clearing than a prairie. Oaks, maples, and willows surround a meadow filled with tall-grasses and marshes. Deciduous forests, interspersed with farms and towns, cover former grasslands and oak savannas from here to the Mississippi River, 150 miles to the west.

It's only after you walk out into Chiwaukee and spend some time among the grasses and wildflowers that you begin to appreciate the wonders of this landscape. In late spring acres of white and pink Shooting Stars blanket the beach ridges, while Canada Geese trumpet in nearby marshes. In late summer Prairie Blazing Stars and Compass Plants brighten 7-foot-high stands of Big Bluestem and Indian Grass.

Despite its small size, Chiwaukee Prairie ranks among the richest grassland remnants in the upper Midwest. Its wet swales and dry beach ridges, created 10,000 years ago as a giant glacier melted from the Lake Michigan Basin, support an array of distinct plant communities. Oak savannas and dry sand prairies grow on the beach ridges and dunes; fens, sedge meadows, and mesic prairies thrive in swales and potholes. These communities harbor

Above: Shooting Stars (Dodecatheon meadia) *carpet the ancient beach ridges and swales of Chiwaukee Prairie in May. (Photo by Joseph Kayne)*

more than 400 plant species, including 10 on the Wisconsin rare and threatened list.

Preserving this rich prairie remnant required perseverance. In the early 1960s two local citizens purchased a strip of remnant prairie along the railway tracks, where sparks from passing trains had ignited the grass often enough to ward off encroachment by surrounding forests. Alarmed over a developer's proposal to build a subdivision and 1,000-slip marina at the site, they and other local activists approached the Nature Conservancy for help with acquiring an additional 300 acres.

The land had been divided into 1,200 lots, and advocates pieced the preserve together one lot at a time, negotiating with individual landowners scattered all over the world. By 1974, when the U.S. Department of the Interior designated Chiwaukee Prairie a Registered National Landmark, more than 200 acres had been saved. By 2003 all but 100 lots had been acquired.

Today a stewardship committee works to restore and maintain the grassland, which is jointly managed by the Nature Conservancy, the Wisconsin Department of Natural Resources, the University of Wisconsin—Parkside, and the Chiwaukee Prairie Preservation Fund. On the third Saturday of each month, work parties gather to remove brush, pull weeds, plant native forbs, and carry out prescribed burns. Land acquisition efforts continue. The name "Chiwaukee" (a hybrid of Chicago and Milwaukee) was coined by a would-be developer of the property during the 1920s.

FENS

About 5 acres of the wetlands at Chiwaukee Prairie are classified as fens, saturated marshes where a constant influx of groundwater slows oxidation of plant material. Because the decay rate in these saturated wetlands is so slow, their soil consists of a thick mat of partly decayed remains of sedges, mosses, and other plants. This spongy soil material is called peat.

Fens are similar to peat bogs, famous for entrapping humans in their mire and for heating Irish homes for generations. But in peat bogs the expanding layer of organic material is raised above the water table, so that the only nutrients available to plants are those delivered by snow and rainwater. Since fens receive a constant influx of nutrient-laden groundwater, they are much richer in plant life.

The cold, wet conditions in fens favor plants adapted to northern climates, including some species that disappeared from most of the prairie region at the end of the Ice Age. In the fens of Chi-

Cottongrass (Erio-phorum *sp.*) *is actu-ally a sedge that thrives in fens and other freshwater marshes.*

waukee you may find Marsh Marigold, an early-blooming, hardy perennial with large heart-shaped leaves and bright yellow flowers; Rush Aster, a late-blooming white- to lavender-flowered aster that flourishes in cold bogs and swamps; or Cottongrass, a sedge that bears its seeds in bunches resembling cotton swabs.

Certain mammals and birds thrive in fens as well. The Water Shrew is a sleek 6-inch-long mammal with stiff hairs on its hind feet that aid in swimming. It feeds on aquatic insects, slugs, earthworms, and small fish. The Southern Bog Lemming nests in clumps of moss or grass and feeds on leaves, stems, fruits, and roots. Swamp Sparrows chatter from perches on willows or bulrushes. They raise their young in grass nests constructed in low bushes, grass tussocks, or mats of dense sedges.

SHOOTING STARS

In tallgrass prairies from Oklahoma to Minnesota, fields of Shooting Stars (*Dodecatheon meadia*) announce the arrival of spring. They appear in early April in the south and bloom well into June in Illinois and Wisconsin, blanketing some prairie remnants. It seems astonishing that such a delicate and striking wildflower could bloom in such abundance. However, loss of native habitat has pushed this species onto endangered and threatened lists in Michigan, Minnesota, Pennsylvania, New York, and several southern states.

Named for its nodding flowers with petals swept backward like the tail of a comet, this member of the primrose family thrives on calcareous and other rocky soils in moist and dry prairies. It also grows in dry forests from Wisconsin and Virginia south to Texas and Georgia. A similar species, *Dodecatheon pulchellum*, blooms in damp prairie meadows, moist hillsides, and open forests throughout much of North America, including the high plains and Rocky Mountains.

KEEPERS OF THE FIRE

From about 1500 to 1833 the Potawatomi lived near the shores of Lake Michigan, where the grassland sea washed over scattered islands of deciduous forest. They had migrated west from the Atlantic seaboard, traveling with two closely related tribes, the Ojibwe and Ottawa. Within this Anishinabe confederacy, the Ojibwe were known as faith keepers, the Ottawa as traders, and the Potawatomi as keepers of the sacred fires.

The Potawatomi lived along waterways and used lightweight birch bark canoes for travel and trade. During the seventeenth century they allied with the French, trading flotillas of furs for cloth, iron kettles, beads, and rifles. Their fortunes began to unravel when the British drove the French from the region after the 1763 French and Indian War.

By 1829 they had ceded 70 percent of their land to the United States government in return for annuities. In the 1833 Treaty of Chicago, they traded the last of their lands in the Great Lakes region for a reservation west of the Mississippi River. Thirteen years later these lands also were taken from them.

As dozens of Potawatomi died along the "trail of death" westward, 2,000 holdouts fled to northern Wisconsin and Canada. These "strolling bands" stayed in the north, where individuals subsisted as day laborers, lumberjacks, and farm workers. Remarkably, these survivors eventually acquired several thousand acres of land, reorganizing in the early 1900s as the Forest County Potawatomi Community.

In 1988 the United States government finally recognized the community as a tribe and granted reservation status to their 11,444 acres. Today the community manages a casino and conference center, a logging cooperative, and an imported Red Deer herd, while providing education and health care for its members.

In 1998 the Potawatomi began sharing gambling revenues with the Red Cliff Band of the Ojibwe. In *Indian Nations of Wisconsin,* Ojibwe historian Patty Loew writes, "In their success, the Potawatomi believe they have not forgotten the ancient obligations that bind them politically and culturally to their *Ne shna bek* (Anishinabe) family. 'Bodewadmi'—Little Brother—continues to fulfill his nurturing role as 'Keeper of the Fire.' "

Hiking

There are no maintained hiking trails, but visitors are encouraged to explore lightly from adjacent roads and on short paths heading south from the parking area.

Camping

Camping is not permitted. Nearby public campgrounds include:

ILLINOIS BEACH STATE PARK, 10 miles south of Chiwaukee off SR 32 (Sheridan Road).
BONG STATE RECREATION AREA, 9 miles west of I-94 on SR 142.

Best Times to Visit

Shooting Stars, Prairie Violets, and Marsh Marigolds bloom in May; Wild Iris, Yellow Stargrass, Spiderwort, and Cottongrass in early June. In summer hundreds of Monarch butterflies perch on colorful wildflowers, including Compass Plant, Prairie Blazing Star, Butterfly Milkweed, and Leadplant. The grasses are usually tallest and most colorful in September and early October, when geese, ducks, Sandhill Cranes, and raptors sweep south along the western shore of Lake Michigan.

Information

THE NATURE CONSERVANCY, 633 W. Main Street, Madison, WI 53703; 608-251-8140.

How to Get There

From I-94 south of Kenosha, go east on SR 165 for 6.3 miles. Turn south on SR 32 (Sheridan Road) for about 1 mile. Turn left on 116th Street (Tobin Road) for 0.7 miles. Turn right on The First Court (Marina Road). Go 5 blocks and turn right on 121st Street. Go 1 block to Second Avenue, turn right, and continue to 119th Street.

From downtown Kenosha, take Sheridan Road south about 4 miles to 116th Street, then follow directions above.

CHIWAUKEE PRAIRIE STATE NATURAL AREA

WEATHER
MEAN TEMPERATURES AND PRECIPITATION

MONTH	HIGH (°F)	LOW (°F)	PRECIP.	SNOW
January	28	12	1.3"	12.5"
April	52	36	3.4"	1.7"
July	79	61	4.0"	0.0"
October	60	42	2.5"	0.3"

Mean annual precipitation is 33.1 inches. July, August, and September are the wettest months. Summer temperatures are cooled by the waters of Lake Michigan, but humidities run high. Severe thunderstorms can occur throughout the warmer months. Data are for Kenosha, Wisconsin.

SELECTED WILDLIFE OF SPECIAL INTEREST

MAMMALS: Thirteen-lined Ground Squirrel, Franklin's Ground Squirrel, Eastern Gray Squirrel, Woodchuck, Coyote, Red Fox, White-tailed Deer.

BIRDS: Canada Goose, Virginia Rail, American Woodcock, Marsh Wren, Yellow Warbler, Common Yellowthroat, Swamp Sparrow, Dickcissel, Eastern Meadowlark.

AMPHIBIANS AND REPTILES: Northern Cricket Frog, Western Chorus Frog, Northern Leopard Frog, Tiger Salamander, Eastern Hog-nosed Snake, Western Foxsnake, Blanding's Turtle.

OTHER WISCONSIN SITES

AVOCA PRAIRIE-SAVANNA (Department of Natural Resources, Tower Hill State Park, Highway C, Spring Green, WI 53588; 608-588-2116). More than 1,880 acres of prairie are dominated by Little Bluestem and Junegrass. From Avoca go east 1.5 miles on SR 133. Turn north on Hay Lane Road. Parking area is 0.3 miles beyond Marsh Creek, which may be impassable in wet weather.

KETTLE MORAINE STATE PARK (Department of Natural Resources, 101 South Webster Street, Madison, WI 53703; 262-594-6200). Wet prairie, fens, dry-mesic prairie, and oak woodlands thrive on 250 acres. The preserve shelters two state-threatened plant species. From Eagle go north 2.25 miles on SR 67 to gated access road. Follow the lane west 0.5 miles to preserve.

SPRING GREEN PRESERVE (The Nature Conservancy, 633 West Main Street, Madison, WI 53703; 608-251-8140). Prickly pear cactus, Leadplant, and Compass Plant grow on sandy soils on this 589-acre preserve in the Wisconsin River Valley. Nature trail. From intersection of US 14 and SR 23 near Spring Green, go north 0.5 miles on SR 23, and turn right on Jones Road. Proceed 0.75 miles and turn left onto dirt access road marked Angelo Lane.

THE HOGBACK (The Nature Conservancy, 633 West Main Street, Madison, WI 53703; 608-251-8140). A mix of dry prairie, oak savanna, forests, and wetlands grows on a steep hogback rising several hundred feet above Citron Valley. Wildflowers include Bird's-Foot Violet and Shooting Star. More than 960 acres. From Prairie du Chien, take SR 27 and SR 179 about 20 miles northeast to Steuben. From the city park in Steuben go west, then bear right across the Kickapoo River. At the "T" intersection, go left 0.6 miles on Citron Valley Road to Hughes. Bear right, continue 2.5 miles, and turn left. Continue for 1 mile and look for sign and kiosk.

THOMSON MEMORIAL PRAIRIE (The Nature Conservancy, 633 West Main Street, Madison, WI 53703; 608-251-8140). This 175-acre dry prairie remnant grows over limestone bedrock that discouraged farmers from plowing the soil. Pasque Flowers, Green Milkweeds, and Bird's-Foot Violets thrive here, along with numerous butterflies. From Mt. Horeb go west on US 18/151 to CR F. Turn south and continue for 1 mile to intersection with CR Z. Bear right and continue for 0.5 miles to the preserve, on the right side of CR F.

UNIVERSITY OF WISCONSIN ARBORETUM (1207 Seminole Highway, Madison, WI 53711; 608-263-7888). Located on the shores of Madison's Lake Wingra, this peaceful 1,260-acre arboretum shelters a cross-section of Wisconsin's natural plant communities, including the world's oldest restored prairie. In early fall Indian Grass and Big Bluestem grow up to 10 feet high. North of SR 12 at intersection of McCaffery Drive and Seminole Highway.

Pasque Flowers bloom in April and May at several Wisconsin prairie preserves, including Thompson Memorial Prairie.

WYOMING

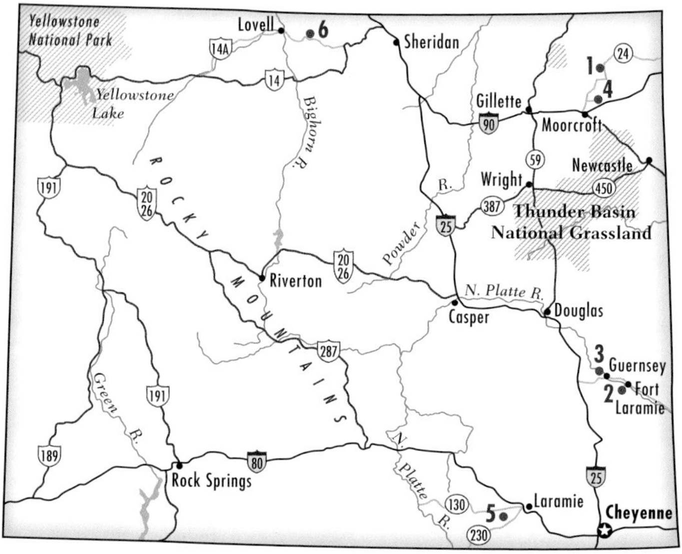
Yellowstone National Park
Lovell
6
Sheridan
14A
14
24
1
4
Yellowstone Lake
Bighorn R.
Gillette
90
Moorcroft
59
Newcastle
ROCKY MOUNTAINS
191
20 26
Powder R.
Wright
450
387
Thunder Basin National Grassland
25
Riverton
N. Platte R.
Douglas
Casper
3
Guernsey
287
2
Fort Laramie
Green R.
189
80
Rock Springs
N. Platte R.
130
Laramie
5
230
Cheyenne

THUNDER BASIN NATIONAL GRASSLAND

OTHER WYOMING SITES:

1. Devils Tower National Monument
2. Fort Laramie National Historic Site
3. Guernsey State Park
4. Keyhole State Park
5. Laramie Plains Lakes
6. Medicine Wheel National Historic Landmark

A lot of mixed-grass prairie and sagebrush, a bit of badlands, some forests, four small rivers, numerous creeks, one of the world's largest Pronghorn herds, one of the last remaining prairie Elk herds, a healthy population of Greater Sage-Grouse, and the largest surface coal mine in North America constitute the 572,000-acre Thunder Basin National Grassland.

Many tracts are small and surrounded by ranches or croplands, forming a checkerboard of public and private lands. However, six roadless areas are pristine enough that environmental advocates lobbied to have them designated wilderness in the 1990s. The Forest Service recommended one of these areas, Cow Creek Buttes, as the Cow Creek Historic Rangeland Special Interest Area, a designation that provides some wilderness protection. Wildlife biologists considered the Cheyenne River area a high priority for reintroduction of Black-footed Ferrets, but an outbreak of sylvatic plague in 2001 delayed the effort.

The various parcels of Thunder Basin are widely separated but fall roughly into three sections. The Fiddleback Area between Douglas and Gillette includes the Cheyenne River Valley and the Red and Rochelle Hills. The Upton/Osage Recreation Area between Gillette and Newcastle includes several reservoirs and

Above: Greater Sage-Grouse foraging in Big Sagebrush. (Photo by Glenn Cushman)

pine-covered hills leading toward the Black Hills in the east. And the Spring Creek Unit north of Gillette includes Weston Reservoir.

MINING AND DRILLING

In a few minutes of driving along SR 59 it's not unusual to see a dozen coal trains on the tracks and more than a dozen oil wells. It's a hint that coal mining and oil drilling are major endeavors at Thunder Basin.

Layers of sandstone, shale, and siltstone lie thousands of feet thick. Trapped within these layers are vast deposits of coal, oil, and gas. To tap this resource, six coal mines operate on the grassland, including Black Thunder, the largest surface coal mine in North America. More than 300 oil and gas wells also operate on Thunder Basin with several hundred more on private land within the grassland boundaries. The Bear Creek Uranium Mine, which is in the final stages of reclamation, opened in 1976 and produced about 500,000 tons of ore a year until production stopped in 1985.

Black Thunder Mine annually produces 67 million tons of coal and reclaims between 300 and 500 acres each year. Reclamation workers strip the topsoil before mining begins, saving it for later reuse. When mining is finished, the area is regraded and contoured to its original topography. Workers spread topsoil and reseed with native grasses, trying to restore the land to its pre-mining condition. Deer, Elk, Pronghorns, Badgers, Coyotes, and foxes are often sighted in the reclaimed areas. Tours of several of the coal mines can be arranged.

Bentonite (the clay that makes dirt roads so slippery) was also formerly mined to use as a lubricant for drilling and to seal stock ponds. Thirty-three of the bentonite pits are being converted to wildlife habitat and fishing areas.

GREATER SAGE-GROUSE

Early on a spring morning when it's still too dark to see, a sound like Yellowstone's mud pots throbs from the lek where Greater Sage-Grouse (*Centrocercus urophasianus*) gather to strut and compete for females. Gradually the males emerge from the dusk, white ruffs gleaming like ermine stoles. They fan out their long spikey tail feathers and raise their delicate neck plumes. They inflate and deflate two mustard yellow chest sacs, producing the mud plopping sound that can be heard for 1 to 2 miles. Brushing their wings against the stiff feathers of the ruff, males make a wheezy *swish, swish* noise as they display.

Greater Sage-Grouse display at Thunder Basin National Grassland from mid-March through May. (Photo by Richard Holmes)

Sometimes cocks fly at each other, but usually the less dominant male retreats, making himself sleek and small. When two cocks are roughly equal in strength, they stand side by side, facing opposite directions, each trying to look bigger than the other. Wing fights occasionally erupt, but often the combatants lose interest and walk away.

It's one of the most exciting courtship displays in the West, but chances of observing it may dim unless sagebrush habitat can be protected. Although Greater Sage-Grouse also eat insects, the leaves and buds of Big Sagebrush are their most important food and, in winter, are critical to their survival. The hens also need sagebrush and tall grasses to shelter the shallow scrapes on the ground where they lay 7 to 9 eggs.

First described by Lewis and Clark near the headwaters of the Missouri, the "Cock of the Plains" is the largest member of the grouse family, weighing up to 7 pounds. At the time of the Lewis and Clark Expedition, sage-grouse probably numbered close to 2 million. The anthropologist and conservationist George Bird Grinnel wrote that sage-grouse flying over his camp in the late 1800s "reminded me of the oldtime flights of Passenger Pigeons that I used to see when I was a boy . . . there must have been thousands of them."

Clait Braun, one of the country's foremost grouse experts, says that since 1950 the North American breeding population has decreased 45 to 80 percent. He estimates the current breeding population to be only 140,000 to 160,000, including the Gunnison

Sage-Grouse (*Centrocercus minimus*), which was recognized as a separate species in 2000. Sage-grouse have been extirpated from five states and one Canadian province but are still found in 11 states and two provinces. Wyoming and Montana have the largest remaining breeding populations, with more than 20,000 birds in each state. However, even this number is far below historic or potential levels.

The main problem is loss of habitat. In some states more than 70 percent of the sagebrush range has been converted to farming. Sagebrush has also lost ground to mining, ranching, and urban development. Remaining habitat is often fragmented by fences, roads, and power lines and is degraded by prescribed burns, the spread of cheatgrass, use of herbicides, and a management style that favors grass for livestock.

Sage-grouse are also adversely affected by drought and by predation by Red Foxes, Badgers, raptors, and ravens that take chicks, and ground squirrels that steal eggs. Surprisingly, Coyotes may actually benefit the grouse by keeping the fox population under control. In a Wyoming study, predation caused 94 percent of nest failures. Predation increases when habitat size decreases or is fragmented, offering less cover for the grouse.

SAGEBRUSH

The future of the sage-grouse is inextricably linked to sagebrush, a plant sacred to Plains Indians, who mimicked grouse in their dances and used various sage species for healing teas and salves. "All species of wild sage were probably used as medicine," writes ethnobotanist Kelly Kindscher, who reports that many tribes burned it in sweat lodges and as incense in purification rites. The spicy-smelling leaves were rubbed on people or objects that had been defiled and were sometimes used as deodorant. Sagebrush was also taken for menstrual irregularity and pain, to induce abortions, and to cure headaches, stomachaches, nosebleed, and skin problems.

The medicinal sages are primarily Pasture Sage (*Artemisia ludoviciana*) and Fringed Sage (*A. frigida*), whereas *A. tridentata*, Big Sagebrush, is the species beloved by sage-grouse. Another bird commonly associated with sagebrush habitat is the Wild Turkey. However, chefs who have stuffed their turkeys with sagebrush report that it tastes like creosote. Sage seasoning actually comes from a *Salvia*, not an *Artemisia*.

Many people still use sagebrush ceremonially. Others, however, regard it as of no economic value and do not regret its demise. But if sage-grouse are to survive, so must the sagebrush.

TEPEE RINGS TO HOMESTEADS

Humans are thought to have lived in the Thunder Basin area for at least 11,000 years. Over 1,000 prehistoric and a hundred historic sites have been recorded, including tepee rings, prehistoric hunting camps, and homesteads. In the 1920s and 1930s nearly every section contained a homestead. The Dorr Place in the Fiddleback section of the grassland was homesteaded by William and Mabel Dorr in 1915. It includes the original log house, a 1920s home, a bunkhouse, a corral, and a tin bar. It is being restored and will eventually be open to the public.

HIKING

Hiking is permitted anywhere on the grassland, but beware of rattlesnakes. About 19 miles of "single-track" in the Upton/Osage Area are open for motorized use as well as hiking. A map is posted at the trailhead about 4 miles east of Upton on FR 914.

CAMPING

Dispersed camping is permitted anywhere on the grassland, including the Soda Well picnic area a few miles north of Gillette.

BEST TIMES TO VISIT

Mid-March through May is when Greater Sage-Grouse display, with the most agreeable weather usually occurring in May. Spring wildflowers and mild temperatures persist through June. September and October also bring pleasant weather, and cottonwoods and prairie grasses turn to gold. Overwintering Bald and Golden Eagles highlight the winter season.

INFORMATION

THUNDER BASIN NATIONAL GRASSLAND, Douglas Ranger District, 2250 E. Richards, Douglas, WY 82633; 307-358-4690.

HOW TO GET THERE

The major part of Thunder Basin lies east of SR 59, which connects Douglas and Gillette, and south of US 16, which connects Gillette and Newcastle. SR 450 cuts east/west through the approximate center of the grassland between Wright and Newcastle. One of the most scenic sections is along the Dull Center and Clareton Roads, connecting Bill and SR 450. Numerous gravel roads also provide access. **NOTE:** A Thunder Basin National Grass-land map, available at the above visitor center, is essential for exploring this grassland.

THUNDER BASIN NATIONAL GRASSLAND

WEATHER
MEAN TEMPERATURES AND PRECIPITATION

MONTH	HIGH (°F)	LOW (°F)	PRECIP.	SNOW
January	33	6	0.5"	10.7"
April	56	29	1.5"	12.6"
July	87	54	1.2"	0.0"
October	61	33	1.0"	6.3"

Mean annual precipitation is around 12 inches. Strong westerly winds blow throughout the winter and spring. April and May blizzards leave many backroads impassable. Data are for Casper, Wyoming.

SELECTED WILDLIFE OF SPECIAL INTEREST

MAMMALS: Wyoming Ground Squirrel, Thirteen-lined Ground Squirrel, Black-tailed Prairie Dog, Coyote, Swift Fox, Red Fox, Long-tailed Weasel, Badger, Bobcat, Elk, Mule Deer, Pronghorn.

BIRDS: Bald Eagle, Ferruginous Hawk, Golden Eagle, Prairie Falcon, Greater Sage-Grouse, Sharp-tailed Grouse, Mountain Plover, Upland Sandpiper, Burrowing Owl, Short-eared Owl, Sage Thrasher, Brown Thrasher, McCown's Longspur.

AMPHIBIANS AND REPTILES: Great Plains Toad, Woodhouse's Toad, Northern Leopard Frog, Plains Spadefoot, Tiger Salamander, Greater Short-horned Lizard, Common Sagebrush Lizard, Western Rattlesnake.

OTHER WYOMING SITES

DEVILS TOWER NATIONAL MONUMENT (Box 10, Devils Tower, WY 82714; 307-467-5283). The stark shaft of gray igneous rock thrusts 1,267 feet above the surrounding forest and prairie. The tower is sacred to many American Indians, who have given it poetic names such as *Mato Tipila* ("Bear's Tepee"—Lakota) and *Tsao-aa* ("Tree Rock"—Kiowa). About 400 acres of wheatgrass-needlegrass prairie, including a thriving prairie dog colony, stretch out from the base of the tower. Hiking, camping. Thirty-three miles north of Moorcroft on SR 24.

FORT LARAMIE NATIONAL HISTORIC SITE (HC 72, Box 389, Fort Laramie, WY, 82212; 307-837-2221). Set in shortgrass prairie along the Laramie River, this historic trading and military post has been restored to the way it looked in the 1880s. Some original structures have survived intact. Museum exhibits, volunteers in period dress, and interpretive signs bring history alive. About 3 miles southwest of the town of Fort Laramie off US 26.

GUERNSEY STATE PARK (Box 429, Guernsey, WY 82214; 307-836-2334). A museum built by the Civilian Conservation Corps, a large lake, and prairie grasses highlight this park, located 1 mile northwest of Guernsey off US 26 along the North Platte River. Boating, camping. The Oregon Trail Historic Site, featuring ruts worn 5 to 6 feet deep by covered wagons, and the Register Cliff Historic Site where thousands of pioneers carved their names are also located near Guernsey.

KEYHOLE STATE PARK (353 McKean Road, Moorcroft, WY 82721; 307-756-3596). Set in mixed-grass prairie along the shore of Keyhole Reservoir at the western edge of the Black Hills, this park attracts a variety of birds and wildlife. Boating, camping. About 6 miles northeast of Moorcroft via SR 24 and CR 113.

LARAMIE PLAINS LAKES (Wyoming Game and Fish Department, 528 S. Adams Street, Laramie, WY 82070; 307-745-4046). Shortgrass prairie surrounds wetlands and seven lakes stocked with Rainbow Trout. Camping. Look for pronghorns and waterfowl. About 15 miles southwest of Laramie; from SR 130 turn south on Big Hollow Road and follow signs.

MEDICINE WHEEL NATIONAL HISTORIC LANDMARK (Bighorn National Forest, Box 367, Lovell, WY 82431; 307-548-6541). A 1.5-mile trail leads to what may have been an early astronomical observatory. Built between 1200 and 1700 A.D., it is sacred to many Indian peoples. Rolling hills of native grassland are interspersed with conifer forest at an elevation close to 10,000 feet. On US 14A between Sheridan and Lovell.

Several hundred acres of wheatgrass-needlegrass prairie surround Devils Tower, a Plains Indian sacred site. (Photo by Glenn Cushman)

Prairie Cordgrass at Fort Laramie National Historic Site

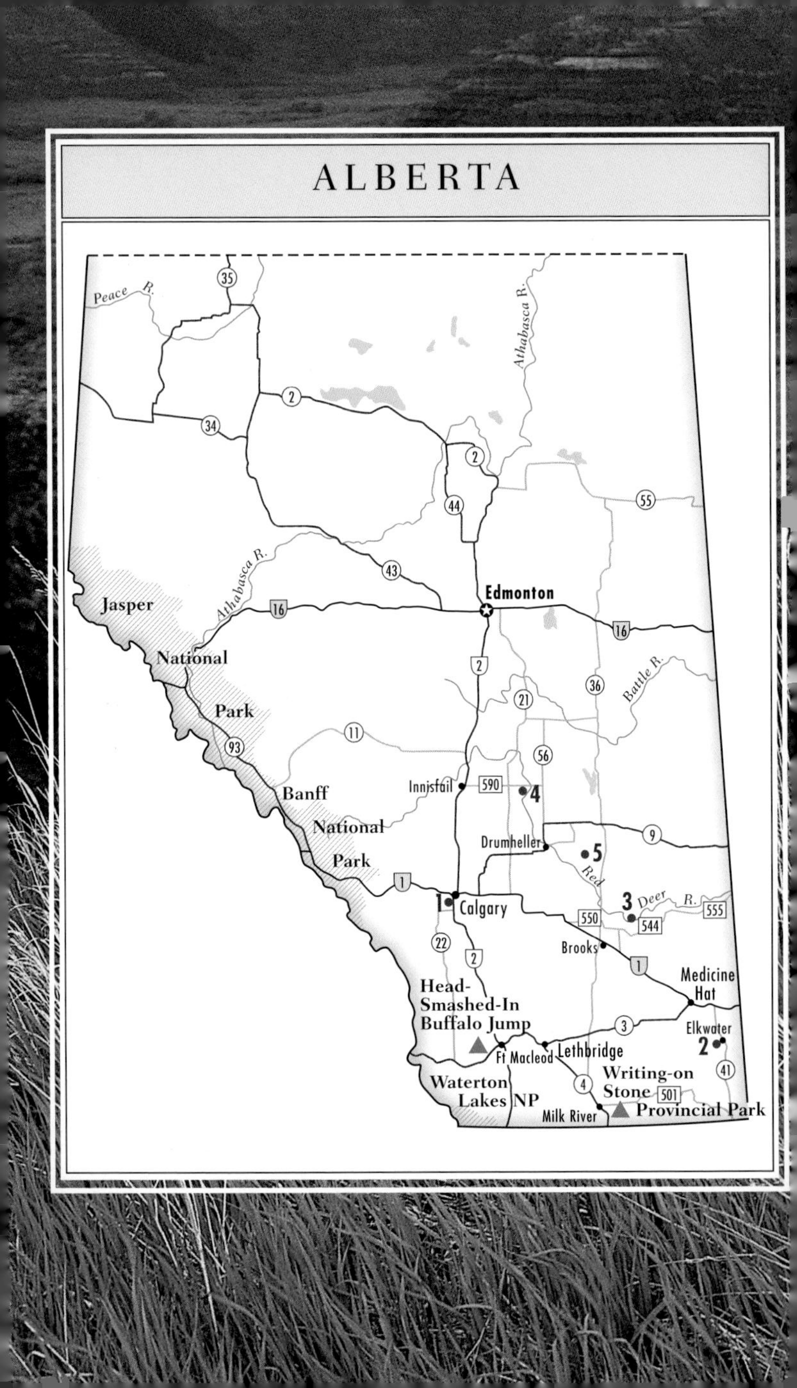

ALBERTA

Peace R.

35

2

34

Athabasca R.

2

44

55

Jasper

National

Athabasca R.

43

16

Edmonton

16

Park

93

2

Battle R.

21

36

11

56

Banff

Innisfail

590

4

National

Drumheller

5

9

Park

Red

3 Deer R.

555

1

550

544

Calgary

Brooks

1

22

Medicine
Hat

2

Head-
Smashed-In
Buffalo Jump

3

Elkwater

2

41

Ft Macleod

Lethbridge

Writing-on
Stone

4

501

Waterton
Lakes NP

Milk River

Provincial Park

HEAD-SMASHED-IN BUFFALO JUMP

WRITING-ON-STONE PROVINCIAL PARK

OTHER ALBERTA SITES:

1. Ann and Sandy Cross Conservation Area
2. Cypress Hills Interprovincial Park
3. Dinosaur Provincial Park
4. Dry Island Buffalo Jump Provincial Park
5. Hand Hills Ecological Reserve

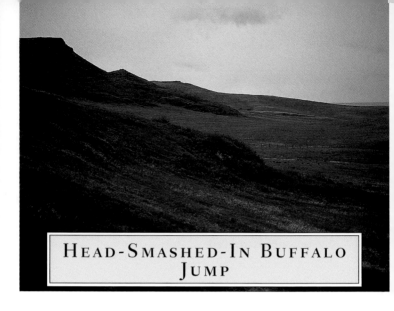

HEAD-SMASHED-IN BUFFALO JUMP

Once upon a time, according to Piegan lore, a young brave stood under a ledge to watch the buffalo fall to their deaths in front of him. The hunt was unusually successful, many Bison hurtled over the cliff, and the man's skull was crushed by the falling carcasses. Because of this tragedy, the Piegan, one of the tribes of the Blackfoot Confederacy, called the place *Estipah-skikikini-knots* or "Where he got his head smashed in." It is one of the oldest, largest, and best-preserved buffalo jump sites in North America.

Designated a UNESCO World Heritage Site in 1981, this archaeological treasure covers almost 3,000 acres. The five-level interpretive center vividly depicts the natural and human history of the region from prehistoric times to the arrival of the Europeans and is the starting point for exploring the area.

The top level of the building opens out onto the mixed-grass prairie at the end of the Porcupine Hills. From this vantage point at the top of the jump, Rough Fescue, Blue Grama, needle-grasses, and sagebrushes stretch out as far as the eye can see. The steep escarpment, 33 to 60 feet high, extends for more than 300 feet.

Across the prairie to the north on the highest of the Porcupine

Above: Rough Fescue prairie, early June. (Photo by Glenn Cushman)

Head-Smashed-In Buffalo Jump becomes a waterfall after a late spring rainstorm. (Photo by Glenn Cushman)

Hills is the Vision Quest site. Many young men seeking spiritual guidance came here to fast and pray. On a clear day the Canadian Rockies loom to the west. Occasionally Bison, escaped from nearby ranches, wander across the plains, and sometimes Lynx are sighted in the far reaches of the hills.

If you're lucky enough to visit during a hard rain, waterfalls instead of Bison leap over the sandstone precipice.

PISSKAN

Various myths from different tribes explain the connection between the people and the buffalo. A Crow story tells how Old Man Coyote challenged the buffalo to a race. Coyote ran faster and hid near the precipice, fooling the buffalo into thinking he was still ahead. The buffalo, which can reach speeds of 34 miles per hour, could not stop and plummeted to their deaths, thus providing meat for the hungry people. The Piegan say that in ancient times buffalo were much larger and attacked and ate the people, making Napi, Creator and Trickster/Hero, very sad. To help his people, Napi led the animals to the Porcupine Hills and taught the *Pisskan*, or buffalo jump, method for killing large herds.

Spiritual ceremonies were a fundamental part of the lives of all Indians of the Northern Plains. Before a hunt took place, members of the tribe participated in sacred rites, chanting songs and burning Sweetgrass. Medicine men performed ceremonies using a stone called *Iniskim* that, it was believed, could call to the buffalo.

As the time of the hunt neared, runners went out onto the prairie to round up the herd into the staging area in Olsen Creek

Valley. Stone cairns were built and embellished with branches that rustled in the wind. The cairns, placed 16 to 20 feet apart, formed V-shaped game drives directing the Bison toward the cliff. Meat-drying racks were erected, roasting pits were dug, and finally, dogs were muzzled so as not to spook the grazing Bison. Moving slowly and quietly, hunters dressed in Bison or Coyote skins decoyed the animals from the staging area toward the cliff. At the right moment, people hidden behind the cairns stampeded the herd over the jump and butchered them on the prairie below.

After the kill, quartzite rocks were heated in fires fueled with buffalo chips, and the meat was boiled and roasted in pits. For many generations the people used water from a creek originating in underground springs near the processing area. A rancher dammed the creek in the mid-1940s, however, and it never regained its former copious flow, even when the dam was removed.

Archaeologists have found Bison bones piled up 33 feet deep below the jump and estimate that during many centuries of use, 150,000 Bison were stampeded over the cliff. Hunts took place here for about 5,700 years until the Bison began to disappear in the mid-nineteenth century. (See p. 365 in Custer State Park for more information on Bison.)

SWEETGRASS

Some of Canada's First Nations believed Sweetgrass (*Hierochloë hirta*) was the first plant to cover the earth, and many Northern Plains Indians used it for perfume and incense as well as in healing teas and salves. It is often burned in ceremonies, left as an offering, and woven into sweet-smelling baskets.

To the Cheyenne, Sweetgrass symbolized the renewal of life. They purified objects, such as medicine rattles, by passing them through the aromatic smoke. Hidatsas practiced a form of "healing touch." After passing their hands through the smoke, they held them over a wound without touching it and then would place tallow on it, according to Kelly Kindscher in *Medicinal Wild Plants of the Prairie.*

Sweetgrass's vanilla-like fragrance comes from coumarin, an organic compound also found in lavender, licorice, strawberries, apricots, and cinnamon. Coumarin has been used as flavoring in candy, tobacco, soft drinks, and as an aromatic in perfumes and is used medicinally as an anti-coagulant. It may serve as a pesticide for the plants that produce it.

Also called Vanilla Grass, Holy Grass, and *Zubrovka* ("Place where the Bison graze" in Polish), this circumboreal grass grows from 8 to 24 inches high. Its showy 3-flowered spikelets bloom in June and form pyramid-shaped panicles. Look for it in wet prairies, marshes, streambanks, and lake shores. In Alberta it often occurs in wheatgrass-sedge communities where its rhizomes and roots form a dense mat beneath the sandy loam. It rarely grows abundantly at any one location, however, and overharvesting may be causing wild stands to decline.

Head-Smashed-In may be too dry to support stands of Sweetgrass. But the grass does grow in the nearby Waterton area and in the Sweet Grass Hills of Montana. On the Great Plains it ranges from Alberta to Manitoba and south into Montana, the Dakotas, and northwest Iowa.

HIKING

HEAD-SMASHED-IN BUFFALO JUMP TRAIL (0.6 miles or 1 km), keyed to a brochure available at the interpretive center, leads to a tepee ring, the kill site, the processing area, and an archaeological dig.

CAMPING

Tepee camping (10 per tepee) and a variety of cultural experiences are offered to registrants, but there are no campgrounds. Old Man River Campground is about 10 miles (16 km) east of the jump, and several other campgrounds are near Fort Macleod.

BEST TIMES TO VISIT

Golden legumes and blue penstemons mix with greening grasses in May and June. Drumming and dancing take place every Wednesday in July and August. A one-day native crafts fair and festival is held in November. Throughout the year many special educational events, such as storytelling, demonstrations, and lectures, are offered.

INFORMATION

HEAD-SMASHED-IN BUFFALO JUMP, Box 1977, Fort Macleod, AB T0L 0Z0; 403-553-2731.

HOW TO GET THERE

From Fort Macleod go west on Hwy. 3, then north on Hwy. 2 for a total of about 5 miles (8 km). Turn west on Hwy. 785 and follow the signs for about 11 miles (18 km) to the parking lots where shuttles take you to the interpretive center.

HEAD-SMASHED-IN BUFFALO JUMP

WEATHER
MEAN TEMPERATURES AND PRECIPITATION

MONTH	HIGH (°F)	LOW (°F)	PRECIP.	SNOW
January	27	6	0.85"	8.8"
April	54	30	1.35"	6.5"
July	79	52	1.75"	0.0"
October	58	33	0.85"	4.2"

Mean annual precipitation is 16.3 inches. Late winter and early spring bring strong winds, and severe thunderstorms are possible during summer. June–August temperatures have ranged from 29°F to 103°F. Data are for Lethbridge, Alberta.

SELECTED WILDLIFE OF SPECIAL INTEREST

MAMMALS: White-tailed Jackrabbit, Richardson's Ground Squirrel, Yellow-bellied Marmot, Porcupine, Coyote, Bobcat, Mule Deer, Pronghorn, Bison.

BIRDS: Swainson's Hawk (m), Red-tailed Hawk, Golden Eagle (m), Ruffed Grouse, Northern Saw-whet Owl.

AMPHIBIANS AND REPTILES: Tiger Salamander, Common Gartersnake.

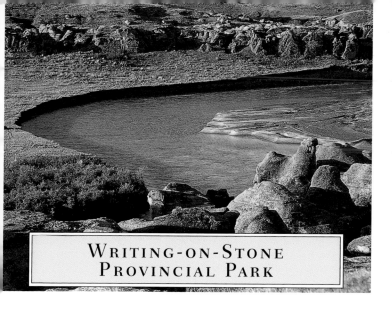

WRITING-ON-STONE
PROVINCIAL PARK

You can almost hear horses whinnying and feel bullets whizzing as stick figures defend and attack clusters of tepees in a vivid petroglyph at Writing-on-Stone Provincial Park. This 4,400-acre park in southern Alberta protects the largest concentration of plains indigenous rock art as well as one of the largest expanses of mixed-grass prairie in Alberta. Summer visitors can also visit a reconstructed Northwest Mounted Police outpost on guided tours.

Wandering among goblinlike formations, called hoodoos, in a maze of sheer sandstone cliffs and outcroppings, a visitor may see White-tailed Jackrabbits nibbling on native grasses such as Blue Grama, Junegrass, Northern Wheatgrass, and Indian Ricegrass. Mule Deer and White-tailed Deer munch on the Saskatoon Serviceberry bushes in the coulees. On summer evenings seven of the nine species of bat indigenous to Alberta flit above the campground, possibly zeroing in on Polyphemus, Cecropia, and Sphinx Moths.

Below, the Milk River makes oxbow meanders. The apt name was bestowed on the river by Lewis and Clark, who thought the muddy waters looked like tea laced with lots of milk. In flood stage the river undercuts its banks, and huge chunks of soil plop down with a splash like an enormous Beaver. Across the river to

Above: Hoodoos form mazes along the Milk River in Writing-on-Stone Provincial Park. (Photo by Ruth Carol Cushman)

the south, the Sweet Grass Hills thrust up into the Big Sky Country of Montana.

ROCK ART

The Blackfoot people call this valley *Áísínai'pi* ("where the drawings have appeared") and consider the art sacred, created by the spirits. They visit the site with reverence, seeking spiritual guidance. In the past many Blackfoot visitors added their drawings to the sandstone cliffs, and in still earlier times, artists from the Shoshone, Nakota, and Gros Ventre nations may have also left their marks on the walls.

Archaeologists believe people may have camped here 3,500 years ago and that some of the petroglyphs (carvings) and pictographs (paintings) might be 5,000 years old. Although it's impossible to date precisely, most rock art at this site was probably created within the last 500 years. For pictographs, the artists mixed minerals such as crushed iron ore with either water or Bison fat, and they also used charcoal. Usually they incised the petroglyphs into the sandstone with sharpened bone, antler, or stone.

The pictures often depict warriors with shields, headdresses, bows, and spears. Animals the people hunted, such as Bison,

This shield petroglyph is visible from the Hoodoo Trail. (Photo by Glenn Cushman)

bear, deer, and Elk, are prominently featured. After European contact, depictions of battles show horses and guns. No one knows for sure what the art means. The purpose of some of the drawings may have been ceremonial or "magical," an entreaty to the spirits for help. Many panels probably record actual events. Others may recount dreams received in vision quests.

A few sites, including a famous scene that may commemorate a Blackfoot battle that occurred in 1866, can be seen from the Hoodoo Trail. This priceless art has endured the elements for centuries but is easily damaged by humans. Even such seemingly benign acts as tracing the drawings on paper or touching them with oily hands can harm them. The park's largest concentration of these images may be seen only on guided tours into the archaeological preserve from mid-May to September.

HOODOOS

Wind and water have sculpted the reddish sandstone into weird and wonderful formations called hoodoos. "Windows" frame the distant Sweet Grass Hills, and sharp clefts give views down into the Milk River. Harder sandstone layers cap the underlying softer layers and help protect them from further erosion. According to legend, if you sleep under a hoodoo, it may become angry and throw down its head to crush you.

Many of these phantasmagoric figures form a maze just east of the road leading to the campground. Off-trail exploring in this area is permitted. The Hoodoo Trail, west of the road, is named for these goblins turned to stone.

WHITE-TAILED JACKRABBITS

White-tailed Jackrabbits are really hares, not rabbits, as the young are born fully furred, with open eyes. The enormous black-tipped ears of adults help dissipate heat and detect predators. Their protective coloration blends into the background, changing from grizzled brownish gray in summer (except for a white tail) to pure white or pale gray in winter. During the March-to-August breeding season you might be lucky enough to observe them capering and leapfrogging over one another. They are easiest to observe in early morning or late afternoon since they rest in forms (shallow scrapes) under a bush during midday.

These kangaroo-like creatures can jump 20 feet and maintain speeds of 36 miles per hour. Some reports say they have forced foxes to retreat by kicking vigorously. They can sprint 45 miles per hour and run in zigzag patterns to escape such predators as hawks, foxes, Lynx, Coyotes, and Bobcats. The Algonquins re-

White-tailed Jackrabbits are at home in open country, including the alpine tundra of the central Rockies and the shortgrass prairies of southern Alberta.

garded Michabou or the Great Hare as a Trickster/Hero and the creator of earth. According to one story, Great Hare employs magical powers to escape from Wildcat, making mile-long leaps and creating fanciful illusions to outwit his befuddled enemy. Wildcat vows to devour Hare or lose his tail. As a result, Wildcat becomes Bobcat.

White-tailed Jackrabbits range from southern Alberta and southwestern Ontario south to northeastern California, Colorado, Kansas, and Wisconsin in prairies, shrublands, mountain parklands, and alpine tundra.

SASKATOON SERVICEBERRY

One of the first shrubs to flower in spring, Saskatoon Serviceberry puts out dense clusters of 5-petaled white flowers in May and June and bears succulent purple berries in July and August. Hairstreak butterflies and other insects gorge on the nectar. Sapsuckers feed on the sap, and many birds fatten on the nutritious fruits that are high in vitamin C, iron, calcium, protein, sugars, and phenols. Deer and rabbits browse the twigs; Beavers, foxes, squirrels, Raccoons, and skunks feast on fruit, bark, and twigs.

Humans so love the bountiful bush that they have given it at least a dozen names and named the city of Saskatoon in its honor. Native peoples dried the berries for soups, stews, sausages, and pemmican and made decoctions from the bark to treat snow blindness, stomachaches, and earaches, as well as to ease childbirth. Today people relish pies, jellies, jams, and delectable wines made from saskatoon fruit.

The word "saskatoon" may be derived from the Blackfoot or

Cree name for the berry: *Misaskatomina* or *Misaskquahtoomina*. Many of its various names reflect seasonal events tied to Saskatoon Serviceberry. Some berries begin to show color in June, hence, "Juneberry." The welcome shade cast by the small tree when the circuit rider arrived to conduct religious services on the frontier led to the names "serviceberry" and "sarvisberry," and the names "shadblow" and "shadbush" probably come from the simultaneous blooming of saskatoon and spawning of shad. Some Alberta researchers are tracking the blooming time of serviceberry, aspen, and other plants as a possible indicator of global warming.

This hardy member of the rose family ranges widely across the northern Great Plains. It is tolerant of drought, cold, and heat and does not require pollination to set fruit. It is used to revegetate mined areas because of its tolerance of acid spoil. Several cultivars with larger flowers and fruit and brighter fall foliage are available for home gardens.

Hiking

The coulee areas south of the Milk River have been designated a hiking zone, but there are no developed trails. Hikers should sign in at the office and obtain a map of the backcountry.

HOODOO TRAIL (1.5 miles or 2.5 km) starts at the campground and winds through hoodoos and along the banks of the river to the famous battle scene petroglyph. A self-guided tour booklet is available from the office or in a box at the trailhead.

Camping

A large cottonwood and willow grove provides shade to the campground on the banks of the Milk River.

Best Times to Visit

Guided tours to the rock art are offered from mid-May to September. However, temperatures can reach the high 90s in midsummer. Sharp-tailed Grouse dance and White-tailed Jackrabbits cavort in early spring. Pronghorn and deer fawns generally appear in late May and early June along with multicolored penstemons, golden legumes and mustards, and white evening-primroses and Saskatoon Serviceberies. Although many of the art panels are off-limits during the off-season, there are several self-guided tours and fewer people.

WRITING-ON-STONE PROVINCIAL PARK, Box 297, Milk River, AB T0K 1M0; 403-647-2364. Free tickets for the rock art tours are available from the Interpreters' Office on a first-come, first-served basis one hour before each tour begins.

How to Get There

From the town of Milk River drive east on Hwy. 501 for about 19 miles (32 km) and follow the signs south on Hwy. 500 for another 6 miles (10 km).

WRITING-ON-STONE PROVINCIAL PARK

WEATHER
MEAN TEMPERATURES AND PRECIPITATION

MONTH	HIGH (°F)	LOW (°F)	PRECIP.	SNOW
January	29	7	0.4"	8.8"
April	56	31	0.9"	6.5"
July	82	52	1.4"	0.0"
October	31	10	0.4"	4.2"

Mean annual precipitation is 13.5 inches. Summer (June–August) temperatures have ranged from 30°F to 105°F. May and June are the wettest months. Data are for Sunburst, Montana.

SELECTED WILDLIFE OF SPECIAL INTEREST

MAMMALS: Nuttall's Cottontail, White-tailed Jackrabbit, Yellow-bellied Marmot, Beaver, Bushy-tailed Woodrat, Porcupine, Coyote, Badger, Mule Deer, White-tailed Deer, Pronghorn.

BIRDS: Ferruginous Hawk, Golden Eagle, Prairie Falcon, Sharp-tailed Grouse, Long-billed Curlew, Marbled Godwit, Burrowing Owl, Short-eared Owl, Common Nighthawk, Bank Swallow, Rock Wren, Brown Thrasher, Sprague's Pipit, Baird's Sparrow, Clay-colored Sparrow, Chestnut-collared Longspur.

AMPHIBIANS AND REPTILES: Boreal Chorus Frog, Northern Leopard Frog, Plains Spadefoot, Tiger Salamander, Western Rattlesnake, Bullsnake.

OTHER ALBERTA SITES

ANN AND SANDY CROSS CONSERVATION AREA (Box 20, Site 23, R.R. #8, Calgary, AB T2J 2T9; 403-931-9001). The Nature Conservancy of Canada has preserved 4,800 acres of Rough Fescue prairie, restored prairie, and aspen parkland in a peaceful retreat adjacent to a busy metropolis. By appointment. Hiking. One mile (1.6 km) west of Calgary on Hwy. 22X and 1 mile south on 160th Street SW.

CYPRESS HILLS INTERPROVINCIAL PARK. See Saskatchewan.

DINOSAUR PROVINCIAL PARK (Box 60, Patricia, AB T0J 2K0; 403-378-4342). This United Nations World Heritage Site (18,116 acres) adjacent to Red Deer River contains one of the richest fossil beds in the world as well as hoodoos, badlands, coulees, prairie, and superb interpretive exhibits. Hiking, camping. Thirty miles (48 km) northeast of Brooks via Hwy. 873 and 544. The nearby Royal Tyrrell Museum, about 4 miles (6.4 km) northwest of Drumheller on Hwy. 837, contains some of the best dinosaur exhibits in the world; phone 1-888-440-4240 to check on museum hours.

DRY ISLAND BUFFALO JUMP PROVINCIAL PARK (Box 1918, Provincial Bldg. Drumheller, AB T0J 0Y0; 403-823-1750). A flat-topped mesa covered with prairie grasses rises 660 feet above Red Deer River and offers views of a 3,000-year-old buffalo jump. The park contains mixed-grass prairie, badlands, aspen parkland, White Spruce forest. About 31 miles (50 km) east of Innisfail on Hwy. 590.

HAND HILLS ECOLOGICAL RESERVE (Box 1918, Provincial Building, Drumheller, AB T0J 0Y0; 403-528-5228). Native peoples quarried stone for their tools in the Hand Hills. Tepee rings, hearths, and an old quarry site can be found in this fescue and mixed-grass prairie and aspen parkland. Foot access only. Contact office before visiting. About 17.5 miles (28 km) southeast of Drumheller, adjacent to the northwest shore of Little Fish Lake. Walk in about 0.6 miles (1 km) from Hwy. 73. Campsites are available at nearby Little Fish Lake Provincial Park on Hwy. 851.

MANITOBA

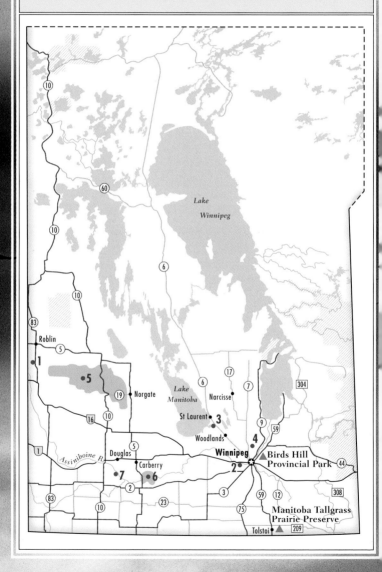

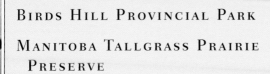

BIRDS HILL PROVINCIAL PARK

MANITOBA TALLGRASS PRAIRIE PRESERVE

OTHER MANITOBA SITES:

1. Asessipi Provincial Park
2. Beaudry Provincial Park
3. Lake Francis Wildlife Management Area
4. Oak Hammock Marsh
5. Riding Mountain National Park
6. Spruce Woods Provincial Park
7. Yellow Quill Prairie

BIRDS HILL PROVINCIAL PARK

Three-flowered Avens tint the prairie a pale damask rose in spring, and golden Marsh Marigolds light up the deep, dark bogs. An occasional Indigo Bunting flashes feathers as blue as the blooming penstemons in summer. Big Bluestem turns the prairie to wine, and encroaching aspen, birch, and larch rim the grassland with gold in autumn.

This 8,704-acre park showcases a mosaic of communities in close proximity: mixed-grass prairies, wet meadows, cedar bogs, aspen-oak parklands, boreal forests, and esker ridges molded by glaciers. As the glaciers retreated some ten thousand years ago, water melting within them tunneled through the ice, carrying debris. This sand and gravel debris was left behind to form snakelike ridges called eskers. Several eskers met, geologists believe, to form Birds Hill, about 15 miles northeast of Winnipeg in Manitoba. The varying elevations of the hills create many different ecosystems, which support a diversity of plants and animals.

These hills also brim with immigrant history. James Bird, who arrived in 1788 as a writer with the Hudson's Bay Company, was granted more than 1,000 acres on the east side of the Red River when he retired. This land forms the nucleus of Birds Hill Provincial Park, named for the Bird family. Settlers from Germany,

Above: A rainbow heralds the end of a summer storm at Birds Hill Provincial Park. (Photo by Glenn Cushman)

Poland, and Ukraine farmed in the area during the late nineteenth and early twentieth centuries. Remnants of their communities remain in the park, which opened in 1967 to celebrate Canada's 100th birthday.

Recreational and educational opportunities abound. A circle driving tour passes an extensive "Avens Prairie," historic homesteads, and self-guided trails. One of these trails is named Nimowin, a Cree word meaning "peaceful" or "quiet," and that's what strikes you about this park. It's a refuge for nature and for people who need nature next to the busy urban life of Winnipeg.

THREE-FLOWERED AVENS

A single plant of Three-flowered Avens is relatively inconspicuous, with muted pinkish purplish sepals and bracts enclosing 5 tiny creamy petals. The small flowers, 3 to a stalk, look as though they are still in bud. But when thousands of them spread across a prairie meadow, it's as though a pink haze enveloped the land, inspiring the name "Torch Flower."

This member of the rose family is just as delightful when the flowers fade. The feathery, silvery styles wave in the breeze until midsummer, leading to the names "Prairie Smoke" and "Old Man's Whiskers." The Blackfeet called this plant with nodding flowers *So-ya-its* (lies-on-its-belly). They used it medicinally, making a mouthwash for canker sores and sore throat and an eyewash, a tea, and a salve from the roots and other plant parts.

Geum triflorum grows in prairies and open woodlands from southern Canada into the northern United States and is often used in rock gardens. Stop number 3 on the auto driving tour is one of the best places to see large aggregations of avens.

Fields of Three-flowered Avens ("Prairie Smoke," Geum triflorum) form fluffy seed heads in June.

Mind-boggling numbers of Red-sided Gartersnakes (*Thamnophis sirtalis parietalis,* a subspecies of the Common Gartersnake) aggregate in Manitoba less than 100 miles (160 km) north of Birds Hill. It's believed to be the largest concentration of snakes anywhere in the world and may be the largest concentration of any vertebrate species. As many as 25,000 may hibernate together in a single den the size of a living room.

When they emerge from hibernation in late April to mid-May, the colorfully striped snakes form mating balls of up to 100 bodies in one writhing mass. Rick Shine (University of Sydney) and Robert Mason (Oregon State University) are studying the phenomenon of males mimicking the scent of females to become the nucleus of such a ball. They theorize that such "she-males" benefit from the heat generated at the center of a mass of bodies and are also protected from crows and other birds, which gather in large numbers to feast on the emerging snakes.

After a two- to three-week orgy, the snakes disperse to nearby marshes where they feed on frogs, toads, leeches, and other small animals. They return to the vicinity of the dens in September, remaining active until cool October weather forces them inside.

Hibernating sites are below the frost line in fissures or sinkholes in limestone bedrock. In recent years some die-offs occurred when snakes failed to go deep enough below the surface. As the snakes travel to and from their dens, they are also at risk from automobiles. Drift fences and tunnels under roads help make the route safer, and "Snake Crossing" signs urge drivers to reduce speed.

As many as 25,000 Red-sided Gartersnakes sometimes hibernate in a single den in winter. In spring they come together in enormous mating balls that may provide warmth and protection to the snakes in the center. (Photo by Robert T. Mason)

All gartersnakes are harmless, and visitors are allowed to handle them. However, in spring, females (larger than the males) should not be touched to avoid stressing them. Collecting is forbidden.

Red-sided Gartersnakes occur at Birds Hill but only in nominal numbers. To see them by the tens of thousands, go to Narcisse Wildlife Management Area 3.75 miles (6 km) north of the town of Narcisse on Hwy. 17 (81 miles or 130 km north of Winnipeg) and follow the snake den signs. A 1.8-mile (3 km) interpretive trail leads to the site. Entry into the dens is prohibited, but there are viewing platforms at each hibernaculum. Phone 1-800-214-6497 to check on the timing of emergence.

HIKING

A network of hiking, cross-country skiing, and horseback riding trails crisscrosses the back country and is shown on the map available at the park entrance. In addition, the following self-guided trails go through a variety of natural habitats.

BUR OAK (0.6 miles or 1 km for short loop) begins at stop number 7 on the auto tour and passes through a stand of gnarled Bur Oaks.

CEDAR BOG (2.2 miles or 3.5 km) begins at stop number 1 on the auto tour and circles through prairie, aspen-oak parkland, and bogs.

NIMOWIN (1.1 miles or 1.8 km) begins at the end of Nimowin Road and loops through Big Bluestem prairie and areas being restored. It is dedicated to the idea of peace in the world and with nature.

PINE RIDGE (1.5 miles or 2.4 km) begins at Stop number 5 on the auto tour and traverses Old School Road, passing such historical sites as the school, the store, and several homesteads.

CAMPING

A spacious campground along South Drive is open May to mid-October. Watch for Wild Turkeys.

BEST TIMES TO VISIT

Red-sided Gartersnakes emerge from dens from late April to mid-May, with highest numbers seen around Mother's Day. Three-flowered Avens, Marsh Marigolds, and several orchids bloom in May and June as White-tailed Deer are giving birth. The Winnipeg Folk Festival takes place each July, and autumn colors peak in late September. Cross-country skiers and snowshoers occasionally glimpse a visiting Snowy or Great Gray Owl in winter.

INFORMATION

BIRDS HILL DISTRICT OFFICE, Box 183, R.R. #2, Dugald, MB R0E 0K0; 204-222-9151.

Two fine museums are located in nearby Winnipeg: the Manitoba Museum of Man and Nature (depicts the relationship of people and their environment), at Main Street and Rupert Avenue, and the Living Prairie Museum (30 acres of unplowed tallgrass prairie), at 2795 Ness Avenue.

HOW TO GET THERE

From Winnipeg take Hwy. 59 north 15 miles (24 km) and follow the signs. The east side of the park is accessible from Hwy. 206.

BIRDS HILL PROVINCIAL PARK

WEATHER
MEAN TEMPERATURES AND PRECIPITATION

MONTH	HIGH (°F)	LOW (°F)	PRECIP.	SNOW
January	8	-12	0.8"	9.2"
April	50	28	1.4"	4.0"
July	80	56	2.8"	0.0"
October	52	32	1.2"	2.0"

Mean annual precipitation is 21.4 inches, with almost half falling as rain in June, July, and August. Heaviest snows often occur in early spring. Data are for Winnipeg, Manitoba.

SELECTED WILDLIFE OF SPECIAL INTEREST

MAMMALS: Snowshoe Hare, White-tailed Jackrabbit, Least Chipmunk, Thirteen-lined Ground Squirrel, Coyote, Black Bear, Short-tailed Weasel, Mink, Mountain Lion, Lynx, White-tailed Deer.

BIRDS: Broad-winged Hawk, Ruffed Grouse, Sharp-tailed Grouse, Wild Turkey, Snowy Owl (w), Great Gray Owl (w), Pileated Woodpecker, Gray Catbird, American Redstart, Ovenbird, Clay-colored Sparrow, Indigo Bunting, Bobolink, Common Redpoll.

AMPHIBIANS AND REPTILES: Canadian Toad, Gray Treefrog, Spring Peeper, Northern Leopard Frog, Wood Frog, Plains Gartersnake, Red-sided Gartersnake.

MANITOBA TALLGRASS PRAIRIE PRESERVE

An invisible Yellow Rail clicks softly somewhere in the marsh. A Marbled Godwit sits on a snag. Behind him, charred fields that were burned just weeks earlier have turned emerald green. Sandhill Cranes leap, bow, and cavort in the Big Bluestem as they perform spring courtship dances. Later they will mate and raise young on one of the last remnants of Canada's tallgrass prairie.

The Manitoba Tallgrass Prairie Preserve, almost touching the border with Minnesota, was saved because of the efforts of people who cared. The effort started in 1987 when the Manitoba Naturalists Society started looking for native tallgrass prairie. They found very little, and what they did find often covered less than 3 acres. A few tracts near the towns of Tolstoi and Gardenton looked promising, however, and in 1989 the Critical Wildlife Habitat Program, a coalition of seven conservation groups, began buying land.

What spared this small stretch of prairie was the fact that the substrate was too rocky to plow, as the early Ukrainian settlers found to their *beedda* (misery). Today the preserve covers more than 6,000 acres and is broken into three blocks. The southern block contains large, deep marshes, whereas the northern block is

Big Bluestem grows 6 feet high in Manitoba's tallgrass-aspen parklands in late summer.

In fall the vital activities of aspen leaves decline as temperatures fall and days shorten; chlorophyll is no longer replenished, and existing yellow pigments in the leaves create dazzling color displays. (Photo by Glenn Cushman)

drier, with scattered sedge meadows. The central block is a mix of small prairie openings and large tracts of aspen and oak. In order to reduce habitat fragmentation, The Critical Wildlife Habitat Program continues to enlarge the preserve through purchases and conservation easements. In 2002 the Nature Conservancy of Canada purchased an additional 5,000 acres, bisected by the Rat River, just north of the preserve.

Marbled Godwits nest throughout the northern prairie region and winter along the Pacific, Gulf, and Atlantic coasts. Some fly all the way to Brazil and Chile. (Photo by Richard W. Holmes)

An aggressive prescribed burning program keeps aspens and other trees at bay, and naturalists pull Leafy Spurge and other invasive weeds by hand. The reward is a resurgence of such native grasses as Indian Grass, Prairie Cordgrass, Prairie Dropseed, Big Bluestem, Porcupine Grass, and one of the largest populations of Western Prairie Fringed Orchids in the world. The preserve provides a haven for other rare species, such as Gray Wolf, Yellow Rail, Powesheik and Dakota Skipper butterflies, and Adder's Tongue Fern.

BLACK LIGHTS AND WHITE ORCHIDS

Biologists have counted as many as 21,000 Western Prairie Fringed Orchids at the Manitoba Tallgrass Prairie Preserve and on private land surrounding the preserve, even though this rare plant is quickly disappearing from other places. It is threatened in both the United States and Canada because its traditional habitat of wet tallgrass prairie is being destroyed and because it depends on just one type of insect, long-tongued hawkmoths, for pollination. As the prairie habitat shrinks, orchid patches become more fragmented, making it difficult for the moths to find them.

Zoologist Christie Borkowsky is experimenting with ultraviolet, or black, lights in an effort to increase pollination rates on the preserve. She hopes ultraviolet lights in orchid patches will attract more moths, whose eyes can detect UV light, from outlying areas. If successful, this technique could benefit other rare plants pollinated by moths.

Ten other orchid species, including the Yellow Lady's-Slipper, the Showy Lady's-Slipper, and the endangered Small White Lady's-Slipper, also grow on the preserve. For more information on Western Prairie Fringed Orchids, see Sheyenne National Grassland, North Dakota.

ENCROACHING ASPEN

Native Americans called Quaking Aspen "the tree that talks to itself" because of the whispering sound made by the leaves. Petioles that attach the leaves to twigs are flattened perpendicular to the plane of the blade and act as a pivot, causing the leaves to tremble and rustle in the slightest breeze. Various Indian tribes made a tonic from aspen bark, which contains substances similar to aspirin.

Populus tremuloides is the most widespread tree species in North America, due in part to its tolerance for a wide range of climatic conditions. Its distribution covers 112 degrees of longitude and 35 degrees of latitude. At the limits of its range, near timber-line and at northern latitudes, aspen become smaller and scrawnier.

On the Manitoba Tallgrass Prairie Preserve, aspen provide sustenance and shelter for many creatures. Beaver eat the bark and twigs and use branches and trunks for dam building; Moose, Elk, and deer browse on both twigs and leaves; and cavity-nesting birds use holes in the soft, easily excavated wood. In autumn the leaves glitter and glow in luminous tones of yellow. Their beauty and usefulness make aspen a universally favorite tree; however, they can invade and displace the prairie.

Although aspen can reproduce by seeding, its most frequent method is through cloning. The trunk may be killed, but new trees spring from the original rootstock, spreading rapidly over disturbed areas or grasslands. Encroaching trees covering many acres may all stem from the root of a single individual or may be a mosaic of several clones. In 1992 botanists reported a single clone covering 106 acres in Utah. They estimated that it weighed more than 6,000 tons and consisted of some 47,000 connected stems.

Aspens are among the first trees to colonize the site of a fire, yet, ironically, fire is also the tool that keeps them in check on the prairie. They retreat if fires occur frequently enough to destroy the root nutrients needed for cloning to occur. The Manitoba Tallgrass Prairie Preserve and other reserves throughout the northern plains all use frequent prescribed burns to prevent aspen from overrunning the prairie.

WHAT TIME IS SPRING?

For many years plant ecologist Elisabeth Beaubien of the University of Alberta has been tracking the blooming times of certain plants as possible indicators of global warming. She has found that in Edmonton, Alberta, the timing of the first aspen bloom has advanced by almost a month during the last 100 years.

In mid- to late August, gentians suddenly appear in wet fields, their vivid blues contrasting with gold and pink grasses—a last burst of summer in the midst of autumn's encroaching gold. Worldwide, the family contains hundreds of species blooming in various shades of pink, purple, green, and white as well as blue. Most flowers have 4 or 5 petals and a funnel-shaped corolla that opens only in sunlight. Generally, gentians do not tolerate heavy grazing, which tends to dry out the soil.

Three species grow on the Manitoba Tallgrass Prairie Preserve, including the Closed Gentian (*Gentiana andrewsii*), sometimes called Bottle Gentian. This intriguing late bloomer often continues to flaunt its blue corolla into mid-September. However, the corolla never completely opens, so it can be pollinated only by bumblebees strong enough to force the petals open and crawl inside. The bees benefit from exclusive access to rich nectar, and in return, they are especially "loyal" to this gentian. Northern or Oblong-leaved Gentian (*G. affinis*) and two subspecies of Fringed Gentian (*Gentianopsis crinita*) also occur here.

The Roman historian Pliny wrote that gentians were named for King Gentius of Illyria, who made a concoction from the plant's leaves and roots to cure plague. Dakota and Winnebago Indians made a tonic from the roots of some gentian species to improve appetite and aid digestion, and the Mesquakies used the root of the Closed Gentian for snakebite.

Northern Gentians (Gentiana affinis) unfurl in late summer in wet prairies from Manitoba west to Alberta and south into the mountains of Colorado and New Mexico.

"Rails are curious characters," writes William Burt in his lyrical book *Shadowbirds*. "Unbirdlike, they are fleet on foot and clumsy in the air; they keep to the thick of marshes, where they live their lives unseen . . . . Rails are prowlers in places of mud and shadow, slinkers in the reed and grass, jittery non-descripts that shrink from view and slip silently away."

And yet birdwatchers like Burt drive far distances and slosh through muck and mosquitoes in the dead of night to catch a glimpse of one of the rarest of rails, the Yellow Rail. This quail-like bird has dull yellow and brownish plumage and an unmusical voice. Perhaps it's the thrill of finding something rare and elusive that appeals to railophiles.

Yellow Rails winter in coastal marshes from Texas to North Carolina and breed from Alberta to eastern Canada and south to the upper tier of states bordering Canada. They usually nest on the drier margins of sedge and cordgrass marshes with fresh or brackish water less than 8 inches deep. There they forage for snails, insects, and seeds and weave a cuplike nest from the sedges and grasses, camouflaging it with a canopy of dead vegetation. Yellow Rails can be heard, and sometimes seen, from early May to mid-July at the Manitoba Tallgrass Prairie Preserve.

Hearing a Yellow Rail is much more likely than sighting one, so listen for the distinctive 5-beat, metallic clicking, "like the crackle of a hundred bug zappers on a gnatty night," says Burt. Its cousin, the Sora, also nests on the preserve and is more apt to creep into view. Both rails can sometimes be coaxed from hiding by tapping two stones together.

Douglas Marsh, about 190 miles (304 km) west of the Manitoba Tallgrass Prairie Preserve, may harbor the largest number of Yellow Rails in the world. In 1995 ornithologists estimated that 500 pairs nested in the sedge meadows there, representing about 11.6 percent of the global population, and in 1993, 108 calls were recorded in a five-minute period. Sadly, numbers seem to have declined in recent years. The marsh is just south of the town of Douglas, about 16 miles (25 km) west of Carberry.

HIKING

THE PRAIRIE SHORE TRAIL (1 mile or 1.6 km) is keyed to a brochure available at the trailhead 1.5 miles (2.4 km) east of Tolstoi and loops through tallgrass prairie, sedge meadows, aspen groves, and oak woodlands.

Camping

Camping is not permitted on the preserve, but there is a campground at St. Malo Provincial Park, on SR 59 about 20 miles (32 km) north of the preserve.

Best Times to Visit

Sandhill Cranes and Sharp-tailed Grouse dance from mid-April to early June, while Yellow Rails click from early May to mid-July. Watch for warblers in breeding plumage in late spring. Several orchid species, including Small White Lady's-Slippers, bloom in early June; the Western Prairie Fringed Orchid, in early July; and Hooded Ladies'-Tresses, in late August. Gentians bring the wildflower spectacle to a close in September, when aspen turn golden and pinkish tallgrasses reach their full height.

Information

CRITICAL WILDLIFE HABITAT PROGRAM, Box 24, 200 Saulteaux Crescent, Winnipeg, MB R3J 3W3; 204-945-7775.

How to Get There

From Tolstoi, drive east on Hwy. 209. In 1.5 miles (2.4 km) the road comes to the Prairie Shore Trail and continues through the south block of the preserve to Gardenton. From Gardenton the road swings north and skirts the eastern edge of the central block. After crossing Hwy. 201, continue north on Beckett School Road into the north block, passing the headquarters building. The road deadends in the north block.

MANITOBA TALLGRASS PRAIRIE PRESERVE

WEATHER
MEAN TEMPERATURES AND PRECIPITATION

MONTH	HIGH (°F)	LOW (°F)	PRECIP.	SNOW
January	10	-9	0.7"	9.2"
April	50	30	1.3"	4.0"
July	81	57	2.6"	0.0"
October	35	52	1.3"	2.0"

Mean annual precipitation is 18.6 inches. June and July are the wettest months. Summer (June–August) temperatures have ranged from 109°F to 24°F. Data are for Lancaster, Minnesota (temperatures and precipitation) and Winnipeg, Manitoba (snow).

SELECTED WILDLIFE OF SPECIAL INTEREST

MAMMALS: Masked Shrew, White-tailed Jackrabbit, Richardson's Ground Squirrel, Thirteen-lined Ground Squirrel, Northern Flying Squirrel, Badger, Coyote, Gray Wolf (very rare), Fisher, Elk, White-tailed Deer, Moose.

BIRDS: Sharp-tailed Grouse, Yellow Rail, Sandhill Crane, Marbled Godwit, Upland Sandpiper, American Woodcock, Great Crested Flycatcher, Philadelphia Vireo, Sedge Wren, American Redstart, Clay-colored Sparrow, LeConte's Sparrow, Bobolink.

AMPHIBIANS AND REPTILES: Blue-spotted Salamander, Tiger Salamander, Northern Leopard Frog, Wood Frog, Smooth Green Snake, Red-bellied Snake, Red-sided Gartersnake.

ASESSIPI PROVINCIAL PARK (Department of Natural Resources, Box 849, Roblin, MB R0L 1P0; 204-937-2181). About 5,760 acres of mixed-grass prairie and aspen parkland lie along the shore of Shell River and the human-made Lake of the Prairies. Camping, boating, and hiking. About 21 miles (34 km) south of Roblin on Hwy. 83.

BEAUDRY PROVINCIAL PARK (Department of Natural Resources, 200 Saulteaux Crescent, Winnipeg, MB R3J 3W3; 204-945-7257). Tallgrass prairie is being restored at this 2,320-acre park along the Assiniboine River. Hiking and canoeing. Go 6.2 miles (10 km) west of Winnipeg on Hwy. 241.

LAKE FRANCIS WILDLIFE MANAGEMENT AREA (Box 6000, Gimli, MB R0C 1B0). Sixteen thousand acres of mesic tallgrass prairie, marshes, aspen bluffs, and shoreline lie along Lake Francis, a critical stop-over for migrating warblers. From Winnipeg, go northwest on Hwy. 6 for about 19 miles (30 km) and west on Hwy. 411 for 10 miles (16 km).

OAK HAMMOCK MARSH (Interpretive Centre, Stonewall Box 1160, Oak Hammock Marsh MB R0C 2Z0; 1-800-665-3825). This 9,000-acre Wildlife Management Area encompasses 160 acres of contiguous tallgrass prairie as well as restored marsh, wet meadows, willow shrub, and aspen-oak parkland. Designated a "Wetland of International Importance" and an "Important Bird Area," it provides habitat for 296 bird species. Hiking. Interpretive Centre, open daily, offers excellent educational programs and exhibits. On Hwy. 220 about 13 miles (20 km) north of Winnipeg.

RIDING MOUNTAIN NATIONAL PARK (Wasagaming, MB, R0J 2H0; 204-848-7275). This 750,000-acre park contains Rough Fescue prairie, boreal forest, deciduous forest, aspen parkland, and numerous lakes. A small Bison herd grazes the grasslands around Lake Audy. Moose, Elk, Black Bear, and deer are often sighted, and Great Gray Owls and Gray Wolves are occasionally seen. Camping, canoeing, hiking. Hwy. 10 bisects the park about 35 miles (56 km) north of Trans-Canada 1. Numerous secondary roads, such as scenic Hwy. 19, also access the park.

SPRUCE WOODS PROVINCIAL PARK (Department of Natural Resources, Box 900, Carberry, MB R0K 0H0; 204-834-8800). The Assiniboine River cuts through this 66,593-acre park containing sand dunes, mixed-grass prairie, a relict boreal forest, and oxbow lakes. An alluring trail leads to Spirit Sands (moving sand dunes sacred to early inhabitants) and the Devil's Punch Bowl (pools of blue-green water in a basin below the dunes). Camping, canoeing, and hiking. About 17 miles (27 km) south of Carberry on Hwy. 5.

YELLOW QUILL PRAIRIE (Nature Conservancy of Canada, 200-611 Corydon Avenue, Winnipeg, MB R3L 0P3; 204-942-4845). Mixed-grass prairie and aspen parkland cover 2,080 acres of this Nature Conservancy preserve. Call before visiting. From Douglas drive south on Hwy. 340 about 15 miles (24 km) and turn east on the last road before crossing Assiniboine River. Continue east about 1 mile to a dirt road at the northwest corner of the project and go south 1 mile to the southwest corner of the property. Access points are along the southern boundary, about 2.5 and 3 miles (5 km) from this corner.

Prairie grasses maintain a tenuous foothold in wind-driven dunes at Spruce Woods Provincial Park. (Photo by Glenn Cushman)

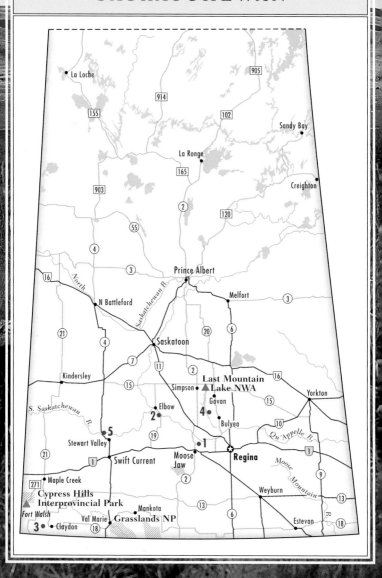

SASKATCHEWAN

La Loche

905

914

155

102

Sandy Bay

903

La Ronge

165

Creighton

55

120

2

4

3

16

Prince Albert

North Saskatchewan R.

N Battleford

Melfort

3

21

4

Saskatoon

20

6

7

11

2

Kindersley

15

Last Mountain
Lake NWA

16

Simpson

Gavan

Yorkton

Elbow

2

4

15

S. Saskatchewan R.

5

19

Bulyea

10

Stewart Valley

1

Qu'Appelle R.

21

1

Swift Current

Moose Jaw

Regina

Moose

1

2

Mountain

9

271

Maple Creek

Weyburn

13

**Cypress Hills
Interprovincial Park**

Mankota

13

Fort Walsh

Val Marie

Grasslands NP

6

Estevan

18

3

Claydon

18

CYPRESS HILLS INTERPROVINCIAL PARK

GRASSLANDS NATIONAL PARK

LAST MOUNTAIN LAKE NATIONAL WILDLIFE AREA

OTHER SASKATCHEWAN SITES:

1. Buffalo Pound Recreation Park
2. Douglas Natural Environment Park
3. Old Man on His Back Prairie and Heritage Conservation Area
4. Rowan's Ravine Recreation Park
5. Saskatchewan Landing Natural Environment Park

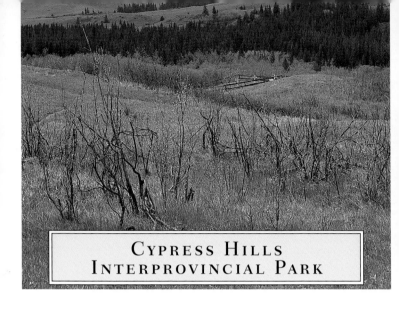

CYPRESS HILLS
INTERPROVINCIAL PARK

Surrounded by a sea of grass, two forested islands rise from the plains on the border of Alberta and Saskatchewan. The Cree named these hills *myun-a-tuh-gow* (beautiful highlands); the Crow, *ketwius netumoo* (hills that shouldn't be). Explorer John Palliser proclaimed them "a perfect oasis in the desert." And the Métis (French-Indian fur traders) dubbed them *Montagne de Cyprès* when they mistook Lodgepole Pines for the Jack Pines, or *cyprès*, of eastern Canada.

Some 15,000 years ago glaciers covered most of this region, known as the Palliser Triangle. However, a portion of the Cypress Hills summit escaped glaciation. As the glaciers began to retreat, forests covered the landscape. Later, as the climate continued to warm, the forests gave way to grass, but relict forests of Lodgepole Pine, White Spruce, and Quaking Aspen remained on the relatively moist and elevated Cypress Hills.

The Lodgepole Pines that inspired the park's name dominate the landscape. They require fire to open their cones and release the seeds, so most of today's giants germinated after the last great fire in 1886. Rough Fescue dominates the mixed-grass prairie, and 18 species of orchids, many of them uncommon elsewhere in

*Above: Wolf Willow (*Elaeagnus commutata, *in the foreground) grows in an old cemetery at Fort Walsh, Cypress Hills Interprovincial Park. (Photo by Glenn Cushman)*

Fairy Slipper-Orchids (Calypso bulbosa) *and other orchids bloom in June in the park's grasslands and forests.* (*Photo by Glenn Cushman*)

Canada, also find refuge here. Botanizers feel a tingle in the spine when they find Fairy Slipper Orchids, Yellow Lady's-Slippers, Sparrow's Egg Lady's-Slippers, White Adder's-Mouth Orchids, coral-roots, and the Blunt-leaved Bog Orchid that is actually pollinated by mosquitoes. One of only two known Common Poorwill nesting populations north of the 49th parallel may be found at Cypress Hills.

Canada's first and only interprovincial park was created in 1989 when Alberta and Saskatchewan merged two already existing parks. It covers almost 91,000 acres and attains the highest elevation between the Canadian Rockies and Labrador. The east block of hills, not in the park, is partly on the Nekaneet Reserve and contains the First Nations' Healing Lodge.

The west block, wilder and less developed than the other sections, contains the spectacular Conglomerate Cliffs and Adams Lake, where Trumpeter Swans have nested. The center block contains a resort area, panoramic views from Bald Butte and Lookout Point, and Loch Leven, where Red-necked Grebes sometimes nest. An auto tour beginning at Loch Leven is keyed to a leaflet available at the information centers. Check on road conditions, however, as Gap Road and several others are impassable in wet weather.

ROUGH FESCUE

Rough Fescue grassland, an ecosystem unique to western Canada and parts of northern Montana, flourishes at lower elevations and on the plateaus. Pockets of it also exist as far east as Riding Mountain National Park in Manitoba. Rough Fescue needs about 20 inches of precipitation per year and grows in rich black soils.

Botanists think this highly nutritious bunchgrass evolved along with winter grazing by Bison. It provides good fall and winter forage for wildlife and livestock and responds well to moderate late-season grazing. Because it decreases under overgrazing, it's an indicator of well-managed rangelands.

In pre-settlement days fescue prairie stretched from the Waterton Lakes to central Saskatchewan, but most of it has been replaced by cereal grain crops. Now only about 10 percent of the original grassland survives. Protection of this native grass is a high priority at Cypress Hills, where biologists are investigating various management techniques, including livestock grazing and "patch" timber cutting, to curtail encroaching trees.

Good places for viewing Rough Fescue prairie are on the auto tour, along Gap Road, on Hwy. 271 en route to Fort Walsh, and on private ranches throughout southwestern Alberta.

Wolf Willow

"It is wolf willow, and not the town or anyone in it, that brings me home," writes Wallace Stegner near the beginning of his lyrical memoir *Wolf Willow.* Searching for something he can't quite identify, he visits his childhood home not far from the Cypress Hills and suddenly catches a familiar smell. "[P]ungent and pervasive, is the smell that has always meant my childhood . . . [I]t is as evocative as Proust's madeleine and tea." He pulls off a handful of leaves, inhales the tantalizing fragrance, and writes, "the queer adult compulsion to return to one's beginning is assuaged…and a hunger is satisfied. The sensuous little savage that I once was is still intact inside me."

It takes some detective work to discover just what plant Stegner is describing. It's not a willow and has nothing to do with wolves. The mystery plant, which biologists identify as *Elaeagnus commutata,* is also called Silverberry and is a member of the Oleaster family. Its dry mealy berries are silver; its leaves silvery gray; and the tiny funnel-shaped flowers silvery yellow. The shrub blooms in June, producing a perfume that some people love and others find overpowering.

Like its relative, Russian Olive, Wolf Willow can be invasive. It is also a nitrogen-fixer that is used in shelterbelts and to rehabilitate mine spoils. Wildlife, especially Moose, browse on the leaves and fruit. In Alaska, native peoples eat the berries cooked in Moose fat and use the large pits as beads.

Wolf Willow grows throughout the northern plains in relatively moist habitats, especially those that have been overgrazed. Thick stands can be seen (and smelled) at Fort Walsh.

Moose

With a pendulous nose, humped back, short body, and enormous spread-out antlers, a Moose looks decidedly ungainly. An Abenaki myth relates that Glooskap, the Algonquin culture hero, created a race of giant Moose. When he saw they were too big for the people to kill, he squeezed them till they were smaller, but he did it unevenly, resulting in the misshapen look of today's Moose.

The Indians of the Northern Plains were careful to show respect for this animal that, like the Bison on the Great Plains, was a commissary for their needs. According to Henry Reeves and Richard McCabe in *Ecology and Management of the North American Moose,* Indian hunters took special precautions not to spill Moose blood on snow, as such disrespect could bring on a blizzard. They sometimes left antlers in trees so the Moose's spirit could see the sunrise and reassure his kin not to fear the hunt.

During the rut (mid-September to November), bulls, weighing 1,300 pounds or more, stamp out pitholes where they urinate copiously and wallow, saturating themselves with pungent pheromones. The cows also wallow in these pits and moan piteously when ready for mating. The dewlap or bell, a hairy flap that hangs from the neck of both males and females, emits sexual scents during the rut. The antlers, measuring up to 64 inches tip to tip, also emit pheromones and are usually shed in late November. The female bears one or two calves in May or June and defends them fiercely.

Not native to Cypress Hills, Moose were introduced in 1956 and now number about 275. Look for them at dusk or dawn around Beaver ponds and swampy areas where they munch on grasses, sedges, wildflowers, shrubs, and willows, consuming up to 50 pounds of plants per day. Adept swimmers, they dive up to 18 feet to feed on aquatic plants and swim distances up to 12 miles. Watch for them also in roadside ditches where they slurp up mud to satisfy their craving for salt and minerals.

Circumpolar in distribution, Moose occur mainly in boreal forests and aspen parklands. In North America they range from Alaska across Canada and have extended their range south as far as Colorado.

Fort Walsh and the Mounties

In the early 1870s Abe Farwell and Moses Solomon established trading posts in the Cypress Hills. The illegal whiskey they and others sold provoked fights and led to the name "Whoop-Up Country." On June 1, 1873, one of these arguments led to the Cypress Hills Massacre.

A group of wolf hunters on the trail of stolen horses rode north across the Montana line. They gathered to drink at Farwell's trading post, where a group of Assiniboin were also camped. The Indians left after the horse problem seemed to have been resolved. Then another horse was reported missing, and the wolfers rode in pursuit. Here accounts become hazy. But when the smoke cleared, 20 to 30 Assiniboins and one wolfer were dead, and the horse, which had merely wandered off, was found grazing nearby.

This massacre so aroused public opinion that the North West Mounted Police, forerunner to the Royal Canadian Mounted Police, was founded to establish the rule of law in the West. In 1875 James Morrow Walsh led 30 helmeted, red-coated men to set up Fort Walsh. He tried to help the various tribes under his jurisdiction and befriended Sitting Bull and the small band of Lakota who sought refuge for a few years in the Cypress Hills after the Battle of Little Bighorn.

It is a tribute to the charismatic James Walsh that the red coat became a symbol of justice and legitimacy to many peoples of the First Nations, in contrast to the hatred felt by the Plains Indians for a soldier's uniform in the United States.

The fort was abandoned in 1883, and a few years later the buildings burned. They were rebuilt when the Remount Ranch was established to raise the black horses used by the Mounties. Later the horses were moved, and Fort Walsh became a National Historic Site. Guided tours are offered to the restored buildings and other sites.

HIKING AND BOATING

In addition to more than a dozen trails that loop and interconnect throughout the park, a portion of the Trans Canada Trail (the trail linking Canada "from sea to sea to sea") traverses the park. Inquire about this long-distance trail at one of the visitor centers. Here are a few of the shorter trails.

HIGHLAND TRAIL (1.25 miles or 2 km) starts near the Lone Pine Campground and loops around Beaver ponds, passing through diverse habitats.

WHISPERING PINES (1.5 miles or 2.5 km) starts near the Loch Leven picnic area and circles through Lodgepole Pines. Interpretive signs describe this ecosystem.

NATIVE PRAIRIE TRAIL (1.1 miles or 1.8 km) begins just past the entrance to Bald Butte and loops across a plateau blanketed with grasses and wildflowers.

Canoeing is permitted on Loch Leven and on Elkwater Lake (where motor boating is also allowed).

CAMPING

In the center block, 14 campgrounds with 559 sites in lodgepole and aspen forests offer a range of services. Maps and permits are available at the campground office. More rustic sites are located along Battle Creek in the west block, and a full range of services is also available on the Alberta side.

BEST TIMES TO VISIT

Sharp-tailed Grouse dance on the golf fairway in the center block (and in other less obvious places) from May through early June. Also in June, Trumpeter Swans sometimes nest on Adams Lake, and Red-necked Grebes on Loch Leven. Many orchid species as well as Shooting Stars, penstemons, and larkspurs bloom in June. Aspen turn butter yellow, and Elk bugle from mid-September into October. Moose also enter rut from mid-September to November, and Moose calves are born in May and June. Throughout winter cross-country skiing and snowshoeing are popular on 15 miles (24 km) of groomed trails.

INFORMATION

CYPRESS HILLS INTERPROVINCIAL PARK, Box 850, Maple Creek, SK S0N 1N0; 306-662-5411 or Box 12, Elkwater, AB T0J 1C0; 403-893-3777. Visitor centers are located in the Elkwater townsite, in the center block, and at Fort Walsh.

HOW TO GET THERE

To reach the center block take Hwy. 21 south 23 miles (37 km) from Trans-Canada 1 to the park entry road. For Fort Walsh, take Hwy. 271 southeast from Maple Creek for 27 miles (43 km). For the Alberta side, take Hwy. 41 south about 21 miles (34 km) from Trans-Canada 1 or north 50 miles (80 km) from the Wild Horse Canadian border crossing.

CYPRESS HILLS INTERPROVINCIAL PARK

WEATHER
MEAN TEMPERATURES AND PRECIPITATION

MONTH	HIGH (°F)	LOW (°F)	PRECIP.	SNOW
January	24	3	0.8"	6.4"
April	55	32	1.1"	3.8"
July	83	55	1.6"	0.0"
October	58	33	0.7"	2.8"

Mean annual precipitation is 13.3 inches. June is the wettest month, averaging 2.5 inches. Blizzards can occur as late as April. Data are for Medicine Hat, Alberta.

SELECTED WILDLIFE OF SPECIAL INTEREST

MAMMALS: Masked Shrew, Snowshoe Hare, White-tailed Jackrabbit, Richardson's Ground Squirrel, Thirteen-lined Ground Squirrel, Coyote, Short-tailed Weasel, Lynx, Elk, Moose, Pronghorn.

BIRDS: Common Loon (m), Red-necked Grebe, Tundra Swan (m), Trumpeter Swan, Ruffed Grouse, Sharp-tailed Grouse, Black Tern, Common Nighthawk, Common Poorwill, Gray Catbird, Sprague's Pipit, American Redstart, Ovenbird, Red Crossbill.

AMPHIBIANS AND REPTILES: Great Plains Toad, Canadian Toad, Northern Leopard Frog, Red-sided (Common) Gartersnake, Painted Turtle.

GRASSLANDS NATIONAL PARK

Wind rages not only in winter but throughout the year on the nearly treeless prairie of Grasslands National Park. With few trees to blunt its force, the velocity of wind on the open prairie can be ten times what it would be deep in a forest. Locals quip that "one day the wind quit blowing, and all the people fell over." It may not be that much of an exaggeration. Old buildings lean precariously away from the wind, and thrashing grasses almost make you seasick.

Archaeologists have recorded more than 3,000 cultural sites, mainly from pre-contact hunting cultures, and think the park may contain the largest number of such sites in Canada. Gros Ventre, Cree, Assiniboine, Blackfoot, Dakota, and Lakota all camped and hunted in this area prior to European settlement and left behind tepee rings, Bison drive lanes, campsites, medicine wheels, and vision quest sites. One projectile point has been dated to 10,000 years ago.

Buttes, badlands, plateaus, and coulees add topographic interest to the park, which is divided into two sections. The west block, dissected by the Frenchman River, is larger and, at present, more accessible than the east block. A 17.5-mile auto tour loops through the west block past a prairie dog town, a Bison rubbing

Above: Abandoned buildings lean in the direction of the wind at the edge of Grasslands National Park. (Photo by Glenn Cushman)

stone, tepee rings, 70-mile Butte, and old homesteads. The east block includes the Killdeer Badlands, where dinosaur fossils were found in 1874.

In the Frenchman River Valley a Black-tailed Prairie Dog colony marks the northern limit of this species' range and attracts chorusing Coyotes, Burrowing Owls, and an occasional lumbering Badger. To survive the severe winters of Saskatchewan, prairie dogs at this longitude actually do experience cycles of hibernation, unlike their southern relatives who remain active throughout winter. The core body temperature of hibernating prairie dogs drops below 88°F, occasionally as low as 45°F, as measured by temperature devices implanted in their stomachs.

Established in 1988 and officially opened in 2001, this park is a work in progress. To restore degraded grasslands and former croplands, ecologists are reintroducing native species. They are also using grazing and herbicides to control the spread of introduced Crested Wheatgrass.

Land is being acquired on a "willing seller/willing buyer" basis, and currently totals more than 118,000 acres. Eventually the park will cover 224,000 acres of uninterrupted mixed-grass prairie. More than 40 species of grass, including Needle-and-Thread, Blue Grama, and various wheatgrasses, intermingle with sagebrushes, cacti, Chokecherries, serviceberries, wild roses, penstemons, mustards, legumes, and lilies.

DEATH CAMAS AND PRAIRIE ONIONS

Two look-alike members of the lily family, one of them deadly, the other delicious, often grow next to each other on northern prairies and are abundant on the Two Trees Interpretive Trail. Both bloom in May and June, producing heads of small whitish flowers and grasslike leaves. Wild onions (*Allium* spp.) have long been a pungent treat for people. (See Goose Lake Prairie, Illinois, for more information on wild onions.) However, all parts of Death Camas (*Zigadenus venenosus*) contain steroid alkaloids poisonous to humans and to livestock.

Unfortunately, some early settlers confused the two and died as a result. Ethnobotanist Kelly Kindscher, curious about the taste of Death Camas and how it could be confused with onions, actually tried it, stating, "I would discourage anyone from doing the same . . . It was extremely bitter and tasted poisonous." The motto "Never gamble and never guess" should be engraved into the minds of all wild-food aficionados.

North American Indians did use Death Camas medicinally. According to Kindscher, the Blackfeet and Shoshones mashed the

Death Camas (Zigadenus ve-nenosus) *blooms in western prairies and conifer woodlands from May through July.*

roots to make a poultice for leg aches and swollen knees, and the Paiutes used it for burns, rattlesnake bites, arthritis pain, and swellings.

SWIFT FOX REINTRODUCTION

Mee Yah Chah, "the lousy one" in the language of the Oglala Lakota, once ranged from the foothills of the Canadian Rockies to southwestern Manitoba. Though Swift Fox fur is somewhat coarse, the Hudson's Bay Company marketed an average of 4,682 pelts each year between 1853 and 1877. Swift Foxes were poisoned accidentally in campaigns against Coyotes and wolves and lost habitat when shortgrass and mixed-grass prairies were converted to croplands.

These carrion eaters depended heavily on the leftovers from wolf kills, especially Bison carcasses. After the Bison and their wolf predators disappeared, foxes in the far north starved during severe winters, whereas Swift Foxes in the south found other food sources. The last native Swift Fox in Canada was sighted near Manyberries, Alberta, in 1938, and in 1978 the species was listed as extirpated in Canada.

In 1983 a reintroduction program began in southern Alberta and Saskatchewan, using foxes bred from animals acquired from Wyoming, Colorado, and South Dakota. The Swift Fox Recovery Team used a "soft release" method the first year, holding and feeding the animals over winter in pens at the release site. Predators attracted by the food killed some foxes, and many foxes disappeared after being released. Only about 5 percent survived. In subsequent years the team released wild foxes captured from the United States. These wild foxes fared better, possibly because they had developed better survival skills. Survival rates also improved when the team set up temporary protective shelters and released foxes directly onto the prairie.

A total of 841 captive-bred and 91 wild foxes had been released when government funding for the program ceased in 1997. Wildlife biologists continue to monitor the foxes in an effort to determine what is crucial to their survival. They estimate there are now between 500 and 600 Canadian Swift Foxes in the wild. About 100 are established in the Grasslands Park region, mostly in privately managed pastures. Some have wandered into Montana, and one was sighted as far east as Manitoba.

At least for now, the program has succeeded, due largely to the availability of native prairie habitat large enough to sustain the foxes. Low predator populations, adequate food supplies, and milder winters have also helped. The survivors seem to pass on knowledge of den locations and food sources, a key to establishing a self-sustaining population.

It is ironic that in the United States where remnant populations still exist, Swift Foxes are legally trapped and hunted, whereas in Canada, where the original wild population was extirpated, Swift Foxes are totally protected. (See Pawnee National Grassland, Colorado, for more information.)

OPERATION BURROWING OWL

In 1987 Saskatchewan initiated Operation Burrowing Owl, a public/private partnership designed to arrest this owl's alarming decline on the Canadian prairies. The program protects nesting habitat on private lands by involving landowners in conservation efforts. Enrolled landowners receive monetary compensation based on the number of Burrowing Owls nesting on their properties.

Burrowing Owl numbers in Saskatchewan plummeted from an estimated 1,500 breeding pairs in 1989 to around 400 pairs in 1995. Alberta has experienced a similar decline, and fewer than five nesting pairs remain in Manitoba. Poisoning of Richardson's

Ground Squirrel and other rodent colonies, where the owls nest, has contributed to the decline. However, fragmentation of native prairies, which leads to greater owl mortality from predation and collisions with cars, has probably caused the most damage.

Biologists throughout the Canadian prairie region are working to save the species. Captive breeding programs in British Columbia and Saskatchewan have released hundreds of owls into the wild. Researchers have installed artificial nest boxes underground at breeding sites and have experimented with supplemental feeding of nesting owls. A new Burrowing Owl Interpretive Centre in Moose Jaw allows visitors to observe captive-reared owls and learn about owl conservation.

A total of 675 Saskatchewan landowners had joined Operation Burrowing Owl by 1994. However, most participants surveyed in 2001 said they were discouraged by the lack of owls on their properties. Scientists fear that this and other conservation programs may have come too late to save Burrowing Owls in Canada.

For more information about Burrowing Owls, see Badlands National Park, South Dakota. To find out about programs at the Burrowing Owl Interpretive Centre, call 306-692-8710.

HIKING

TWO TREES INTERPRETIVE TRAIL (0.9 miles or 1.5 km), keyed to a brochure available at the visitor center, loops around the top of a plateau offering panoramic views of the Frenchman River Valley and of 70-mile Butte. Drive south from the visitor center about 4 miles (6.4 km) and follow the signs.

Cross-country hiking is also permitted, and many interesting routes wind through valleys and coulees.

CAMPING

There are no campgrounds, toilet facilities, or drinkable water within the park, but two areas have been designated for car camping, and back-country camping is encouraged. Register at the visitor center in Val Marie or at Rodeo Ranch Museum (summers only) at nearby Wood Mountain. Campgrounds are available in Val Marie, Mankota, and at Wood Mountain Regional Park.

BEST TIMES TO VISIT

Greater Sage-Grouse and Sharp-tailed Grouse dance in April. In late April and May, Burrowing Owls and other migratory birds return. Saskatoon Serviceberries, Chokecherries, Pasque Flowers, and various species of legumes and lilies bloom in late May and June. June is also when Sprague's Pipits and Lark Buntings nest. In late August and September the prairie grasses turn varying shades of dusky rose and gold.

INFORMATION

GRASSLANDS NATIONAL PARK, Box 150, Val Marie, SK, S0N 2T0; 306-298-2257. The Visitor Reception Center, at the junction of Hwy. 4 and Center Street in Val Marie, includes exhibits, brochures, and cassettes, which may be borrowed for the auto tour. A good road map is essential.

HOW TO GET THERE

For the west block, take Hwy. 18 east for 9 miles (14.5 km) from Val Marie or about 33 miles (53 km) west from Mankota. At the sign, turn south on a gravel road and continue for another 2.5 miles (4 km) to the park entrance. For the east block, take Hwy. 18 south from Wood Mountain Regional Park for 18 miles (29 km); turn west on a gravel road and continue for 1.5 miles (2.5 km) to the entry point. Roads may be impassable when wet, so inquire locally about conditions.

GRASSLANDS NATIONAL PARK

WEATHER
MEAN TEMPERATURES AND PRECIPITATION

MONTH	HIGH (°F)	LOW (°F)	PRECIP.	SNOW
January	20	-1	0.4"	6.9"
April	56	29	0.9"	4.8"
July	84	53	2.1"	0.0"
October	58	31	0.6"	3.5"

Mean annual precipitation is 12.7 inches. Winter (December–February) temperatures have ranged from 71°F to -51°F; summer (June–August) temperatures, from 108°F to 22°F. Data are for Whitewater, Montana (temperatures and precipitation) and Swift Current, Saskatchewan (snow).

SELECTED WILDLIFE OF SPECIAL INTEREST

MAMMALS: White-tailed Jackrabbit, Black-tailed Prairie Dog, Coyote, Swift Fox, Long-tailed Weasel, Badger, Bobcat, Mule Deer, White-tailed Deer, Pronghorn.

BIRDS: Swainson's Hawk, Ferruginous Hawk, Prairie Falcon, Greater Sage-Grouse, Sharp-tailed Grouse, Upland Sandpiper, Long-billed Curlew, Marbled Godwit, Burrowing Owl, Short-eared Owl, Loggerhead Shrike, Sprague's Pipit, Lark Bunting, Baird's Sparrow.

AMPHIBIANS AND REPTILES: Boreal Chorus Frog, Northern Leopard Frog, Tiger Salamander, Greater Short-horned Lizard, Eastern Racer, Western Rattlesnake, Western Hog-nosed Snake.

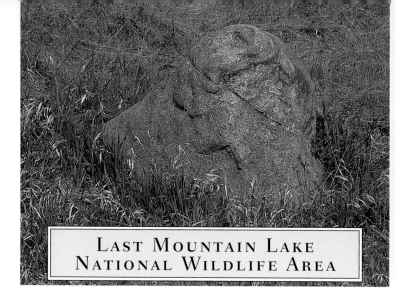

LAST MOUNTAIN LAKE
NATIONAL WILDLIFE AREA

North America's oldest federal bird sanctuary, established in 1887, lies on 37,000 acres at the interface of the mixed-grass prairie and the Rough Fescue prairie and is within both the Central and Mississippi Flyways. Birds fly through Central and South America to feed in the diverse habitats around the northern end of Last Mountain Lake.

During peak migration in spring and fall, more than 280 species of birds have been observed, including up to 50,000 Sandhill Cranes, 250,000 ducks, and 400,000 Snow Geese. Many of the spring arrivals, including six species of grebe, American White Pelicans, Piping Plovers, and Baird's Sparrows, stay to nest in summer.

This officially designated "Wetland of International Importance" also includes a well-managed native grassland with needle-grasses, wheatgrasses, Blue Grama, and Rough Fescue stretching out to the horizon. About 500 acres of barley are planted to lure birds onto the protected area and away from nearby agricultural fields. This is the scene evoked by the word "prairie": flat and green or golden, depending on the season, with the incessant sound of wind and of the birds that ride the wind.

Above: Several Bison rubbing stones can be seen at Last Mountain Lake National Wildlife Area, even though the Bison have long since vanished. (Photo by Glenn Cushman)

What you see depends on the weather cycle. In 1857 explorer John Palliser saw the Saskatchewan prairies during a drought and called them a desert, whereas botanist-explorer John Macoun came through in 1879 and described the area around Last Mountain Lake as the flower garden of the Northwest. "Often, whole acres would be red and purple with beautiful flowers and the air laden with the perfume of roses," he wrote in his journal. You may see scarlet Wood Lilies (the official provincial flower), Golden Peas, and blue penstemons—or you may see sere grasses and cracked mud.

A 10-mile (16 km) auto tour starting at the information kiosk near the headquarters passes a Bison rubbing stone, an observation tower, two self-guided walks, and several viewing stops along the lake and marshes. Several provincial parks, a regional park, and Stalwart National Wildlife Area also cluster around Last Mountain Lake, which stretches 55 miles long and 2 miles wide.

WATER BALLET

In springtime, grebes perform highly ritualized dances to attract a mate or strengthen the pair-bonding between mates. The dances range from very complex ceremonies performed by Western Grebes to the relatively sedate displays of Pied-billed Grebes. Since six of the seven North American species of grebe breed at Last Mountain Lake, chances of seeing a performance are good from May into July. Dance season reaches its height in June, when Pied-billed, Horned, Red-necked, Eared, Western, and Clark's Grebes dip and dive and dash across the water with grace and passion.

Western Grebes, noted on a sanctuary checklist as common, are possibly the flashiest and splashiest of the dancers, although they are incapable of walking on land. Their dance routine includes various stylized elements, which the bonded pair stages in synchronization. To begin the dance, the birds approach each other riding low in the water, pointing their bills and dipping and shaking their heads. Then, side by side, they raise their upper bodies out of the water with wings slightly lifted and run rapidly across the surface. After "rushing" for up to 65 feet, they dive head first into the lake.

"Barging" occurs when the grebes, side by side in a vertical or "penguin" posture, move slowly forward, turning their bills in unison and trilling. In the "weed ceremony" the birds dive into the lake for organic debris. Rising into a vertical posture and facing each other, they hold the weeds in upward-pointing bills. They may move forward in this position or swim in circles. Ritualized body preening often follows the various "steps" in the dance.

A Western Grebe stretches its neck and croaks to impress a potential mate or to deter a potential rival.

Other grebe species follow somewhat similar patterns, employing synchronized head movements, penguin postures, rushing, barging, and weed dancing. Most grebes build floating nests of organic material. Awkward on land and relatively weak in flight, they are the Fred Astaire and Ginger Rogers of water dancing.

NESTING WHITE PELICANS

American White Pelicans shift their nesting colonies from place to place as climate change and human activities alter food supplies and habitats. Between 1954 and 1987, pelicans disappeared from their nesting grounds at Last Mountain Lake. Since then the species has successfully bred each year at the north end of the lake, and numbers now fluctuate from 750 to 1,500 annually.

Pelicans usually locate their breeding colonies on predator-proof islands, often shared with Double-crested Cormorants. Some 20 colonies remain in the United States and more than 40 in Canada. Numbers have steadily increased since the banning of DDT in 1972, but the birds still suffer from human disturbances, such as boating, near their breeding grounds.

These stately white birds winter along the coast and inland waterways of the Gulf of Mexico as far east as Florida, west to the southern California coast, and south into Central America. They generally return to Last Mountain Lake in mid-April and begin nesting as soon as the ice has melted. Breeding adults of both sexes are decked out with bright orange bills and legs, a large knob on the upper mandible, and white plumes adorning the head. They fly 50 miles or more from their nests in search of food.

With wingspans of 9 feet and weighing up to 17 pounds, Amer-

American White Pelicans fish in lakes and ponds throughout the prairie region, but they nest only on islands surrounded by large bodies of water.

ican White Pelicans are unmistakable as they flap and glide in unison over prairie lakes and ponds or sail in for a water landing, their webbed feet acting like skis. They often fish cooperatively, swimming close together to encircle their prey. When pelicans dip their bills and open their mouths, up to 4 gallons of water flows into their expandable pouches. The water drains from the pouch when the pelican lifts its head, leaving only the fish, which is swallowed in one gulp, inspiring Dixon Merritt's famous line, "his bill will hold more than his belican."

HIKING

GRASSLAND NATURE TRAIL (1.25 miles or 2 km) begins just before stop 5 on the auto tour and is keyed to a brochure available at the kiosk.

WETLAND NATURE TRAIL (1 mile or 1.6 km) begins at the picnic/parking area northeast of headquarters or at stop 10 on the auto tour and is also keyed to a brochure available at the kiosk.

CAMPING

Camping is not permitted at the sanctuary, but Last Mountain Lake Regional Park Campground, on the northeast side of the lake about 9 miles (14.4 km) west of Govan, is open May 15 to September 3. The only migratory songbird banding station open to the public in Saskatchewan is located here.

Best Times to Visit

Spring migration is variable but generally best from mid-April to late May. Sharp-tailed Grouse dance in April and May, pelicans nest from late April through May, and grebes dance in May and June. White-tailed Deer give birth in June as blue penstemons, magenta locoweeds, and shelterbelts of golden flowered Siberian Pea-Shrubs bloom. Fall shorebird migration occurs from mid-July through August; waterfowl migration, from September into early October. In winter, Snowy Owls and Rough-legged Hawks are common visitors.

Information

CANADIAN WILDLIFE SERVICE, 115 Perimeter Road, Saskatoon, SK S7N 0X4; 306-975-4087, or Box 280, Simpson, SK S0G 4M0; 306-836-2022. The information kiosk, across the road from the headquarters, contains brochures and tapes for the auto tour as well as other brochures, maps, and exhibits.

How to Get There

Last Mountain Lake is located about 50 miles (80 km) northwest of Regina. From the west side of the lake, take Hwy. 2 to Simpson and look for the brown National Wildlife Area sign. Turn east at the cemetery onto a gravel road and continue about 9 miles (14 km) to the blue headquarters sign. Turn south and continue for another 1.9 miles (3 km). From the east side of the lake, take Hwy. 20 north from Govan for about 7 miles (11 km) and look for the brown sign. Turn west on the gravel road and travel about 6 miles (10 km); curve north for about 1.9 miles (3 km) to the first corner and turn west. Continue another 3.7 miles (6 km) to the blue headquarters sign.

LAST MOUNTAIN LAKE NATIONAL WILDLIFE AREA

WEATHER
MEAN TEMPERATURES AND PRECIPITATION

MONTH	HIGH (°F)	LOW (°F)	PRECIP.	SNOW
January	12	-7	0.7"	7.8"
April	51	28	0.9"	3.2"
July	80	53	2.3"	0.0"
October	53	29	0.8"	2.8"

Mean annual precipitation is 15.8 inches. Half of this amount falls in June, July, and August. Extremes are the norm in this part of Saskatchewan. Recorded temperatures have ranged from 112°F to -58°F. Data are for Regina, Saskatchewan.

SELECTED WILDLIFE OF SPECIAL INTEREST

MAMMALS: Arctic Shrew, Masked Shrew, White-tailed Jackrabbit, Richardson's Ground Squirrel, Thirteen-lined Ground Squirrel, Porcupine, Coyote, Red Fox, Short-tailed Weasel, Long-tailed Weasel, Badger, White-tailed Deer, Moose (rare).

BIRDS: Red-necked Grebe, Western Grebe, Tundra Swan (m), Rough-legged Hawk (w), Ferruginous Hawk, Sharp-tailed Grouse, Yellow Rail, Sandhill Crane (m), Whooping Crane (m), Piping Plover, Marbled Godwit, Snowy Owl (w), Short-eared Owl, Baird's Sparrow, Lapland Longspur, Bobolink.

AMPHIBIANS AND REPTILES: Canadian Toad, Boreal Chorus Frog, Wood Frog, Tiger Salamander, Plains Gartersnake.

OTHER SASKATCHEWAN SITES

BUFFALO POUND RECREATION PARK (306-110 Ominica Street W., Moose Jaw, SK S6H 6V2; 306-694-3659). Plains Indians once confined Bison in circular enclosures among the sand hills of this area. In 1972, almost a century after the Bison were exterminated in Canada, they were reintroduced to this 4,769-acre park in the Qu'Appelle Valley. Hiking, boating, camping. About 15 miles (24 km) north of Trans-Canada 1 via Hwy. 301, or about 20 miles (32 km) from Moose Jaw via Hwy. 2 and 202.

DOUGLAS PROVINCIAL PARK (Box 39, Elbow, SK S0H 1J0; 306-854-6266). Active sand dunes up to 82 feet high loom over pioneering Indian Ricegrass, Canada Wild Rye, and Prairie Sandreed in this 10,956-acre park in the Missouri Coteau region. Mixed-grass prairie, shrublands, and aspen forests grow on the eastern shore of Lake Diefenbaker. Hiking, boating, camping. Almost 9 miles (14.5 km) southeast of Elbow on Hwy. 19.

OLD MAN ON HIS BACK PRAIRIE AND HERITAGE CONSERVATION AREA (Nature Conservancy of Canada, Box 448, Eastend, SK S0N 0T0; 306-295-3696). In 1996 Peter and Sharon Butala donated 1,000 acres and sold 12,000 acres of their ranch to the Nature Conservancy of Canada. Sharon Butala lovingly describes this semiarid mixed-grass prairie in her book *Old Man on His Back*. By appointment only. From the village of Claydon, drive west on an unnamed gravel road for 10 miles (16 km) to the headquarters.

ROWAN'S RAVINE RECREATION PARK (Box 370, Strasbourg, SK S0G 4V0; 306-725-5200). Although it is only 667 acres in size, this park on the eastern shore of Last Mountain Lake showcases mixed-grass prairie, marshes, and sand beaches. The few groves of trees were all hand-planted back when prairies were something to be "improved." Hiking, boating, camping. Go 14 miles (22.4 km) west of Bulyea on Hwy. 220.

SASKATCHEWAN LANDING NATURAL ENVIRONMENT PARK (Box 419, Kyle SK S0L 1T0; 306-375-5525). This 13,837-acre park on the western end of Lake Diefenbaker features an auto tour through native mixed-grass prairie and past tepee rings, a Bison rubbing stone, wooded coulees, and viewpoints. The restored nineteenth-century Goodwin House near the historic crossing of the Saskatchewan River has excellent exhibits. Hiking, boating, camping. On Hwy. 4 about 31 miles (50 km) north of Swift Current. The Matador Ranch country northeast of the park demonstrates the success of sound land management on prairies in private ownership.

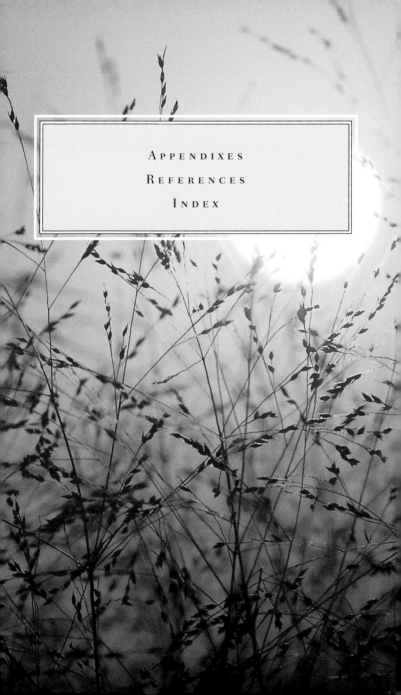

APPENDIXES

REFERENCES

INDEX

APPENDIX I
PRAIRIE PRESERVES IN INDIANA,
MICHIGAN, OHIO, AND ONTARIO

INDIANA

BEAVER LAKE NATURE PRESERVE (Department of Natural Resources, 402 W. Washington Street, Room W267, Indianapolis, IN 46204; 219-992-3019). This tranquil 640-acre preserve protects marshes and sand prairies. Green Milkweed blooms in early summer. Permission to enter must be obtained from the manager at Lasalle State Fish and Wildlife Area (see phone number listed above). From Enos go 3 miles north on US 41, then 1 mile east and 1 mile north. At the adjacent Kankakee Sands Preserve, the Nature Conservancy has begun restoration of more than 7,000 acres of former prairies and oak savannas; check the TNC Web site for updates.

HOOSIER PRAIRIE NATURE PRESERVE (Department of Natural Resources, 402 W. Washington Street, Room W267, Indianapolis, IN 46204; 317-232-4052). Sandwiched into an industrial area south of Chicago, this 439-acre mix of black oak savannas, sand prairie openings, wet prairies, and marshes supports a high diversity of native plants and has been designated a National Natural Landmark. Hiking trail. From US 41 about 5 miles north of US 30, go east on Main Street toward Griffith. The parking lot is on the right just past Kennedy Avenue.

INDIANA DUNES NATIONAL LAKESHORE (1100 N. Mineral Springs Road, Porter, IN 46304; 219-926-7561). This national park stretches 15 miles along Lake Michigan and encompasses 15,000 acres of dunes, forests, swamps, savannas, and prairies. More than 1,100 species of plants have been recorded here, including dozens of prairie grasses. Flocks of migrating shorebirds stop over in spring and early fall. Northwest of US 12, between Burns Harbor and Michigan City.

SPINN PRAIRIE NATURE PRESERVE (The Nature Conservancy, 1505 N.

Delaware Street, Suite 200, Indianapolis, IN 46202; 317-951-8818). A 29-acre oak savanna contains relatively high-quality tallgrass prairie remnants. From Reynolds go north on US 421 for 2 miles. Go east 0.2 miles and turn right at the "T" intersection. The preserve is on your right.

STOUTSBURG SAVANNA NATURE PRESERVE (Department of Natural Resources, 402 W. Washington Street, Room W267, Indianapolis, IN 46204; 317-232-4052). Grasses grow over head-high in prairie remnants scattered among dunes and oak savannas. From I-65 take SR 10 about 7 miles east to CR 350W. Go south 1 mile to CR 1100N. Turn left and go 0.5 miles to the beginning of the preserve, which follows the road for 0.75 miles.

MICHIGAN

ALGONAC STATE PARK (8732 River Road, Marine City, MI 48039; 810-765-5605). About 35 acres of tallgrass prairie remnants survive among several thousand acres of forest and savanna along the St. Clair River. The park's lake plain prairies and oak savannas support 19 species on the state endangered, threatened, and special concern list. Camping, hiking, skiing. From I-94 Exit 243, drive 20 miles east.

BOWERMAN PRAIRIE (Barry State Game Area, 1805 S. Yankee Springs Road, Middleville, MI 49333; 269-795-3280). Wet prairie, mesic prairie, and sand barrens persist on 45 acres in this public hunting area in southwestern Michigan. Camping, hiking, skiing. From US 131 Exit 61, go east about 7 miles.

OHIO

ERIE SAND BARRENS STATE NATURE PRESERVE (Department of Natural Resources, 1889 Fountain Square Court, F-1, Columbus, OH 43224; 614-265-6453). Remnant beach ridges with dry sand prairie and wet meadows support an abundance of native prairie wildflowers and butterflies. Nature trail. In Erie County 9 miles south of Sandusky. From the junction of US 2 and SR 4, follow SR 4 south 5 miles to Mason Road. Go 2.5 miles east on Mason Road to Taylor Road, then 1.5 miles to Scheid Road. The preserve entrance and parking area are on the south side of Scheid Road just beyond Taylor Road.

IRWIN PRAIRIE STATE NATURE PRESERVE (Department of Natural Resources, 1889 Fountain Square Court, F-1, Columbus, OH 43224; 614-265-6453). This 215-acre preserve protects a high-quality remnant of the once expansive Irwin prairie. Boardwalk and observation platform. Ten miles west of Toledo. From I-475/US 20 intersection, follow US 20 west for 3 miles to Centennial Road, go south 1 mile to Bancroft Street, then west on Bancroft to the preserve entrance.

KITTY TODD NATURE PRESERVE (The Nature Conservancy, 10420 Old State Line Road, Toledo, OH; 419-867-1521). About 575 acres of protected lands protect a mosaic of habitats, including oak savanna, wet prairie, and dry dunes in western Ohio's oak openings region. This is the only known location in the state for the endangered "Karner" Melissa Blue butterfly. Nature trail. Open 9 to 5 weekdays and on the first full weekend of each month. From I-475 on the west side of Toledo, take Airport Highway (SR 2) west toward the Toledo Express Airport. Turn right on Eber Road and follow it until it deadends into Old State Line Road. Turn left and follow the signs to the preserve office and parking lot.

SMITH CEMETERY PRAIRIE (Department of Natural Resources, 1889 Fountain Square Court, F-1, Columbus, OH 43224; 614-265-6453). Many of the highest-quality prairie remnants in the Midwest are in cemeteries or along railway rights of way. This 0.6-acre parcel supports native wildflowers and stands of Big Bluestem. Take SR 161 west from Plain City for 2 miles. Turn south on Kramer/Chapel Road, then go west on Boyd Road. The cemetery is on the north side of Boyd Road.

ONTARIO

OJIBWAY PRAIRIE COMPLEX (Ojibway Nature Centre, 5200 Matchette Road, Windsor, ON N9C 4E8; 519-966-5852). This 864-acre network consists of five natural areas within a 10-minute drive of downtown Windsor: Ojibway Park, Tallgrass Prairie Heritage Park, Black Oak Heritage Park, the Ontario Prairie Provincial Nature Reserve, and the Spring Garden Area of Natural and Scientific Interest. These remnant tallgrass prairies and oak savannas contain more than 117 provincially rare plants, including Yellow Stargrass, Gray-headed Coneflower, and Culver's Root. In spring the preserves become migrant traps with up to 12 warbler species seen perching in a single Chokecherry bush. Some 239 bird species, including nesting Indigo Buntings, have been recorded.

From E. C. Row Expressway in Windsor take Matchette Road south 0.6 miles (1 km) to the Ojibway Nature Centre, which offers excellent educational programs and exhibits. The other units of the complex are within a few blocks.

APPENDIX II
COMMON AND SCIENTIFIC NAMES
OF PLANTS MENTIONED IN TEXT

Scientific names are from Kartesz, John T., and Rosemarie Kartesz. 1996. *A Synonymized Checklist of the Vascular Flora of the United States, Canada, and Greenland.* Scientific synonyms are from McGregor, Ronald L., et al. 1986. *Flora of the Great Plains.*

TREES

American Elm (*Ulmus americana*)
Balsam Poplar (*Populus balsamifera*)
Basswood, Linden (*Tilia americana*)
Bigtooth Aspen (*Populus grandidentata*)
Blackjack Oak (*Quercus marilandica*)
Black Oak (*Q. velutina*)
Box Elder (*Acer negundo*)
Bur Oak (*Quercus macrocarpa*)
Chinkapin Oak (*Q. muhlenbergii*)
Douglas-fir (*Pseudotsuga menziesii*)
Eastern Red Cedar (*Juniperus virginiana*)
Eastern Redbud (*Cercis canadensis*)
Green Ash (*Fraxinus pennsylvanica*)
Hackberry (*Celtis occidentalis*)
Hickory (*Carya* spp.)
Jack Pine (*Pinus banksiana*)
Larch (*Larix* spp.)
Limber Pine (*Pinus flexilis*)
Linden, Basswood (*Tilia americana*)
Lodgepole Pine (*Pinus contorta*)
Maple (*Acer* spp.)
Mulberry (*Morus* spp.)
One-seeded Juniper (*Juniperus monosperma*)

Paper Birch *(Betula papyrifera)*
Persimmon *(Diospyros virginiana)*
Piñon Pine *(Pinus edulis)*
Plains Cottonwood *(Populus deltoides)*
Ponderosa Pine *(Pinus ponderosa)*
Post Oak *(Quercus stellata)*
Quaking Aspen *(Populus tremuloides)*
Rocky Mountain Juniper *(Juniperus scopulorum)*
Russian Olive *(Elaeagnus angustifolia)*
Shinnery Oak *(Quercus mohriana)*
Siberian Elm *(Ulmus pumila)*
Silver Maple *(Acer saccharinum)*
Soapberry *(Sapindus saponaria)*
Sycamore *(Platanus occidentalis)*
Walnut *(Juglans* spp.)
Wavy-Leaf Oak *(Quercus undulata)*
White Spruce *(Picea glauca)*
Willow *(Salix* spp.)

Shrubs

Big Sagebrush *(Artemisia tridentata)*
Buffaloberry, Bullberry *(Shepherdia argentea)*
Buffalo Currant *(Ribes odoratum)*
Bullberry, Buffaloberry *(Shepherdia argentea)*
Chokecherry *(Prunus virginiana)*
Creeping Juniper *(Juniperus horizontalis)*
Dogwood *(Cornus* spp.)
Elderberry *(Sambucus racemosa)*
Gambel Oak *(Quercus gambelii)*
Greasewood *(Sarcobatus vermiculatus)*
Hawthorn *(Crataegus* spp.)
Hazelnut *(Corylus americana)*
Honey Mesquite *(Prosopis glandulosa)*
Juneberry, Serviceberry *(Amelanchier arborea)*
Mesquite *(Prosopis glandulosa)*
Mountain-Mahogany *(Cercocarpus montanus)*
New Jersey Tea *(Ceanothus americanus)*
Peachleaf Willow *(Salix amygdaloides)*
Raspberry *(Rubus* spp.)
Salt Cedar, Tamarisk *(Tamarix* spp.)
Sand Cherry *(Prunus pumila)*
Sand Sagebrush *(Artemisia filifolia)*
Saskatoon Serviceberry *(Amelanchier alnifolia)*
Serviceberry, Juneberry *(Amelanchier* spp.)

Silverberry, Wolf Willow (*Elaeagnus commutata*)
Skunkbrush (*Rhus aromatica*)
Smooth Sumac (*R. glabra*)
Snowberry, buckbrush (*Symphoricarpos* spp.)
Tamarisk, Salt Cedar (*Tamarix* spp.)
Wax Currant (*Ribes cereum*)
Wild Plum (*Prunus americana*)
Wolf Willow, Silverberry (*Elaeagnus commutata*)

GRASSES AND SEDGES

Alkali Sacaton (*Sporobolus airoides*)
Big Bluestem (*Andropogon gerardii*)
Black Grama (*Bouteloua eriopoda*)
Blowout Grass, Sandhill Muhly (*Muhlenbergia pungens*)
Bluebunch Wheatgrass (*Agropyron spicatum*)
Blue Grama (*Bouteloua gracilis*)
Buffalo Grass (*Buchloë dactyloides*)
Canada Wild Rye (*Elymus canadensis*)
Cheatgrass (*Bromus tectorum*)
Composite Dropseed (*Porobolus silveanus*)
Cottongrass (*Eriophorum* spp.)
Crested Wheatgrass (*Agropyron cristatum*)
Green Needlegrass (*Nassella viridula, Stipa viridula*)
Gyp Grama (*Bouteloua breviseta*)
Hairy Grama (*B. hirsuta*)
Idaho Fescue (*Festuca idahoensis*)
Indian Grass (*Sorghastrum nutans*)
Indian Ricegrass (*Achnatherum hymenoides, Oryzopsis hymenoides*)
Junegrass (*Koeleria macrantha*)
Little Bluestem (*Schizachyrium scoparium, Andropogon scoparius*)
Needle-and-Thread (*Hesperostipa comata, Stipa comata*)
Northern Sweetgrass (*Hierochloë hirta, H. odorata*)
Porcupine Grass (*Hesperostipa spartea, Stipa spartea*)
Prairie Cordgrass, Sloughgrass (*Spartina pectinata*)
Prairie Dropseed (*Sporobolus heterolepis*)
Prairie Sandreed (*Calamovilfa longifolia*)
Rough Fescue (*Festuca campestris*)
Sand Bluestem (*Andropogon hallii*)
Sand Dropseed (*Sporobolus cryptandrus*)
Sandberg's Bluegrass (*Poa sandbergii*)
Sandhill Muhly, Blowout Grass (*Muhlenbergia pungens*)
Sideoats Grama (*Bouteloua curtipendula*)

Silver Bluestem *(Bothriochloa saccharoides, Andropogon saccha-roides)*
Silveus Dropseed, Composite Dropseed *(Sporobolus silveanus)*
Sloughgrass, Prairie Cordgrass *(Spartina pectinata)*
Smooth Brome *(Bromus inermis)*
Sweetgrass *(Hierochloë hirta, H. odorata)*
Switchgrass *(Panicum virgatum)*
Tall Dropseed *(Sporobolus compositus)*
Tall Fescue *(Festuca arundinacea)*
Three-Awn *(Aristida purpurea)*
Western Wheatgrass *(Pascopyrum smithii, Agropyron smithii)*
Wild Rice *(Zizania aquatica)*

FERNS

Adder's Tongue Fern *(Ophioglossum* spp.)
Marsh Fern *(Thelypteris palustris)*
Sensitive Fern *(Onaclea sensibilis)*
Spinulose Wood Fern *(Dryopteris spinulosa)*

FORBS

Arrowhead *(Sagittaria* spp.)
Arrowhead Violet *(Viola sagittata)*
Bigflower Coreopsis *(Coreopsis grandiflora)*
Bird's-Foot Trefoil *(Lotus corniculatus)*
Bird's-Foot Violet *(Viola pedata)*
Black-eyed Susan *(Rudbeckia hirta)*
Blanket Flower *(Gaillardia* spp.)
Blazing Star, Gayfeather *(Liatris* spp.)
Blowout Penstemon *(Penstemon haydenii)*
Blue-eyed Grass *(Sisyrinchium angustifolium)*
Blue False Indigo *(Baptisia australis)*
Blunt-leaved Bog Orchid *(Habenaria obtusata)*
Bog Aster, Swamp Aster *(Aster puniceus)*
Buck Bean, Golden Pea *(Thermopsis rhombifolia)*
Buffalo Gourd *(Cucurbita foetidissima)*
Bur Marigold *(Bidens aristosa)*
Bush Morning-Glory *(Ipomoea leptophylla)*
Butterfly Milkweed *(Asclepias tuberosa)*
Canada Goldenrod *(Solidago canadensis)*
Carolina Anemone *(Anemone caroliniana)*
Cattail *(Typha* spp.)
Ceramic Milk Vetch *(Astragalus ceramicus)*
Cholla *(Opuntia imbricata, Cylindropuntia vivipara)*

Closed Gentian, Bottle Gentian (*Gentiana rubricaulis, G. andrewsii*)
Cobaea Penstemon (*Penstemon cobaea*)
Common Milkweed (*Asclepias syriaca*)
Common Spiderwort (*Tradescantia ohiensis*)
Common Sunflower (*Helianthus annuus*)
Compass Plant (*Silphium laciniatum*)
Coreopsis (*Coreopsis* spp.)
Cowboy's Delight, Scarlet Globemallow (*Sphaeralcea coccinea*)
Crested Penstemon (*Penstemon eriantherus*)
Cryptantha (*Cryptantha* spp.)
Culver's Root (*Veronicastrum virginicum*)
Death Camas (*Zigadenus* spp.)
Dotted Gayfeather (*Liatris punctata*)
Downy Gentian (*Gentiana puberulenta*)
Early Easter Daisy (*Townsendia exscapa, T. hookerii*)
Fairy Slipper Orchid (*Calypso bulbosa*)
Forked Aster (*Eurybia furcata*)
Four-point Evening-Primrose (*Oenothera rhombipetala*)
Foxglove Penstemon (*Penstemon digitalis*)
Fringed Gentian (*Gentianopsis crinita*)
Fringed Sage (*Artemisia frigida*)
Gayfeather, Blazing Star (*Liatris* spp.)
Giant Eveningstar (*Mentzelia decapetala*)
Gilia Penstemon (*Penstemon ambiguus*)
Golden Aster (*Heterotheca* spp.)
Golden Pea, Buck Bean (*Thermopsis rhombifolia*)
Grass-of-Parnassus (*Parnassia glauca*)
Grass Pink Orchid (*Calopogon tuberosus*)
Gray-headed Coneflower (*Ratibida pinnata*)
Green Milkweed (*Asclepias viridiflora*)
Ground-Plum Milk Vetch (*Astragalus missouriensis*)
Gumbo Evening-Primrose (*Oenothera caespitosa*)
Heath Aster (*Simphyotrichum ericoides, Aster ericoides*)
Hill's Thistle (*Cirsium hillii*)
Hog Peanut (*Amphicarpaea bracteata*)
Hooded Lady's-Tresses (*Spiranthes romanzoffiana*)
Jack-in-the-Pulpit (*Arisaema triphyllum*)
Jerusalem Artichoke (*Helianthus tuberosus*)
Kittentails (*Besseya bullii*)
Knapweed (*Centaurea* spp.)
Large Beardtongue, Shell-leaf Penstemon (*Penstemon grandiflorus*)
Larkspur (*Delphinium* spp.)
Leadplant (*Amorpha canescens*)

Leafy Spurge (*Euphorbia esula*)
Locoweed (*Oxytropis* spp.)
Loesel's Twayblade (*Liparis loeselii*)
Lupine (*Lupinus* spp.)
Mariposa Lily (*Calochortus gunnisonii*)
Marsh Marigold (*Caltha palustris*)
Maximilian Sunflower (*Helianthus maximilianii*)
May-Apple (*Podophyllum peltatum*)
Mead's Milkweed (*Asclepias meadii*)
Michigan Lily (*Lilium michiganense*)
Missouri Evening-Primrose (*Oenothera macrocarpa*)
Nodding Ladies'-Tresses (*Spiranthes cernua*)
Nodding Onion (*Allium cernuum*)
Northern Green Orchid (*Platanthera hyperborea, Habenaria hyperborea*)
Northern (Oblong-leaved) Gentian (*Gentiana affinis*)
Nuttall's Sunflower (*Helianthus nuttallii*)
Nuttall's Violet (*Viola nuttallii*)
Paintbrush (*Castilleja* spp.)
Pale Evening-Primrose (*Oenothera latifolia*)
Pale Purple Coneflower (*Echinacea pallida*)
Pasque Flower (*Pulsatilla patens, Anemone patens*)
Pasture Sage (*Artemisia ludoviciana*)
Pecos Puzzle Sunflower (*Helianthus paradoxus*)
Pincushion Cactus (*Coryphantha* spp.)
Plains Eveningstar (*Mentzelia nuda*)
Plains Phlox (*Phlox andicola*)
Poison Ivy (*Toxicodendron* spp.)
Prairie Blazing Star (*Liatris pycnostachya*)
Prairie Bush Clover (*Lespedeza leptostachya*)
Prairie Coneflower (*Ratibida columnifera*)
Prairie Dock (*Silphium terebinthinaceum*)
Prairie Evening-Primrose (*Oenothera albicaulus*)
Prairie Larkspur (*Delphinium virescens*)
Prairie Onion (*Allium stellatum*)
Prairie Phlox (*Phlox pilosa*)
Prairie Rose (*Rosa* spp.)
Prairie Spiderwort (*Tradescantia occidentalis*)
Prairie Smoke, Three-flowered Avens (*Geum triflorum*)
Prairie Sunflower (*Helianthus petiolaris*)
Prairie Turnip (*Pediomelum esculentum, Psoralea esculenta*)
Prairie Violet (*Viola pedatifida*)
Prickly Pear (*Opuntia* spp.)
Puccoon (*Lithospermum* spp.)
Purple Coneflower (*Echinacea* spp.)

Purple Loco (*Oxytropis lambertii*)
Purple Loosestrife (*Lythrum salicaria*)
Purple Prairie Clover (*Dalea purpurea*)
Ragged Fringed Orchid (*Platanthera lacera*)
Raspberry (*Rubus idaeus*)
Rocky Mountain Bee Plant (*Cleome serrulata*)
Rose Vervain (*Glandularia canadensis, Verbena canadensis*)
Rosin Weed (*Silphium integrifolium*)
Rough-seeded Fameflower (*Talinum rugospermum*)
Royal Catchfly (*Silene regia*)
Rush Aster (*Symphyotrichum boreale, Aster junciformis*)
Sago Pondweed (*Stuckenia pectinatus, Potamogeton pectinatus*)
Sand Lily (*Leucocrinum montanum*)
Sand Verbena (*Abronia fragrans*)
Sandwort (*Arenaria* spp.)
Scarlet Globemallow, Cowboy's Delight (*Sphaeralcea coccinea*)
Shell-leaf Penstemon, Giant Beardtongue (*Penstemon grandi-florus*)
Shooting Star (*Dodecatheon frenchii, D. meadia; D. pulchellum*)
Showy Lady's-Slipper (*Cypripedium reginae*)
Showy Goldenrod (*Solidago speciosa*)
Showy Milkweed (*Asclepias speciosa*)
Showy Orchis (*Galearis spectabilis*)
Showy White Evening-Primrose (*Oenothera speciosa*)
Siberian Pea-Shrub (*Caragana arborescens*)
Small White Lady's-Slipper (*Cypripedium candidum*)
Snakeweed (*Gutierrezia sarothrae*)
Soapweed, Yucca (*Yucca glauca*)
Sparrow's Egg Lady's-Slipper (*Cypripedium passerinum*)
Spider Milkweed (*Asclepias viridis*)
Spiderwort (*Tradescantia* spp.)
Standing Milk Vetch (*Astragalus adsurgens*)
Stiff Goldenrod (*Solidago rigida*)
Swamp Aster, Bog Aster (*Aster puniceus*)
Swamp Dock (*Rumex verticillatus*)
Sweet Flag (*Acorus americanus, A. calamus*)
Textile Onion (*Allium textile*)
Three-flowered Avens, Prairie Smoke (*Geum triflorum*)
Trillium (*Trillium* spp.)
Trumpet Gilia (*Ipomopsis longiflora*)
Tube-flowered Penstemon (*Penstemon tubiflorus*)
Tulip Gentian (*Eustoma exaltatum, E. grandiflorum*)
Two-grooved Milk Vetch (*Astragalus bisulcatus*)
Ute Ladies'-Tresses (*Spiranthes diluvialis*)
Western Prairie Fringed Orchid (*Platanthera praeclara*)

Western Wallflower (*Erysimum capitatum, E. asperum*)
White Penstemon, White Beardtongue (*Penstemon albidus*)
White Adder's-Mouth Orchid (*Malaxis monophylla*)
White Turtlehead (*Chelone glabra*)
Wild Indigo (*Baptisia* spp.)
Wild Iris (*Iris* spp.)
Wild Licorice (*Glycyrrhiza lepidota*)
Wild Mint (*Mentha* spp.)
Wild Onion (*Allium* spp.)
Wild Parsnip (*Pastinaca sativa*)
Wild Rose (*Rosa* spp.)
Wild Sarsaparilla (*Aralia nudicaulis*)
Wild Strawberry (*Fragaria* spp.)
Willow Aster (*Symphyotrichum praeltum, Aster praealtus*)
Wintergreen (*Pyrola* spp.)
Wood Lily (*Lilium philadelphicum*)
Yellow Lady's-Slipper (*Cypripedium calceolus*)
Yellow Stargrass (*Hypoxis hirsuta*)
Yucca, Soapweed (*Yucca glauca, Yucca* spp.)

REFERENCES

GENERAL ECOLOGY

Adelman, Charlotte, and Bernard L. Schwartz. 2001. *Prairie Directory of North America*. Wilmette, Illinois: Lawndale Enterprises.

Allmann, Laurie. 1996. *Far from Tame, Reflections from the Heart of a Continent*. Minneapolis: University of Minnesota Press.

Bleed, Ann, and Charles Flowerday, eds. 1989. *An Atlas of the Sand Hills*. Lincoln: Conservation and Survey Division, University of Nebraska.

Bock, Carl, and Jane Bock. 2000. *The View from Bald Hill, Thirty Years in an Arizona Grassland*. Tucson: University of Arizona Press.

Botkin, Daniel B. 1995. *Our Natural History: the Lessons of Lewis and Clark*. New York: G. B. Putnam's Sons.

Bragg, T. B. 1982. Seasonal variations in fuel and fuel consumption by fires in a bluestem prairie. *Ecology* 63: 7–11.

Brown, Lauren. 1985. *Grasslands*. New York: Alfred A. Knopf.

Butala, Sharon. 2002. *Old Man on His Back*. Toronto: HarperCollins Canada.

Chapman, Kim Alan, Adelheid Fischer, and Mary Kinsella Ziegenhagen. 1998. *Valley of Grass: Tallgrass Prairie and Parkland of the Red River Region*. St. Cloud: North Star Press.

Collins, Joseph T., ed. 1985. *Natural Kansas*. Lawrence: University Press of Kansas.

Collins, S. L., A. K. Knapp, J. M. Briggs, J. M. Blair, and E. M. Steinauer. 1998. Modulation of diversity by grazing and mowing in native tallgrass prairie. *Science* 280: 745–747.

Collins, S. L., and L. L. Wallace. 1990. *Fire in North American Tallgrass Prairies*. Norman: University of Oklahoma Press.

Costello, David F. 1969. *The Prairie World*. New York: Thomas Y. Crowell.

Cushman, Ruth Carol, and Stephen R. Jones. 1988. *The Shortgrass Prairie*. Boulder: Pruett Publishing Company.

Engle, David M., and Terence G. Bidwell. 2001. The response of central North American prairies to seasonal fire. *Journal of Range Management* 54: 2–10.

Flores, Dan. 1990. *Caprock Canyonlands*. Austin: University of Texas Press.

Hartnett, D. C., K. R. Hickman, and L. E. Fischer. 1996. The effects of bison grazing, fire, and topography on floristic diversity in tallgrass prairie. *Journal of Range Management* 49: 413–420.

Johnson, S. R., and A. Bouzaher, eds. 1996. *Conservation of Great Plains Ecosystems*. Boston: Kluwer Academic Publishers.

Jones, Stephen R. 2000. *The Last Prairie, a Sandhills Journal*. New York: Ragged Mountain Press/McGraw-Hill.

Knapp, Alan K., John M. Briggs, David C. Hartnett, and Scott L. Collins. 1998. *Grassland Dynamics: Long-Term Ecological Research in Tallgrass Prairie*. New York and Oxford: Oxford University Press.

Kricher, John C., and Gordon Morrison. 1993. *Ecology of Western Forests*. Peterson Field Guide Series. Boston: Houghton Mifflin Co.

Larrabee, Aimee, and John Altman. 2001. *The Last Stand of the Tall Grass Prairie*. New York: Friedman/Fairfax Publishing.

Leopold, Aldo. 1966. *A Sand County Almanac*. New York: Oxford University Press.

Licht, Daniel. 1997. *Ecology and Economics of the Great Plains*. Lincoln: University of Nebraska Press.

Madson, John. 1995. *Where the Sky Began, Land of the Tallgrass Prairie*. Ames: Iowa State University Press.

Manning, Richard. 1995. *Grassland: The History, Biology, Politics, and Promise of the American Prairie*. New York: Viking.

Mathews, John Joseph. 1981. *Talking to the Moon*. Norman: University of Oklahoma Press.

McClain, W. E. 1994. Occurrence of prairie and forest fires in Illinois and other midwestern states, 1679–1854. *Erigenia* 13: 79–90.

McFall, Don, and Jean Karnes, eds. 1995. *A Directory of Illinois Nature Preserves, Volumes 1 and 2*. Illinois Department of Natural Resources, One Natural Resources Way, Springfield, IL 62702-1271.

Minnesota Department of Natural Resources. 1999. *A Guide to Minnesota's Scientific and Natural Areas*. Minnesota Department of Natural Resources, 500 Lafayette Road, Box 25, St. Paul, MN 55155.

Mutel, Cornelia F. 1989. *Fragile Giants: a Natural History of the Loess Hills*. Iowa City: University of Iowa Press.

Nature Conservancy of Minnesota, The. 2000. *A Guide to the Nature Conservancy's Preserves in Minnesota*. Minneapolis: The Nature Conservancy.

Packard, Stephen, and Cornelia F. Mutel. 1997. *The Tallgrass Restoration Handbook*. Washington, D.C.: Island Press.

Reichman, O. J. 1987. *Konza Prairie: a Tallgrass Natural History*. Lawrence: University of Kansas Press.

Samson, Fred B., and Fritz L. Knopf, eds. 1996. *Prairie Conservation: Preserving North America's Most Endangered Ecosystem.* Washington, D.C.: Island Press.

Smith, Annick. 1996. *Big Bluestem, Journey into the Tall Grass.* Tulsa: Council Oak Books.

Steiert, Jim. 1995. *Playas: Jewels of the Plains.* Lubbock: Texas Tech University Press.

Steinauer, Ernest M., and Thomas B. Bragg. 1987. Ponderosa Pine invasion of Nebraska Sandhills prairie. *American Midlands Naturalist* 118: 358–65.

Stubbendieck, James. 1986. *An Identification of Prairie in National Park Units in the Great Plains.* (National Park Service Occasional Papers No. 7) Washington, D.C.: Government Printing Office.

Tester, John R. 1995. *Minnesota's Natural Heritage, an Ecological Perspective.* Minneapolis and London: University of Minnesota Press.

Wauer, Roland H. 1999. *Heralds of Spring in Texas.* College Station: Texas A & M University Press.

Weaver, John Ernest. 1954. *North American Prairie.* Lincoln: Johnsen.

Zimmerman, John L. 1990. *Cheyenne Bottoms, Wetland in Jeopardy.* Lawrence: University Press of Kansas.

GEOLOGY, PALEONTOLOGY, AND ARCHAEOLOGY

Buchanan, Rex. 1984. *Kansas Geology.* Lawrence: University Press of Kansas.

Maher, Harmon D. Jr., George F. Engelmann, and Robert D. Schuster. 2003. *Roadside Geology of Nebraska.* Missoula: Mountain Press Publishing Company.

Strömberg, Caroline A. E. 2002. The origin and spread of grass-dominated ecosystems in the late Tertiary of North America: preliminary results concerning the evolution of hypsodonty. *Palaeo* 177: 59–75.

Unklesbay, A. G., and Jerry D. Vineyard. 1992. *Missouri Geology: Three Billion Years of Volcanoes, Seas, Sediments, and Erosion.* Columbia and London: University of Missouri Press.

Ward, Peter Douglas. 2000. *Rivers in Time: The Search for Clues to Earth's Mass Extinctions.* New York: Columbia University Press.

Wiggers, Raymond. 1997. *Geology Underfoot in Illinois.* Missoula: Mountain Press Publishing Co.

Wood, W. Raymond, ed. 1998. *Archeology on the Great Plains.* Manhattan: University Press of Kansas.

PLANTS AND FUNGI

Bailey, Robert G. 1995. *Descriptions of the Ecoregions of the United States.* Washington, D.C.: U.S. Department of Agriculture.

Gilmore, Melvin R. 1977. *Uses of Plants by the Indians of the Missouri River Region*. Lincoln and London: University of Nebraska Press.

Johnson, James R., and James T. Nichols. 1982. *Plants of South Dakota Grasslands*. Bulletin 566, Agricultural Experiment Station, South Dakota University. Brookings, SD.

Kartesz, John T., and Rosemarie Kartesz. 1996. *A Synonymized Checklist of the Vascular Flora of the United States, Canada, and Greenland*. Portland, Oregon: Timber Press.

Kindscher, Kelly. 1987. *Edible Wild Plants of the Prairie, an Ethnobotanical Guide*. Lawrence: University Press of Kansas.

Kindscher, Kelly. 1992. *Medicinal Wild Plants of the Prairie, an Ethnobotanical Guide*. Lawrence: University Press of Kansas.

Küchler, August William. 1977. *Potential Natural Vegetation of the Coterminous United States*. Manual to Accompany the Map. New York: American Geographical Society.

Ladd, Doug, and Frank Oberle. 1995. *Tallgrass Prairie Wildflowers*. Helena, MT: Falcon Press.

McGregor, Ronald L., T. M. Barkley, Ralph E. Brooks, and Eileen K. Schofield. 1986. *Flora of the Great Plains*. Lawrence: University Press of Kansas.

Moyle, John B., and Evelyn W. Moyle. 2001. *Northland Wildflowers, the Comprehensive Guide to the Minnesota Region*. Minneapolis: University of Minnesota Press.

Niehaus, Theodore F., Charles L. Ripper, and Virginia Savage. 1984. *Southwestern and Texas Wildflowers*. Peterson Field Guide Series. Boston: Houghton Mifflin Co.

Rogers, Ken E. 2000. *Magnificent Mesquite*. Austin: University of Texas Press.

Scott, Michael L., Jonathan M. Freedman, and Gregor T. Auble. 1996. Fluvial process and the establishment of bottomland trees. *Geomorphology* 14: 327–339.

Sheviak, Charles L., and Marlin L. Bowles. 1986. The prairie fringed orchids: a pollinator-isolated species pair. *Rhodora* 88: 267–290.

Vance, F. R., J. R. Jowsey, J. S. McLean, and F. A. Switzer. 1999. *Wildflowers of the Northern Great Plains*. 3rd ed. Minneapolis: University of Minnesota Press.

WILDLIFE

American Ornithologists' Union. 2001. *Check-list of North American Birds*. 7th ed. Washington, D.C.: American Ornithologists' Union.

Benedict, R.A., P.W. Freeman, and H.H. Genoways. 1996. "Prairie Legacies — Mammals." In *Prairie Conservation* (Fred B. Sansom and Fritz L. Knopf, eds.). Washington, D.C.: Island Press.

Bent, Arthur Cleveland. 1919–1968. *Life Histories of North American . . . Birds.* U.S. National Museum Bulletin, Washington, D.C., 21 Vols. Reprinted by Dover Publications.

Biondini, Mario E., Allen A. Steuter, and Robert G. Hamilton. Bison use of fire-managed remnant prairies. 1999. *Journal of Range Management* 52: 454–461.

Braun, Clait E. 1998. Sage grouse declines in western North America. http://www.rangenet.org/projects/grouse/grouse01.html.

Burt, William H. 1976. *A Field Guide to the Mammals.* 3rd ed. Peterson Field Guide Series. Boston: Houghton Mifflin Co.

Burt, William. 1994. *Shadowbirds: a Quest for Rails.* New York: Lyons & Burford.

Busby, William H., and John L. Zimmerman. 2001. *Kansas Breeding Bird Atlas.* Lawrence: University Press of Kansas.

Christiansen, Tom. 2000. What happened to all the sage grouse? *Wyoming Wildlife News,* March–April: 11–14.

Cokinos, Christopher. 2000. *Hope Is the Thing with Feathers: A Personal Chronicle of Vanished Birds.* New York: Warner Books.

Crother, Brian I., ed. 2001. *Scientific and Standard English Names of Amphibians and Reptiles of North America North of Mexico.* Society for the Study of Amphibians and Reptiles, Herpetological Circular No. 29. Department of Biology, St. Louis University.

Dary, David A. 1974. *The Buffalo Book, the Saga of an American Symbol.* New York: Avon Books.

Dodd, C. Kenneth. 2001. *North American Box Turtles, a Natural History.* Norman: University of Oklahoma Press.

Dundas, Heather, and J. Jensen. 1994/95. Burrowing Owl status and conservation programs. *Bird Trends* 4: 21–22.

Evans, Howard Ensign. 1993. *Life on a Little-known Planet.* New York: Lyons and Burford.

Fitzgerald, James P., Carron A. Meaney, and David M. Armstrong. 1994. *Mammals of Colorado.* Denver: Denver Museum of Natural History and University Press of Colorado.

Franzmann, Albert W., and Charles C. Schwartz, compilers and eds. 1997. *Ecology and Management of the North American Moose.* Washington: Smithsonian Institution Press.

Headstrom, Richard. 1973. *Spiders of the United States.* New York and London: A. S. Lawrence & Co.

Herkert, J. R. 1994. Breeding bird communities of Midwestern prairie fragments: the effects of prescribed burning and habitat-area. *Natural Areas Journal* 14: 128–135.

Herman, K. J. 1998. The New Mexico dragonfly notebook. http://www.rt66.com/~kherman/odonata/notebook.html.

Hoogland, John T. 1995. *The Black-tailed Prairie Dog: Social Life of a Burrowing Mammal.* Chicago: University of Chicago Press.

Ivan, Jake, comp. 2001. Observation of Piping Plovers in the U.S. Al-kali Lakes core area: 2001 field effort: summary report (unpub-lished).

Johnsgard, Paul A. 2002. *North American Owls, Biology and Natural History*. Washington and London: Smithsonian Institution Press.

Johnsgard, Paul A. 1990. *Hawks, Eagles, and Falcons of North America, Biology and Natural History*. Washington and London: Smithsonian Institution Press.

Johnsgard, Paul A. 2001. *Prairie Birds*. Lawrence: University of Kansas Press.

Jones, Clyde, Robert S. Hoffmann, Dale W. Rice, Mark D. Engstrom, Robert D. Bradley, et al. 1997. Revised Checklist of North American Mammals North of Mexico, 1997. Museum of Texas Tech University, Occasional Papers No. 173.

Kantrud, H. A., and K. F. Higgins. 1992. The nest and nest site char-acteristics of some ground-nesting, non-passerine birds of northern grasslands. *Prairie Naturalist* 24: 67–84.

Kingery, Hugh, ed. 1998. *Colorado Breeding Bird Atlas*. Denver: Col-orado Bird Atlas Partnership.

Knapp, Alan K., John M. Blair, John M. Briggs, Scott L. Collins, David C. Hartnett, et al. 1999. The keystone role of Bison in North Ameri-can tallgrass prairie. *Bioscience* 48: 39–55.

Knopf, F. L. 1994. Avian assemblages on altered grasslands. *Studies in Avian Biology* 15: 247–257.

Lantz, Gary. 2001. For the love of a horned lizard. *National Wildlife* 39 (Aug.–Sep.): 68.

McHugh, Tom. 1972. *The Time of the Buffalo*. New York: Alfred A. Knopf.

Matthiessen, Peter. 1981. *The Wind Birds*. New York: Viking.

Mech, L. David. 1970. *The Wolf: The Ecology and Behavior of an En-dangered Species*. Garden City, New York: Natural History Press.

Milius, Susan. 1999. U.S. fireflies flashing in unison. *Science News* 155 (March 13): 168–170.

Miller, Brian, Richard Redding, and Steve Forrest. 1996. *Prairie Night: Black-footed Ferrets and the Recovery of Endangered Species*. Washington, D.C.: Smithsonian Institution Press.

Opler, Paul, and Amy Bartlett Wright. 1999. *Peterson Field Guide to Western Butterflies*. Boston: Houghton Mifflin Co.

Petranka, James W. 1998. *Salamanders of the United States and Canada*. Washington, D.C.: Smithsonian Institution Press.

Poole, Alan, and Frank Gill, eds. 1992–1997. The Birds of North America. Nos. 1–320. Philadelphia and Washington, D.C.: Academy of Natural Sciences and American Ornithologists' Union.

———. 1998–2002. The Birds of North America. Nos. 321–716. Philadelphia: The Birds of North America, Inc.

Putnam, Rory. 1988. *The Natural History of Deer*. Ithaca: Comstock.

Pyle, Robert Michael. 1992. *The Audubon Society Field Guide to North American Butterflies*. New York: Alfred A. Knopf Inc.

———. 1999. *Chasing Monarchs: Migrating with the Butterflies of Passage*. Boston: Houghton Mifflin Co.

Ryden, Hope. 1975. *God's Dog*. New York: Coward, McCann & Geoghegan.

Sauer, J. R., J. E. Hines, and J. Fallon. 2003. The North American breeding bird survey results and analysis. Version 2003.1. Patuxent Wildlife Research Center, Laurel, MD. http://www.mbr.nbs.gov/bbs/bbs/.html.

Scientific Committee on the Status of Endangered Wildlife in Canada (COSEWIC). 2002. *Canada's Endangered Species*. Ottawa: Committee on the Status of Endangered Wildlife in Canada.

Shaw, Charles E., and Sheldon Campbell. 1974. *Snakes of the American West*. New York: Alfred A. Knopf.

Shine, R., B. Phillips, H. Waye, M. LeMaster, and R. T. Mason. 2001. Animal behavior: benefits of female mimicry in snakes. *Nature* 414: 267.

Silsby, Jill. 2001. *Dragonflies of the World*. Washington, D.C.: Smithsonian Institution Press.

Slobodchikoff, C. N., J. Kiriazis, C. Fischer, and E. Creef. 1991. Semantic information distinguishing individual predators in the alarm calls of Gunnison's prairie dogs. *Animal Behavior* 42: 713–719.

Stebbins, Robert C., and Nathan W. Cohen. 1995. *A Natural History of Amphibians*. Princeton: Princeton University Press.

Turbak, Gary, and Alan Carey. 1987. *Twilight Hunters: Wolves, Coyotes, and Foxes*. Flagstaff: Northland Press.

U.S. Geological Survey, Northern Prairie Wildlife Research Center. 1998. *Swift Fox Symposium: Ecology and Conservation of Swift Foxes in a Changing World*. Northern Prairie Wildlife Research Center Home Page. http://www.npwrc.usgs.gov/resource/1998/swiftfox/swiftfox.htm.

University of Michigan. Museum of Zoology. 2002. Cicada Web sites. http://insects.ummz.lsa.umich.edu/fauna/Michigan_Cicadas.

Van Wormer, Joe. 1969a. *World of the American Elk*. Philadelphia: J. B. Lippincott.

Van Wormer, Joe. 1969b. *World of the Pronghorn*. Philadelphia: J. B. Lippincott.

Wilcove, David S. 1999. *The Condor's Shadow: The Loss and Recovery of Wildlife in America*. New York: W. H. Freeman and Company.

Williams, K. S., and C. Simon. 1995. The ecology, behavior and evolution of periodical cicadas. *Annual Review of Entomology* 40: 269–295.

Black Elk. 1972. *Black Elk Speaks, as Told through John G. Neihardt.* New York: Simon & Schuster.

Brave Bird, Mary, and Richard Erdoes. 1990. *Lakota Woman.* New York: Harper Perennial.

Catlin, George. 1989. *North American Indians.* New York and London: Viking.

Dorsey, George. 1997. *The Pawnee Mythology.* Lincoln: University of Nebraska Press.

Erdoes, Richard, and Alfonzo Ortiz. 1984. *American Indian Myths and Legends.* New York: Pantheon Books.

Loew, Patty. 2001. *Indian Nations of Wisconsin.* Madison: Wisconsin Historical Society Press.

Mathews, John Joseph. 1932. *Wah'Kon-Tah: The Osage and the White Man's Road.* Norman: University of Oklahoma Press.

Momaday, N. Scott. 2001. *The Way to Rainy Mountain.* Albuquerque: University of New Mexico Press.

Reid, Gordon. 2002. *Head-Smashed-In.* Calgary: Fifth House Publishers.

Smith, Rex Alan. 1975. *Moon of the Popping Trees.* Lincoln: University of Nebraska Press.

Standing Bear, Luther. 1988. *My Indian Boyhood.* Lincoln: University of Nebraska Press.

Unrau, William E. 1971. *The Kansa Indians, a History of the Wind People, 1673–1873.* Norman: University of Oklahoma Press.

EXPLORATION AND PIONEER HISTORY

Ambrose, Stephen E. 1997. *Undaunted Courage: Meriwether Lewis, Thomas Jefferson, and the Opening of the American West.* New York: Simon & Schuster.

Borland, Hal. 1984. *High, Wide, and Lonesome.* Tucson: University of Arizona Press.

Cather, Willa. 1954. *My Antonia.* Boston: Houghton Mifflin.

Featherstonhaugh, George. 1970. *A Canoe Voyage up the Minnay Sotor, with an Account of the Lead and Copper Deposits in Wisconsin.* St. Paul: Minnesota Historical Society.

Frémont, John Charles. 1956. *Narratives of Exploration and Adventure.* Edited by Allan Nevins. New York: Longmans, Green.

Garland, Hamlin. 1928. *The Son of the Middle Border.* New York: McMillan.

Irving, Washington. 1956. *A Tour on the Prairies.* Edited with an introductory essay by John Francis McDermott. Norman: University of Oklahoma Press.

Lewis, Meriwether. 1902. *History of the Expedition under the Command of Captains Lewis and Clark,* prepared for the press by Paul Allen. Chicago: A. C. McClurg.

Parkman, Francis. 1946. *The Oregon Trail.* Garden City: Doubleday.

Sandoz, Mari. 1961. *Love Song to the Plains.* New York: Harper.

Steele, Eliza. 1975, 1841. *Summer Journey in the West.* New York: Arno Press.

Stegner, Wallace. 1955. *Wolf Willow.* Lincoln: University of Nebraska Press.

Wilder, Laura Ingalls. 1935. *Little House on the Prairie.* New York and San Francisco: Harper and Row.

General Web sites

www.greatplains.org (General database on the Great Plains)

www.nature.org (The Nature Conservancy)

www.npwrc.usgs.gov (Northern Prairie Wildlife Research Center)

www.r6.fws.gov/refuges (National Wildlife Refuges)

www.cws-scf.ec.gc.ca (Canadian Wildlife Service)

INDEX

Page numbers in **boldface** refer to pages on which photographs appear.

THE PETERSON SERIES®

PETERSON FIELD GUIDES®

BIRDS

FISH

INSECTS

MAMMALS

PETERSON FIELD GUIDES® continued

ECOLOGY

PLANTS

EARTH AND SKY

PETERSON FIELD GUIDES® continued

REPTILES AND AMPHIBIANS

EASTERN REPTILES AND AMPHIBIANS Eastern and
central North America 90452-8
WESTERN REPTILES AND AMPHIBIANS Western
North America, including Baja California
93611-X

SEASHORE

SHELLS OF THE ATLANTIC Atlantic and Gulf coasts
and the West Indies 0-618-16439-1
PACIFIC COAST SHELLS North American Pacific coast, including
Hawaii and the Gulf of California 18322-7
ATLANTIC SEASHORE Bay of Fundy to Cape Hatteras 0-618-00209-X
CORAL REEFS Caribbean and Florida 0-618-00211-1
SOUTHEAST AND CARIBBEAN SEASHORES Cape Hatteras to the Gulf
Coast, Florida, and the Caribbean 97516-6

PETERSON FIRST GUIDES®

PETERSON FIELD GUIDE AUDIOS

EASTERN BIRDING BY EAR
cassettes 0-618-22591-9
CD 0-618-22590-0
EASTERN MORE BIRDING BY EAR
cassettes 97529-8
CD 97530-1
WESTERN BIRDING BY EAR
cassettes 97526-3
CD 97525-5

BACKYARD BIRDSONG
cassettes 0-618-22593-5
CD 0-618-22592-7
EASTERN BIRD SONGS, Revised
CD 0-618-22594-3
WESTERN BIRD SONGS, Revised
CD 97519-0

PETERSON FIELD GUIDE COLORING BOOKS

BIRDS 32521-8
BUTTERFLIES 34675-4
MAMMALS 44091-2
REPTILES AND AMPHIBIANS 37704-8

PETERSON FLASHGUIDES™

ATLANTIC COASTAL BIRDS 79286-X
PACIFIC COASTAL BIRDS 79287-8
EASTERN TRAILSIDE BIRDS 79288-6
WESTERN TRAILSIDE BIRDS 79289-4
HAWKS 79291-6
BACKYARD BIRDS 79290-8
TREES 82998-4
ANIMAL TRACKS 82997-6
BUTTERFLIES 82996-8
ROADSIDE WILDFLOWERS 82995-X
BIRDS OF THE MIDWEST 86733-9
WATERFOWL 86734-7

PETERSON FIELD GUIDES can be purchased at your local bookstore or by calling our toll-free number, (800) 225-3362.

When referring to title by corresponding ISBN number, preface with 0-395, unless title is listed with 0-618.